The Cutleaf Reader

Volume Two

EDITED BY

**Keith Lesmeister, Denton Loving,
Kelly March, and Walter Robinson**

The Cutleaf Reader, Volume Two

Edited by Keith Lesmeister, Denton Loving, Kelly March, and Walter Robinson

Anthology

ISBN 978-1-958094-07-5

Book & Cover Design : EK Larken

❋

Cutleaf and The Cutleaf Reader are projects of EastOver Press.

Advisory Board: Christopher Castellanti, Jasmin Darznik, Libby Flores, Jill McCorkle, Lynne Sharon Schwartz, Joan Wickersham, and Paul Yoon

❋

EastOver Press encourages the use of our publications in educational settings. For questions about educational discounts, contact us at www.EastOverpress.com or info@eastoverpress.com.

Published in the United States of America by

EASTOVER
— PRESS —
Rochester, Massachusetts
www.EastOverPress.com

The Cutleaf Reader

VOLUME TWO

www.CutleafJournal.com

CONTENTS

NONFICTION

POETRY

FICTION

A Note from EastOver Press

Cutleaf and *The Cutleaf Reader* are both projects of EastOver Press, a small, independent publisher of fiction, nonfiction and poetry. Some of the authors in *Cutleaf* also have books published by EastOver Press, and if you like their work published in this anthology, we encourage you to seek out their books at EastOverPress.com.

Other writers featured in *Cutleaf* in 2022 have put out books with other presses in the past year, and we also encourage you to seek out their works.

Contributors to *Cutleaf* with recent books from EastOver Press:
Darius Stewart, *Intimacies in Borrowed Light*
Khanh Ha, *All The Rivers Flow Into the Sea*
Louise Marburg, *You Have Reached Your Destination*
Kate Hanson Foster, *Crow Funeral*

Contributors to *Cutleaf* with recent books from other publishers:
June Gervais, *Jobs for Girls with Artistic Flair* (Viking)
Rolli, *Plumstuff: Poems and Drawings* (8th House Books)
Moriel Rothman-Zecher, *Before All The World* (Fararr, Straus, Giroux)
Victoria Buitron, *A Body Across Two Hemispheres: A Memoir in Essays* (Woodhall Press)
Shawna Kay Rodenberg, *Kin* (Bloomsbury)
Elise Gregory, *The Clayfields* (Cornerstone Press)

Introduction

Welcome to the second volume of the *The Cutleaf Reader*, a print anthology of work published in the online journal during 2022.

We know that some readers prefer a screen and some prefer paper, so at the end of every year we publish this anthology of the work previously published online to satisfy our paper-loving readers. We hope these two versions can bring the widest possible audience to the work written by the authors of *Cutleaf*.

When we started *Cutleaf*—in the middle of a pandemic, and run by people living in four different states—we expected to need at least a year to get going, but from the beginning we have been surprised and delighted by the work submitted to a new journal by a wide range of writers. That delight has extended into the second year of the journal, and we continue to be impressed at the quality and variety of the writing we can feature in *Cutleaf*.

In 2022, we tried to stay true to our mission of publishing work that both responds to our common experience and reflects our differences. We hope you will agree that we have come close to that goal in this anthology. *Cutleaf* publishes work of all shapes and sizes. In this anthology you will read flash fiction and longer stories, hybrid essays and more traditional nonfiction formats, and poetry of many different styles and approaches.

The four of us who edit *Cutleaf* are all writers ourselves. As writing is a (mostly) solitary activity, we have sought to build connections with the wider writing community through *Cutleaf* and the other work of EastOver Press. We hope that in our second year, we have continued to "help uplift and support that community," as my fellow editor Keith Lesmeister put it in the introduction to the first volume of *The Cutleaf Reader*.

As we move forward into the third year of the journal, we seek to uphold the success of the first two years and broaden our reach within the literary community and beyond. But most of all, we want to still have fun working with each other and with you, the readers and writers of *Cutleaf.* This project has been a joy for us during difficult times, and we are happy to share it with you.

Walter M. Robinson
ROCHESTER, MASSACHUSETTS

NONFICTION

Hussain Ahmed

Half The Sky is Grey with Shame

ﺍ

We are back in the city
where I learned to read in English

and prayed in the Arabic I was made
to believe God understands better.

If I want to make Aljanah,
I need to learn the difference

between 'ka' and "kha'
and to learn to sing

pages of qasida from heart, even if
I don't know what they mean.

ﺏ

The cloud was baked into fragments. The mango tree outside
the mosque had grown wild, its branches cast shades over the
rusty train track. The cars' skeletons in front of our old house
were in a nearly perfect line, as I believe we would all be on
the day of resurrection. When we left, the air was filled with
smoke and some of the cars were still shedding their uphol-
steries to the fire. The curfew had been relaxed, we were head-
ed out of Kaduna before the sun mounts the blue altar, of a
sky that witnessed too much death, but interceded with rain
when it got tired of the blood.

Departures are irreversible, even when you return, some parts
of you would not come with you into the city. The walls are
scarred with murals of palm and machetes, there is grief in
the air.

ﺙ

I was barely eight years when it happened,
I don't remember praying Fajr.

The house we lived in
was filled with echoes.

That morning, I doubted there was
anyone else left in the house

or they were, but too scared to breathe –
to remain unnoticed for the flying swords

or the Angel of death, that roamed
the streets of Kaduna with pride.

We tiptoed down the staircase,
with bags of clothes and pictures.

There was a car waiting down the road
to take us to an underground car park.

Many of such had resurrected in all corners of Kaduna,
to help evacuate us from the city.

I believed leaving was because we had other places to go,
because we had far more things to lose.

ﺕ

Everyone has a gate they want closed only at night. I want
mine opened but I desired no one to walk through it.

God's house must not be left unattended, so Baba did not
travel with us.

For someone who had a room that always reeks of incense, he
doesn't get sick of the burning sky.

Baba led salaat in a city that has half its sky grey with shame.
& the wind clustered – with the whispers of everyone lost to
the eclipse.

ﺝ

I rehearsed loneliness
until it became a cloud

over a new city
waiting to be plundered.

Except, I own the boxes
or I will, through inheritance.

The frames on the walls – are
a batch of untold histories,

everyone I know in the pictures
looks younger,   happier –   or dead.

I have since learned
to spell magic with my eyes closed

in a bid to reimagine this city of wanderers.

ح

I was born a year before the last eclipse, it took seven years before
the next one in 1999. I am never tired of hearing the stories of
how we survived the first, *you almost got us all killed with your wailings.*
Mama would always say with a smile, "I had to place a pillow over
your head anytime you starts to cry, but I'm careful to not press
too hard so you don't suffocate". There are several versions of
how we survived, but in my Baba's version, I was a siren in a ghost
town, seeking to sing the wounded to sleep.

I lost my Grandfather to the last crisis, he was thrown inside the
well in their backyard. His library was set on fire and the fence of
the house where he dreamed to nurse the new army of preach-
ers and teachers was demolished to fill up the well, while he was
inside of it. There are several versions of how many days he sur-
vived inside the well, he was heard saying the adhan. Even though
he couldn't see the sun, he knew the prayer time by heart. He
doesn't need an alarm to know when it was time for his forehead
to be planted in the wet soil.

خ

He was buried in the makabarta in Tudun Wada,
in the middle of a horizon of brown grasses,

labeled with dust of memories. Each with their date of departure.

It's a taboo to read the names on the graves, but in all my visits

I remember the warnings after reading at least fifteen names or more.

I'm taken aback anytime I saw a grave plate with an age that is about mine or younger.

We visit his grave every year before the start of Ramadan, because we sing better with empty stomachs, because we are a vase of refracting pebbles.

ا

Once, before I was old enough to visit the graveyard, Baba comes home with tea leaves, plucked from the cemetery. We believed a part of our grandfather nestles in our bodies anytime we sip from the tea. His grave was the biggest I have seen, maybe the widest in the whole of Tudun Wada. He was buried with a son, a student and two strangers whose names no one knew, not even my Baba.

ذ

The city swallowed my ancestors and every rosary Baba owned.

The air is a blunt thorn in our lungs to curb the stench of the dead, and

to stop their ghosts from roaming the streets at night.

It was the same for everyone entering the city for the first time.

We sought refuge beyond the barrack gates, like most people from the neighborhood.

We rode for hours until we were seven hundred miles away,

to the embrace of waiting families,
families I knew from the pictures on the walls.

ر

For three years, we lost somethings we adored more than
Baba's prayer rug or his ash colored Fiat, my sister died of
typhoid. What survived a giant fire did not survive the spirits
inside the water. There is something that weakens the tendons
that held our bones, and worst, it kills. *Only a stranger would
suffer from it,* one of the myths I believed.

I was home, but I am a stranger. Whatever lives in the water
my Baba drank as a child, I'm not immune to it, as any of my
siblings.

ز

Holy Mariam, Mother of God, pray for us in heaven.

س

On the balcony of an old but newly painted hospital,
on a tarred street where we learned to ride bicycle,

Mama and Baba's sister were seated outside.
Maryam was without a cloth, or so I remembered it.

The electricity was out, it was crowded with patients,
and that was because their services are cheap,

I hear people say it was rare for people to die in the hospital.
I have been there myself since we arrived Ilorin,

the spirits in the water are finding it hard
to recognize my Baba's gene in mine or in my siblings.

We got sick before every full moon.
but I was a bit consistent with fever of all sorts.

ش

I recognize the heat inside the hospital, it could make one
want to get well soon enough, or to the least miss the fresh air
strutting outside. I overhead Baba's sister tell a friend whose
child was at the hospital for a scheduled injection, that my

sister is heavy, "she'll need to vomit, and she'll be alright, maybe we will be going home soon. She looks well already, can't you see?".

"Yes, I pray that Allah will purge her blood and bones of diseases." She said, before fading into the waves of patients.

For almost a week, Mama did not change her clothes or came home for anything, but a day before Maryam died, I saw her walked through the space we made into football field outside the compound and did not make eye contact. I knew she saw me and was mad I had the strength to play when my sister has not been home for a week. I followed her inside the compound, she reduced her pace to respond to the greetings and prayers from the women seated outside their doors, taking in the fresh air.

She changed her clothes without taking her bath or brushing her teeth, she left in new clothes and with a spec of light on her face that suggests what I heard earlier was maybe the truth, Maryam will be come tomorrow.

Maryam was home – lifeless,
after she emptied the boxes in her body.

That was all I know of her death.

I was nine and naïve about how loss swells
inside a body to render it breathless,

all I knew was to aspire
to be a goalkeeper in a soccer field

and maybe one day return to Kaduna,
where the spirits in the water recognizes my genes,

where there is a God
that understands my accent

Although, I never heard him speak

ض

On the veranda, women gathered on my mama's side of the family house, crying harder and harder as if to remind God of how fluent they were in the language of grief. Women are trusted to mourn in the open, the men only say prayers and pretend there is no enough water in their body to be shed for something they lost, something they once loved. I sat and wondered why there was need no cry and mumble unprintable words as they try unsuccessfully to ask questions and demand answer from God, but they look into the eyes of the closest person consoling them and yell. Why?

ط

I could not bear the congregation
of crying women,

so I stared at the ceiling,
decorated with the seed of some red berries

that only get sold during the rainy seasons.
I took turns counting the seeds over and over

to distract my eyes from the crying.
It was before I got used to mourning.

I am to learn to say prayers for the dead
like my uncles and my grandfather, who

comes out of his room at intervals
to ask the women to lower their cry,

with an assuring tone, as if to confirm to them,
that a God that gave command to the angel of death

could hear whispers from quaking hearts.

ظ

For a minute or less, the crying would reduce and then after he went back to his room, the tempo would rise and continue for a long time, until a new mourner runs into the house to heighten the wailing with their fresh voices.

I wanted so much not to cry, to shed the weight of pains trapped in my small body. The pain is not one I know to name, it is a strange voice that poured out of my mama's mouth as she continues to listen to so many reasons why she must be thankful to the God that took her daughter.

I didn't witness
how Maryam was lowered

inside the earth
in the family house's backyard,

I was too young to witness
the ritual of janazah.

ع

She was buried amongst her ancestors. Men and women who built the house she lived in before her death. For days, or even weeks, my heart was filled with fear. I was afraid I'll see her sit on the grave if I walked passed it alone. I believed she wouldn't be shy to speak to me, but I was worried she wouldn't speak in a language I will understand. I avoided the backyard at nights and the restroom, built against the fence that bordered the mosque and the family house. Her grave was small, but I guessed would fit a three-year-old.

A cousin told me the dead in the backyard communicate amongst themselves, and now my sister will have so much to learn from her great grandparents.

"How would they know her and what would they be discussing" I asked him

"They will tell her stories of the times before Nigeria got her independence, before there was a single car roaming the streets of Ilorin"

I want to hear those stories too, but I don't want to die to hear them.

غ

Thirteen years after we left Ilorin,
I walked inside the family house.

There is a giant water storage tank
just above the well

that was once our only reliable source of water,
it swallowed so much space,

it shrunk the memory I had of the house.
There is a solar on top of the roofs

I recognized this house,
but there's been layers of paints over its wall,

like a scar smeared with mascara,
I could see beneath the orange painting,

no matter how long I stayed away,
I can still see the balcony

where I blow charcoals to embers
on evenings when we had something to cook.

ف

Some of the women did not recognized me, I had grown big
they would say after I reminded them of my name and whose
son I was. On my way to the restroom, the heaps were levelled
like the small field outside the house where we once gathered
on most evening to play football. I thought I could see the past
in the new face the house wore, but I was wrong. The bones
of my ancestors in the backyard were deemed old enough to
be sand and they've been erased with my sister's. I could have
asked my mama's father why they decided to erase the sign that
my sister was laid here in the house, but I didn't, I was too mad
to trust that I will ask gently, so I tucked my shock away.

ق

If I had not witnessed the women's wailing, or
if that memory wasn't a louse in my hair,

I would argue that the backyard
had no memory of any of our ancestors

or my sister's, and that memory is a mirage
beneath a mirror of a frozen floor.

Daniel R. Ball

Review of a Late-Minted Ween Fan

Ween. The very name seems to connote the small and discounted, perhaps evoking a penis joke. Principal members: Gene and Dean Ween (these are not their real names). A glance at their repertoire reveals bizarreness practically unparalleled: grunge rock, sea shanties, gnarly jams, or heartfelt portraits of love and addiction that you'd swear on first listen must be some kind of joke. "Bananas and Blow" offers a manic, twisted answer to Jimmy Buffet's "Margaritaville". Their self-described "dark, acid rock record," The Mollusk, was an inspiration to the creator of Sponge-Bob SquarePants. And oh yeah, you bet your ass they have a country album. I was never really into music as a kid. I didn't go to shows or collect albums. So I missed the boat for timely entrance into Ween fandom and I only really started listening to anything more than an occasional blare of "Ocean Man," which everyone agrees is entry level Ween, in my late twenties. Maybe that's a good thing, all things considered; they say not to meet your heroes, and Gene Ween is my fucking hero.

✳

My obsession with Ween started shortly after I made the decision to stop seeing my psychiatrist. That doesn't sound healthy, and it's not, but there it is. Seeing him in the first place was one of the more drawn out and difficult things I've had to do for myself. It took holding the hand of one of my dear friends during my final MFA residency to force me to click "send" on the appointment request. It took the same hand-holding to finally admit that I wasn't doing fine, that things weren't getting better, that I was spending most days hating myself and feeling paralyzed with guilt about that very paralysis, all the while telling my friends, family, mentors, and anyone who would listen that being in New York, being married, being young and being a writer were a kind of Shangri-La. I'd use that word, "Shangri-La", hate myself a little more the moment it left my lips, wondering if the person hearing it had any idea of the extent of my bullshittery.

So I ballsed up and made an appointment with exactly what I wanted: a pill pusher. I wanted an easy way to be better. In my mind I had to go to a doctor because I had a medical problem to fix. This doctor spoke in a calming voice and feigned concern as he ran through the diagnostic checklist and family history, raising an eyebrow at my past history of cutting. I followed my end of the script: I'm depressed, I've been depressed for a long time, I want to make it better – but I don't want to lose my boner. This last bit was the extensively-googled linchpin for walking out with my prescription for an initial titration of Bupropion Hydrochloride.

✻

When you make yourself known as a band that delights in goofiness and crafts every song and album from within a deep bubble of irony, it can be easy for someone – even a fan – to think that you don't care about anything. Ween's chameleon-like shift between styles and general disdain for "depth" or cultural loyalty can be seen in the album 12 Golden Country Greats, or in the wannabe prog rock artsy-ness of The Mollusk. But this is the great contradiction of Ween. They're seriously joking – or they're joking, seriously. If all there is to life is getting high and acting like a rock star, then by God that's what you do. It's part of what endears the band to ski bums and those with the hearts of ski bums.

Which is not to say that Ween didn't put an incredible amount of effort into their art. Yes, they did a lot of drugs. Yes, they laughed at the very thought of taking themselves seriously. But everything they produced was created with awareness and purpose, and to anyone willing to listen, it shows.

Ween's work invites questioning. Are they rock stars, or are they making fun of rock stars? Are their own fans failing to get the joke, or are they a necessary part of the joke? If you are alternately absurd, what does it mean when people take you seriously? Is meaning dressed up in nonsense still meaning?

In the world of Ween, what is real?

For me, getting healthy was about the dogged pursuit of some kind of answer to that question. It says something that I unironically took comfort in the song "Exactly Where I'm At", from Ween's seventh album, White Pepper. It starts with a lo-fi drumbeat, into which the quiet narrator's voice emerges synchronously with a tinny guitar riff:

> *Let's begin with the past in front,*
> *And all the things that you really don't care about, now.*
> *You'd be exactly where I'm at.*

And to think you've got a grip, well,
Look at yourself, your lips are like two flaps of fat.
They go front and back, and flappity flappity flap...

The grungy systoles and diastoles continue for a few measures, building with quiet intensity as if the narrator is willing himself to continue while waiting for the curtain to rise. Then, with a crescendo of high-hat cymbal, that lo-fi quality reminiscent of Ween's early days on self-recorded tapes is dropped, replaced with a rich and driving bassline and a full, rounded sound into which the now clear narrator leads:

I'm on stage; it's all an act.
I'm really scared that I may fall back on the abstract.
You'd be exactly where I'm at.

If you're to be the roaming eye, then
Pry it open; let me tell you why it sees
The harsh realities.

This is one of those striking moments in Ween lyrics: the sudden fidelity of the instrumentals reflects the trueness of the line, scuttling any notion that this is merely a joke band by bringing a long-felt clarity, that, yes, somehow, they've made it. And yet the voice of Gene, in all humility, still insists that the very real earned fame, the very fact that he's on stage, is "all an act" – both figuratively and literally.

I love this lyric. I love this song. Where most of Ween can seem deliberately exclusive or enigmatic with its bizarre lyrics, tonal shifts and overall attitude, here instead is something radically inclusive, that in fact demands the listener take a moment to empathize with the narrator. Then, after that moment of reflection during the very brief lyrics, we can enjoy the rest of the – again, genuinely talented – instrumentals.

Waxing poetic about "Exactly Where I'm At" like this might lead you to think that the song is an anomaly, but no, it is 100% Ween. And those goofy ones I mentioned before? Those are 100% Ween too.

If I'm feeling lost or stuck, this is my go-to jam. I'll sit there at my desk with my headphones blaring, my head filled with the cautiously optimistic work of the guitars. It's funny how now in retrospect I can split my life into before and after Ween. This is my new self-injury, finger-drumming on the corner of the desk hard enough to make it feel like my knuckles will bleed, waiting for the return of the lo-fi in the fadeout that will bring me back into the unreality of reality.

✳

I'm all too well acquainted with the scent of my wife's lover's perfume. It's spicy, musk-forward, yet altogether unmistakably feminine. I'll catch a note reminiscent of it seemingly everywhere I go. Is it something in the air, some autumnal essence that the perfumer faithfully reproduced? Or did some stray molecules stow away in our linens, somehow evading annihilation in the laundry, only to drive me momentarily mad as they take flight? It's as if she's omnipresent, an olfactory apparition. I'll note it when I'm working with soil or watering houseplants; out of nowhere the musky scent will rise, life and fertility distilled and brought out of the loam, and as I breathe it in I'm helpless to picture anything other than her.

The whole thing was difficult for me to process or accept at first. For a long time I hated her, the very thought of her. Even more I hated myself for hating her. She was, after all, so many things that I am not, can never be. She is a woman. I'll never have her dark hair, her olive eyes, her sensuous figure, her throaty laugh. I'm no lout, but I'll never have her intoxicating presence, her deceptive confidence, her effortless allure. At the same time as all that jealous loathing, I was in awe of her. When she tells you about her life, it's as if she's lived multiple lives, and all I wanted was to let her continue the spell, consume my life and steal my youth like some Twilight Zone villainess.

I once had a long conversation with her parked in a rental car in front of a liquor store in San Francisco. I don't really remember much of what I said to her. I do remember that I couldn't look her in the eye the entire time, opting to stare in front at the dashboard as I prattled on about trust and love and whatever else. But she listened until I ran out of words and told her as much. And then we went in and bought the bottle of whiskey we had to get. We both prefer Talisker because we have good taste.

She's a doctor, but it's not just that she saves lives. It's that she cares for people, even those who are dying and those whom we'd say have lost their mind. And she does it all without losing her own humanity or ever compromising on her will to bring more goodness – more life – into the world.

It's no wonder my wife likes her.

I talked about her to my psychiatrist in one or two of my brief attempts at sneaking in some of the therapy I knew I needed into our 15-minute medication checkups. ("I'm really more of a psycho-pharmacologist," he'd said during my first visit, as he jotted down the number of a referral I'd never call.)

In typical fashion he heard me and took a note or two in my file, raised eyebrows betraying the pedestrian scandal of a patient with a bisexual wife. I omitted that I knew how this sort of story would end: in divorce, or, in my more dramatic moments, my suicide. Instead I preferred to water down the constant strain in my mind, finding myself saying aloud something like, "It's fine, you know, I want my wife to be happy, and I want us to keep being in love, and I know that even with all of this, that will never change…"

Come to think of it, maybe he wasn't such a bad therapist after all.

※

There isn't always a meaning, an answer, a way you're supposed to feel. I'm talking about Ween again, of course. Their love of pastiche, their seemingly endless appetite for goofing off, and their partying weirdo fanbase all make this clear on their own. Yet, even in the mode of pastiche, certain songs like "Stay Forever" and "It's Gonna be (Alright)" are just simple and sweet to the point that you have to wonder whether it's an inside joke you're outside of. It seems almost selfish that fans like me will still have our favorites in spite of this, those we either want to share with everyone we know or else keep quietly "ours." And isn't that enough to make the whole thing matter?

One of the consistent fan favorites at Ween's live shows is "Awesome Sound." The lyrics consist entirely of the thrice-repeated phrase, "I've got an awesome sound, going down", followed by the grungily shouted, "I've got a pork roll, egg, cheese, and bacon!" All of this is nestled in five to fifteen or more minutes of heavy andante rock beat and sweet guitar work. It's the epitome of Ween playing the role of rock stars. You could say that the whole spectacle is "all an act." But for the fan rocking out in the audience – be they a tried and true down-with-the-brown follower, or an East Coast breakfast sandwich enthusiast, or just someone who needs to escape life for a while in that brief respite of awesome sound – does knowing it's role-playing make it any less real?

Try as Ween might to portray themselves as just fucking off, there is always something in there. This in turn gives them the freedom to let what's good about a song come out in its own right; if everything is a joke, then nothing is a joke either. How else could a rock group get away with sea shanties on their best album? Yet there sits "She Wanted to Leave", the final song of The Mollusk. It starts with an aptly piratical 3/4, and details the short story of how a band of scoundrels board the narrator's ship and kidnap his true love. The narrator's first reaction is one of righteous indignation, and he orders his men to fire on the interloping ship. It's only upon his true love's plea for him not to shoot that he realizes that, in fact, he's not the good guy here. She wanted to leave, after all, made all the more abundantly clear: "I've never loved thee." Forced to reckon not only with this loss but with the fact that everything he's sought in his life has been a lie, the narrator concedes as the tempo slows, "So go fetch your bottle of rum, dear friends, and fill up my glass to the rim, for I'm not the man I used to be: now, I'm one of them."

For perhaps obvious reasons, this song resonates with me. But just to say that it's relatable is weak, a half-truth. What it is for me is a provoker. It taps into not only the jealousy and fear that your true love might leave, but more so that you might be "one of them," the very scoundrel for which the narrator first pinned the men who board his ship, a selfish prick who would steal someone away without care for what she wants or what's "right." There's comfort for me in the way this little story is framed. For the listener, what starts as empathy for the ostensibly attacked and violated narrator quickly turns into understanding that the narrator deserves no empathy. It only takes seeing the true picture with the narrator's bias removed. I for one am left with gratitude that I can drop that pretense of empathy, that I can say, confidently, that I am not the narrator; I am not "one of them."

As if to confirm this, or to add insult to injury, the song concludes with a plaintive bit of fourth wall-breaking. After that final line, "Now, I'm one of them," the music fades to silence, but the rhythmic oceanic ambience of wind and waves continues. We can imagine the narrator standing at the bow of his ship in silence, now that there is nothing left: all that remains of him (and Ween's album) is the soulless sea.

But then, in a fantastic illustration of Weenian absurdity/ profundity, music returns. Out of the left speaker, still muffled by the waves, a staccato piano begins, and soon joining it, a chintzy accordion-esque ensemble playing the melody from the goofy showtune that begins the album, "Dancing in the Show." It's not just the fact of the reprise that makes this brilliant, it's the continued use of very visual sound. The tune begins softly, balanced far to the left ear, and then gradually sweeps to center, then off to the right, where it finally fades away with distance. Then the waves overtake the sound once again, and the track ends. It creates the image in sound of a small vessel, in my mind an overloaded rowboat, carrying the slipshod members of a band so much like Ween who have taken to the seas with utter lack of purpose or care, and who pass the narrator of "She Wanted to Leave" just to briefly pull him from his humiliated reverie, remind us all that there's something delightful in absurdity, and then disappear over the horizon to leave him alone once more in his miserable new reality.

✳

Burned in my memory: we're at a wedding in southern France at a fairytale chateau outside of Aix-en-Provence. Leading up to the trip I'd felt the tug of an ongoing depressive episode. At this point I've been off medication for a while, so I keep the familiar symptoms quiet, as is my default, both for fear of ruining the trip and out of embarrassment that I'm not yet "better."

My wife and I are with a couple of friends, and more we know from New York are here too. It's all quite beautiful, lucky and bourgeois. I even keep my composure when she arrives after a delayed flight. I see my wife's face light up as she checks her phone for the tenth time, and I know she wants nothing more than to jump up and run to her, though she's keeping her cool in front of the others.

It's only later in the evening, in all the abundance of wine and stimuli, that I feel the full ponderous pull of depression. I can't dance or chitchat, and everywhere I put myself I feel searingly out of place. My thoughts take on that familiar accusatory vocal quality that drowns out all sound and reason: "What the fuck are you doing here? Nobody here is your friend. Nobody cares that you're here." I find myself pacing in an unlit portion of the garden, telling myself I'm just taking a breather, but I cannot bring myself to step back toward the noise and light of the party. Eventually my wife comes and finds me. She sits me down at our table in the corner and tries to calm me down but I start crying. I put my head down on the table. I can't breathe.

Someone else comes over to the table, and of course, it's her. She's just come over from the dance floor: there's a glisten of sweat on her brow and her face is relaxed the way it gets when she drinks but her eyes are bright with youth and vim. I lift my head and I'm sure that she sees that my face is all red and shitty looking, but she doesn't make a thing of it. She just looks at me and asks, earnestly, "Can we go back to being silly?"

It's one of the most perfect things anyone has ever said to me.

✳

On January 24th, 2011, Ween embarks on a tour. The first major show will be in Vancouver. The tour will be the last the band plays before their breakup.

To say the show is a disaster doesn't quite capture it. There's something altogether more eerie about it, all visible in what little footage of the night is available. The way the set never really gets off the ground and instead looks and sounds like some kind of extended sound check, with band members milling around on the stage, tuning instruments and holding brief one-to-one conferences, the way Gene Ween's wilder than usual hair looks in the spotlight, the way his voice takes on the tone of a pained, intoxicated plea as he tries to power through "Birthday Boy", the way members of the audience seem torn between entertainment and concern as they cheer a supine Gene on, even when he's the only one left onstage, willing themselves to believe that this is not a meltdown but rather just part of "the true Ween experience"… it all makes for a sinking sort of feeling. We all know how the rock-star-at-rock-bottom narrative ends.

Maybe that's the Achilles heel of the fuck-all immortality that brought about the rise of Ween. Whether it meant slapping together a dorky pastiche track for the hell of it, or doing a shit-ton of coke for the hell of it, Ween would always stay the course. Embracing the idea that everything's a joke if you take it seriously may let you do anything, may blunt any misguided attempt at criticism, but it also must insist on a kind of transcendence that may inevitably lead to a hard and complete fall. The Vancouver show was a wakeup call for Aaron Freeman. He could no longer go on laughing in the face of alcohol and drug abuse, could no longer goof away the obvious pain of depression and a divorce – in short, he could no longer be Gene Ween.

Fortunately, though, Freeman's career doesn't end there. It's not the expected story, with fans proving their loyalty by expressing their profound loss as yet another celebrity overdose death story hits the internet. No – Freeman, in fact, soon releases another album.

The new band he creates is also called Freeman, and their eponymous album is unsurprisingly Ween-like. When I first heard a couple of songs on the album without context, I thought in fact they were some Ween songs I simply hadn't heard. All of the songs on the album share some of that dreamy psychedelic charm and sedate groove spiked with alt-rock flair. But taken as a whole, the album differs from any Ween album because it omits the sinister undertone that drives the narrative reality of Ween's work. Freeman sounds almost Eden-like at times. Songs like "There is a Form" emit a sunshine-y air. It's as if Aaron Freeman wants to drive home the fact that he escaped his existence as Gene Ween – Free Man, get it?

But there's one song on the album that lacks this border-line-saccharine happiness. "Covert Discretion", the very first song, instead provides Aaron Freeman's account of the incident in Vancouver. It's very metered, with a repetitive structure that guides you through each stanza, all set to a sobering acoustic guitar. In stark contrast to essentially anything Ween had produced, Freeman's song begins one night before the Vancouver show:

> *Covert discretion, in the hotel room,*
> *Ain't it always the same?*
>
> *Another gig now, got an aching head,*
> *And I'm back on display.*
>
> *Ain't no thing though, all the fans agree:*
> *We killed it tonight.*

Gone is any rock-star pretense, any "Awesome Sound" braggadocio. Instead we have a human, vulnerable and alone in his hotel room. This setting and narrator are much more akin to that brief voice in "Exactly Where I'm At", the fruition of the lyrics,

"I'm on stage, it's all an act. I'm really scared," and yet it lacks even that song's drive and will to press on through musical verve. Freeman sings as if his being real were something he'd need to hide, as if how badly he was spiraling could be hidden from anyone. Continuing his "covert" misery, we find the lonely narrator going down into the hotel lobby, where a few fans linger. For a little while, at least, he can prop up that party-going rock star illusion. With this, of course, comes drugs. They'll be shared in the bathroom, to which he suggests with increasing bitterness, "Let's be super cool", even as the song continues with its methodical, melancholic, droning melody.

The Vancouver show would bring this all to a head. The climactic moment of Gene's downfall occurs before we've boarded the bus to the Vancouver show. It's here we see his language shift from "Yeah I'm down with the Brown" – trying to convince himself more than the drunken fans he's with– to something much more cynical and true:

What a special thing, I'm your trophy boy.
Get the fuck out my face.

'Cause you will go home satisfied,
And I'll be blacked out for the night.

By running through the memory in real time, pinpointing the moment of Gene's failure to pretend any longer, "Covert Discretion" elevates the whole history of the moment, preempting the obvious accusation that Freeman was the "bad guy" here. Instead it brings his overt depression to the forefront, and the question becomes, did nobody care to help?

What follows this moment is the only lyrical break. During the four-bar interlude evoking his blackout, Freeman strums his guitar with heavy strikes. You can practically feel his thumb and forefinger cutting against the strings. This isn't a song he wants to do; it's a story he has to tell.

When the lyrics resume, there isn't all that much new ground to cover. The rest of the story about the show just has to fall into place. We hear of Freeman, self-confirming his worthlessness, "On the bus now. They won't look at me. Man, it's always the same." That "Exactly Where I'm At" idea returns in the humble apology, "I wasn't tryin' to blow your fantasy." Then, in a very subtle dynamic shift, the song slows and softens at the line,

"Another chance now. I'm on the stage again," as if there's still a chance that the fate of the evening might shift. As if there's still a chance for Gene Ween. But of course, Freeman must deliver the simple, defeated line that sums up the whole show: "But this time I don't fly."

There's no break between the stanza covering the show and that of its aftermath. A few last details come in about how the same bandmates who left Gene "alone up there to die" call the next day, "makin' sure I'm alive." Granted, for someone as fucked up as Freeman was, it would be a legitimate concern, if a bit base. But it's the calls he sees as half-hearted, those saying "Man you gotta end this, just walk away," that lead him to the final line of the quiet acoustic story:

So save your judgments for someone else,
And be grateful I saved me from myself.

Then, as if in final defiance of the expected rock bottom overdose/suicide narrative – you can't put Gene Ween in a box! – electric guitar now swells along with driving rock bass and drums as Freeman delivers the manic, many-times repeated final lyric, "Fuck you all, I've got a reason to live, and I'm never gonna die." That doesn't sound healthy, and it's not, but there it is.

❊

Not only would Freeman and his career survive, but Ween would get back together a few years after that "final" performance. You can still see Gene, Dean, and the rest on tour today.

Given this practically unprecedented rebound, it's understandable that Freeman would have some measure of embarrassment or regret for creating the final "fuck you" that the song was ultimately meant to be. There are very few instances reported of the song being performed live, and Ween and their fans have focused on moving forward as well as enjoying the favorites that made them.

But on some level, I'm sure Aaron Freeman regrets none of the words or sentiments he immortalized with the song. It was, and will always be, the story of who he was, and who Ween were, encapsulated in that moment, and the hindsight logic of the story as told in "Covert Discretion" is what allows the history of Ween to have any sort of truth to it at all. Without that truth, it really would be "all an act." Without Freeman's raw contemporary honesty in the song, Ween's work could be seen as nothing more than the silly pastiche they created with facetious abandon.

I'm so damn glad they got a happy ending.

✳

My favorite thing about the whole Ween story is that theirs is not the message of the millennial platitude "don't let your dreams be dreams." Rather, it's that giving up on your dreams, to an extent, is part of becoming an adult. That, more than anything else, is why I treat Ween as if they were my therapist, or more simply, believe that Ween even helped me through some shit.

Really, it was just good timing that I'd stumble into admiration of Aaron Freeman, a person who figured this fact out the hard way, at the same time I was beginning to figure it out for myself. If Freeman could shed the burden of Gene Ween, then I could shed the childish, false and hollow idea of what it meant to be whole: to be a "real" writer; to have a "perfect" marriage.

It's only in peeling away the sanctimonious truths I thought I knew about love that I could look back at what I left to see something truer. And only then could I even think about getting back up on the stage again.

✳

I wanted to end this essay there, with this note of acceptance, of light at the end of the tunnel. But real stories don't fit into boxes.

The woman my wife was seeing – damn it, I have to write the woman my wife loved – is no longer in contact with her. I can imagine myself years ago being smugly satisfied at the idea of it, as though it were a victory, but instead I'm left with the hollow truths of biology and fate, narrators so heartless and unstoppable that no protagonist or antagonist could compete.

My wife and I are new parents, and the birth of our daughter has led to a total re-definition of love that we never anticipated. It is a new kind of struggle, exhaustive in its joyousness, that we want nothing more than to share: look, look what we've managed to do, look how wondrous the world is. But through the eyes of someone struggling with fertility, scourged with the grief of loss and weighed down by the specter of what might never be, what avenue is there to share in any of that joy? How could we ask that of her?

For a few months after the news of my wife's pregnancy, they maintain increasingly strained and distant contact, but soon their will to prop up the façade erodes. And so, with a phone call, the relationship ends.

My best friend texts me when we're going through this, when I'm trying to figure out how to feel, trying to assign a reason to it. "Did you love her a little bit?" they ask me. "Of course I did," I respond, as though just saying it could be enough to shut the book, close the show.

I find myself wishing that she's still a part of our lives, as if her being present were the only way to make any of it real. But no closure is ever found in despair. I never found an answer through medication, nor could I ever quite write my way out of my trouble, keeping it real by keeping it silly the way I always thought Ween could.

Then again, a kind of answer can be found in Ween, in "Transdermal Celebration" from the album Quebec. The song is the Book of Revelation performed with hallucinatory compassion in place of violent finality, providing a haunting yet quietly hopeful portrait of a man lost. The chorus begins, "Hey, hey, a million miles to mark A."

And no matter how many times I listen, I consistently mishear it as "Hey, hey, a million miles from O.K."

That's what it's all about, isn't it? It hasn't been easy, and I'm sure there will always be some things that I'd prefer to hide from. There will always be more pain to persevere through, and more joys to see if I do. All there is left is to continue forward, hoping that I've got the words right, hoping that happy endings can be real, hoping, even if I'm still another half a million miles from O.K., that we'll get there.

Lori Brack

A Blur in the Field

Regarding a Kansas farm, there are documents – maps, photographs, and a handwritten journal, its ink gone brown. If you squint at the 1916 county atlas and plat book, you can make out a farmer's first and last name inked on a wedge of land tucked under a curve of the Arkansas River. The farmer named this place Jingletown.

Jake farmed, built, and gardened there. He grew and sold wheat, corn, and melons. He called the first structure Jingle-house, built while he lived at his parents' farm, worked on after family chores.

In 1907 when Jake was 19, he began a daily work record and continued writing each day until he was 30. By giving Jingletown a name and keeping track of it in his journal, Jake made the place live, filled it with speculation. I envision the garden, barn, one field, a side of the house easily as if I'd been there. Years on, Jingletown became the mythical homeland where my mother was born, the place occupied by one family — Jake and Iva, their five children, dogs and cats, horses, pigs and cows. Because I cannot discover why it was named, I invent a lilac bush hung with silverware and old keys, or a bottle tree in the wind, or the ring of harness over horses' necks.

January 15, 1911: Burnt brush and measured Jingletown in a.m. The measurements were North End 72½ rods. South side 122 rods. West end 68½ rods.

❋

I have a photograph of my mother on Jake's birthday the year he died in a car crash, age 49. She sits behind the new gravestone surrounded by flowers – prairie garden zinnias mostly. She is freckled and round-cheeked, age twelve. Her curled hair brushes the shoulders of her dress. On the bottom margin, her mother noted: *Dad's birthday – August 24, 1938.*

Though I swear she had been unconscious of the calendar for weeks, she died in 2001 on the same date. My mother looks at me out of the picture on the day of her death 63 years later.

Her gaze brushes Jake's gravestone and branches from the 1930s photographic paper to me, where it puts down roots.

He was dead years before I was born. I've read and reread each journal page and not once does a common address – rural route or road number – appear. On the last pages, though, he made a list of fruit trees he planted, mostly cherry and apple varieties, an apricot, a peach or two. Within a few years, Jake's orchard dream would dwindle and die from flooding or drought. He plowed it under and planted corn and wheat. He cultivated cantaloupe on the sandy riverbank and trucked loads of them to town, noting in his ledger the pounds and proceeds from each trip. Sometimes he took one of the children along.

As drought and dust storms brought meager crops and the Great Depression weakened grain prices, Jake took his family and left home, trading it for a job and house in town. He sold the land and soon lost his life. Whatever remains of Jingletown fills the creases of the ledger he covered with words, tangled among his penmanship.

✳

Maps, like dreams of flying, bestow power. Split from myself as in dreams, I and someone not-I survey from above, trying to make out the owners of each pastel acre. In 1916, a mapmaker drew the irregular shapes of farms, made approximations based on land surveys, and marked bridges and roads, inked river flow between banks.

Talking to myself, I hover over the beige digital emptiness I find, a whole screenful of nothing except light blue river and white road: Dartmouth Rd intersects SE 10 Rd that ends in a loop like a magnifying glass, one single circle amid the map's parallels.

June 8, 1918: Hoed till noon. Father and mother came down. Went after alfalfa. Came back and hoed till dark. Finished cantaloupes. Total eclipse of sun this evening about 6 p.m.

✳

She lines them up where the light is. My grandmother's daughters and sons, or anyone she can gather when she discovers the camera under the mess. What's a broom or dust rag to a magic box that keeps the faces of those she loves? Her finger steadies on the button, she clicks: freckles and overalls, one kitten, horses, a goat hitched to the little cart, her husband holding out his big hands. She clicks: hollyhocks beside the porch, friends who dropped in, a

neighbor wearing a sheet and a cardboard crown. When grand-
mother's photos come back from the drugstore in town, she inks
names in the margins and always includes the white horse, the
dog with his tongue out, the blur in the birdcage atop a Model T.

✳

When she was grown, my mother had a fruit empire – bright
cherries on two backyard trees. The subjects she could rally –
her children, her eldest sister – stooped under limbs and climbed
ladders wearing bleach bottles with holes cut into them, fastened
around our waists with rope. We reached into the tree, pulled and
dropped each cherry into the bottle, a cascade of shiny marbles
piling up without temptation to taste even one sour fruit.

Once, we went to find Jingletown. Mother, who raised us 30
miles away in town, was seeking sand hill plums, and her sister,
still a farmwoman living even farther away, remembered plums
had grown around the homestead. The cherry-picking bleach
bottles rolled around the trunk of the big Dodge my mother
piloted over dirt roads.

Like her taste for jelly and her stubborn insistence we go
on this quest, sand hill plums are damn near invincible. They're
native to the sandy prairies of Kansas and love a drought. In
spring, they bloom white and in the heat of summer, they put
out small red fruit, each round plum frosted with a white film.
Thickets are thorny, and stems are covered with small leaves that
turn down at the tip. Despite my willingness to help, I couldn't
spot plum brush from the back seat. The homestead was a set-
ting for family stories, not a place I knew how to recognize.

The sisters did not know the way to their birthplace, but they
kept trying – false turnings into other drives, backing and retrac-
ing, craning to see anything familiar at intersections. Neither of
them had been home in more than thirty years.

✳

On both sides, I come from families that use names to
claim, to tease, to connect. My father invented nicknames for his
wife, his children, and most of his many siblings. I was Glims.
My sister was Russki, my brother Rocky. Mom was Jackson. His
flamboyant elder sister was Paganucci. My father had his original
reasons, but they seem less important than his inventive daily
act of twirling out an aspect of who we were. On jovial days, I
was Glim-ronia – a riff on Louis Jordan's 1945 jump blues hit

"Caldonia," a dance song from a decade before I was born. My
dad would holler with glee, "Glim-ronia! Glim-ronia! What make
your big head so hard?" My mother might interject, "She got it
from you."

Place names, though. They should stick. Poets can rename
a river because of light or weather or mood, but if you want to
navigate, you need permanence to count on. Naming invents the
landscape, marks off a vista or makes a dream visible, pulls the
past into the present, privileges a worldview. The same year my
dad was listening to "Caldonia" on a thick 78-rpm disk, English
professor George R. Stewart published *Names on the Land.*
Stewart was interested in the human motivation behind how
we distinguished places as we settled. He expounds, "Thus the
names lay thickly over the land, and the Americans spoke of
them, great and little, easily and carelessly ... not thinking how
they came to be. Yet, the names had grown out of the life, and
the lifeblood, of all those who had gone before."

My grandmother, annotating her husband's journal after his
death, clicked her blue ballpoint and wrote in the margin at the
top of April 1910: "Jingletown was the name given the little farm
when Daddy squatted on it. Was lots of brush and shrubs there."
Instead of clarifying, this note only deepens the mystery – her
passive voice ignores the namer though she must have known
who it was. And I'm still no closer to what jingled.

*Oct. 15, 1911: "Hart and his auto got lost. I showed them the way to
the road."*

✺

Here is a minor chapter for the myth of place: my son and I
walked an abandoned railroad right-of-way one recent spring, a
wild and unmarked rural Kansas trail where we found no human
traces amid the sharp rocks used to steady rails, pulled up long
ago. Wild roses and tall tufted grasses grew around the signposts
bearing arcane symbols meant for train engineers. Most were
hacked off and strewn in the grass where my son spied our only
souvenir – a silver jingle bell sparkling among the weeds, big as a
sweet cherry with its metal pit rolling free.

✺

Kansas seasons – planting and growth, harvest and freeze
– shaped me and won't let me abandon their shifting chaos
of light and leaves and clouds. How April might blizzard, and

August might rain and rain. The coming on of change – I am addicted to it in my cells. The easy reasons are sky and horizon, the near-impossibility of getting too far from the soil. In Kansas, wind carries the news: rain, pollen, ash. Seasons speak clearer than the ephemeral ways we trace comings and goings. For instance, every blustery winter – Decembers with or without dry prairie snow, flat gray Januarys of my childhood, or the hovering climate-change winters post-millennium – I am aware the year ends and begins in darkness like a fleeting life that emerges from the womb only to fall to earth, to fall under it.

Why do I come back or stay when the ground is hard with labor and strain?

February 10, 1911: Cloudy. Very windy. Plastered house in Jingletown. Hauled up load of wood in eve.

February 15, 1911: Oiled set of harness in a.m. Painted house and porch in afternoon. Quite cool in a.m. Pleasant in p.m. Cloudy in eve.

February 18, 1911: Rained all night, turned to snow about 2 a.m. Ground was white by daylight. Snowed all day. Drifting bad all afternoon. Down to Jingletown to feed calves.

✳

Using the century-old plat book map as guide, I trace the closest town and enter its name into Google maps. I use my fingers to move around the countryside until I recognize a particular river curve. Click, and a brown and green pattern replaces the map's emptiness near where I find what I'm seeking. You will see a green, anvil-shaped patch edged by a swath of trees crowded against the river. And in its upper left corner, you will find a circle of road that loops and catches a small patch of land overgrown and littered with what might be buildings. Zoom in on a house with its roof fallen in, another building losing its siding, fence shadow. You have arrived at Jingletown – the same road in and out, and no way of getting to the river unless you walk across the field. It is hardly spring and the plums aren't leafed yet, the trees barely budding. You float, bird perspective, feel ancestors breathe from the ground. You think you catch a glimpse of them under your eyes roving over field, road, river. You wish for a way to see the past as overlay, x-ray – bones and skin of how you got *here*. You click out, then farther, wait for the focus, click broad and broader, until you drift bewildered in satellite omniscience, perceive from space how distant you are from home.

Mother Tongue

I play videos on my phone of the Belizean chef Sean Kuylen cooking every night. I'm not making any food; I'm in bed and can't sleep. I close my eyes every few words to revel in the way he sounds, especially how he pronounces each word. *Ai nayli bon aaf mi aiybrow*, he says, while flambéing a butter sauce for black cake, a Belizean take on holiday fruit cake. He's nearly burned off his eyebrow setting the sauce ablaze with a culinary torch. I smile at the way he pronounces the word 'burn' like 'bun.'

Each night like clockwork, Sean's voice lulls me to sleep. He sounds exactly like my grandmother, who was also born and raised in Belize. They speak what Belizeans call Broken English. I later learned the official name of the language is Kriol, and it's a version of the Creole spoken by Caribbeans that is specific to Belize.

My grandmother and I hadn't been close since we lived together in California during my childhood. We grew apart when I left for college, and in my adulthood, only talked a couple of times a year on the phone.

My mother kept tabs on her. Last December, my mother told me that my grandmother was in the hospital with a debilitating stomach pain. In March, the hospital called to tell my mother that my grandmother's kidneys were failing, and she would not live much longer. It was the height of the pandemic, but I dropped everything and booked a flight to California. Close or not, I didn't want my grandmother to die alone, and I wanted to say goodbye.

I hadn't seen her in seven years. I wondered what her failing kidneys had done to her. I worried most about her speech, fearing I wouldn't understand her.

I walked into the hospital room and announced myself. I approached her slowly and pulled down my gold sequined mask to kiss her forehead. I caught her eyes glimmering and asked, "Do you want a mask like mine?"

She nodded and interjected, *"Bot Ai noh waahn fi mi maas bee soh bizi bizi.*" I sighed with relief. But I don't want my mask to be too busy, she had said.

We spent the next two days together, talking when she felt like it. When she didn't, I just watched her sleep.

The next morning, she passed away. I stuck around to sign paperwork and arrange cremation services, and then flew home.

※

For weeks after my grandmother's death, I couldn't sleep. I didn't miss her, because I didn't really know her. I didn't know anything about her interests or passions, or much about her life before she was my grandmother.

But I knew what she sounded like. And that's what I missed.

Although I couldn't speak a word of Kriol, I understood every one of hers.

Mikays, nuh, mek wee geh bak faas. Hurry up, okay, so we can get back quickly.

Lef mi loan; yoo di dischrak mi fahn di teevee. Leave me alone; you're distracting me from the TV.

Chef Sean's voice brought me back to my childhood. The ten of us—my mother, siblings, cousins, aunts, uncles, grandmother, and I—crammed into a small house in a middle class suburb so that the kids could go to a good school.

My grandmother watched us while the adults worked. She didn't watch us the way that professionals provide childcare nowadays. She was there in case anything broke or caught on fire. She stayed on her side of the house—everything white and pristine—watching *Oprah* in her rocking chair and occasionally yelling to the other side where we played. *Unu pikni beta stap di goh aan soh.* You children better stop carrying on that way.

We quieted down immediately.

I understood my grandmother so well that I didn't know she was speaking a different language. I didn't even detect an accent. Then, when I was seven, she took me on a trip with her to the grocery store. She asked the cashier at the register, "*Ya ku chaynj dis dala intu foa kwaatas fi mi?*"

The cashier waved his hand at me, pulling my attention away from the candy offerings at checkout.

"Hey kid, what is she saying?" he demanded. "I cannot understand her. What does she want?"

"She needs change for a dollar," I said, annoyed that he didn't

understand what seemed perfectly understandable to me. The ca-
shier's face illuminated and then I knew.

My grandmother hurried me along, muttering an insult
about *yenkees* on our way out.

❋

My grandmother's six children ditched their accents soon after
the family emigrated from Belize in the early 70s. They wanted to
thrive in America, and thought their Broken English would hinder
their success.

By the time my siblings, cousins, and I were growing up in the
90s, they all spoke Proper English at home. But, when my genera-
tion wasn't around, or they thought we couldn't hear them, they fell
back into the comfort of Kriol. It came out after a deep sigh, pent
up all day and relieved to be released. In Kriol, they complained
about their low-paying jobs and conspired about how to get the
rent paid or Christmas gifts under the tree.

We only heard their Kriol by accident when a word slipped out
that didn't exist in English. "It's cold in here, *hais* up the window,"
they said.

We snickered and chided, "It's 'raise' the window."

The only intentional Kriol we heard came from my grandma.
It had none of the self-consciousness of my mom's and her
siblings' speech. It sounded unashamed and pure. I savored that
sound.

I assumed my grandmother couldn't ditch her accent. Perhaps
that's true. Or maybe she didn't want to.

By the time I knew her, my grandmother had stopped working.
She didn't know how to drive. She left the house only to go to the
grocery store or the doctor's office. She didn't interact much with
strangers. As a child, I thought she didn't feel comfortable out in
the world. She had a 2nd grade reading level. She had an accent.
She didn't want to play the 'where are you from?' guessing game
with *yenkees*.

But my grandmother got on a plane in Belize by herself, bring-
ing along her 2nd grade reading level and accent and not much else.
She landed at JFK International Airport and found a place to live in
Brooklyn. She got a job cleaning houses in Manhattan and saved up
enough money to send for her kids. She filled out immigration pa-
perwork and counted money and went grocery shopping and took
the subway, all with her 2nd grade reading level and accent.

Maybe she didn't want to turn it off. Maybe she loved the way she sounded as much as I did.

※

My mother had no Belizean accent during my childhood. In addition to buying into the myth of assimilation, her reason for purposefully losing her accent was more personal. In middle school, her classmates bullied her, constantly slinging xenophobic insults and even assaulting her. So she raised her kids to speak Proper English, not wanting us to have a similar experience.

Then my mother had a stroke in her early fifties, and her accent came raging back.

The sound of my mother's new voice disquieted me. I didn't recognize it. The stroke caused verbal apraxia, a motor speech problem defined by slurred and airy speech and difficulty with pronunciation. My mother sounded like a flighty Belizean schoolgirl, a younger version of herself whom I'd never met.

Unlike my grandmother's Kriol, my mother's brought me no pleasure. It reminded me of her weakened health. In her voice, I heard the stroke, the heart transplant before the stroke, and the heart failure before that. It highlighted her inability to control her faculties the way she'd done before. She wasn't healthy enough to push her accent down like she had for forty years. I knew how important self-control was for her, and how much it pained her to lose it.

Embarrassed, she asked me to speak to the waiters at restaurants. "*Ai kyaahn* with *mi* voice," she whispered in a mix of Kriol and English while cowering behind the menu. I can't with my voice.

I felt for her, back to fearing she would be bullied for her accent.

I went away to law school and called to check up on her every few days. The apraxia reached its height in the mornings. She fought to get every word out and strained to find the English equivalent. I grew accustomed to hearing her inner monologue. *Now, how mi fa seh dis eena Inglish?* Now, how do I say this in English?

I stopped calling in the mornings. Not just because I didn't like to hear her struggle or sound sick. I didn't like the shame I heard in her voice.

On her birthday one year, I had an eight-hour final exam. I broke my rule and called her in the morning on my walk to class.

"Hello my daughter, are you ready to ace your Torts exam?"

she asked in clear, easy, perfectly-accented English. I heard the mother who raised me. I stopped in shock.

"Are you there?" she asked. Same Proper English. I couldn't believe it.

"Sorry, I'm here," I jolted out of my reverie. "Happy birthday! Yes, I think I'm ready for Torts."

"Thank you. You got this. Your hard work will totally pay off." Even her American diction had returned.

The next day, I called her early, excited that my mom was back.

But she wasn't.

"*Heloa mi daata,*" she said slowly, as if to contain the Kriol. It spilled out anyway. "*How di egzam mi gaahn?*" How did the exam go?

I swallowed my disappointment and pretended not to notice. I didn't want her to feel ashamed.

I went back to evening calls, but it didn't matter. I never knew who would answer when I called, or what language she would speak.

✳

Even with full command of my faculties, I can't master a Belizean accent. I can't say anything in Kriol. I listen to Chef Sean and repeat his words. I don't sound anything like him.

But in my head, we sound the same. Our Kriol is thick but breezy. One morning, making breakfast, I ran to the stove thinking, *Ai hafta mek shoar mi noh bon op di oatmeel.* Yet out of my mouth came: I have to make sure I don't burn the oatmeal.

I don't have a connection to place, despite being stuck in the same one until I went to college. I have no geographic allegiances. I don't root for any sports teams or Olympic delegations. I'm American, but nothing in my home growing up hinted of America: no Fourth of July festivities, *Turner Classic Movie* nights, or Hamburger Helper dinners. My family is Belizean, but I didn't go to Belize until I was 29 years old. I ate tamales at Christmas and heard stories of Hurricane Hattie in 1961, but I didn't know Belize City from Belmopan.

My connection is, has always been, to sound. To words I can't spell with meanings I don't remember learning. A language that I can pronounce only in my head.

✳

Chef Sean says a few words I've never heard before. The closer I listen, the more I hear how healthy, happy, and alive he sounds. It reminds me that my grandmother is not.

I turn it off. I Google the unknown Kriol words, hoping some enterprising Belizean has made a YouTube channel for *yenkees* like me.

To my great fortune, I come across a Kriol-to-English dictionary created in 2007 at the behest of the then-governor-general of Belize, Sir Colville Young. In the forward, he explains the necessity for the text: "Appreciation of and literacy in one's mother tongue is essential for self-enrichment and expression of identity."

I pore over the dictionary's guide and grammar notes, the etymologies from Spain, Africa, Britain, and the Miskito people. I guess at the spelling of words my grandmother and mother used and rejoice when I find them. I go down the illustrative sentences one by one and guess the meanings before reading the English translation. When I get it right, I cheer inside like a kid who has just aced her multiplication tables.

There in the words is my connection to my grandmother, my culture, my country. As Sir Colville decreed, there I am.

Sir Colville also writes that because English is the most widely spoken language, it is often said to be the most useful. Not for me. Not for connecting to culture, for keeping a person's memory alive, for finding what was there all along. For these, there is only your mother tongue.

So now I call my mother at different times of the day. I learn Kriol so I can speak to her in whatever language I hear on the line.

Heloa mi daata, unu di kohn bai fa di paati? Hi my daughter, are you guys coming by the party?

Ahaahn Ma, wee waahn kohn rong chree. Yes, Mom, we will come around three.

Her voice perks up as we keep talking. The pride I hear fills me with warmth.

I savor the sounds. I cherish my mother's survival, and the endurance of her language too.

Before bed, I close my eyes and hear my grandmother in the hospital, at the grocery store, on her side of the house. I talk to her out loud in Kriol, getting up to check the dictionary if I get stuck. I tell her I love her and miss her. Sometimes I just tell her the things I wish I could've said. *Grani, Ai waahn mek sure fi yoo maas noh soh bizi bizi.* Grandma, I will make sure that your mask is not too busy.

Victoria Buitron

Sextonic Plates

Ithought my parents were having sex in their bedroom. I placed a pillow over my ear, hummed a Backstreet Boys' song and envisioned flying monkeys from the Wizard of Oz or a tsunami wave toppling a house like matchsticks, and just waited for the slight booms to stop. I heard no voices, but the idea that someone was having sex was the only option because every thirty seconds the sliding windows of my room would budge—a timed pounding—and I wanted to believe it wasn't my parents but that King Kong was miles away striding toward us. King Kong and flying monkeys weren't real, but the idea my parents could be having sex in the next room was unfortunately quite possible.

When my mother opened my bedroom door and asked me if I was responsible for the house shaking, my initial hypothesis dissolved the way a spiderweb fissures with the help of a swaying hand.

"Wait, so you're telling me it's not you?" I said.

Before she could answer, sleepy eyes widening and eyelashes still caked with a bit of mascara, she pointed to the roof and screamed: "Ahí están. ¡Ya los vi!"

Who she saw beyond the zinc roof baffled me, since I wasn't aware she could see through walls. But it was enough that a few seconds later I caught a glimpse of my father in grey boxers running from their room. Gun in his hand. Black sneakers untied. So fast he seemed like a tanned ghost intent on chasing invisible ones.

He had a gun, but maybe the others my mom saw had one, too.

She shoved my brother and I into our Jack and Jill bathroom and made sure not to turn on the lights. We stood in pitch black, hugging each other and waiting to hear screams. I could no longer envision scenes from films or song clips to distract me—all I could hear was the steady flow of blood in my neck. I couldn't cry, but I waited for a man's wail, or footsteps, or my father screaming that we were safe.

My uncle and his wife, Iris, lived in the other section of the house, just on the other side of the bathroom wall.

"Are you okay? We thought we were imagining things. Pedro

took a gun too. They're outside the gates now," she spoke to us in whispers through the walls, the words quick, stumbling into each other like cartwheels. I envisioned her close to the window, her skin translucent under the shadow of the yard's lights, trying to make out limbs and men.

We heard a gunshot. Just one.

A few seconds later Iris told us my father and his brother had returned, and we could leave our hiding places to meet them among the mango trees. My father had let out a warning shot into the night to frighten imaginary thieves, to show neighbors he had no qualms about shooting a gun. The ground still moved as if a tree fell every minute not a long ways away. When I reached our yard and looked beyond the gates, I noticed neighbors standing on their balconies as if ready to confront a villain. Lights were turned on, and people strode to the street corner as perplexed as we were with the bumps in the night. No one could discern what it was.

My father, still in his boxers, stomach bulging, his belly button deep enough to hold a peach pit, said: "I don't know what the hell that is, but I hope it stops."

Iris believed that maybe the apocalypse was here, and that this is how it started. We made fun of my mother and her ability to see through walls. My younger brother, eleven years old, stood in between my mother and one of the mango trees, waiting for permission to head back to sleep. My uncle wondered if someone had positioned a huge Sony boom box in the heart of our town, and that every few moments we could feel the thwacks from the bass.

"Tío, that's ridiculous," I said. "I for sure thought someone was having sex."

"What do you think we are? Bulls?" my father placed a hand over his face, laughed so much his belly trembled, and then grabbed onto a tree so he wouldn't lose his balance. How could I think something so mundane, so natural, could move the entire house? I avoided looking at my parents' faces, but we all stood there, laughter comforting us amid the unknown.

As we made our way back to the house, my brother and I headed our parents' room. The four of us had never slept together on the same bed, and the last time I spent a night with them was before I was a teenager, when I was sick and needed their closeness to comfort me. The idea of going to sleep alone that night—not understanding what was happening and why—made me wish that actual thieves had tried to make their way into our home. That would have been a reasonable explanation. A human one.

We lay on the bed, our eyes as awake as an owl's, waiting for the adrenaline inside of us to dissipate and the ground's rumble to stop terrifying us. We waited until the dark swapped into light. Until the vibrations became a memory.

While we prepared breakfast, friends of my parents called with the neighborhood report. A man stood on his laundry-lined rooftop to see if the culprit was a monster that resembled a giant serpent. Another placed a chair in his dining room, gripping a machete, waiting for what emerged from underground. He wanted to be ready, but his wife scoffed and went back to sleep. All around our town, people heard the thumps, and like us, found it menacing and waited to defend themselves.

But as the day continued, we learned that a volcano hundreds of miles away had erupted in the Andes, the western highlands. A tectonic plate that neighbored it, and that stretched all the way to us—Milagro, Ecuador—moved with every burst of magma that became lava.

It was just the land. The insides of the earth. Not a human explanation, but a scientific one.

Now that we were reassured, we spent the day pointing to ghost thieves, asking my uncle if he needed a new boom box, and comparing my dad to Rambo. My jaw hurt by the end of the day from the laughter. I went to sleep that night knowing that unlike the apocalypse, my parents doing it in the next room wouldn't bring the house down around us.

Sara Siddiqui Chansarkar

The Making of Mango Pickle

The summer breeze sways bunches of green mangoes left and right on the neighbor's tree which stretches its limbs into your courtyard. The fruit reminds you of the mango pickle you haven't made in a long time—you made it last 30 years ago. You decide to make it this summer and pack it for your six married daughters to give them a taste of their mother's recipe before you are too frail and forgetful to follow the multi-step process that spans across days.

Day One:
You weave your silver-gray hair into a thin braid and take a rickshaw to the subzi-mandi to purchase raw mangoes. There, you bargain with the fruit vendors and buy six kilograms from the seller who offers to load the produce into your rickshaw. With your husband's pension halved after his death last year, you spend wisely, watching each paisa. Next, you stop at the plasticware shop and press the shopkeeper for a deal—you are buying not one but six plastic jars after all. On the way home, as the rickshaw swerves along the narrow streets, your thoughts do, too.

The last time you went out to buy mangoes for pickling, your husband stayed home to watch 11-month-old Aalia—your first-born daughter. Having mastered the crawl, she used to race around the house, tumbling utensils stacked in the kitchen, scooping mud from the potted plants lined along the courtyard. When you returned from the market, you expected her to rush into your arms, but she was sleeping, exhausted like a runner. Her skin wasn't warm, her nose wasn't blocked. All she needed was some rest, you thought.

Day Two:
After the morning Fajr namaz, you pull your hair into a bun and check the mangoes for firmness by pressing them between your palms. Only the hard ones go into the pickle. You arrange the spices—hing, turmeric, red chillies, coriander, fennel, mustard,

and fenugreek—in a platter and lay them out to dry in the veran-
dah. The smell of hing dredges up more memories.

The last time you collected spices for the pickle, Aalia fussed
and cried, rubbed her face against your shoulder. You applied a
paste of hing and water—a remedy for bellyache—to her abdo-
men. The salve calmed her into a nap.

After the mid-day Dhuhr namaz, you fetch the mango-
chopping apparatus—a sharp blade hinged to a wooden block—
from the storeroom. You place the mangoes on the chopping
block, one by one, and bring down the blade on them repeatedly
until you have even one-inch pieces.

The last time you chopped mangoes for the pickle, Aalia
awoke from the nap with a cough. You brewed ginger tea to
soothe her throat but she hated its taste, turned her head away
from the spoon you pressed to her lips. You pinched her nose to
force the liquid down her throat. She wailed. Your breast com-
forted her.

Day Three:

You roast the sun-crisped spices on a tawa, constantly stir-
ring until the sweet aroma of fennel balances the bitter essence
of fenugreek. After the spices have cooled down, you grind them
to a coarse powder in the electric mixer.

Last time, you used the sil-batta—a grinding stone kept in
a corner of the courtyard— to grind the pickle spices as Aalia
lay on a dhurrie beside you. You made silly faces for her but she
didn't chuckle, only stared at you with weary eyes.

You rub the spice mixture on the mango chunks, the earthy
whiff of spices combining with the raw tanginess of the fruit.
You heat mustard oil—the natural preservative that inhibits the
growth of fungus—until it smokes. When the oil cools down,
you pour it over the mango pieces.

The last time you heated mustard oil for the pickle, you set
aside some for making khairuti—an ointment made by melting
wax in the hot oil—as recommended by the lady next door. You
applied the salve over Aalia's ailing chest, and it eased her cough
a little, but her face grew smaller, her cheeks leached color, her
eyes sank deeper into the sockets, as did your heart.

Day Four:

You use a dry spoon to transfer the mango pieces into a ceramic pickle jar and shake it to avoid the spice mixture accumulating unevenly.

The last time you filled the jar with the pickled mangoes, your husband decided to take Aalia to the hospital. You cooked paranthas for the bus trip. The dough yielding under your knuckles, transforming into discs under the rolling pin, made you feel hopeful, in control.

With the mango pieces settled in the jar, you look for a cloth to cover the jar. The fabric should be strong and also thin to allow sunlight to permeate through it. You sift through your husband's clothes in the bottom shelf of the almirah and pull out his white muslin kurta with an iron burn on the front.

The last time you ironed this kurta for your husband to wear on the hospital trip, he pressed a hand to sleeping Aalia's forehead. Then, his scream—the guttural howl of a sacrificial lamb on Bakra-Eid. You dropped the iron and clutched Aalia, her head fell deep into your palm, cool and round like a cabbage. You swaddled her in your dupatta, the smell of the burning kurta swirling around you.

You consider using a square from your husband's burnt kurta to cover the jar, but the fabric is too fragile. So, you tear off a piece from your faded linen dupatta instead and tie it around the mouth of the jar.

Last time, the covered pickle jar stood in the kitchen as women wrapped Aalia in a white kafan, sprinkled her with rose attar. Your husband carried her out in his arms. Women held you back as you ran after him; then, you fainted. When you came to, you heard your child crying at a distance. You grabbed her rattle and shook it, but her wails didn't stop; you shook it harder and harder, then smashed the toy on the wall.

You keep the jar out in the verandah and pray to Allah to hold the rains so that the sun can broil the pickle to tender perfection for your daughters—six more girls after Aalia.

Last time, your pickle didn't see a speck of sunlight. After Aalia left, you abandoned the mixture. Its oil turned black, gray-green mold hair grew on the mango pieces.

Days Five - Fifteen

You keep the jar in the sun every morning and bring it inside at sunset right before your Maghrib namaz.

After fifteen days, when the pickle is ready, you line up the six new plastic jars on the kitchen counter. As you scoop the pickle into the containers, your fingers tremble, a tightness grips your chest—you don't have six daughters, but seven. You slip your outdoor shoes on and rush to the market for another jar. After you've distributed the pickle among the seven containers, you place six of them on the top rack, mentally marking on them the months of your daughters' annual visits.

The seventh jar, you place in front of your eyes, on the slab by the window. A ray of sunlight shines on it and you see her in the golden pool. Not with her sickly skin but the full-moon face she was born with, her black, button-like eyes gazing at you. Aalia.

The Anatomy of Desire

I was stuck working late in my West Village office one snowy January night when two phone calls came in, both from life-long friends with the happy news of their first pregnancies. I was alone in a cubicle, holding a cup of bad office coffee, and I felt like a train station the moment the train departs—exhaled. I was 30. I wanted to want a baby. More precisely, I wanted to want anything as much as my friends wanted their babies. In truth, when babies cried, I felt nothing. If they giggled I might smile, but with nowhere near the wattage I afforded to even the ugliest dog. I had reached a pinnacle moment of society's narrative about women: well-employed, well-married, no longer exactly young. I knew what desire was; I just didn't have it toward babies. But everywhere around me, the babies were on their way. I rose from my desk after the second call, stretched, and walked to the picture windows in the office kitchen. I watched the blurred lights from the high rises along the Hudson. A New York City ice rain was falling, the kind that leaves you gasping when it hits the neck between your scarf and hat. The green gleam of the Statue of Liberty shone through the rain, the dark bay pooling under her light.

I had promised to work late, but as I stood at the window I decided I didn't want to. So I went to the gym instead.

How often do we do this—pay attention to what we actually want? And then simply do that thing instead of its opposite? There are people who excel at doing what they want, who culti-vate an ability to listen to their desires and then take appropriate action. I was not one of those people. I was a creature of the "should" persuasion. I should work late, even if my shoulders are knotted and I am miserable at my computer. I should get to bed at a reasonable hour, not read poetry until 3 a.m. near a drafty window, buried happily under three blankets. I should pursue a practical, reasonable career instead of trying to be a writer. Instead of art. I should eat salads, stretch, floss. Send thank you notes, too.

At the gym I'd planned to jog slowly on the treadmill for just a few minutes, but when I hit the ten-minute mark I started all-out running. It felt good. I was weary and lost, and my legs wanted to run, so I let them. I ran three miles, a distance I'd never gone before. I ran so hard I almost cried, my side cramping, my body dripping.

And then I really was crying, openly weeping on the treadmill—elated.

✳

I was 21 years old when I had my first spinal surgery. Some people develop a bad back in frumpy middle age but I'd sprouted mine as a pre-teen, degenerative discs collapsing down my spine like a broken ladder. In the recovery room, I was told by a neurosurgeon with kind eyes and a Santa Claus demeanor: no running. No roller coasters or long car rides. Don't carry anything heavier than a gallon of milk. Be careful. You'll have this problem for the rest of your life.

I nodded, young and terrorized. I moved from my college apartment back to my childhood home to recover. For my first post-surgical outing, my mother drove me through the suburbs of central New Jersey, down Durham Avenue from Edison to South Plainfield, past the condos and the strip malls and the bustling gardening centers set up in asphalt parking lots. We landed at Kohls.

I hated Kohls. Its organized piles of affordable shoes and reasonably patterned dinnerware brought forth a strange despair on a good day, and this was not a good day. I wandered through the desolate aisles in sweatpants and a tattered college t-shirt, pale and dark-eyed under snapping fluorescent lights. The walk back across the parking lot felt like crossing the moon, and by the time I slipped into the passenger seat I was silently crying. My mother took me home without saying a word. She tucked me into my childhood bed. She brought me water. She kissed me goodnight. I thought I would never feel strong again.

"Everyone who is born holds dual citizenship, in the kingdom of the well and in the kingdom of the sick," Susan Sontag wrote in *Illness as a Metaphor.* "Although we all prefer to use the good passport, sooner or later each of us is obliged, at least for a spell, to identify ourselves as citizens of that other place."

I knew I wasn't actually sick. A degenerative spine didn't

make me an invalid, nor would a bad knee, a bum shoulder. These are mechanical failures. These things are not cancer. And yet it was my first experience with genuine pain or physical helplessness. I had nerve damage in my feet. I'd spent my final months of college in a nauseated Vicodin haze. I understood for the first time how delicate, how devastating, lies the border between the healthy and the sick. I became afraid.

I spent the rest of my 20s in slow motion. I learned to make safe choices, to be inactive, to be tentative. And although I took care of my fragile, asshole spine, played by the rules, did everything I'd been told that I should, when I was 28 it happened again.

Again, that liquid, unbearable pain. Again, emergency surgery. Again, the kindly doctor in the recovery room.

"We meet again," he said, still jolly.

"Lucky us," I said, trying not to throw up on him.

He sat beside me, held my hand, and said the third time would be much worse. A spinal fusion was my only remaining option, which would limit my mobility permanently and perhaps not resolve the pain. I would have to be even more careful. I slipped in and out of morphine dreams as he spoke. I watched my legs jerk and twitch under the blankets, feeling like a marionette—the nerves of my spinal column so inflamed they sparked like a live wire, sending bad electricity down my limbs. The morphine didn't cut it, but Dilaudid did, a level-up opioid I hadn't known existed. When relief arrived, so cool and silent, I sank into it. I imagined myself underwater: graceful, weightless. Sliding seamlessly through the blue dark.

❋

I recovered again, but more slowly this time. When I imagined my future, I pictured a gradual decay of health, a descent into wheelchairs and nerve damage and narcotics. I started physical therapy, and when the pain persisted, I was sent to pain management, a branch of medicine my late-20s self was horrified to learn existed. I developed near-debilitating anxiety. A doctor's gentle touch on my lower back during a routine visit left me gasping, dissolving on the examining table like a panicky toddler.

Two months after my second surgery, which had been deemed successful, I attended a wedding, during which I danced. For exactly three songs. I woke the next morning locked in the fetal position in a hotel bed. I shook my husband awake and asked him for a balled-up pair of socks. He looked on in consternation as I shoved them into my mouth, bit hard, and inched sideways out of bed. I landed on the carpet on my hands and knees, grunting through cotton, primal with pain. A half-hour later the Vicodin kicked in. I spent the rest of the day pain-free but sweating through nausea, my face pressed to the cold tiles of the bathroom floor.

My mother came to help. When the storm passed, I curled up in bed, spent, and said, "If I have to live like this forever-"

"You'll kill yourself. I know." She kissed the top of my head and switched the TV on. Unreasonably comforted, I slept.

In time, I recovered again. I kept plodding ahead, collecting birthdays. I lived a flat-toned, careful life. Some good things had happened along the way in my 20s, of course. I had married a man I loved—the helpful sock-holder—and gotten a decent job. And yet I felt older than my years, joyless and stagnant, and my days had taken on a slogging quality. I heaved myself out of bed every morning. Convinced myself into the shower. Shit-talked my body into its clothes, its shoes, out the door.

✳

The summer I turned 30, when all those babies started popping up from the ether, a non-parent friend invited me on a safari. A real safari, in the actual Serengeti, in a rickety off-road 4-by-4, because that's how that's done. To join would entail four days of bumping and jostling over dirt roads, in the middle of the African plains, where no one could fish me out if something went wrong.

I knew I should not do this. It was financially extravagant and medically risky. A responsible person would have said no, but I found myself lying awake at night, tortured with indecision, staring at the streetlight out my window. One night, rationalizing it out in the dark, I realized I couldn't bear to become a person who *didn't go to Africa*. I said yes instead. And felt an instant rush of relief.

That first day, in the jostling, I was terrified. I gripped my seat so tightly, trying not to bounce, that my palms cramped. A friend held up a full handle of whiskey and I grabbed it with both hands, laughing, the glass clanging against my teeth. That first night in the Serengeti I slept slathered in DEET under white clouds of mosquito netting, my pants tucked into my socks so ants couldn't crawl in. At sunrise, just outside our cabins, a hyena loped by. The blister-bright African sun rose over a horizon of scrub brush and brown earth, a landscape so stark and so wide I could see the curvature of the Earth, the land drifting away just like an ocean. At breakfast, my friends and I sat together in an open-air lodge with cool tiled floors while servals, wild African cats that look like tiny cheetahs, clambered overhead on exposed wooden beams. The morning air was spicy, like campfire and curry. As we poked with furrowed brows at unidentifiable fruit, a flock of blazing green birds arrived and splashed around in a dark, stone-lined pond. They were delicate and songful and gloriously bright. Right then an old friend leaned over the breakfast table and said, "They're called lovebirds," and I felt a full-bodied flood of joy, and I knew, I knew, for once in my life I had done something right.

❋

I could write thousands of words about what specifically went wrong with my spine when I was young; about how in being so careful, in staying so still, I had only amplified the stiffness that was part of my problem in the first place. But all that really matters is this: I did things on that trip that should have hurt me, things I'd spent a decade trying *not* to do, and I walked away just fine. Better, in fact.

I began treating my body differently. I hired a personal trainer—another extravagance—to learn about strength training, something I'd always longed to try. I started from scratch and, by the end of that summer, imagined myself a superhero under a barbell. One day, feeling strong, I decided I wanted to run after all. I started small and safe on a treadmill, jogging for one minute at a time—literally sixty seconds, terrified of injury—but minute led to minute, then mile to mile, small braveries to other small braveries. My first race came just nine months later, a ten-miler, and when I crossed the finish line I felt as light and lean as a bird. I wept on the way home, shaking with exhaustion as I drove up the New Jersey Turnpike, windows down and wind in my sweaty hair while I crammed bananas into my mouth.

At one point I pulled over to let the crying jags shudder through me. I was 32 years old and athletic for the first time in my life. I'd spent my entire youth feeling awkward, sitting out gym class alone on the bleachers. Longing for an athleticism or grace I thought I couldn't have, so I'd never before bothered to try. I wanted to feel victorious, and I did, but I was sorrowful too. I wondered how many other moments of my own life I'd missed, out of caution or practicality. My car shook on the side of the highway as the trucks blasted by. I ran my hands along my thigh muscles through my running pants. They were so fucking beautiful. It had taken me so long to find them.

✸

These days it's been years since I've had an episode of acute pain, but I live with what I call a "body headache" in which my hips ache and my back creaks. I have no feeling in two toes of my left foot. On bad days a crackling electricity runs down the outside of my left calf. When I was 29 and it wouldn't stop firing, I had a nerve conduction study to test my legs for nerve damage. A very tough friend of mine had had this test done once. "It's the most painful thing that's ever happened to me," he'd said solemnly. I lay on a cold metal table in a hospital gown and was told to relax, then injected with tiny needles that sent electrical currents pulsing through my limbs to check for a response.

As I lay there like Frankenstein's creature, legs firing away, I looked out the filthy window at New York's humid skies and thought, *well this is unpleasant, but I've felt worse*, and then I felt ferociously strong. I walked back to my train the long way through Times Square, my legs moving freely beneath me, sore and twitchy but working fine. Legs like little spark plugs. Legs like a marionette, flashing under a pretty dress. When I was a teenager my father died of cancer, and his legs rotted with gangrene while he was in hospice. A few years later his brother, my beloved uncle, lost a leg to diabetes, then died a slow and painful death as well. My mother's legs are lined with varicose veins and she thinks they are ugly but all I see are beautiful tracks of blood and movement; life pulsing just under her skin.

At the base of my back are two vertical scars. I call them my railroad tracks. I'd like to tattoo a real railroad track over them someday. I'd like to turn these scars into symbols of motion. If I could time-travel, I'd find high school April and tell her this: someday, your skin will be hot with sunlight and sweat, then cooled by a sudden breeze, and you'll walk up the driveway after a run as the sun streaks in the distance and maybe a dog barks, and your legs will ache from exertion, not flawed skeletal dynamics, not bad anatomy, and inside you'll strip out of your sweat-drenched clothes, step into your clean shower, and let the warmth slide down your shoulders. You'll feel the exquisite pleasure of soap on a washcloth, let it slide over your full breasts and soft stomach and the curves of your slightly-too-ample hips, and they will not be perfect, not one inch of you has ever been, or will ever be, perfect, and yet the pride will be astonishing: to be there at all, deep in your 30s, a woman for once in full possession of her body instead of bullied by it.

You will run your fingers over your railroad tracks. You'll think about your missing discs, your lack of mechanical cushion. You will be grateful for your hipbones, your collarbone, for the joint-and-socket way you click together. Like lines of type on a page.

＊

I'm in the final stretch of my 30s now. My four-year-old will wake soon and demand the full attention of my body: my neck to snuggle in, my hands to offer up her pink cup of milk and to cook her perfectly buttered waffles. Her eyes are blue and endless and her cries and her laugh both rise from her gut, blood-filled and strong. She teaches me about trusting desire every day. Announcing what she wants. Insisting upon it. She hasn't yet learned any other way of being. I hope she never will.

I didn't feel a speck of maternal desire until north of my 35th birthday, and even then it was just a low-light flicker, unsteady, unsure. But one day I'd spotted a small girl, perhaps four years old, walking ahead of me on a train platform. Her hair was long and dark, and out of nowhere I wanted, fiercely, to smooth her ponytail. And then I started seeing ponytailed girls everywhere, dozens of them, with hopeful eyes and upturned noses and hands that were reaching, always reaching, for their mothers.

It wasn't much, of course. Certainly not enough to bet a life on. And yet.

The answers to my happiness had been with me the whole time, pulsing away under my skin. It was my feet that walked me into every bookstore of my life, my tight muscles that unfurled behind the shield of a novel. It was my whole body thrumming, electric with joy, when I walked onto a snow-frosted Vermont campus at age 32 to begin a creative writing program. It was my legs that burst into a run on that treadmill, proving that I was capable of more than I had become. And it was my hands that, in time, itched to smooth a little girl's hair. We all understand what desire is, though we've been trained to associate the word with sex instead of with the body at large. But there is a silent conversation happening within our bodies every day, buried under the ordinary noise of our lives. Like the distant freight train I've heard without noticing every single night of my city-adjacent life. It's a lullaby soundtrack, ever-present at the pitch-bottom of sleep. Calling me to wake up, to pay attention. To run.

Hanna Ferguson

A Little Marshmallow Ghost

Armageddon
A 1998 film directed by Michael Bay, which pulls on the heartstrings via Liv Tylor and Ben Affleck's tortuously precarious future together. The world is ending! It's always been ending, Liv, very slowly, one person at a time.

Black veined brown
Another name for the Monarch Butterfly, scientific name *Danaus plexipus*. The female glues sand-sized lacy domes on the undersides of leaves and leaves them in the care of their own tiny minds. They swell into pea-pod sized caterpillars who then boil themselves down and spread like toffee into stained glass miniatures. Four batches hatch a year, but only the fourth does anything remarkable. Don't romanticize them, I know it's tempting, but they don't know what they're doing. They don't know that the fate of their species depends on how thickly they can hang themselves on the drooping arms of oyamel firs. They don't see that their life is only the domino that gets the next one going. They don't want anything more out of life than to do this great thing, this mindless feat, and reproduce so that the next generation can do this great thing, this mindless feat, and reproduce so that the next generation can do this great—

Cemetery
A small cemetery set into the side of a hill was the site of my first unofficial date with my fiancé. We walked slowly in the cushion of fall air, reading and talking about last names and messages on headstones. A maple tree bloomed yellow over our heads. I didn't think about death the whole time because the terror of love was far nearer. Upon hearing about this date my friend says, "Where it starts and where it ends!"

Danse Macabre
As if we needed a reminder.

Endymion

Endymion was an Aeolian shepherd who lived at Olympia in Elis. The goddess of the moon, Selene, saw him sleeping one night as she passed her silver hands over his pasture, and his beauty so struck her that she asked Zeus to grant him eternal, youthful sleep that she might gaze at his face nightly for eternity. She appeared to him in dreams.

Futile, adjective

French *futile* or Latin *futilis*, that easily pours out, leaky, hence untrustworthy, vain, useless. Some phrases that mean futile: painting rocks, to pound sand, to put lipstick on a pig, to whistle in the wind, to grasp at straws. Some things that pour out easily: water from my baby-blue watering can, milk from the half-gallon jug, sugar from the 1-cup measuring cup. Some things that are leaky: hoses that aren't screwed on tightly, polychloroprene balloons, the shower head in my college dormitory. Some things that are untrustworthy: oracles. Some things that are vain: plans. Some things that are useless: promises.

Ghost

A tiny ghost, small and blobby like a marshmallow: the form in which God appears in my mind as I watch my fiancé's grandfather look down into the casket at his wife's face for the last time. This room is weirdly shaped and people are struggling to decide how quiet they ought to keep their voices. "To God a thousand years is like a day and a day is like a thousand years." God is hovering at the shoulder of the widower, in his eighties, who stands shorter than me now and with an underbite, his hand covering hers, which are folded, which look like plastic. A thousand years is a long time to watch someone be so sad.

Henry V, Act 5, Scene 1

What I was reading when my lover came and laid beside me as I sat on his bed. A thunderstorm was gathering. His breathing evened and slowed. I put my hand on his brown, wooly head, attendant to his freckles and begonia cheeks, his eyelashes like mink, his peony lips. The pang of complete adoration, the desire to touch but not disturb, to keep utterly, shuddered and purled in my gut. I wondered if he dreamt of me.

Isopropyl alcohol

Isopropyl alcohol is the household variety also known as rubbing alcohol. It is an effective disinfectant and a sterile way to kill an insect without deforming its body, which proved very useful to my brother during his bug-collecting years. A monarch butterfly dragged itself along the road, unable to fly, missing some legs, resolutely pointing south. Unwilling to let this specimen – of no use to its species now – waste itself, my brother and mom put it in a clean peanut butter jar with a cotton ball soaked in alcohol. I sat on the front step and watched the butterfly's spiked feet slide against the sides of the jar. It could see the world right there. Its legs began to slow until they were twitching, and then they were altogether still.

Jones, Davy

Supernatural ruler of the Seven Seas, captain of the Flying Dutchman in Pirates of the Caribbean: Dead Man's Chest, immortal ferrier of souls. Jones asks any sailor whose ship he overtakes a single question: "Do you fear death?" He delivers this line with gumption, relish, and spluttering due to the tentacles on his face. There are two answers to this question. If no, or any variant thereof, the sailor is immediately killed. If yes, he becomes a member of the deathless crew. Jones falsely assumes that anyone who answers no wishes to die immediately rather than join the crew, and that anyone who answers yes wishes to join the crew rather than face his fear. Being a man of impulse himself, Jones cannot see that sometimes people are surprising, sometimes they can see death more clearly when it's closer.

Kittens

My mother always comforted me with, "But at least you made them comfortable, at least they felt some love, that's all you can do," when the abandoned kittens I rescued from my grandparents' farm died. Countless babies for whom I dipped my pinky finger in fake milk in the middle of the night to make sure it was warm but not hot; for whom I pressed my palm to the heating pad to make sure it was neither warmer nor colder than the soft underside of their missing mother; for whom I moistened a paper towel and rubbed their anuses so their intestines wouldn't explode; for whom I set alarms for 2:30am, 4:30am, 6:30am; for whom I picked out soft scraps of fleece fabric to serve as burial shrouds when I found them cold and stiff in the morning; for whom I cried knowing that some time while I slept the very last little breath was pressed out from those lungs and though they were comfortable, they weren't being held.

Lab-created diamond

My research indicated a lab-created diamond was more environmentally friendly, so that's what he got me. Emerald cut on 18K gold. He said, "Will you marry me?" And what I want that to mean is that I'll never lose him, that it's a guarantee I'll get him for a long, long time. I want it to mean something about forever, whatever forever means, and I think as long as I believe it does mean forever, then it does. So I said yes to the gauzy outline of forever I could see in his eyes. The lab-created diamond looks no different than the regular kind, it still makes rainbows on my walls.

Marmalade tabby

The color of the day-old kitten I found on my grandparents' driveway. It had crusty sunburnt splotches from lying in the sun on the cement all day. For an hour I washed the maggots from its tummy and the crooks of its arms and from under its chin, the warm water my *not yet* to their *yes*.

Necromancy

Necromancy is the practice of trying to communicate with the dead. People usually do it to learn about the future, as though the dead by no longer participating in the present are suddenly privy to that withheld information. It's like when you play the game Mafia or Werewolf with your friends and once you die you get to keep your eyes open and see who's who. Except in that game you can't talk until it's all over. The point isn't that we should forget the dead, or let them go, or believe we'll never see them again. The point is that you can't know how it will go, and that's what separates you from the dead. You have to play the game.

Ornithology

Caroline Van Hermert is an author and ornithologist. She used to spend her time catching birds in giant nets and killing them so she could study how pollution and environmental change were causing beak deformities. Hundreds of birds. Mew gulls, hairy woodpeckers, black-billed magpies, warblers, nuthatches, crows. What faith she had, to kill and kill, all for the bird of the future, the bird yet to be. How sad it must have made her to do that. You have to love birds an awful lot to kill so many of them.

Promise

Classical Latin *promiterre*, to send forth, to promise, to predict, from the prefix pro- forward, and verb mittere, to let go. A promise is a prediction in the sense that when I answer you, when I promise I will love you forever I thrust myself forward into the future like an arm through a window. Of course, I can't predict the future (which is from Latin, futurus, which is the future participle of the verb to be) because it has yet to be. But a promise is the best I can do. I predict that I will love you forever and with every second of my life, with every beat of my heart I must work to make it true. There is no passivity here, there is no waiting for what will happen to happen, I am not a crystal gazer blowing gold and roses with my breath. A promise is not a paper boat set into the stream of time. A promise is a sending forth. What am I sending forth? My own self. My own hands to do the loving, the dishes, the proof-reading, the touching, the laundry, the desk job, the picking out, the picking up. I am sending forth my words like butterflies, like birds with messages tied onto their scaly ankles, to meet us in what is yet to be, to wait for you and me to get there with our bodies. It may turn out I cannot keep my promise. It may turn out that my forever lasts longer than yours, or yours longer than mine. But we both must acknowledge that and then put it away. The promise is only worth something if we act like it's worth something. If every step I take until the end is a step toward my promise to you, then that is all that matters. The promise isn't dependent on if we both ever get to forever, because we probably won't. No, we won't. But if we both decide forever means as long as we can, as far as we can, as hard as we can, then, yes. Yes, yes.

Question

Can I say "I will" instead of "I do"? It seems more future-oriented.

"Remembrance of what is now passing"

The Lord of May tries to cheer his melancholy Lady, on the day of their wedding, under the perfume of the May Pole, the sun glinting on their dark curls, flowers draped heavy over their chests, by saying the very remembrance of this moment, now passing, will be the brightest glimmer in their lives. Yes, says she with a quiet smile, that is why I am sad. It is already passing.

Spiritus Sanctus

Latin for holy spirit or holy ghost. The third person of the Trinity, the Triune God of most Christian denominations. In the Bible, the Holy Spirit appears as a wind, a breath, a glob of flame. We consider a spirit to be the remnant of something that has died, synonymous with a ghost, a perspective which emphasizes the death of the body, rather than the movement of the life. The Holy Spirit is the life breath of God, that which entered the dust-made body of man to make him living. Maybe when people die their scrap of breath flies back to the Holy Spirit like a bird to its flock. In Early Christian marriage ceremonies, the wedding ring was touched to each finger: "In the name of the Father (thumb), Son (pointer finger), and Holy Spirit (middle finger), Amen (ring finger)." The promise of love as long as life sits next to the Breath of God, which forever whispers blessings from one knuckle to the other.

Tactile

According to Gary Chapman, tactility is my top love language, the most impactful way I experience love from other people. I cannot, like the moon, content myself to gaze on my beloved. I have to have him. If I cannot feel the pressure of his arms around my ribs, the weight of his head on my chest, the contraction of twined fingers with every step, step, step, then he might as well be a phantom, an apparition. Life is different from her sister Death because her lips are warm.

Utah State Route 24

When I was driving on this road with my brothers and sister and mother and the love of my life, the world felt vast and old, and in my bones I felt the sheerness of the breast of the globe upon which we traveled, in between nothing and nowhere, red earth stretching out and out like a tanned hide. We were on our way to Goblin Valley to witness the wonders of time worn away by time. We call it a destination, as though we knew anything of destiny, how brash. Look out the window, there, you've arrived, you've arrived, here again, you've arrived.

"Vampires"

"Vampires"—full title "If We Were Vampires"—is a song by Jason Isbell, released in 2017, which won the Grammy for Best American Roots Song. I can't listen to it anymore. But that's okay.

"William!"

The final line of Elizabeth Swann, Pirate King of the Brethren Court, lover of William Turner, in the Pirates of the Caribbean film series. She could have ruled the seas as the King of Pirates, finally having escaped a domestic fate. But she doesn't. She waits on an island for William, replacement of Davy Jones, new immortal ferrier of souls, captain of the Flying Dutchman, to come back to her for one day every ten years. It wasn't about being Pirate King for her, it was about him, having him.

X marks the spot

Typically on pirate maps, the location of a treasure which the pirates will go after is designated by a letter X. But we don't watch the movie for the place where the treasure is. We watch the movie for what happens in between. For the sword fights, for the quippy retorts, for the romance and the danger and the moments in which characters' eyes meet and suddenly they have to get married right now, in the middle of the battle, in the middle of the hurricane.

"You're The Reason Our Kids Are Ugly"

A 1978 song by Loretta Lynn and Conway Twitty that my fiancé put on his love song playlist. I don't even mind. It feels like a brave, quivering joke, a flame we cup our hands around. Hypothetical children, hypothetical ugliness, veritable love.

Zinger

Sugar dissolves and is gone. For why have we tongues but to taste it while we can?

Hanna Ferguson

Extant

From somewhere in the trees behind our hostel comes a primordial screeching early in the mornings. In the mist, in the cool, waking up feels like a Jurassic park scene. This place, this back side of the city, is mostly bushy jungle. Mist clings to the canopy as the sun rises, and out of this dewy cool comes the murderous cry. We keep the window open at night because it's still about 26 C when we go to sleep; three bodies in a bedroom and 12 in a house make for warm nights. The house is navy blue stucco with thick white trim. Trellises with magenta flowers crawling over them frame the doorways and cover the patio. The back side of the house, the side where our room is, is submerged in the ground so the bottom of our window is at ground level. We climb in and out of it, stepping up through the inside sill, and then standing up outside, our heads almost level with the roof. Some mornings, when my roommates are still pretending to be asleep with their pillows over their heads to block the noise, I climb out the window and listen to the bird call bouncing off the mountain that looms over us. In my head I go through the list of New Zealand birds I researched before we came, trying to match the sound to a face.

The kākāpō, a flightless, green, shaggy parrot, once was the favorite food of Haast's eagle—a bird of prey the size of a seated Saint Bernard. Thankfully, this eagle is extinct and no longer prowls the skies, or New Zealand would be a far less popular travel destination. Today the crowd-favorite New Zealand bird is the kiwi, but the cultural importance of kākāpō stretches back just as far. The main consumers of kākāpō while they were abundant were the Māori people who roasted them in pits with hot stones, or boiled them in hollowed-out gourds. They used kākāpō feathers to construct cloaks so warm that a Māori saying preserves this no-longer-possible attire, "You have a kākāpō cape and still you complain of the cold." It's said to a person who's being unreasonable, who can't be pleased. The Te Papa Tongarewa ("container of treasures") has a kākāpō cape in its collection, preserved behind glass so any visitors to New Zealand's capital can see it. The cloak is made out of 11,000 feathers.

It's impossible not to be a tourist when you've never been somewhere before. It feels like a residue that itches on my skin. It's even more difficult to not be a tourist when your traveling companions are solely occupied with the most touristy things they can find. Half of the group complains loudly about the bird that wakes us in the mornings and walks to Starbucks everyday to sit under the canopy of a small green umbrella, choosing which pictures of themselves on the beach to post today. They hate the bird because seven am is far too early when you stay up every night enjoying the liberties of a drinking age lower than your native country's. The second half of the group is intent on paying extraordinary amounts of money to come as close to dying as possible. Together we've all done things like zip-lining and white water rafting and surfing, but they go out on their own and dirt bike down mountains and throw themselves off cliffs. They keep doing things that sound worse than drinking a coffee that contains seventy grams of sugar. I walk to Starbucks, but I don't buy anything.

It seems so unfair that the kākāpō evolved perfectly for a place that no longer exists. The kākāpō once spent its days tucked under the branch of a tawa tree that it climbed using its long, hooked toes. It meandered through the forest as the sun set, rummaging for snacks, not missing the use of its wings in any way. Only the eagles of the day and the laughing owl of the night might have threatened its placidity. What peace of mind it must have brought to the kākāpō to know that simply by existing it fulfilled the purpose of its species, that its habitats satisfied destiny. And then, one day while the kākāpō is out on its evening stroll, a little brown creature comes bounding towards it, bites it on the neck, and eats everything but the beak. By the 1920s, kākāpō were extinct on New Zealand's north island.

"You don't want a beige life," the canyoning guide tells us, "You want it to be resplendent and iridescent and blinding." My friends nod their heads but suddenly I'm dizzy. What color is my life? What color is resplendent? Surely resplendency is not a color, but a sumptuous refraction of light absorbed. How should my life look? Like soap bubbles, like feathers, butterfly wings, seashell nacre? Sequins? Diamonds? I look down at my hands and feel a hole swell in my chest. How do I get resplendency when there is nothing about me, nothing inherent, nothing built-in, that makes me feel that way? Why does it take a wetsuit and a helmet and repelling gear and a harness and a surfboard and a kayak and a splash guard and a lifejacket and a seventeen hour plane ride for my life to feel blinding, for me to feel resplendent? That night I go to sleep wanting the earth to swallow me, the earth and all her waterfalls.

Because they are nocturnal and flightless and clumsy, kākāpō were almost eliminated completely when rats, dogs, and stoats were introduced by Polynesian and European settlers. It's easy to imagine dazzling, barrel-chested Europeans stomping their boots into the nubile soils of virgin islands and unleashing hoards of hounds upon the helpless endemics. But this only happened after the Polynesian settlers arrived and did a good bit of damage. To be fair, New Zealand was the last substantial, habitable place on earth to be settled by humans, so its doom was delayed. What existed before humans arrived was a green hedgy forest inhabited mostly by birds. In fact, New Zealand's only native, non-aquatic mammals are three species of bat, as though the mammals too, wanted to be birds. Humans found New Zealand somewhere around 1300 CE and the kākāpō let out a great, sad sigh.

This place is not my home, and who's to say whose home it really is. Is it home for those who were here first? For those who were here bigger, stronger? For those who were here gentler? For those who were here last? But it is certain, factual, irrefutable, established, that this place is not my home. Even though they tell me not to, I keep tucking stones and leaves into my pockets, shells and shards. Maybe if I can bring a small pile of it with me, then that glittering, luminous burn in my belly will stay with me too? Maybe I can absorb, just a little, just a speck of the magic, and become less dependent on where I am and more on what I am. The human body is hopelessly adaptable. I can do too many things. I don't have a beak that was clearly meant for prying open seeds, nor a spine built for extreme flexion to hunt antelope, nor skin so camouflaged with tree bark that not even my own mother could find me. If I was bioluminescent like a jellyfish then finding resplendency, brilliance, purpose, would not be so hard.

The male kākāpō, who is about the size of a hiking back-pack, creates an indent in the earth called a bowl, and plods little paths into the ground leading in and out of the bowl for females to follow. Kākāpō mate only when their favorite food, the rimu tree, produces a bumper crop. The male settles himself in the little bowl like a chicken in a roost and produces a booming call by inflating a sack in his throat. The sound is at such a low frequency that to human ears it is quiet, just a thumping like a hand over a PVC pipe. But the sound actually travels for miles. Female kākāpō hear it and begin waddling through the forest with their large, pinkish, zygodactyl feet. Predators hear the sound and find dinner waiting for them, already in a bowl.

Humans are certainly all one species, but I'm beginning to wonder if there aren't different kinds of us. There are people here who live in the hostel full time and live to surf, eat to surf, sleep to surf. Our kayaking guide is from England, but he couldn't get these mountains out of his head, so he stayed. Some people thirst for a place like these, it is their beak, their bent, their blending in. What am I, then? I'm waiting for the right wings to sprout, for the right scales to grow, for my body to make clear to me where it belongs on this great, big world. Maybe I am a worm, coming out from the darkness only when it rains, only when streetlights can glint the water off my back.

New Zealand advertises itself excellently. It maintains an image of complete authenticity, untouched nature, pure and clean, while also getting loads of tourists to come. New Zealand is home to 4.8 million people, and in a year will host 3.8 million tourists. They come, we came, for the bays throwing off cloaks of diamond light, mountains musky and cool, waterfalls around every bend, and the best surfing in the world. The climate is also literally perfect exactly when the midwest is a hellscape. It's too late though, I can never be from here, no matter how welcoming people are. Sometime since its colonization, New Zealand had a bit of a transition in how it welcomes visitors. When the first Europeans arrived – a Dutch crew – they were met by Māori in carven canoes. Somehow there was a row and four Dutch men were killed. Their captain named the area Murderer's Bay. In 2014, it was renamed Golden Bay.

It turns out there's a bird preserve right next to our hostel. We walk behind it on a skinny path through the bush that leads to a restaurant someone has selected for dinner. Through the bird park fence I see the neat paths that lead visitors from one enclosure to the next. In the nearest one is a large greenish bird. I can't quite make out what bird it is through the trees, a kea? A kākāpō? It lets out a call like "EEEEEEEaaaaa, EEE-aaaaaaa." My friends, single file in front of me, recognize the sound. "You!" they shout, laughing, "sleep in, we beg you!" The path is not really official, so the wild bush pushes us up against the chain-link fencing that surrounds the bird park. We move branches aside with our hands. It's curious being in a place where there's not a single animal that could hurt us. The worst thing we could meet in the bush is a common brushtail possum, which is honestly one of the cutest animals in existence. The possum, while adorable, is New Zealand's greatest pest, and we took a ziplining tour during which the guide showed us the handy traps that shoot possums right through the brain with a little spike. The little spike-shooter goes "native things only!" and bam, the possum falls dead to the ground below.

The kākāpō is a habitat generalist, meaning it can be happy anywhere it's not being eaten by stoats or nest-robbed by rats or thrashed by someone's loose dog. They needn't worry about that anymore though, since the 208 kākāpō still in existence have been relocated to a handful of islands just off New Zealand where nothing nasty can eat them. Every kākāpō is named and equipped with a radio-transmitter. Despite their geographical location and pitiful population count, kākāpō are still making their mark on the world. They're internet famous as the "party parrot" emoji on the communication platform Slack. There they appear in various shades of neon blue, coral, and purple. They can be found holding a cup of coffee or a slice of pizza, wearing sunglasses or sporting a mustache. The kākāpō on whom the emoji was based is named Sirocco. His mother's name is Zephyr, his father's name is Felix.

The face of the canyoning guide as he implored us not to live beige lives rises in my mind when I try to sleep. He looked so worried, as though beigeness was worse than death. But I just know that when I get home to the dearth that is winter, all the glitter will drain out of me and all I'll be is tan. But who am I to think I can take any of this place with me? It isn't mine. What right have I. All those birds, here for ages, for eons, shunted out of their homes, pushed to extinction, only to be caught at the last second, welcomed back to certain spaces, revered, modified. All those people to whom the same thing happened. Now you're

an emoji, be thankful you're not extinct. Now your culture is a
souvenir, be thankful you're still around. And my home is not
enough? My home, rooted in the mud of the Mississippi like a
mollusk, going nowhere, safer than salt. Can we not let one bird
greet the mountain in the morning in the cool of its shadow? But
nothing starts where it ends up, the very earth is moving, the very
stars are sailing away. Everything came on a canoe or a breeze or
a promise. It has always been this way, and I saw that even the
glowworms made their heavens out of mud.

The Boys

Let's say it begins in Beijing with the boys, perhaps a little boy who toddles from his mother to a blade of grass, a bright greenish twig secretly calling to him, pulling him toward its demanding hum. He bends over in his red apron-like garment, its sturdy straps tied around his waist and thighs, his naked buttocks thrust out into the air. Or maybe it begins with a boy in diapers, peeking from behind a bamboo curtain while we Americans eat soft, moist tofu in an upstairs restaurant, our chopsticks clicking. "Chinese tofu!" we squeal, the taste so succulent, so rich, we keep turning the lazy-susan, round and round, reaching for more. Or perhaps it begins with the startled face of a bristly headed boy poked by my umbrella as I am pushed and shoved by curious crowds through the last ornate gate of the Forbidden City. Our bodies are packed so close I wonder how the adults free an arm to touch the thick red walls, their fingers caressing that rough painted surface for happiness, good fortune, and the miracle of love, while the boy gazes steadily at me, his round face as smooth as polished stone. He looks more startled than hurt, but that face, it's such a sweet boy's face, I keep saying, "I'm sorry, I'm so sorry" long after he's turned away.

Much later I'll realize it begins with Kim and Mieka, two boys who run dutifully towards me in the park after Harry, their English language coach, calls out, "A teacher. Come meet the teacher," as if he's discovered a prize. And there I am trapped in my duties, caught in a profession I want to leave behind as I wander through Hepingli Park on this bright July morning. There are times when I long to be just a citizen, irrelevant to the world, bemused or indifferent, self-absorbed and myopic, useless to anyone, merely a traveler, scavenging for scraps of delight that mean nothing to anyone else. But now I have been found. A teacher. I know the part.

Kim, the taller boy, reaches out to shake my hand, his own hand so soft it makes me blush. Then Mieka, his mouth tucked sideways to repress a grin. He knows this is all a show for the

English coach, Harry. What does Mieka care? Left to his own desires, he'd probably give me a high five and sprint off to swimming or badminton or talking loud to his friends. But now, like me, he's caught. He turns that round puckish face towards me, his two front teeth overlapping, his forehead so narrow he is all dark eyes and black brows. His hair, barely a bristle of dark fuzz, reveals an emerging cowlick. I smile. For him I will be a teacher. While he shifts from foot to foot, Kim stands attentively, staring at me with dark, solemn eyes behind wire-rimmed glasses. His eyes say, "I'm here. I'm listening. I'm a boy who is going places."

"*Nice to meet you,*" Kim says precisely, in a voice as soft as his hand. "*How are you?*" comes out stronger, more assured. I imagine he will be a businessman someday, traveling the world, calling from a distant shore, surprised at how easily his words shift – like a warm, sweet breath — from Mandarin to English and back to Mandarin.

"*Nice,*" Mieka says, tossing out the one word he knows, mimicking his friend. He too holds out his hand even as the coach says emphatically "*to meet you!*"

Let's say it begins with two handshakes and becomes the inevitable conversation of *How old? How much you like? What you do here? How long you stay? Where you live?*

"No, no," Harry intones. "Never ask age."

Kim frowns at the mistake, but quickly recovers. "Where from?"

Ahhh, near Chicago. A smile.

It begins when Harry, the English coach, saw me sitting alone in the park at 8:30 on a Sunday morning in July. As he walked past, he turned and smiled at me, then idled near the pond, glancing my way. I sat on a stone bench on a tiled square beneath the shade of poplar trees and watched an old man across from me fiddle with something I couldn't quite comprehend. At first, I thought he was opening a tube, like a Pringles tube of potato chips, perhaps his breakfast, but instead of breakfast, it became a long, flat brush he attached to a stick. Still, I didn't understand. The old man, dressed in a loose white t-shirt and baggy pants with a faded blue hat squashed flat on his head, glanced slyly at me – the interloper – then went back to his work. I watched as he limped to the pond and dipped the brush into the still water. Then, to my surprise, he limped back and began to paint: long, rhythmic sweeps on the gray tiled ground, a calligraphy of brushed water.

"Oh," I murmured. "Beautiful."

It was then that Harry appeared by my side. "Can you tell me what he is writing?" I asked after Harry had introduced himself.

Harry stepped closer to the man, gazing at the winged characters. "He is writing poetry," he said. "Here, look, he is writing about faraway places." He stared at me. "You see? About heaven and earth. You understand heaven and earth?"

I nodded, uncertain if I did.

"He is saying we must get as far away as we can."

I imagine he means that our spiritual selves must try to grasp heaven, must try to hold both heaven and earth in our bodies, finding a heaven both within and beyond this earth. *As far away as we can*. And though I know he means this philosophically, I can't help thinking of the literal, of how much time I've spent trying to get as far away as I can, as if faraway places might save me, might allow me to find a heaven within by exploring the world without.

But it's more than that. I have expected the world to save me from silence, to infuse me with speech. Often as a child I was too frightened to speak. Each night I lay in bed, a ghost-child beside my sister, the one who talked so much her 5th grade teacher kept her in for an entire year of recess. She talked and she read. She read at the dinner table, talked in church, read in the middle of softball games and talked all through the movies we paid $8 to see. She told my parents everything she did as if she had no censors, no shame, had nothing to hide, but how could that be? I was a child full of cautions, ellipses, living in an insular world, always watching. I watched the physical irritation of my father, how his eyes jerked and his mouth narrowed at the slightest interruption. I watched that same face relax with sudden, irrepressible joy, his jaw softened, all his teeth showing. I watched my sister sneeze and forget to catch the sneeze with a Kleenex, and then forget that sneezes mattered, that the sneeze *went* somewhere. I watched the rain puddle the yard, making huge, pond-sized puddles where frogs, tiny as walnuts, leapt and splashed. I watched and in the moment of watching, I was happy.

Only later, when the spell was broken, did I perceive how

quiet I had been, and in such moments, I believed it was the silence that made me invisible, unreachable, a girl hiding behind the door. From this premise came a private admonition: I must become a grand and fanciful creature, a creature who wanted to talk. Surely a faraway place would be my rescue, my tutor. A faraway place would become my experience, something to talk about, to take home as my prize. And yet ironically, each new place – London in my 20s; Dublin in my 30s; Florence in my 50s — pulled me back into silence, into my watchful, watching self.

Perhaps that's why I notice the boys in Beijing, so mischievous, so surprising. Yesterday I watched three little boys following their parents into the Yonghegong Lama Temple. The oldest boy knelt, bowing at one of the altars, his hands holding his incense sticks upright as he bent low, his forehead almost touching the ground. He looked reverent, devout. I watched as he rose in one fluid motion and very carefully placed his incense stick on the altar. And then to my surprise, he turned to his brothers, two fingers holding his nose, his grin barely stifled.

I laughed.

The boys. I see them everywhere. With backpacks and Mickey Mouse t-shirts. With orange flip-flips and tennis shoes. With #10 written on the brim of their caps. With fishing rods and badminton rackets. With cell phones and bicycles. They sneak into my consciousness and take me away from myself, and for a moment I forget to worry. I am watching.

"Goodbye. Nice to talk," Kim says when I tell them I must leave the park for a meeting.

"I am so glad to have met you," I say. "I am so glad to have come to your country, to your city, Beijing."

Harry smiles a gleeful smile. Then he prods Mieka.

"Good," Mieka says, his eyebrows raised as if he hopes this is right. He smiles at me and then he takes a small step forward so that he is slightly in front of Kim. "Good," he says again, more assertive this time.

And I nod, repeating his word – *Good!* – but what I'm seeing are the sensuous curves and arches of the poet's characters, their bones thickening into symbols of heaven and earth, then fading, becoming fragments, as fleeting as rain evaporating into clouds. As I walk away, I carry them inside even as they vanish in the mid-day sun.

Molly Gaudry

Origin Story: An Essay

I. NEW WORK

The last time Ab saw her biological half-brother, Jiwon, he was six years old and unwilling to release her leg, which he had wrapped himself around like a baby panda. He sobbed, in Korean, "I don't want you to go to California," which sounded like *Cali-por-nee-ah*. She recognized "bogoshipo," *I miss you,* and her Korean name, "Sun-Yeong," followed by "noona," *sister.*

That was the summer of 1999, and Ab had just turned eighteen the month before, during a Homeland Tour for Korean adoptees that ended about a week before she moved into her biological father's house to live with him and his wife and their two children. Deji, nine years old, didn't love how Ab's presence suddenly demoted her position in the family from firstborn daughter to, well, not the firstborn daughter. Jiwon, six, had acted out on Ab's first night in their house and smacked her across the face, and when she pinched the skin above his elbow, hard, in retaliation and out of view of the parents and aunts and uncles who had gathered for the occasion, he looked at her in surprise, clearly weighing his options to either start screaming about it or do what he actually did, which was to crawl into her lap and hand over the controller to his Nintendo.

All summer, the two of them played *Super Mario Bros.* Jiwon babbled in Korean at her and howled at her terrible moves, groaning and sighing his displeasure at seeing her guy, Luigi, die repeatedly. As she improved, though, resurrecting the game's secrets from the graveyard of her childhood memories, and as she progressed past his highest level, he celebrated her and Luigi's advancements, transfixed by the game and Ab's ability to play. And as the weeks went by, sitting side by side in their gaming chairs, she picked up her brother's various expressions and learned the different intonations of the same words when spoken in delight or frustration. After only a few weeks, Ab was surprised to discover that she was fluent in six-year-old Korean.

Nights, the family slept together on the floor. The father on the farthest end, closest to the door, and then the stepmother, then Deji, then Ab, and then Jiwon, who, every morning, she discovered, had wriggled his way into being her little spoon. After a week of this, she began to wake early in order to hug him close and smell the crown of his head, inhaling the baby brother she never knew she had.

But Jiwon was twenty-six now. Ab was thirty-eight. Twenty years had passed without any correspondence from anyone in the family, until last night when Jiwon reached out via Facebook, first by sending a friend request, and then by following up with a message to say he was in California and wanted to meet. Ab explained that she lived in Utah now but confused the issue by saying she wasn't there at the moment. She would be back tomorrow, she told him, and she asked if she could pay for his flight to Salt Lake City. She planned it so that after she got home in the morning she could clean her apartment and make up her second bedroom for him. She scheduled his flight to get in late in the evening.

Now, Jiwon was at her door.

She heard his knock. She didn't know why she let him knock. Since she didn't drive highways at night, she had booked him an Uber from the airport and tracked his ride and knew he was outside. She took a deep breath and looked up at her ceiling as if praying, then exhaled and opened up.

"Come in, come in!"

Ab took his Adidas duffel bag and put it in his room, which was by the door. She showed him the bathroom across the hall, which would be his, then led him into the living/dining area and gestured for him to take a seat, wondering if he would choose the couch or the table. He sat at the table. So would she have.

"Water?" she said. "Beer?"

Jiwon indicated beer, and Ab remembered that their father was a HITE and soju drinker. As she walked back from the kitchen with two Yuenglings and handed one over, she studied his face. No trace of the chubby kid she remembered. He was strong-looking, muscular, taller than she would have thought. His hair was curly now like Ab's, although he probably permed it. She didn't remember anyone else in the family having curly hair, except their aunt.

As Ab drank, she peeled the label from her Yuengling bottle.

She wondered if Jiwon might be offended by the brand name even though it wasn't actually Chinese. Better Yuengling than Sapporo, she supposed, particularly as there was no HITE to be found at her local Smith's grocery. From what she could tell, Jiwon didn't care. As he drank, and as she watched him, she felt an overwhelming urge to inhale the crown of his head but of course that impulse revealed a yearning for a past that was long gone.

"Our father is dead," Jiwon said, suddenly.

"I'm sorry," she said.

She didn't know what else to say.

The father he spoke of was his father, not hers. Ab's dad lived in Ohio. She was surprised, though, to feel so little upon hearing Jiwon's news. Except perhaps sadness because she felt so little upon hearing his news. Yes, perhaps sadness, tinged with twenty years of resurfaced guilt for leaving that summer without warning, weeks before she should have, without any explanation.

"I thought you would want to know," Jiwon said. "I could only tell you if I saw you again, in person. Please understand me."

"I do," Ab said. "Thank you."

She added, "I'm glad you're here."

"I've missed you," she said, after a while.

But it wasn't really *him* she missed, right? It was the six-year-old him she missed and had wondered about over the years, although not with any real frequency, truth be told. Honestly, she had convinced herself long ago that he'd been so young, right? He'd probably forgotten all about her.

✳

Around midnight, Jiwon was close to passing out and Ab helped him into bed. By then, they'd moved on to shots, which Ab did not toss back as he did but sipped, although she heartily encouraged him to: "Geonbae!" she said, laughing, conjuring up twenty years of dusty old phrases she'd long since thought she forgot. "Jjan!"

She closed his door and quietly began cleaning up, wondering what they would do for the rest of his visit. The truth was it wasn't a great time for him to be there. She was between campus visits. Her first had not gone well. After her job talk, the post-colonialist got the first question. "But what are you doing to dismantle the canon?"

Ab had opened the door to his question, regrettably, by going off script and making a joke midway through her talk about not hating the canon. She was potentially if not likely a diversity candidate, so Ab had meant to signal that as a nonwhite creative writer and an experimental one at that she had been trained to be a generalist and could in fact teach canonical texts in introductory literature courses. She was not prepared for a question about what she had assumed was one of her strengths—a solid grasp of the Western tradition—which had been in an instant turned against her.

She could have drawn attention to her sample syllabi, featuring an expansive range of contemporary authors working in different genres and forms. She could have said that, after Angela Flournoy, she too tried to write "against unreality" by, for instance, centering characters that looked like she did. Or she could have said that in her own new work, like that of certain contemporaries she admired such as LaTanya McQueen and Robert Lopez, Ab too was reckoning with her own confusing assimilated behaviors and questioning the extent of her own internalized white supremacist beliefs. And if none of that felt particularly appropriate for the moment, she might have simply suggested that the hybrid forms she specialized in reflected back the mixed and multiple identities of her own lived experiences, her students', and when you really thought about it just about everyone's. But Ab did not say any of these things. She froze and never recovered. On the drive to the airport, the search chair informed her that hers was their third and final campus visit. Predictably, it took only two weeks to find out she did not get the job.

Her second failed visit was much fresher. She'd only gotten home this morning, and she hadn't even unpacked yet. For this job talk, she had been asked to address the question: How does form perform content? So she prepared a talk titled "The Lyric Essay: A Broken Form for Broken Narratives," and she had intended to make the case that the fragmented hybrid-genre's form, reliant on juxtaposition and white space, could perform a writer's deliberate withholding, reflecting the writer's choice to *not* tell, or to tell only what they knew and on their own terms, which could be particularly useful for those whose stories were full of holes or for those who could take back their power by not disclosing and not revealing their trauma as soft-core entertainment for the consumption of others.

To help make her point, she began with an anecdote: *During the summer of 1999, at the same time that a translator provided by the South Korean government told me that my biological father wanted to meet me, a producer from* The Montel Williams Show *told my dad, in Ohio, that his biological mother was searching for him. When I called my dad to tell him not to come pick me up from the airport as planned, that I was staying in Korea for the rest of the summer because I wanted to meet and move in with my biological father and his family, he said, "I wasn't going to tell you this," then proceeded to tell me about the producer from* The Montel Williams Show. *"So," he said, "I guess we're both making the only choice we can live with. We'll probably both regret it."*

This was the essay Ab had tried to write, she told everyone in the lecture hall, but for years it just stalled out after this opening. *The Montel Williams Show* was too good a detail to be true, but it was true. There just wasn't anything she could do with it, because her dad never had never done anything with it. Another writer, she said, had suggested Ab just make *that* the essay, and to explore the divergent paths taken by a daughter and her dad, both adopted, the former transnationally at the age of three and the latter domestically when only a few days old, and to try to get at deep human truths about life and love and countries and borders and family. No matter how sensible that suggestion may have been, it still made Ab uncomfortable. Her dad's story wasn't hers to write. So the years went by, and Ab never wrote about her own adoption either. But she did write about absence and loss, again and again, which in a way was like writing around her adoption, and her first book of essays, many of them lyric, were in fact full of holes that were representative of not knowing, representative of all that she did not know and might never know.

As Ab read from her pages, she felt as if she were trying to sell Swiss cheese. She felt like a fraud at the podium, but her audience on this campus was generous and their questions were kinder, gentler. She even saw a few grad students taking notes. But then the nonfiction professor raised her hand. "There seems to be a hole in your own argument, speaking of holes," she said. "It seems to me that speculative nonfiction also allows a writer to tell her own story, 'full of holes' as you say, but rather than simply say, 'My story is full of holes and this is the best I can do—these bits and pieces of fragmented memories,' can't spec-nonfic create space for imaginative possibilities and allow the writer to more honestly and bravely explore those absences or gaps? For instance, your own 'failed' essay, as you called it, could have explored the hypothetical musings of 'what if he had gone on the show?' and 'what if you had not stayed in Korea?' If part of your project, as you say, is for writers to address or confront past trauma by adopting this broken form for broken narratives—why frame such writing, such healing, let's call it, so negatively? Is there space, do you think, for spec-nonfic in your teaching or in your classroom, perhaps even alongside the lyric essay and/or the other hybrid forms you have yourself adopted?"

Even as Ab recognized the leading nature of the professor's question, and thought to herself, "Just say yes, of course there's room!" she, instead, rejected it entirely. She wasn't even sure why, other than she was afraid of another horrifying silence like the one after the postcolonialist's question, and so she compensated by not taking even half a second to think before speaking. Instead, she doubled down on her first/worst answer, and it was only toward the tail end, she realized, that she was defensive because of the nonfiction professor's use of "adopting" and "adopted." Before Ab even finished her answer, she was convinced she would not get the job.

She might have drowned her sorrows in her hotel room after dinner, during which assembled faculty members had been genial enough and even to some extent welcoming, but when she excused herself to go to the bathroom and checked her phone she found Jiwon's friend request. She accepted and scrolled through his photographs as long as she could before she began to worry they'd send someone to come check on her. All through dessert she tried her best to engage and to not appear to be too distracted but of course she was incredibly distracted.

In her hotel room, she received his message. An hour later, she responded. An hour after that, she booked his flight from LAX to Salt Lake, which she had to put on a credit card. Was it necessary to buy the ticket for him? Probably not, but she still felt so terribly guilty about that summer.

✳

In the morning, Jiwon stumbled out of his room and

yawned.

Ab remembered those early mornings curled up with him on the floor and she couldn't quite mentally compute how that child was now this man. She was crouched over looking at her potatoes in the oven, which were coming along all right and beginning to brown. The onions and peppers were getting darker at the edges, too.

Jiwon sat at the table again in the same chair he'd occupied the night before.

Ab stood and opened the fridge. She poured two glasses of orange juice and took one over to him with a mug of coffee. "Milk? Cream? Sugar?"

He shook his head. She remembered their father drank his coffee black, too.

Back in the kitchen, Ab topped off her own mug and spooned in about twice the amount of sugar she normally used because she was nervous and because she tended to indulge whenever she was nervous. "How did you sleep?"

"Fine," he said. "Thank you."

She nodded.

"Are you married? I thought you would be married."

Ab shook her head. She felt like a robot, nodding and shaking. "I'm not married," she said. "Not yet," she added, and then suddenly she was irrationally upset about why she'd felt the need to add that. "Are you married?"

"No," Jiwon said. "Not yet."

"Is Deji?"

Jiwon smiled. "Yes, she is happy."

Ab said, "Good. That's good. That's really good," and again she felt like a robot.

At this point, she decided she could probably get started on the bacon. She only bought MorningStar strips and worried that Jiwon wouldn't know what to make of them. She pulled the frozen pink-and-coral strips apart anyway and put them into her nonstick pan and started pressing them into the heat with the back of her spatula, for no reason other than she needed something to do.

Before she could stop herself, she said, "How's your mother?"

This was one of the more pressing questions Ab wanted an answer to but had felt too guilty to ask. She was a little afraid of what Jiwon might say, actually. It was because of his mother that

Ab had left so abruptly that summer. Not because of anything bad she had done, but, instead, because she had been so kind. Too kind.

He paused. Without answering her question, he asked, "Do you have her skirt?"

Ab smiled. Her stepmother had worked in a clothing boutique, and one day she brought back a bunch of clothes for Ab to try on. There was also a leather miniskirt, which was not from the boutique but from her own closet. She had indicated to Ab that she should take it if it fit, which it did. Ab protested, saying it was too nice a gift, but her stepmother insisted. "I'm too old," she said. "You take it." Ab had pointed to Deji and said, "No, save it for Deji, for later," but her stepmother pushed it into Ab's chest and said, "You. It's yours. You take it." So Ab did. She tucked it into her suitcase and took it with her back to America.

Ab nodded. "Yes," she said. "Tell her I still have it." Although she had never worn it, she had never been able to part with it.

"Okay," Jiwon said.

"Okay," he said again.

Ab found a mixing bowl and started cracking eggs. She figured they could each eat about three so she cleared half the carton, tossed the shells, and began to whisk. She didn't use milk or salt or pepper or anything like that. She just whisked until the eggs were airy. When the bacon was done she turned the heat way down, removed the pan from the burner, divvied up the strips between their plates, and then returned the pan to its burner. She poured in the eggs and began to stir, slowly. Once they were perfectly fluffy and a bright golden yellow but still a little wet looking, she split them down the middle and put one half on Jiwon's plate and the other on her own. Then she opened the oven, grabbed a towel, and pulled out the potatoes. She divvied these up, too, but not all of them. If Jiwon was still hungry after finishing his plate, there'd at least be more potatoes for him. She put their plates on the table, went back to the kitchen for napkins and forks, and brought them to the table.

Quietly, they ate.

Their silence wasn't uncomfortable. If anything, it came as a relief. She had a mild hangover, and she assumed his was worse. There was a bottle of ibuprofen on the table if he needed it, which she left there for him after taking three herself upon waking.

Ab remembered all the meals they shared in Korea that summer. She remembered the way their father made midnight ramen and put the crusty leftover dinner rice into his bowl before pouring in the noodles and broth. She remembered trying to teach her stepmother to make garlic mashed potatoes, except the potatoes they had were waxier than those she was used to and the end result was not good at all. She remembered that despite all her protesting, everyone ate her gross potatoes that night as if she were some kind of cooking prodigy. But most of all, Ab remembered the fruit. Like the potatoes, the fruit there was different. The berries were different, the melons were different.

She remembered living in South Philly, too, for a year after her first master's degree, and she remembered the Asian market down the street, not far from the room she rented, and how on a whim one afternoon she bought a white peach. She remembered the tearing of its skin between her teeth. She remembered its juice on her tongue and chin, and how just one bite shot her back to that morning thunderstorm a decade previous beneath which she'd met her father and, later, his wife, their daughter, their son, whose six-year-old body curled at night beside her eighteen-year-old anger on the living room floor where the rest of them slept and where she stared into the lush green hills, choking back thoughts, searching those giant white cranes within that thick white morning fog for meaning, the incense burning its citronella spiral through the night.

❋

Jiwon, as it turned out, was getting an MBA from Yonsei University, and he had a good deal of homework, he said, which he had brought with him. Together, they set up their work stations at the dining room table, and they spent the rest of the morning in silence, drinking coffee, occasionally looking at one another and smiling. Sometimes awkwardly. Sometimes not.

Ab needed to be concentrating on her job talk. For this visit, the search chair instructed her to present new work, something unpublished and written especially for their own students if possible, and this new work should be something risky—Ab might even, in fact, model for students a willingness to risk failure. But, the chair told her, the search committee also wanted her to have fun. Perhaps some fun could emerge from a meta-discussion about her process composing this new work?

Ordinarily, talking about process actually did qualify as one of Ab's definitions of fun, but not under these circumstances, for what seemed to be the cruel amusement of a roomful of strangers who held the fate of her future academic employment in their hands. The fact that she had to come up with three different job talks for three different institutions rankled. She was a creative writer. Wasn't she just supposed to read something published and deal with whatever questions arose afterward? Wasn't that the way it had always been done? And why did this department want her to risk failure? What the hell was that about? She didn't feel like enough of a failure as it was?

Despite having been given the prompt several weeks before, Ab had yet to write a word of this new work. To be fair, there just hadn't been time. Her only option had been to prepare for one visit at a time. If Jiwon hadn't popped up out of nowhere, she would have started on the new work at the airport the next morning. But now, something about Jiwon working at her table with her, being not just a college graduate but pursuing an MBA, reminded her of a particular type of trauma she had read about once that some Korean adoptees experienced after reuniting with their family. Other transnational adoptees from across the globe likely also experienced it, but the data had been compiled specifically on Korean adoptees, and because Ab had experienced it herself she had read the entire article with interest.

Essentially, the Korean War's legacy still informed a dominant myth in the West about why Korean babies were given up. Korea was supposedly a war-torn, third-world nation, and the parents were probably too poor to properly care for a baby. But Ab, like so many others, had been adopted long after the war and during an economic boom. When she moved into her biological father's house, she was entirely unprepared for what awaited her. Deji had a private English tutor who came to the hi-rise apartment a few times a week, and she also had a piano teacher who sat beside her as she practiced scales on the baby grand in the sitting room. There was a playroom with floor-to-ceiling bookshelves filled with children's books and toys and video games. The kids were all right. There was even a woman who came to clean once a week. In the living area where they slept at night, the family had a big-screen television with surround sound. Some evenings, they watched Korean dramas. Other evenings, subtitled

American movies her father brought back from the video store for Ab's enjoyment. Theirs wasn't a bad life. She hadn't been saved, as an elementary teacher once said to her, from working in a rice paddy.

Then there was Ab's stepmother, who turned out to be a complete 180 from what Ab had been told to expect. During the Homeland Tour for adoptees, she had heard all about terrible, evil Korean stepmothers. Because birth records documented only the father's identifying information, adoptees who returned to Korea to search for family often ended up at their father's doorsteps. If their father was married to a woman who was not their biological mother, though, the search was effectively over. Stepmothers, Ab learned, turned orphans away as if their lives depended on it. Some of the adoptees on the Homeland Tour—one from Norway, another from Germany, most memorably—had been pleading with their stepmothers for years, returning to Korea every summer and begging to be invited inside to spend time with their fathers.

But not Ab's stepmother. Ab's stepmother baked a chocolate cake, and when Ab and her father came through the door of the apartment for the first time, the woman and her two children emerged from the kitchen, smiling and clapping. The kids were shy but Jiwon was excited about the cake and eager for Ab to blow out the candles. Deji stuck like Velcro to her mother's side, but after the cake was cut she did as she was told and presented the first slice to Ab, and then ran back to her mother's side again. Ab didn't remember anything else about that day, or even her entry into the apartment, but she remembered the cake and being gobsmacked that her stepmother was celebrating her arrival into her home.

Nothing made sense. Ab had expected poverty. She expected a sullen and deeply unhappy, resentful stepmother. Not chocolate cakes and baby grand pianos and expensive leather skirts. Nothing made any sense at all.

All these years later, at her own table in her own apartment, Ab studied Jiwon's face. He looked up from the books spread out before him and nodded.

She nodded back, smiling.

And then he asked, finally, what she had been waiting for him to ask, the question she had been dreading for the last twenty years, and which sank like a rock in her gut when she got his friend request. "Why did you leave us that summer? Why didn't we ever see you again? Or hear from you?"

II. FAILURE

The last time I saw my biological half-brother, ~~Jiwon~~ Siwon, he was six years old and unwilling to release my leg, which he had wrapped himself around like a baby panda. He sobbed, in Korean, "I don't want you to go to California," which sounded like *Cali-por-nee-ah*. I recognized "bogoshipo," *I miss you*, and my Korean name, "~~Sun-Yeong~~ Sun-Hee," followed by "noona," *sister*.

The truth is, Siwon has never come to find me.

I have no idea if our father is alive or dead. Or if, for that matter, Siwon or my half-sister ~~Deji~~ Haley or my stepmother are alive or dead. I don't know if any of my aunts or uncles is alive or dead. I don't know if my grandmother is alive or dead, although my guess is she's probably dead by now.

The truth is, I did leave them all that summer.

Until now, I've never really looked back.

❋

This is true.

During the summer of 1999, at the same time that my aunt told a translator provided by the South Korean government— who then relayed her message to me—that my father wanted to meet me, a producer from *The Montel Williams Show* told my dad, in Ohio, that his mother was searching for him.

"I have a father?"

The translator didn't understand me. Why should he have? But to my knowledge, there was no father and there had never been a father.

That night, when I called my dad to tell him not to come pick me up from the airport as planned, that I was staying in Korea for the rest of the summer because I wanted to meet and move in with my father and his family, he said, "I thought I was your father."

❋

Unlike so many other adoptions, transnational or domestic, mine was open.

Until the age of three, I lived with my grandmother—or so the story goes. It was only after my grandfather died that my grandmother considered her own mortality and impending inability to care for a child. Her decision to put me up for adoption was made with the support of my aunt, her oldest daughter—the one with curly hair—who happened to be a Catholic nun. Together they decided I would be placed with Holt, a Christian organization, but that I would not go into an orphanage.

Then, even in America, I never lost contact with them. We sent each other letters, cards, drawings, gifts, Dictaphone tapes like the ones my dad used to record patient notes for his clinic's transcriptionist.

And when my mom and I went to Seoul during the 1988 Olympics, we spent a day with my grandmother and my aunt. Via a translator, more of my story came out. Yes, my grandfather had died and that was the primary event that led to my being placed with Holt. But there was also the fact that my father was out of the picture entirely. He was a roadie of all things, traveling with some band. He had dropped me off one day at his mother's house, and no one had seen or heard from him since.

✳

"I have a father?"

I was eighteen years old and the story I knew had suddenly shifted on its axis. Until that moment sitting in that coffee shop across from my aunt and grandmother, the translator beside me, if and when I had ever thought of my roadie father the word "deadbeat" came to mind.

I turned to the translator. "What about my mother?"

When my mom and I visited in '88, our translator at that time had also been asked about my biological mother. He told us my grandmother and aunt knew nothing about her. From then on, if and when I ever thought of her I assumed she was dead, which was the only story I could accept, not least of all because it also helped to justify the actions of a heartbroken, devastated father who ran away to be a roadie.

After a quick back and forth, my translator reported back, "They don't know about your mother. But your father will be here tomorrow."

✳

Although my stepmother pretended not to speak any English when my father was around she spoke quite fluently, actually. During the day when he was at work, and when Haley went off to dance class, and when it was just me and Siwon playing video games in the playroom, she would come get me sometimes and take me out onto the balcony to share a stolen cigarette with me.

"Don't tell your father!" she said, and I never did.

✳

"It's too expensive," I said, fingering the seams of my stepmother's leather miniskirt. I didn't know why she wanted me to try it on, or to take it. I really did think she should save it for Haley. Or keep it for herself, for that matter. "You don't wear it anymore?"

"I'm too old," she said, laughing.

"You should keep it," I said. "Wear it! We're the same size!"

My stepmother laughed and said, "No, you're so skinny."

We really were the same size. She was just being shy or self-conscious or whatever it was that was going through her mind about giving me her skirt. The leather was ridiculously soft, that buttery kind of soft. I'm sure it was expensive. I didn't know why she was insisting on giving it to me. But it seemed to be really important to her—the memories it held, and the gifting of it to me. "I'm too old," she said. "You take it."

"No," I said. "Save it for Haley, for later."

But she pushed it into my chest and said, "It's for you. It's yours. You keep it."

So I did.

I tucked it into my suitcase and took it with me back to America.

I have no idea where it is now.

✳

It wasn't just peaches that summer but nectarines and plums and concord grapes whose skins and pits we piled up, and green and white and yellow melons and fruit I'd never tasted before, but I ate it all because that was how we shared and spoke with one another—well, the fruit and the soju, the fruit and soju and cigarettes. Oh, how we drank every night and how I learned to pour for my elders with both hands as a sign of respect, and how six-shots-in one well-past-midnight Monday that man said, "Do not ask me anymore about your mother," and how his wife, who was everything but the third-world woman I had assumed all South Korean women were, said, "Me," and put my hand beneath her breast, said, "Omah, mother, bio-mom, okay?" and how I looked at her until she said, again, "Okay, you say, bio-mom," and how I did not answer until days later when I watched her cut the evening fruit and then reached and put a piece of melon in my mouth, and, when I swallowed, said, "Okay," and how we shared a cigarette that night on the balcony after every-one else was asleep, and how, a few weeks later, on my last day, the two of us looked out into the early morning fog and watched the cranes soar and listened to them cry, not saying anything but leaning shoulder to shoulder, knowing it was never supposed to last anyway, that I was always meant to return to America and continue on with my life and so was she with hers. But before all that, what we did was eat. We ate that fruit all summer long.

III. FUN?

When you asked me to come here today—to prepare some-thing new and something risky—I thought, "What is my darkest secret, my deepest shame? And is that something I can write about for this talk?"

Ultimately, I decided to take this opportunity to think about how I did, in fact, ghost the family that welcomed me into their home during the summer of 1999. To me, this new work is more nonfiction than it is fictionalized autobiography.

The fictional component, the dramatic element—having the brother show up after twenty years to announce the death of their father—is an exercise in speculative nonfiction.

What would I say to him, if he did show up wondering what happened all those years ago?

How would I feel if I learned our father was dead?

To whom, if anyone, do I owe any explanation for my past behavior?

*

One of the risks I am taking with this piece, upon which rests its potential failure, is of course whether or not the leap from one genre to another "works."

Does it?

I don't know.

But it feels honest to me. Like the most honest piece of writing I have ever put on the page.

*

Another night, several shots in, after she told me to consider her my bio-mom, we were out on the balcony again and sharing another cigarette.

She said, "There's a ritual for mothers and firstborn daughters. We go to hot springs when we turn eighteen. I want to take you, if you want to go with me."

I don't remember what I said to her that night.

A few days later, though, I was on a flight back to the States, completely freaked out about how she shouldn't have wanted to take me to those hot springs, that that needed to be something she did with Haley and with Haley alone.

I don't know why I reacted so immediately, or why I chose to lie to everyone and say that I was so homesick that I just needed to secure the earliest flight I could.

Quickly, my travel arrangements were made, albeit shrouded in confusion—my own, my stepmother's, my father's. And Siwon's, clinging to my leg and begging me not to go.

*

My mom likes to tell the story about how, before my arrival, she had searched for a Korean pediatrician who would be able to speak to me and understand anything I might say in Korean. During my first checkup the doctor's wife was also there, by invitation, and the woman took one look at my hair and said, "So curly!"

My mom, confused, didn't understand. My hair was wavy at best. A little frizzy, maybe. There were no ringlets, no corkscrews.

Throughout childhood and adolescence, however, as we realized all the other Asian girls we encountered had perfectly straight silky black hair, and that my own was coarse and wild, wiry even, and frequently a tangled mess, we understood that for a Korean I did indeed have curly hair.

Many years later, during grad school when *Grey's Anatomy* aired, I remember falling in love immediately with Sandra Oh, whose hair was even curlier than my own.

The two of us, plus my aunt, were the only Asian women I knew of with curly hair.

*

Over the years, what began as the coincidence of our curly hair has led to my slowly developing an entirely different origin story than the one I have disclosed above.

Perhaps by writing it here—by giving it voice, at last—it is, in fact, the new work I am truly sharing with you now.

✳

This is a question that haunts me: Why was my stepmother so willing to accept me?

And this is the answer I have come to believe: That man was not my father. I was not his mistake. I was my aunt's—the nun's—whose curly hair I inherited.

And because he was the youngest son in his family—the roadie, the deadbeat—he could take the fall, as it were, for my aunt.

Who arranged for my adoption with Holt, that Christian agency.

Who, with her mother, met me and my mom when we visited Korea during the Seoul Olympics.

Who looks like me.

Who is—I swear this is true—the only one who looks like me.

Who, when I came back to Korea again when I was eighteen, met me in a coffee shop after the Homeland Tour and told me that my father wanted to meet me.

I had a father? Wasn't he a roadie? A deadbeat?

I believed everyone back then.

I believe none of it now.

What I choose to believe, instead, is that my aunt, the Catholic nun who looks like me and has curly hair like me, is my biological mother.

I believe that, at some point, the family's youngest son agreed to take the blame because it was far more socially acceptable for him to have had a child out of wedlock, and that when I returned again to Korea when I was eighteen they decided to offer me some semblance of a family within the family.

I believe that the reason his wife baked me a cake and welcomed me into her home and gave me her skirt and ate my disgusting garlic mashed potatoes and took shots with me at night and shared her husband's cigarettes with me out on their balcony was that she knew she had no reason to feel threatened by me, for I was not her husband's shameful secret but her sister-in-law's, who had ended up in a nunnery. A self-declared liberal feminist, my "stepmother" was willing to play along.

✳

That day in that coffee shop, after learning my father wanted to meet me, my "aunt" and I took the subway together and she showed me where to get off so I could get back to my hotel. As I stood for my stop, she started sobbing and saying my name over and over again. She pressed something into my hand and wrapped my fingers around it, and she kept her hand around mine so that I couldn't look and see what she had given me.

When the doors opened, she all but pushed me off the subway and out onto the platform. I stood and watched until it pulled away.

She never turned to look back at me through the window.

Of course, I never saw her again.

I have no idea if she is alive or dead.

In my hand, a delicate gold necklace with a tiny diamond pendant, which, unlike the leather skirt, I do still have.

✳

Then again, it's also true that on some level I can appreciate that she is probably not my biological mother.

But I cling to it, this story, this fantasy, this just-barely plausible theory, because like anyone else I want an origin story.

Even when we know them to be unlikely, untrue, we hold on to our narratives, against all reason and against our better sense. Because who are we, otherwise?

How else are we to attempt to make sense of ourselves?

Dustin Hoffman

Mending Fence

You and I, dear neighbor, meet to fell the rotten tree stump that separates our yards. You and I, beloved neighbor, have converged to remove this mess that the previous owners of our houses built this fence around, incorporating all its gnarled bark down to pith. Its height is cut to match the six-foot fence, the size of you, sweet neighbor, so much taller and more dashing than five-foot-six me. Back when the neighbors before us built this fence, this tree straddling their property lines must have been too stubborn to remove. Build around it became the solution. Or maybe this was their joke on us, cursed to resolve their heirloom eyesore. Can you hear them laughing, neighbor, as we shove shoulders against mold-ridden wood?

Our houses are a century old, built so close to the creek bed that our basements flood every spring. Edison neighborhood, Kalamazoo, Michigan—this was papermill land, houses built to convenience the mill workers, to tuck them close to their sulfur-reeking day jobs where they pulped every tree in sight.

Except for this one, dear neighbor. They spared this chunk, this torso of tree, to form our good fence that has kept us good neighbors, though soon a missing-tooth gap will exist between our yards, where your children could spill onto my lawn, and my orange fox dog could sniff her way onto yours, urinate on your garden, where you've been growing vegetables, composting, feeding your children from the earth that once housed the papermills. We've been admiring your sustainability from our second-floor window that looks on your backyard. We've enjoyed your respectful parties, the folk music piped at a moderate volume, the yellow strings of light, the craft beers and local wines. We'd join you, but there has been this tree in the way, filling our fence where a gate could open. This tree and also the lack of invitation.

We push harder, and the six-foot stump sways. Under our shoulders, we feel its heft, dense with pulp and mold and countless insects who've burrowed inside this wood for generations. We count and grunt in unison on the count of three. No need for the trappings of modern masculinity. No power tools. No chainsaw. No tools at all yet. Just two neighbors ramming and grunting and swaying and, finally, then, the give, the two-hundred-year-grown fibers answering our grunts with the tired sighs of wet cracking. We are cavemen, you and I, dear neighbor, sweating and twinned. We should touch each other to celebrate, clap backs, bump chests, kiss cheeks.

The moment for celebration passes, when a green snake swivels out from the tree carcass turned black shards and crumbles. The snake churns toward your yard, and turns toward mine, then back toward your home. You thrust hedge shears into my hands and goad me: *Kill it!*

I would say back to you, beloved neighbor, that this was your idea. This is, technically, your fence, though we both enjoy its privacy from your parties for which we lack invitations. This is Michigan, where the snakes are almost all gentle and good stewards for the gardens that feed our children. This is not my fence. This was not my tree, or, at least, only half so.

But you chant, *kill it, kill it, kill it, man!* and my blood still pumps in sync to yours, our caveman victory of shoulder blade tree toppling. Though you are the kindest neighbor I've ever known, patient with your three children, teaching the neighborhood kids how to fix bikes, planting a tiny library in your front lawn, volunteering to fill sandbags when the spring floods return—here you are now with murder stuck in your throat.

I widen the shears' mouth. Thrust down. Squeeze. I'm more accurate than I would've dreamed. I usually miss in sports, strike out, overthrow, picked late or last for teams. I've never killed any animal, never even tried, in a state where every boy hunts bucks from boyhood. But I am terribly exact in my slaughterous aim. You and I, good-citizen neighbor, our ancestors have gifted the instincts to decapitate a snake to protect your homestead, to protect your children, the child my wife will have one year from now, when the snake might've continued existing inside this rotten stump without any child ever knowing.

Using your shovel, you scoop the snake's body into a black garbage bag. The head you lift last, and you suspend it, so we can both wonder at its removed head aspirating, jaws opening and clenching, fangs drawn, more ferocious in death than we could've imagined, this Medusan curse floating between us. Those golden-ring irises gaze past us, fixed on a world we can't see, past the fence, our bodies, our houses, past the papermills and before the trees were felled to clear way for this neighborhood.

Dearest neighbor, still quivering, you discard the head, too, into the black bag, where it will reunite with body, return to the pulpy remains of its home. And tomorrow, after you level the earth, you'll erect five new slats of fencing. From my second-floor window, I'll study the blond of fresh fencing contrasted by the weathered slats that have kept us good neighbors for these years. Soon the colors will blend. You'll sell, then we'll sell, and the new neighbors will never know the brutal wonders that could separate them.

Ben Kaufman

Unknown Caller

Three generations ago, my ancestors packed Yiddish with their luggage and carried it to the U.S. on boats to escape Europe. My great-grandparents were the last generation in my family whose first language was Yiddish. It was the language of European Jewry for hundreds of years; it supplanted Hebrew as the Jewish language for an entire continent. After arriving in the U.S., it only took one generation for Yiddish to die in my family. *Glitch* is a word from Yiddish. Probably. Etymologists haven't come to a consensus, but most think that *glitch* is derived from the Yiddish '*glitsh*,' which translates to mean "slippery place." The word's English-language history can only be traced back to the mid-20th century, when astronaut John Glenn gave the word a technical definition in his 1962 book, *Into Orbit*: "Literally, a glitch is a spike or change in voltage in an electrical circuit which takes place when the circuit suddenly has a new load put on it." I can't say for sure what the context was; it's a surprisingly hard book to find.

John Glenn, the opposite of a Jew, was a religious Presbyterian from rural Ohio. It's hard to imagine how *glitch* got to him. Glenn makes it sound like he learned it from aeronautical engineering, like he had to explain the definition every time he used it. Did Jews invent space travel? Or did *glitch* simply fill in a gap where no English word existed?

Dictionary-dot-com defines *glitch* as "a defect or malfunction in a machine or plan." That sounds more like Glenn's definition than the original Yiddish. The translation changed the word's identity. Something *slippery* becomes *defective*; poetry becomes circuitry. This is assimilation.

✳

I've been thinking about *glitch* because I had a favorite one on my iPhone. My mom and I call each other around 3 times every day, just to check in. My mom likes to say, "I know you're not doing well when I don't hear from you." She's right. When I don't pick up her calls, my mom always forgets to hang up until a few seconds after the beep. Always. So every time I miss my mom's call, I get two alerts: one missed call and one brief, blank voicemail.

This is where the glitch comes in. The missed calls are labeled 'Eema' (Hebrew for 'Mom'), but the voicemails have always been labeled 'Unknown Caller.' It doesn't happen with any of my other contacts, just her.

The glitch started with my first smartphone, an iPhone 3 which I bought in late 2014 just as the new iPhone 6 was coming out. The glitch appeared with the very first missed call from my mom. For the first few months, I was irritated by red notifications which bubbled up over my phone app like a rash. But over the years, it's become a source of comfort. A reliable, harmless mis-step of a technological tool that constantly outsmarts me. It's the one thing I know which my iPhone doesn't. I know it's a message from my mom.

I always thought it would end someday, I just imagined that *someday* was far enough away that I would have time to prepare. Like, someday-down-the-road I'll have to buy a car to bring my someday-kids to basketball practice. Someday, I'll have to think about the quality of schools in my neighborhood. Someday, my mom will be dead, and she won't call me at all, and I won't press the volume button to mute my phone or flip it upside down on my desk so that I don't see the screen light up.

Every time I've upgraded my phone, I worried the glitch would correct itself. It never did, until two months ago when I upgraded to the iPhone 11. My newest smartphone finally fixed its bug. Joy, meet death. Just like that, an era slipped through my fingers to disappear forever.

Adding the suffix '-*ik*' to the end of Yiddish nouns can turn them into adjectives, similar to the German '-*ig*'. '*Glitshik*' means slippery or elusive. How appropriate.

※

When I saw the missed call *and* voicemail from 'Eema,' I stared at my phone in disbelief before eventually deleting the message and popping two Tums tablets. I called my mom back to tell her about the voicemail glitch for the first time. Initially, she was confused. She hadn't realized she'd been leaving me messages.

"Eema, you leave me a message literally every time you call," I said.

"I do?" she said.

"Yes!" I said.

"Do I say anything?" she said.

"No, Eema, every time you call, you leave me a blank, 3-second message," I said. "I think you just forget to hang up."

Since we talk every day, most conversations only last a few minutes. Our brief chats feel like temperature checks; we talk for just long enough to make sure the other is okay. I can usually tell from her voice that she's lying down in bed alongside Balthus, her battleship grey cat.

This conversation was our longest in weeks. I told her that, for the first time ever, I had gotten a voicemail from 'Eema.'

"I'm kind of reeling to be honest," I said. "I don't know why I was so attached to the glitch."

"Ah, it's a little sad. I totally get it," my mom said. She totally got it.

"End of an era I guess," I said.

"You know," my mom added, "Glitch is a Yiddish word."

✳

These days, Yiddish is making something of a comeback. Yiddish web series pepper my YouTube algorithm. Old Yiddish plays are making the rounds both on- and off-Broadway. Duolingo even recently added Yiddish to its offerings.

But 'new speakers'—an academic term used to describe people who choose to learn and speak a new primary language as a way of reinventing their political, social, and cultural realities—learn their languages with different quirks and norms than those who came before. As with *neofalantes* speaking Galician or with *gaeilgeoirs* speaking Irish, new speakers in Yiddish are creating a new dialect of an antique language. That's because they incorporate knowledge from their first language into their new one. To them, *glitsh* might simply mean glitch.

My great-grandmother's name was Sonia, derived from the Greek word for wisdom. She was born in a tiny Ukrainian village in 1907, 14 years before John Glenn was born.

I wonder what she would think of *glitch*. If I could speak to her now, I'd tell her about the bug on my smartphone. First I'd have to explain smartphones, and digital voicemail. And maybe we'd need a translator. But I know eventually I'd ask if she knew a word for something like that—a slippery place, a technical bug, a malfunction in the machine—in Yiddish. I'd ask her if she thought words meant something solid down through the years, something enduring, or if words might lose their meaning when the world decides to upgrade.

E.M. Mariani

Mother's Teeth

I have bad teeth. I've lost count of the number of root canals. Last week, I had another tooth extracted, following a failed root canal. I wasn't aware that root canals could succeed or fail, but when tooth pain continues after it's been drilled and the pulp extracted and the antibiotics administered, your root canal has failed, and you are sent to the next level of concerned dental professional. Every new dentist asks about my dental history. I have developed a short-hand explanation

"I have six children," I say, "and after every pregnancy, I've had at least one, but up to four root canals. I brush my teeth three times a day; I floss twice daily, at least. I haven't missed a six-month dental check-up in over fifteen years."

The dentists usually say something along the lines of "Oh," followed by an awkward pause. They doubt my truthfulness. Their distrust lingers in the exam room, heavy like the lead apron on my chest while I open wide and bite down on the cardboard film for a few more pictures.

I understand their doubt. My mouth makes no sense. How one can claim excellent oral hygiene and still have a mouth which looks like mine on an x-ray? Instead of the neat lines of teeth, grayish and soft, with healthy roots in strong bones, like the x-rays my kids have, I am a hodge-podge of white splotches, fillings and crowns and fake teeth, drilled into re-grown bone. The x-rays are invariably ugly and puzzling, but my gums are glowingly, beautifully healthy. They don't bleed when poked or prodded. They're not receding. There is no evidence of gum disease, even if dentists have stopped counting the number of my cavities. Instead, they count the number of teeth which haven't yet required work. We're down to the single digits. One of my former dentists told me the gums are the true indicator of oral hygiene. It was shortly after my last child was born, and I was feeling particularly demoralized, undergoing another round of root canal, cavities, and a bonus abscess within a cracked root.

"Your gums look great," he said. "Teeth, you know, a lot of

that is genetic and environmental. Did you have fluoridated water where you grew up?" He paused. "Your gums, though, their health mostly depends on how well you take care of them and you're doing a very good job."

*

Several years ago, I visited a woman for whom I babysat throughout my teen years. She had birthed ten children, though one died in infancy. Mrs. Lawson was a woman I considered strong and wise, having raised a huge family, by all appearances successfully, with minimal chaos and maximum order. She was intelligent, organized, and an enigma. We sat down to tea, and she asked me when I'd last seen a dentist. It was recently, in fact. At that point, I had three children, still within spitting distance of normal family size. My third was about one, and with his babyhood, I'd needed two teeth worked over. Mrs. Lawson advised me in her vaguely Southern drawl that I needed to be careful with my teeth.

"Having so many babies can be difficult on your teeth," she said. "My dentist told me your body will draw out the calcium needed to build your child from your teeth. She said repeated pregnancies will leave your teeth weak and inclined to decay. Be sure to keep up your dental care."

It was motherly advice, kindly given, by a woman who had watched me grow. But I was surprised and puzzled by her words. Not so much because of the advice itself – though I wondered how she presumed to know I would be having "so many babies," even as time proved her correct–but because she said specifically and unapologetically that her dentist was a woman. I could not fathom that Mrs. Frederick P. Lawson would choose a female medical professional for any reason whatever.

The Lawsons lived in the suburban Maryland neighborhood where I grew up. They were something of an oddity in the late 1980s and early 90s. Aggressively evangelical, Mr. Lawson was a successful real estate broker, who peppered most conversations with, 'Praise Jesus!' even when talking to our Jewish next-door neighbors. The Lawson kids, dressed in matching floral dresses, would canvas the neighborhood, delivering handsomely packaged apple butter, and spreading the good news of Lawson Realty. The agency sold the most houses in Daisy Ridge, our tract subdivision of Rockville. Eventually, Mr. Lawson built the largest independent real estate brokerage in Montgomery County. No one was sure how they were so successful, or how their smiling kids in their Laura Ashley dresses and well-crafted bows were so well behaved, all "Yes, ma'ams," and "No, sirs" to the neighbors with whom they spoke as they stood next to their father in his seersucker suit and fedora hat.

For reasons I still don't know, Mrs. Lawson took a liking to me when I was around thirteen. She was pregnant with her fourth child, and she called our house seeking my sixteen-year-old sister. Catherine had babysat for them once or twice, but she did not like the experience.

"They're weird," she said. "It's too quiet. And the kids never complain, even about the chores."

When I told her Catherine wasn't in, she asked me, "How old are you?"

"Twelve," I replied, "but I'll be thirteen next month."

"Do you ever babysit?" she asked. There was a note of fluster in her voice that I remember even all these years later.

"I watch my brother a lot," I said.

"And how old is he?"

"He's four," I said.

"Would you be willing to babysit Friday night?" she asked. "From five till around nine. We're just a few blocks from your house."

I told her I'd have to ask my mother. My mother was surprised at the request. She and Freddy Lawson had a history of several tense exchanges during my parents' house hunt. When we first moved to Daisy Ridge, we lived in a rental house owned by another military family. Our lease ended, but my father's tour at the Pentagon was re-upped so we weren't moving away. My mother decided Daisy Ridge was the neighborhood in which she wanted to plant her roots, regardless of my father's army career. She undertook the effort of finding a house herself, without a realtor. She knew which houses were coming on the market before anyone else. Mom-friends throughout the subdivision fed her information. At a neighborhood gathering, Mr. Lawson, in a tone mixing awe with disdain, told my mother, "I guess you're good at this; maybe I should hire you." At the time, Lawson Realty had no women agents, but here he was admitting he might make an exception for her. Her inside knowledge and his disdain had been confirmed the year before Mrs. Lawson called me, when my parents purchased our house directly from neighbors with neither benefit of nor commission for any realtors at all.

I don't remember whether my mother talked to Mrs. Lawson, or if she had any qualms about her twelve-year-old watching three children, aged seven, four, and two, but she allowed me to go. Over the next five years or so, I became the regular Friday night babysitter for the Lawsons. By that time, they had six children, a parallel I note now, but do not comprehend.

Elin, the oldest child, was so responsible that she barely needed a babysitter. She could cook dinner, change diapers, and tell me where to put the teacups. She also told me in the same helpful voice where the 'switches' were stored, thin plastic rods that were kept in a hallway closet, but explained they were "only for our parents to use." Amelia, second in line, was spunky, funny, prone to singing silly songs she made up on the fly, with goofy dances to accompany. Megan, the third, was sweet, wide-eyed, astonishingly cute. Freddy, Jr., Ryan, and Christine, who was a tiny newborn the last time I babysat for the family, followed in the good order and discipline over ensuing years.

Within Daisy Ridge, there was a mystique about being the Lawson's babysitter. A giant, homeschooling, intensely Evangelical family, dressed in matching wholesome clothing? People wanted to know more.

When asked how their family functioned on the inside, I usually responded, "I don't know." Because I didn't know. There was something different about them, but I couldn't put the pieces together into a clear story. It was normal enough except when it wasn't. I was 13, 14, 15, 16. I played with the kids, fed them, made up rhymes and played imaginative games. We did dishes, folded laundry, cleaned up toys. Normal stuff. And then not: knowing I wasn't a member of their church, the kids called me "a papist" and asked me why I worshipped Mary instead of accepting Jesus as my Lord and Savior. I took the question as curiosity, like I was an anthropological find for them. Mrs. Lawson praised my organization and diligence. She liked that the kids behaved for me, that I rarely gave bad reports at the end of the night. "She's a good example," she'd tell the girls in my hearing. "Studious and industrious and godly." I wasn't sure the state of my soul, but I maintained the illusion. I craved her approval.

The girls found my last name hilarious, an endless joke.

"Elizabeth Mariani," Amelia would say, stating my name simply.

"Yes," I'd respond.

Then she'd shout, "Elizabeth, Marry-Ahnni!"

And I would say, "But who is Ahnni, and I'm way too young to marry him, anyway."

Elin, Amelia, and Megan would collapse into giggles, repeating the command at random intervals when they were supposed to be going to sleep, starting the laughter train all over again. I'd rub their backs, singing lullabies till they dropped off.

One night, after a particularly raucous Mariani session, as the girls were finally dropping off to sleep, Elin, asked me, "Elizabeth, when you get married in real life, can we go to your wedding?"

"Sure," I said.

"Do you promise?" she asked.

"I promise," I replied.

I was probably fifteen. I didn't mind making the promise, but I told them I had to finish high school first. And college. And probably graduate school, too.

"We're not going to college," Elin told me one day. "Girls don't need to know stuff like that in order to run a family in a godly way."

"But it's always helpful to know stuff," I replied.

"That's what the worldly claim," said Elin. She spoke with the authority of a wizened grandmother. "But education in girls becomes defrauding, like immodest bathing suits. Ladies become domineering, and that's not how God intended for them to live. It makes everyone unhappy." She was ten at the time.

I didn't ask further questions. I had come to understand the rules of the Lawson house: the man was the head of the household, and the woman was the heart of the home. In their kitchen, Mr. Lawson had a cabinet filled with treats, just for him. The kids weren't allowed in there; Mrs. Lawson wouldn't consider eating from it. Because Mr. Lawson was the man, he deserved respect and his favorite cookie whenever he wanted it.

In households like my own, the cookie bin was a free-for-all; it was loud and chaotic, and people fussed and argued and fretted over wants and needs, in a constant fluster of papist disorder.

*

The summer after I started babysitting for the Lawsons, I attended a summer camp for creative writing. From my earliest memory, I wanted to be a writer, first Laura Ingalls as portrayed in the 70s television show, then Anne with an 'e' Shirley of Anne of Green Gables. I wanted the life of imagination, but the desire struck me as dangerous to admit. It felt too vulnerable, the risk of failure too great. The camp instructor, a middle-aged man who told a room full of 13-year-olds at lunch about his ongoing divorce and mounting bills, wrote "Fine" and "OK" on my work. It was the same kind of bland praise my parents muttered in passing, if they praised me at all. It was a stark contrast to Mrs. Lawson's effusive and specific approbation: "studious and industrious and godly." I felt warm in her presence.

At our tea, all those years later, Mrs. Lawson said to me, "Isn't it is the most wonderful thing, to devote your life to raising a brood for Christ?"

*

I have tried to be that mother, the one whose life is joyfully fulfilled. Keeping up with laundry and groceries, cleaning scrapes and hurt feelings, managing school projects, and soccer schedules. For a while, I was good at it, at least I think I was. When the children were young, when the sheer number of little people and their physical needs demanded my whole attention, I juggled and coordinated, curating their tiny lives, developing their brains and bodies with zoo trips, libraries, playgrounds. They ate balanced meals. Their birthday cakes, baked from scratch, were elaborate creations, shaped into dinosaurs and lady bugs, decorated with frostings made bright and cheerful with colored gels purchased from the baker's supply shop.

I didn't choose to be this sort of mother because of religious fervor. It just seemed the way to be: after spending the first 26 years of my life achieving in school, in work, in marriage, it felt like relief to pour myself into caring. Loving my children to the point that I would cut myself open for any one of them, bleed myself dry, lop off a limb or a brain and all my wants and needs, if only it would make them healthy, whole, at peace. This was my impulse.

Until it wasn't. Until I began to see the slip ups, the mistakes, the ways I failed the children, missed their needs. My oldest was bullied for a year, taunted and rejected throughout the first and second grades because he wasn't allowed to play the video games the other boys in his tiny class played. I missed it entirely. It wasn't until his sweet, six-year-old-self refused to go to school one morning that I became aware that something might be wrong. And even then, it was my husband who saw a problem and got him to talk. Ten years later, on the cusp of manhood, that experience still shapes his character. You wouldn't know it to meet him now. He is healthy, athletic, has friends, but I see it in his humor. He is funny, quick-witted and dry, but it's the humor of someone who's known hurt he couldn't comprehend.

I am present and devoted, but it's not enough because there is never enough in this kind of mothering project. I am too invested in #5's life. #6 needs more attention. #1 needs more guidance. #2 needs to more balance in her life. #3 cannot cope with conflict. #4 seems to be doing okay at the moment, which means she's overlooked, until (God forbid) she has a crisis and the attention deck gets reshuffled.

✻

Shortly before the latest tooth decided to rot from my head, I decided to switch dentists. In normal circumstances, this wouldn't be a big deal. People switch dentists and doctors all the time, for all sorts of reasons. The problem, however, was that Louisa, the now-former dentist, was also my friend. I told her my decision via text. This isn't as cowardly as it seems. Our friendship was conducted almost entirely over text. We occasionally met for coffee or to run-walk-chat with other mothers. Otherwise, we did everything over text: coordinated carpools, swapped jokes and recipes, offered advice and support. A full friendship, conducted and ended through the blue blurbs of iMessage.

Louisa was first person I befriended when we moved to the area. She was almost a godsend. With my history, I needed a dentist in a new place, and there she was. Our kids were in the same grades. They went to the same school. We attended the same church. Our husbands were both physicians, working for the same university system. Petite, elfin, with wild, frizzy hair, she seemed welcoming and funny. She introduced me to her friends, invited me into the running group she started. We read the same books, discussed the same articles. She seemed like a long-lost sister, sympathetic and caring. At some point, little bits of information, shared in the confidence of friendship, turned into subtle insults, launched when least expected. I barely noticed at first, frequently excused them.

The first direct affront I remember occurred just over two years after we'd met: "Lucy [her daughter] asked me what you do," Louisa texted me one afternoon, "She said, 'All the girls' moms do something... Emily's mom is an accountant, Lily's mom does computer stuff; you're a dentist, but what does Maeve's mom do?'"

"I didn't want to tell her that you're just a mom," Louisa continued, "So I told her you're a writer, since you did take that class."

"I'm not a writer," I replied. "I'd like to be, maybe. but I'm not there."

"But I don't want her to know that being just a mom is an option," she replied, "so she's going to think you're a writer."

Another morning, she texted me asking what I planned to feed my family for dinner that evening. "I'm out of ideas the kids will eat," she wrote. "Sometimes I have to remind myself that I am not actually a stay-at-home mom, even though my kids' lives are basically identical to kids with moms who stay home. It's just too much to keep up this pace—full time mom and full time professional."

This became the crux of our friendship, a contest in competitive mothering. Who was better? Whose kids were smarter? More athletic? Whose kids were going to be more successful, win more prizes, get into better schools, make more money, influence more people?

I gloried in the competitive game. I suspect I maintained the friendship because I was confident I would win. She was obsessed with her children's grades, checking them multiple times per day on the school system's mobile app. "You should get it," she texted me, "the app lets you email teachers directly with questions." She developed a persistent compulsion to know my children's grades. One month she texted me five times, "concerned" about Lucy's test grades in the third grade, "Lucy got an 85 on the math test, but Maeve got a 100," she'd say. "What is Maeve doing to study? I clearly need to change things up with Lucy."

I didn't know what my daughter was doing to study. I didn't know she'd had a test, and I didn't know she'd gotten a 100. In a household with six kids, they're in charge of their own homework. If they need help, they ask someone, most often one of their siblings, who will explain anything better and faster and less distractedly than I would.

There was something creepy about another parent knowing my kid's grades before I did. But Louisa's creepy habits cemented my position as the better, less neurotic mother. I was willing to accept that.

✳

Six years after my tea with Mrs. Lawson, my mother called me, out of breath, shocked.

"Have you heard anything about the Lawsons?" she asked.

I had not. I last called them some four years prior, when I had left a message for Mrs. Lawson, asking if some of her children might be able to babysit my toddlers during my father's funeral. She never called back. I never thought about it again.

"Ed Klein told me there was a lawsuit filed against the church the Lawsons went to," she said.

Ed Klein was my mother's next-door neighbor of nearly thirty years, the Jewish man subjected to Mrs. Lawson's 'Praise Jesus' routine on a regular basis. After my father died, my mother and Ed became brisk-walking partners with a group of seniors on the streets of Daisy Ridge.

"Ed says the Lawson girls accused their father of abusing them and the church of covering it up. Physically and sexually. He asked me what you think? Do you think it's true?"

"I don't know," I said. "I'd have to see it."

She emailed me the civil complaint which was making the digital rounds of the subdivision. I read the accounts relating to 'Grace Goe,' the pseudonym Amelia had used to file the lawsuit. I knew it was Amelia, the second oldest, based on her birth date and description. The accusations were detailed and precise.

A chill ripped through me and settled in my stomach. I knew it was true. Like a flash, I was inside a memory with a clarity never experienced before: Amelia, probably around eight years old, telling me exactly what she reported as an adult in the lawsuit. And I remembered my response to her, something so colossally stupid that as an adult I am appalled at my teenaged self.

"My dad put his toes in my privates," she had said, in her typically spunky way.

"Huh?" I said.

"I was rubbing his feet," she said, "and he put his toe inside my privates."

"It must have been an accident," I said.

At the time, I didn't understand. I remember hearing the words and watching them float through my head. I couldn't form them into a coherent concept. I remember my stomach dropped in vague recognition that something was off. I knew of sexual abuse. I'd watched Afterschool Specials in the mid-80s, like tons of other kids my age. But in those shows, families where abuse occurred were grungy and chaotic. They weren't wealthy and well-behaved in matching Laura Ashley. Abusers weren't successful and powerful and praising Jesus on the manicured lawns of suburban D.C. I was entirely naïve and compliant, willing to take authority on its appearance of authority. To the Lawson parents, I was the perfect babysitter.

"No. It definitely wasn't on accident," she said. "He did it on purpose."

"Just shut up, Amelia!" Elin suddenly interjected.

'Shut-up' was a forbidden phrase in their household. That Elin, obedient, complaint, sweetly responsible Elin, used that phrase should have been another clue that something was terribly wrong. Instead, the girls started bickering. I changed the subject and put it out of my mind.

Reading through the allegations, I remembered more of what I'd seen with blinding clarity, like sunshine hitting your eyes when you step out of a dark building. The plastic switches used to 'spank' the kids. Their upper thighs covered in black and blue eruptions, where the plastic had whipped them. For sassing, for fibbing, for being little kids in a big and confusing world.

I felt sick from the remembering. But there was more.

I remembered one Friday evening, the summer when I was 14. Megan, about three, had angry purple whip marks across the back of her upper leg. The welts were raised, almost blistered.

"Is that from Tuesday?" I asked Elin.

"Uh-huh." She responded. "She lied to my mom, so Mom had to switch her."

I babysat the previous Tuesday afternoon. While giving Megan a bath, I had removed the mother of pearl ring my grandmother gave me for my Confirmation a few months before. At some point when I wasn't looking, a curious three-year old had picked it up and dropped it in the toilet. When I couldn't find it, I became upset, but just a bit. I told Mrs. Lawson. First, she lectured me that it was "a thing," and I shouldn't be attached to the things of this world. Then she and the kids set about looking. Megan promised with all preschool sincerity that she hadn't touched the ring. Over and over, she promised. I went home without the ring, feeling grumpy and ashamed. The next day, Mrs. Lawson called me. She found the ring, she told me. "I tried to think what a three-year-old would do with a ring in a bathroom," she told me. "I stuck my hand down the toilet, and sure enough, that's where it was, sitting at the bottom of the bowl."

I thanked her and felt relieved. I saw Megan's leg a couple days later. I knew I shouldn't have said anything. The ring wasn't important enough for the welts on Megan's legs. I whispered, "I'm sorry" to Megan that Friday night, when I tickled her back, as she dropped off to sleep.

Sitting in my basement, years later, a mother of six myself, I accused my teenaged self. How did I not see the hell these kids were subjected to? What had I been thinking? Even when they turned to me for help, confided in me because they knew I was from the outside world, I failed them. I hadn't thought to tell my parents. Even if I had, I'm not sure what they would have done. I had mentioned something to my college-aged sister, but my description had been confused. "I don't know," she'd said. "That's weird." Afterward, I boxed up those memories, walled off sections of my brain so that I could remain free in my naïve compliance.

A few months after Amelia told me about her father's molestation, Mrs. Lawson called to tell me she'd no longer rely on me for regular Friday night babysitting.

"You've reached the age," she said, "when you are too busy with school and your own life, and you'll become unreliable."

I was confused. I couldn't remember missing any scheduled babysitting engagements. I'd always been reliable, responsible, letting her know well in advance if I had a conflict.

Decades later, I understood.

According to the complaint, the girls continued to tell people they trusted about the abuse for years. Their housekeeper finally brought them to the pastors of the mega-church they attended.

This was several years after Amelia told me. The pastors appeared to cover up the accusations systematically. Mr. Lawson paid for the entire pastoral staff and their families to take an expenses-paid vacation at South Carolina resort. Mrs. Lawson fired the housekeeper just as she fired me. The kids were cut off from anyone they trusted, and the abuse continued.

Allegedly, but clearly so.

✳

For the first few years, my competition with Louisa existed in a comfortable stasis. Until it didn't. One morning Maeve collapsed in a sobbing heap on my bed, refusing to go to school.

"What's the matter?" I asked her.

"It's Lucy," she sobbed. "She's so annoying. She always follows me around, doing what I'm doing. It's like she wants to be me. She won't stop asking my grades—all day! But then, she also wants me to mess up. Like she's just waiting for me to make a mistake so she can brag about how great she is."

I texted Louisa, gently requesting that Lucy stop asking Maeve her grades throughout the day. It was against the school rules anyway.

Louisa replied, "My daughter is a very competitive girl. She needs to be the best. Right now, she sees Maeve as the best – at least in school – so she's aiming for her."

Aiming for her? Like she's a nine-year old target who must be done away with, for the zero-sum superiority prize of the third grade?

Their teacher called me. "I'm concerned," she said. "There's an abnormal amount of competition between Lucy and Maeve. I know they're both strong girls, and I know they have a lot of overlap with school and Irish dance – there are a lot of opportunities to compare. But I feel this competition is coming from one direction, and it's directed at your daughter. Maeve doesn't seem to be handling it well. I've moved them to opposite sides of the classroom. I'm trying to limit their interactions at school, but I wanted you to be aware."

I was aware. Maeve started therapy. She couldn't confront school without anxious meltdowns. I kept this development entirely secret from Louisa.

Louisa called the school, believing that Maeve was bullying Lucy, avoiding her and not including her in games she wanted to play. She wanted Maeve talked to.

Lucy started therapy. Louisa let me know this. She was pretty sure Lucy was being so competitive, so badgering toward Maeve because her grandmother had died, and it was a grief reaction. Grief was an acceptable reason for a kid to go to therapy. Anxious meltdowns and hypercompetitive tendencies were not. Coping with a double-full time perfect mother was certainly no reason for counseling.

At their first feis, the name for Irish dance competition, Maeve beat Lucy in every contest. The results are brutal and clear: kids are ranked, their names posted on the wall for all to see how they placed according to the judges who evaluated them.

Louisa took it hard.

"I don't think Lucy should be around Maeve right now," she texted. "Lucy needs friends who enhance her self-esteem, and Maeve doesn't do that."

A few weeks later, Maeve sat in the chair at her dental check-up, her mouth wide open, sunglasses protecting her eyes from the glare of the examination light. Louisa chatted while checking her teeth.

"You did so well at that feis, Maeve," she said.

Naturally, Maeve couldn't respond, so I replied for her. "Yeah, she really likes Irish. She's dancing everywhere, all the time these days, huh, Maeve?"

There was an undertone of tension between us mothers. I tried to diffuse it, while still staking my kid's claim. To what, I wasn't clear.

"Yeah. Lucy likes it, but I think she likes ballet better. We'll have to see...So, Maeve, are you taking the grade exams at Nations Cap?" she asked. Nations Cap was an upcoming competition.

"What are grade exams?" I asked. I hadn't heard of them.

"They're like standardized tests for dance. They're offered at some competitions. Lucy's friend, Cara was invited to take them. It's part of the process of qualifying for your Irish teaching license. I understand they're by invitation only. I thought maybe you were invited."

And there it was: the taunt. Directed squarely at my kid, sitting in the chair, vulnerable and small, her mouth agape while her teeth were prodded.

"Maeve is nine," I replied, "and since she only started dancing six months ago, we're not thinking about her career."

I said it lightly, but my brain seethed. In the parking lot, I sat
in the car before driving home. I texted two trusted friends, one
who knew Louisa, one who did not. I relayed the scene as close as
I could. Did what I think happened really happen? Am I making it
up, filling in assumptions? I needed outside confirmation to clarify
my sight. Maeve waited in the back seat, increasingly impatient,
"Can we just go?" she asked.

A couple weeks later, I cancelled the older kids' appointments,
and didn't reschedule. I sent Louisa a text, informing her we were
switching dentists. I blamed it on insurance.

"We have the greatest respect for you as a dentist," I wrote,
"but being out of network, we're spending too much time dealing
with insurance, tracking and coordinating payments. I'm sorry,
and I understand if you find this situation upsetting. I really value
our friendship and appreciate everything you have done for our
family!"

✳

About a year after my mother emailed the Lawson's civil
complaint, I was cleaning out my desk drawers. We were moving
back East. Within the desk, I found a note from Mrs. Lawson. The
paper was creamy and thick with her monogram embossed on the
front. It was crumpled and frayed the way notes become when
they spend years furrowed in the back of a drawer. Mrs. Lawson's
smooth penmanship filled the card. It was dated two years earlier, a
couple of months before the girls filed suit. By the time she wrote
the note, she must have known it was coming.

I had forgotten receiving it. It had arrived at a time of crisis
in my young family. At that moment, I felt like a reflection of my
teenage self, desperate for order and approbation. Mrs. Lawson up-
dated me on her children, most of them adults by then. Her words
conveyed complacent maternal pride, the kind you'd expect when
children are mostly grown. She wrote about my children, some-
thing like, "I keep the Christmas card of your precious children in
my Bible and pray for them daily." She recalled what a blessing I'd
been to her, with my diligence and godliness. I'd forgotten I sent
her our Christmas cards. She ended the note much like she had our
tea three children and several root canals before: "It's the greatest
blessing," she wrote, "to raise a brood for Christ."

Looking at the rumpled card, I remembered I sent Mrs. Law-
son a reply, a card I bought at Target filled with my scratchy hand-

writing. I thanked her for her note and for her influence during
my adolescence. I said something about their marriage demon-
strating mutual support and care. My blindness had been so
durable and willful, my betrayal toward those girls so thorough.
I crumpled her note and threw it with the rest of the moving
trash. The note is gone, but the shame lingers still.

✳

At the first check-up with the new dentist after leaving
Louisa, they found five cavities. I'd seen her six months before,
but she hadn't noticed any. The hygienist, scraping and prodding
and counting decay, stopped her sociable chatter as concern
heightened. She typed notes in the online chart and emitted a
shrill laugh when the dentist entered. "All five cavities need to be
filled," he said after his examination. "A couple look like they've
been there a while, but I don't think we have any root canals yet."
Despite such decay, my gums remain healthy.

Emily Mohn-Slate

Mourning a Student

In the days before the memorial service, I keep cycling through where Micah sat in each class. Creative Writing I: the middle of the back row, between Sam and Michael. Creative Writing II: the back right corner, between Thalia and Sam. Special Topics in Fiction: the back right corner, next to Sam. Always in the back near his friend, Sam. Micah was deep-thinking, quiet, funny. The kind of person who has whole cities tucked inside of him. If I work hard enough to picture Micah there, maybe he will return.

I keep turning over two memories: the first is when we work-shopped one of his stories about werewolves taking over a town. In the story, two kids hide in a rickety treehouse while the were-wolves pace below, swiping their claws at the tree trunk. It felt like Stranger Things meets Karen Russell but with a voice that was unmistakably Micah's. Another student said, "God, I love this story. I don't mean to be a fangirl, but I am. I love all your stories, Micah." Everyone agreed, nodding. Micah looked down, smiling painfully, looking like he wanted to burrow into the desk.

The second is an essay he wrote about his diabetes. He wrote about his backpack, how he carried a blood tester and supplies for shots in there, and that he didn't mind. He made some joke about how it was a good excuse to wear a backpack all the time, so he had more room to carry stuff than just his pockets. I read that line in a rush of grading, and I stopped and put down my pen. A window had opened onto his life—what it must be like to be so young and to carry this illness with him everywhere he went.

I try to find Micah's emails, but I can't log in to my university email. A message in a little box tells me to contact an administra-tor. Instead, I go looking for more of his writing in the folders of saved work on my laptop. I find some stories, poems, and essays, a reflection from our fiction class, the journal he created in our Literary Journal Practicum course. If I read it more closely now than when I was rushing to grade, to just make sure he had revised, will I see something I missed before? Will I somehow know him better?

Micah was born in the spring of my freshman year of college. I started teaching him in the spring of his freshman year of college. He had wide hazel eyes, and brown shaggy rock-star hair. His eyebrows were almost permanently raised, which made him look surprised or gently skeptical. He'd often mumble something under his breath that made everyone sitting near him crack up. I'd half-smile and ask, "What did you say?" I remember thinking that if I were his age, I would want to be his friend.

He would push his hair back behind his ears and gaze intently at his computer or his paper. He mostly avoided my gaze when I asked questions of the class. He rarely talked. When I required that everyone give a presentation on their favorite writer, he began by saying, "I hate talking in front of people, so I'll be short." Everyone laughed, then leaned forward to listen. He didn't realize he was good at public speaking; he was so clearly himself.

I saw Micah at the little café on campus near the end of last semester. His hair was longer than I remembered and his eyes were focused on his computer. I thought about going up to him and saying hi, asking how he was, but I was busy. I pretended I didn't see him. I focused on wrapping my scarf and clearing the crumbs off my table. If he had said hello, I would have stopped and talked, but I didn't want to bother him. Or, I didn't want to stop and talk.

The kids are finally asleep. I put my feet up and take a sip of peppermint tea. I haven't had a moment to talk to anyone about Micah since I heard. His face, his obituary, his voice had been buzzing in my head, making it hard to remember what to set up for my daughter's birthday party. I had to look at my list three times before I actually fished the candles out of the junk drawer.

I text Sara and arrange to go to the viewing with her. She was his advisor and taught him in several classes. I post something online about Micah, and one of my former students who was in class with him writes, "Please let me know about any ways the school will memorialize him." I start to text Sara, then remember I'm not teaching there this spring. How do I grieve my student when I'm no longer teaching there?

One of the givens of teaching is that you're never sure what you're saying or doing matters. With a quiet student, that unknowing is amplified. You wonder constantly what's going on in their heads, asking, Are they getting it? Or, the more important question to me, what do they need to hear right now? Or to say? What are they carrying inside that I might help them bring into the world? Since Micah was quiet in class, we had a largely epistolary relationship studded with brief conversations and the occasional head nod. I tried to reach him through my notes on his drafts, or through an email that I hoped he'd read, since he never replied.

Micah was from the town next to where I grew up, and there was something about him that felt kindred to me. Micah was his age in some ways, and in other ways older than his years, maybe because he was a natural observer, or because he had to cope with a complicated illness his whole life. He must have had thousands of awkward conversations in his twenty short years.

I remember feeling bad when he had to turn down the cookies I brought to class, and then worrying if he did take one.

How did you know Micah? his brother, his cousin, his best friend, his parents will ask. *Were you his professor?* they will say.

I worry I will say, "Just his teacher, not a real professor," letting my thoughts about myself linger too long at exactly the moment when my thoughts are supposed to be on someone else. I coach myself beforehand, so I won't utter the words that are always on the tip of my tongue: *Yes, I was. No, I wasn't, not really.*

When you're an adjunct professor, you're constantly aware of your position on the periphery of the department and the university. As you move through your days on campus, or work in the campus coffeeshop, you wonder: is this invitation to teach an upper-level course a hint that soon I might be invited closer into the circle? You carry an id card in your wallet, but your title—Adjunct Instructor—places you in a poorly paid no-man's land between the graduate students, who carry their world in a backpack like you, and the "real" professors, who have offices where they can hang their coats and scuffed desks where they can store their favorite green tea. You still teach and mentor and write letters of recommendation and help plan student readings, but nobody asks, "Would you like to be on this panel? What are you writing these days?"

I'm anxious about going to the viewing. I don't want to think of him in a polished box when I am not yet sure where he is in my memory. I don't want other memories to crowd out the picture I am holding of him.

I'm meeting Sara and some students and we're driving together to the funeral home. I'm a few minutes late, as usual. The students hover like crows in the entryway in black tops and long coats. I feel nervous. I'm not sure why. Maybe because this is the first time I'm seeing other people who are grieving Micah. I keep thinking about the line in the book of James, "What is your life? You are a mist that appears for a little while and then vanishes."

Peter and Angela, two of my former students, climb in my car. The afternoon is cold and bright, so bright I have to wear my sunglasses, but so cold my toes are already freezing in my boots. It's 23 degrees as we drive out to Bellevue, a town built into a hill along the Ohio River.

At the funeral home, we see the rest of our group right away. We bunch together awkwardly in the foyer for a while, next to a poster-sized picture of Micah in his red and white high school band uniform. I hug a few students. Nobody makes eye contact.

His grandmother introduces us to his grandfather, who then points out Micah's mother. We stand around stiffly for long minutes while she talks to a few people. Then his grandfather guides her over to us. Sara and I shake her hand and tell her we taught Micah and she nods and doesn't say anything. "We all loved Micah," I say, but she isn't looking at me. *Maybe we shouldn't have come*, I think. I can't remember anything else I wanted to say.

Sara guides Peter over, and Micah's mother lights up and hugs him. They start talking about the terrible third roommate Micah and Peter had their freshman spring. She smiles and laughs a little. I overhear him say, "You did a good job. Micah was such a good person." Her body caves in a little when he says that.

After we file out again into the foyer, we look at each other, then at the floor. "Does anyone need to get back to campus now? Or do you want to go to Eat n' Park? I could use some pie," I say.

We breathe out collectively when we sit down at the long table in the back room. I go into hostess mode, talking about how I love their pie, how I used to come here all the time in high school. The students seem tired and old. We order fries, mozzarella sticks, fried pickles, pie, coffee. Everyone talks about easy things like what classes they're taking this spring, how their break was, then drift to talk about Micah, then flash back to something easy again. Micah should be with them, eating fries and cracking jokes. I miss Micah. I miss my old students, hearing about their lives. I miss being Prof Mohn-Slate. I feel like I'm having lunch with my ex, that pang of missing. A wall gone up suddenly between us.

We pay the check and are about to get up when a half circle of young men I recognize from the funeral home drift over to our table.

"Are you guys Micah's friends from college?"

"Yeah," a few of the students say. "Are you his friends from high school?"

"Yeah."

They are shaggy, wearing button-down shirts, some with messy ties, a few with sport coats. Their hands are planted in their pockets. We talk for a little while about Micah. They knew Micah before any of us had even met him, when he was playing trombone in the band, writing his first stories, deciding where to go to college.

My students knew him in ways I never will. Because I read his writing, I knew him in ways some others never will. We all circled his life, describing the part we could see from our limited experience, feeling it was the whole truth.

After I drop the students off on campus after Micah's viewing, I drive down Fifth Avenue toward home. I think back to how we told Micah's grandmother we would send her some of his writing. *Shit*, I think, *I shouldn't have told her that*. I know we can share work he published in the student literary journal, which she probably hasn't seen yet. But I can't share work that he turned in for class. He turned it in as an assignment, for only my eyes, for a grade. I can't make that decision for him.

And then I think: I will mourn those stories he won't have time to write, and the letters of recommendation he won't ask me for.

Thinking about Micah's stories brings something into relief for me: In this world where we pass into and out of each others' lives like a mist, I was his teacher. And that is a role that at least gives some order to things.

My students and I sat in a circle together twice a week for two years. We sat there after having read the same things and we talked or didn't talk about them. But we were there twice a week, in that dingy room in the second floor of Falk that was always either too hot or too cold. We connected in large and small ways, some of which had to do with our shared love of writing, and others that had to do with something more mysterious, like the gift of being alive together.

My students didn't care that I was *only* an adjunct professor; they never once signaled that they did not value what I shared with them. What had hobbled me about being an adjunct wasn't the lack of an office or the poor pay (though that mattered), but my view of myself as someone who didn't deserve respect without a particular title. And I could change that, if I decided to, couldn't I?

Months later, I log on to Facebook and one of my former students has posted an audio recording from our class two years earlier. It's a game that I always used to start my fiction unit—I start with a character named Margie who wants a glass of water, then each student has to advance the story in some way.

I close my eyes and listen, seeing each person's face in my mind. It's mid-summer, the air is thick with humidity at my attic desk. The story moves from left to right around the circle. Once I hear Sam's voice, I know Micah is next. His voice is steady, sharp: "But he was an old hippie, so he didn't have any money." Everyone laughs then the voices drop away, and the story moves on.

Anna Nguyen

For Children Who Translate

1.

At my elementary school, each grade level was assigned to study a continent. By swiftly looking at the hallways, one could easily tell which continent was the research object for the specific grade. Every time I craned my neck and moved my eyes upward, I saw the single continent in a bold hue, detached from the world along its geographic borders, on the white walls of our hallways. In fourth grade, the continent was Asia. We were assigned to select a country and make a travel brochure as homework. The teacher asked basic questions: the population size, the spoken languages, religions, and significant dates. In the middle of the folded paper, there was a box to illustrate the country's flag.

The teacher asked us to name three countries, in order of preference. I picked what I thought was the obvious choice for me: Vietnam. The teacher permitted me to "research" Vietnam, writing in red ink, *I know you really want to write about Vietnam.* I wasn't very studious at the time; I simply knew my parents could fill in the gaps.

During one of his visits to the Salvation Army, Ba found a set of used *Funk & Wagnalls'* encyclopedias. From the handmade blond oak bookshelf, I took the V volume and walked to our dining table. I found the entry on Vietnam. There were only five pages, and I didn't understand what I was reading. But all I had to do was answer the categories on each small box of the brochure. I didn't even need to write in complete sentences. One of the sparse photographs featured a bright red flag with a bright yellow star in the middle. I sketched a crude replica into the map box. My star was crooked, and I erased it many times. I felt someone peeking from behind my shoulder.

"No, no, that's not right," Ba said in his gentle, throaty Vietnamese. "The South Vietnamese flag is yellow with three red stripes in the middle. You should draw that." For ten years, Ba fought in the South Vietnamese regime.

"Can you show me?" I asked in Vietnamese. I only spoke English to my brother and sisters at home. I found a piece of scrap paper and handed him a pencil. It was one of the few times my father helped me with my school assignments. He could tutor me in math, but when it came to reading and grammar I had to learn on my own or ask my impatient older siblings.

Pressing the pencil lightly, he sketched a simple rectangle with three horizontal bars in the middle.

"The three lines have to be red. The background is yellow," he instructed.

From my box of crayons, I found the two colors and held them up for his approval.

"Why are the flags different?" I asked my father. I pointed at the photograph in the encyclopedia.

He glanced at the image.

"Two different flags for two different countries," he answered curtly. He left the room.

My teacher returned our assignment. I received a checkmark. In red ink, she had circled my flag, the flag I had carefully lined with my ruler. *The flag is supposed to be red with a yellow star in the middle*, she wrote in cursive. I was embarrassed. I reread the comment-cum-reprimand many times. But I was also confused. My father and I are Vietnamese. And she was a white American. Did my father not know his own flag? Had he been away for so long that he couldn't remember?

When I returned home, I handed my father the incriminating brochure.

"She said it's wrong," I said to him, almost in anger.

My father examined my illustration. My older sister was sitting next to him at the dining table. She leaned forward to examine the offending paper.

"Well, your stripes are a bit thick," he said, "but the star is not our flag." He tossed the paper on top of the newspapers that were scattered on the dining table. Every evening, he would throw the newspapers away.

My sister turned to me. "Are you going to talk to your teacher?"

I didn't answer her. Not because I didn't care, but because I didn't know what to say to the teacher at the time. Or any white teacher teaching about colonial histories and forgotten artifacts.

2.

After living in the United States for twenty-five years, my parents decided to apply for citizenship. I was twelve years old. I don't even remember if they discussed their reasons with us, their four children. All I recall is helping my mother study. She had to memorize one hundred answers to one hundred questions that resemble a basic social studies course. *Who was the first president of the United States? When did the United States declare independence?* There were at least a couple of questions dealing with local politics. *Who is your state governor?*

When my mother returned home from work at the chicken factory, she'd prepare dinner. Rice was always magically cooked, and someone would scoop out six bowls of rice. Ma would pull out leftover dishes from the refrigerator and reheat them. We ate together, at the table in the small kitchen. After dinner, she'd settle in the living room. The TV was usually on, a rented TVB soap on VHS tapes from a Vietnamese market about an hour away, and she'd begin to embroider a complicated rose or bird design for a quilt or a pillowcase.

"Help me study," she commanded, either to my twin sister or me, as she threaded a needle.

I had already finished my homework. My older siblings, then high school students, had disappeared into their bedrooms. They were probably studying or finishing their own homework.

I was not a very good reader. I particularly disliked reading aloud. In the middle of third grade, I had been sent to speech classes, where I would remain until I finished elementary school, because of pronunciation problems. Every Monday, Wednesday, and Friday at eleven o'clock, I spent thirty minutes with other students repeating words and imitating sounds with a hard "r". I needed to enunciate more, the speech teacher told me, in her slight southern accent, as she corrected a list of words that ended with "-er" or "-ar". The monosyllabic word "art" was especially difficult for me. *Ahhh-t*, I'd try to say. My classmates often made jokes at my expense. They called me stupid or slow. *But Ma's English was worse than mine*, I always thought, as if such a comparison provided me with any consolation at all.

Many times, Ma didn't understand my shaky English, so I had to try to translate fragmented phrases in Vietnamese. I could barely translate "What do we call the first ten amendments of the

Constitution?" or "checks and balances." Sometimes, I'd get creative. For "what are the three branches of government," I would conjure a tree in my limited vocabulary.

"What are the three tree limbs of the U.S. government?" I'd say in halting Vietnamese, after Ma couldn't comprehend the English.

"Three tree limbs?" Ma asked, not looking up from her embroidery. Her colorful bird, mainly in dark reds and purple, was only half completed.

"Three..." I searched for a different word. "Three..."

Ba answered from the dark. He always sat far away from us, in the dining room. He rarely turned on the light and sat chain smoking his Marlboro Reds.

"Tree limbs!" Ma exclaimed. She was probably imagining a government tree. "What is the answer again?" Like any student, she tried to memorize the question and answers.

I mispronounced "executive" as "ex-uh-q-tif" until my older sister walked by and corrected me. "Ex-eck-u-tif," I repeated.

Ma repeated in broken syllables a few times before we moved on.

Why didn't Ba need help? I wondered. Once, when we watched and listened to Ma go down the list of questions with my twin sister, I asked him if he wanted my help. The same printed sheets of paper were on the table, some proof of his more solitary studying.

He shrugged. And he lit a cigarette.

I asked the questions out of order. Ba told us the examiners would rearrange the order of questions. He answered quickly, but his accent was, in some ways, harder to understand than my mother's. Later, I found out Ba had taken language and writing courses at a community college in the evenings. Ma did not. I learned how to write checks for her. It was especially useful during her visits at the doctor's clinics, where debit transactions and automatic check printing were not yet available. Ba could write and understand the written language and text, but Ma was more social. She spoke enthusiastically and carelessly to our neighbors and people at the grocery stores. Ba was quiet. I'm not even sure if I remember if he spoke a lot of English at all during my childhood. Even if he was assured in his comprehension skills, I would, or one of my older siblings, would always attend parent-teacher conferences as the reliable interpreter. But this entire citizenship process was almost a mystery to me.

"You don't have to help me anymore, Anna," Ba said, after we went over the one hundred questions.

"Just once?" I asked, confused. Ma said she needed multiple rounds.

"It's okay," he said, unconcerned. And he took out another cigarette. The flame from his silver lighter briefly lit his face.

My twin and I got off of the bus and came home to a red-faced Ma. She was fuming. In one of their rare solo outings, she and my father, dressed in unusually formal clothes, had driven to Fort Smith with a witness to finally take their citizenship test. Ba had passed. Ma had not. And she was complaining about being tricked.

As she relayed the story again, Ba actually looked amused. The receptionist had misunderstood her when she said she couldn't speak English. She was not allowed to take the exam and had to reschedule.

"What does this mean?" I think we asked Ba.

"I need an American passport," he had answered. "I no longer need to carry my green card." But it was neither a celebratory nor a happy moment. Ba had just said this so matter-of-factly. When Ma eventually passed, I didn't attend their Oath of Allegiance ceremonies. Nor did I know such a ceremony existed until much later in my life.

Decades later, when I found myself mindlessly scrolling through Twitter, I'd read emotional tweets about strangers or their parents becoming citizens. Many would mark their anniversary of such a milestone. I knew Ma wasn't sentimental about these particular events in her life, but I felt compelled to ask her why we didn't celebrate.

"Citizenship test?" she repeated over the phone.

"When did you become a citizen?" I asked. "What was the exact year?"

"Two thousand..." Ma began in English. "Two thousand..." Finally, she said, in Vietnamese, "two thousand ten."

I laughed. "That's not right, Ma. That would mean you took the test ten years ago. I was young when you began studying. I was still in elementary school." I didn't tell her I never really understood or knew their plans, or their differences that marked them as "alien" or "permanent residents" when I, their child, was an "American citizen." They never talked about these matters with me. Or perhaps I had never asked them.

"Exactly twenty-five years after Ba and I left Vietnam in 1975." Her voice trailed off, and she began counting.

I solved the arithmetic problem for her.

"If you add twenty-five years, that's 2000. That's some time ago." I said the word "year" in Vietnamese and "2000" in English.

"Two thousand," she repeated in English. "That sounds right."

"Why didn't you celebrate?"

"Celebrate what?"

"Your citizenship."

"People remember those things and celebrate?" Ma asked, in genuine surprise.

"I see it online all of the time." I translated "online" as "on the net."

"Not important to me," Ma said, not dismissively but decisively. "We just did it for paperwork reasons. Ba, when he was alive, and I were told that if we didn't become citizens, people would tamper with our retirement funds. Now, who said that…" She searched her memory for a name.

"Your retirement funds?"

"We don't even know if that's true," Ma said. In the background, I could hear her grandchildren loudly playing with each other. It was expected daily noise whenever we talked on the phone. "But people weren't very nice to us. We did it just in case because we didn't have a lot of rights."

I then suddenly remember her talking in rapid Vietnamese, on that fateful day she was told she couldn't take the exam.

"What happened when you tried to take the citizenship test?" I said. "You said you couldn't speak English and they wouldn't allow you to take it?"

"It's like this," Ma began in her tone of storytelling. "There was a secretary who asked us a bunch of questions. She asked me if my English was good enough to take the test. I told her, honestly, 'not really', and she wouldn't let me finish the thought! I think she only heard 'no'. And then…" Ma's tone grew somewhat huffy, "she asked me why I would take the test if I couldn't speak English. But I could have passed it! I only needed to correctly answer six out of ten questions. If she only listened to me!" Ma was on a memory rampage.

"So what did you do when Ba took the test?"

"I had to wait for him," she said. "There must have been FBI or CIA agents in the room. I couldn't cause a scene."

I was imagining a bureaucratic office in Fort Smith, in western Arkansas. We used to drive to the area almost every other weekend. We always visited a particular, now closed, Vietnamese grocery store. I was always accustomed to my parents speaking Vietnamese to us, but there, they could speak Vietnamese to nearly every patron in the grocery store. It seemed like a magical place for them to speak comfortably. But I couldn't place where this U.S. Citizenship and Immigration Services might be.

"Your English is quite good now," I said suddenly. Ma was still talking about her unjust experience.

"You think so?" Ma said.

"Maybe your English is better than my Vietnamese," I said, thinking aloud. "How are your grandchildren's Vietnamese and English?" When they had Internet access in their home in rural Delaware, the older kid would try to FaceTime me. I always spoke to them in Vietnamese, but I knew their language experiences were similar to their father's, their aunts', and mine.

"They speak both better than you!" Ma said, laughing. "You had a lot of problems in school." She was referring to my special speech classes. "How long did you have to take that class?"

"For too long," I said, almost unkindly. "Why are their language skills better than ours?"

"They have a parent who can speak both fluently," Ma answered. "Their father can help them with their homework."

Ma once told me an extraordinary story of her youth in Vietnam. At fourteen, she stopped attending school because her father would not teach her martial arts. As rebellion, she skipped school and ran away from home, spending her days in the mountains practicing kung fu on her own. I always laugh at this story. I didn't think it was unbelievable or an outright lie; Ma never seemed ashamed about her limited education. But there are moments when it shows. She can read in Vietnamese, but she, unlike my father, writes slowly and crudely and often misspells words.

When we were taught how to begin reading and writing in Vietnamese, it was our father who taught us. Never Ma.

3.

When my father had his first stroke in 2006, his speech became impaired. My older sister and I were in the ICU room with him. He tried to speak to us, but only sounds came out. We couldn't understand him. Both of us, in panicked voices, kept repeating "we don't know what you're saying, Ba." He kept trying, but abruptly stopped. He looked down at the linoleum floor and didn't say anything more. Inconsolable sobs came out. He wouldn't look at us as he wept.

Ba spent months in rehab. His speech improved rather quickly. His right hand was permanently balled into a fist, and he had to walk on a cane using the strength of his left side. He could no longer write letters or checks in his beautiful cursive. No more meticulous loops, curls, and waves that connected together. He practiced writing in his left hand. Shaky lines replaced his once showy handwriting.

Other things had also changed. My parents lived separate lives and never stayed in the same house if they could avoid it. My father began living with my sister, who acted as his primary caregiver. I seemed to move farther and farther away.

At the end of summer 2016, I had flown from Montreal to Fayetteville, Arkansas. I had just barely unpacked after relocating from Boston when my sisters told me he had another stroke and was in a coma. They were told that he may be dying soon.

I only understood fragments of the story. My sister's neighbors saw our father walking around in the front yard in a confused state during the early afternoon on a hot day. Later, they helped pull him out of a storm drain. They mentioned he said something about looking for a cat. Sometime later, on a walk with his dog, someone found my father passed out in his beat-up white Oldsmobile car. He had vomited all over himself and was unresponsive.

My tired sisters finally left the hospital, saying that they were going to return in the early evening. They were scared and worn out.

The nurse gently urged me to ask my father to squeeze my hand, to try to lure him out of the coma. I took his rough and dry hand into mine, and repeated the nurse's order, in Vietnamese. My father lightly squeezed my hand. Encouraged by the response, I pleaded with him to wake up. He had briefly opened his eyes once, when my older sister was present on the afternoon before my arrival, but he quickly closed his eyes. She thought she heard him tell her he was tired. It had been almost 24 hours. I didn't know what to say to Ba, and kept repeating the short sentences that I could say without crying in front of the nurse: *It's Anna. I'm here now. I came all of the way from Canada. I'm here. Wake up. Please.*

Ba's eyes flew open. I screamed "Ba" and started crying loudly. I sat up at once, turned away from my father, and tried to calm my loud, shaky breaths. I could see some curious nurses from outside peering in from the windows. When they caught my eye, they quickly returned to their tasks. I rushed into the bathroom and washed my face with cold water.

The nurse told me he'd return to run some tests on my father. He assured me things would get better, that his waking up was a good sign.

I sat silently next to my father, who seemed dazed. He looked at me with wide, cloudy eyes. His brown skin looked so dull and yellow then.

"It's Anna, remember?" I asked softly.

He nodded. With his good hand, he touched his chest and he continued to look at me. His hand had big black bruises and liver spots. He repeated the motion. He opened his mouth, but no sound came out.

"Are you trying to say something?" I asked, in alarm. I leaned closer, in case I could make out any whisper. But I heard nothing. I turned to look at him again. "Are you in pain?"

He nodded again, and he kept tapping his chest.

New tears began to form, but I took a deep breath.

"I'll get a notebook and pen, Ba," I said, trying to sound calm. But my heart was pounding. I swallowed. "Just wait for me. I'll be right back."

I dashed over to my backpack and pulled out a small Moleskine notebook and a pen. I hurried back.

"Can you write what you want to say?" I asked. I had turned to a new blank page.

Ba took my pen and began writing with his left hand. His hand was shaky, and he wrote hesitantly. From my perspective, it looked like he was just drawing horizontal and vertical lines. At times, he would cross another line. I looked on in horror, but hoped that the lines would eventually be words. Something. Anything.

Ba handed the notebook and pen back to me. And then he looked at me impatiently. His eyes were still wide and confused.

I looked at the indecipherable lines. There were about a dozen lines. Just lines. I didn't know what he was trying to communicate. I willed myself not to cry as I gazed at my father.

"I don't understand, Ba," I croaked. A few tears leaked. "I'm really sorry. I don't know what you're trying to say."

Ba's forehead furrowed. He looked at the notebook page briefly. He then returned his gaze back to me and tapped his chest again.

"I'm really sorry, Ba," I repeated. I took his hand and squeezed it. He squeezed back. He shifted his gaze to the wall in front of him. And he sat like that for a long time.

The last six months of his life were cruel. His voice was barely a whisper. He was now in a wheelchair, too weak and physically unsteady. He had been transferred from the ICU to a regular hospital back to the ICU, and to the rehab center. He had his own room, and the extra bed was occupied by my sisters or me. We had to stay with Ba, to translate for him.

During one of his speech exercises, the heavily pregnant therapist read to us from one of the pamphlets. I listened with slightly raised eyebrows at the tone of her voice. It seemed like she knew how patronizing the aspirational guidelines sounded, but she didn't stop reading nor did she ever look up from the paper. And then she finally began the exercises.

"Name five fruits," the speech therapist said. She looked from Ba to me.

I repeated the command in Vietnamese.

Ba paused, and whispered, "Apple. Banana. Orange." In Vietnamese.

"Oh," I said, feeling foolish for not expecting this. "He said apple, banana, and orange in Vietnamese. Did you want him to speak in English?" I asked, skeptical how one could even separate speech from cognition.

The speech therapist hadn't anticipated this inquiry either.

"In Vietnamese is fine," she responded with uncertainty and with a slight frown. She would just have to trust my translation skills.

I turned to Ba. "Can you name two more?" I gently asked. Ba's eyes turned thoughtful.

"Point to your tattoo," the speech therapist suggested. She had admired my sleeves before she began the session. When I used to visit my parents, I always tried to cover my arms, to avoid tiresome fights. But the summer in Fayetteville was too hot.

I pointed to the pineapple on my left arm. "Can you name this, Ba?"

Ba's eyes rested on my tattoo. He hated my collection.

"Pineapple," he whispered in Vietnamese.

We waited for another fruit. Then the speech therapist improvised. She asked me to point at the other fruits, vegetables, flowers, and the lobster that was tattooed between my shoulder and chest.

Ba looked at the lobster with knitted eyebrows.

"Shrimp?" he said, looking at me with questioning eyes. I couldn't tell if he wanted confirmation or if he was expressing disapproval. I shared a smile with my father.

We were sitting in the cafeteria of the rehab center, eating dinner. Ba's tray was covered in Styrofoam, plastic, and foil. I tore open his plastic utensils, small packets of salt and pepper, and a single napkin, while Ba, using his left hand, opened his fruit cup and milk carton. I looked around the cafeteria. Posters about healthy eating and MyPlate.gov were taped all around the otherwise empty walls. We were seated near the doors, and the other patients were also spread out. There were about a dozen of older folks. Some were eating by themselves; much older patients had a nurse practitioner sitting with them.

Ba offered his roll. At the time, I didn't have an appetite and barely ate. My stomach was always upset. But I took the roll and split the roll in half. I took a small bite.

One of the clinic's social workers stopped by. She had introduced herself earlier, when we were setting up his room at the center.

"I just wanted to check on your dad," she said, giving him a quick glance and smile. "Make sure he eats a little bit more today."

After I relayed the message to him, she continued, "I just read his file, and I have to say it's a surprise that he's still alive."

I just stared at her, unsure of how to respond. I remained

silent. I didn't know what file she had read, but assumed it was a cobbled piece of various testimonies from us and the doctors at the hospital.

She said more platitudes, that they'd work to get him better and that he could benefit from attending community centers with people "like him." Then she moved onto a different table, where an old woman with thick black glasses demanded cake.

I watched Ba eat his food. He had finished his fruit cup, and ate a few more bites of his boiled chicken before pushing his tray away.

Ba finally returned home in early November. Throughout this time, my family had been together temporarily. All six of us for a few days. But we never spoke about the possibility of his passing. We were scared to, and we chose to believe the doctors and rehab professionals when they said he would improve. Even when I called our family doctor after I saw him coughing up blood in his napkin. The doctor, who had told me to calm down and not be hysterical, said he would be okay and to buy cough medicine.

I flew from Montreal to Fayetteville often and stayed for extended periods. When I was in Montreal, I called at least once a day. Ma remained at my sister's home. She would put Ba on the phone. He always sounded tired, but we tried to hold a short conversation.

As the months went by, Ba's hoarse whisper eventually disappeared. At the start of his rehab, when he felt better, his eyes were clear; but they had become permanently cloudy and dull. He could not keep his food or liquids down, and had lost too much weight. He had become skeletal. He could barely stand with assistance. And, yet, he couldn't tell us how he felt. When he didn't speak, he nodded, shook his head, or pointed. He occasionally tapped his chest.

On my last trip to Fayetteville, when I stayed from November until January 5. My father had turned 72 at the start of the new year. I had baked cupcakes, but he never ate one.

I had to catch an early flight back to Montreal. It was about four in the morning. I told my mother I was going to say good-bye to my father. I opened his bedroom door softly and sat by his bed. His eyes weren't closed all of the way, but his chest was moving up and down.

"Ba?" I whispered. No response. "I'm leaving today. I'll try to come back next month. I hope you'll be better by then. I'll be back." I squeezed his hand. He didn't squeeze back. Lowering myself, I hugged my father on one side and stayed in that position for a few seconds before leaving.

The last time I talked to my father was on January 6. By then, whenever we were on the phone, I could hear nothing. No breathing. No sounds. I knew he was holding the phone with his good hand and he was moving his lips. But there was just silence. But I continued to ask him questions, as I had in the previous years when I used to call him daily. But I never knew if he had finished answering when I moved on to a different topic. I couldn't hear him.

He was again admitted to the ER. On the morning of January 10, he passed away in the hospital. I was in Montreal. I wouldn't return to Fayetteville until his funeral, forty-nine days after his death. In the Buddhist ritual, these forty-nine days were a mourning period, to allow us to pray and be assured that Ba's spirit would transition into the afterlife.

When I finally returned to Fayetteville, a photo of my father was on the altar table. At the cemetery, his tombstone was just a few feet away from the graves of his daughter and son. Family members I've never met, their names barely spoken at home. They were only children when they had died, almost a decade before I was born.

During his ceremony, we kneeled on the cold earth and prayed silently. I wished for my father's suffering to end in the afterlife and bowed three times at the grave in front of me.

I didn't linger. Once I got up, I began walking away, not bothering to wipe off any signs of dirt on the knees of my black tights. When there was a safe distance between his gravesite and me, I glanced behind my shoulder. Narrowing my eyes, I could just make out the image on the backside of his tombstone. An engraving of the South Vietnamese flag.

David Ishaya Osu

Wander

1.

Yellow reminds me of my first time in Lagos. That day I made a note in my book: Lagos, our Lagos / yellow buses, yellow pulses / ready madness / Lagos, our Lagos / this is Lagos.

"What's your favourite colour?" I often ask.

2.

I grew up wondering why people called it a blue film. I would ask: what is blue inside the film? Is it the background, or are the people blue? I didn't know anything about a blue film until I watched my first blue film. Blue became a strong patch on my mind.

"There is a colour inside of the fucking, but it is not blue," said Maggie Nelson in her book, *Bluets*.

3.

Most of my favourite photographs are monochromes. I remember photographs of Francesca Woodman. I fell in love with Francesca when I was twenty-two; ironically, it was at that same age she died. The closer I got to her work, the stronger I felt her presence, the sharper the things I felt—life and death.

The socks are odd, yet you wear them, I mused. This was the period I battled with questions about meanings of life, of love, the essence of things:
  • A jealous god is a greedy blur
  • I believe I cannot touch the sky
I would close my eyes, enter a room and be naked. I want to do things without knowing. I point fingers to the dark void, to a standing mirror. I would say things as I imagine them:
  • A snake in a bowl
  • A glass in need
  • A second touch, though
  • There is nothing to ruin or to forgive

4.

"When would you like to die?" I once asked my friends.

5.

My mother, she wants to sleep and not wake up. Something easy, something without pain, like licking chocolate candies till they finish and leave you wanting more. Circles or squares, winds or parallels, call them city codes.

Another form of love is to never die for love.

6.

In her book, *Plainwater*, Anne Carson said, "Shapes of life can change as we look at them," and I concur. In one of her poems, Emily Skaja said, "anyone can be the sky."

7.

I was at an event where the speaker spoke about the nonexistence of the two-gender system in some cultures. Most people in the audience left their mouths agape for a while hearing these facts. I heard someone behind me categorically say: "I'd like to live in a society where I am me, human with no label or fear; I can just be myself."

8.

Personally, one aspect of being oneself is the freedom to be careless. I mean, why would a stranger tap me on the shoulder to kindly inform me that I wore my shirt inside out? We burst into laughter.

"But you know what?" he smiled, "it's fine. There's really nothing wrong, it suits you." Still smiling, we shook hands and went our separate ways.

9.

I had a change of mind on my first night in Lagos. I realised that there was no need for stereotypes. Not necessarily because the stories weren't untrue, but because I needed to see for myself. I needed a first-hand experience, because there are a million other stories or sides to a person or place, because human existence is a complicated diagram, because there are different kinds of salads. *I can have a taste of that. Things are possible.*

"Lagos is a decadent city," my parents warned me. It's not an easy life in Lagos, everyone thinks. This was how Lagos was oversimplified and offered to me to consume. So, when I landed, I made sure my hands stayed with any rails I could get.

With stereotypes pounding in my head as I breathed in Lagos air, what do then I say about the city when it was a total stranger who stood by me and showed me the way? I asked of what routes to take from Berger where the bus stopped, to Oshodi and then Mushin. A journalists' workshop was what brought me into town.

A total stranger: he didn't only draw a map in my mind, to make sure my arrival was safe, he got on each bus that got me closest to my destination. I thanked him very much; his kind gesture both impressed and frightened me. Where did he get the heart to follow me, an unfamiliar face, and to particularly make sure I arrived at my destination? Was it from Lagos he got such a kind and loving heart?

I have gone back to Lagos several times since then. I have moved around the city all by myself. I have wandered around. I have located places; places have located me too. And though I've spent many nights in hotels, I've spent fond times in the bosom of my Lagos friends (most of them artists).

"David, when are you in Lagos? Come around, let's have a good time," they'd say. Their doors are always open.

10.

Embrace: every part of the body feels it, it flows down the spine. Like ripe mangoes, love is tangible. The moment you're in love (or the moment you feel love, and are loved) you forget things, even when the things are right there.

Decisions: I've decided to surrender myself to love, and I've decided to give and receive love for the rest of my life. A little gesture of kindness melts me. Like a fresh sea wave crashing at your feet. It strikes me how ripples travel endlessly—they move from one end to another.

You're in a helpless situation, and someone comes to your rescue. You search for words to express your gratitude, yet the love shown to you as you directly felt it cannot be quantified nor expressed in mere words. You cannot find the language you want to use to say, "thank you," so you simply surrender and say the thanks. You're forever grateful, and the heart knows. Someone else is in a helpless situation, and you come to their rescue; and they're forever grateful; and the heart knows.

It was Elizabeth Gilbert who said: "In the end, though, maybe we must all give up trying to pay back the people in this world who sustain our lives. In the end, maybe it's wiser to surrender before the miraculous scope of human generosity and to just keep saying thank you, forever and sincerely, for a long as we have voices."

11.

I remember a milk mug a woman gifted to me for coming third position in class that term. I was seven or eight and in primary three. Even though I don't remember the woman's name today, I still have that mug and still have sweet feelings inside the mug. Years have passed, I am now twenty-eight, but I've yet to forget that special day—I've yet to forget a gift.

12.

About four weeks after the passing of my dad's friend (Uncle Sam we used to call him), my dad drew his last breath. For this reason I thought to myself: Do friends love each other to the point they'd want to die together?

13.

Death inspires me. And I know why, or maybe not exactly.

14.

I am restless as I write this, and I am tempted to write a list of only God knows what.

15.

Questions that pop in my mind when I'm on the train:

- If there is a God, what part of the sky does this God live in?
- What is the truth? And who makes it the truth?
- What if every source of water available to human beings dries up?
- What happens if, in the next fifty years, everybody decides to not bear a child?

16.

I think of terraced houses: the colours we care our walls must wear, and then how to love a neighbour as myself.

17.

One Monday morning, just before boarding a cab to Wuse in Abuja, a friend phoned. "Where are you?" he asked. I told him I was on the road and invited him to meet me at Salamander Café. We ate and drank. We talked about poems, and about people—art people. We didn't talk about birds. There was no need to blame ourselves for aspiring to blue skies, so we talked about things immediate to us:

- He had just got a new pair of glasses
- I was under pressure, preparing for England.

18.

Sometimes I think I have a mind of milk. Though I'm not sure what that means. Why I always forget the key or pen I was searching for was right in my hand. Or how I remember friends worrying I hadn't had sex at twenty-five.

19.

I have no regrets choosing to commit my life to poetry. I would rather I no longer exist than I no longer read and write poetry. What is a mind devoted to poetry? What is a mind focused on making art?

20.

One question folks often ask about my first sex: "how was it?" I sometimes don't find the words to say what's on my mind, other times I find the words to say what's not on my mind. Almost all times, it ends with a laugh or some instant philosophy.

21.

Art comes not only from beauty or joy of life. I 'become' when I read poems. It comes also from death; hence the decision to devote my time to life and death.

Not minding the shallowness or depth of perception, I entered the following thought in my journal last September:

If war and death are both prolific, why should I then slow down my art? Should I not be prolific in writing and publishing? Death has its active agency, so do I—both of us members of the universe. As long as I am alive, with breath and time, I shall use up all my creative energy to make art, to write and publish poetry, and to love every day of my life, as possible as I can. It's my will.

22.

Having survived car crashes, having watched my father's body go back to dust, having seen and heard stories, I revere death.

There is a passage from Lidia Yuknavitch's novel, *The Small Backs of Children*, that continues to strike me: "Who are we in moments of crisis or despair? Do we become deeper, truer selves, or lift up and away from a self, untethered from regular meanings like moths suddenly drawn toward heat or light? Are we better people when someone might be dying, and if so, why? Are we weaker, or stronger? Are we beautiful, or abject? Serious, or cartoon? Do we secretly long for death to remind us we are alive?"

23.

My memories of childhood are quite blurry. It's either recalling my favourite shirts got mixed up, or recalling the one time I cried in public because dad refused to buy me a shirt I really wanted (it was Christmas). Or recalling names of classmates got mixed up with names of characters in books I have read. I hardly remember the big events of growing up in one long stretch. But remembering my accident is a different thing; it's one story that is both easy and painful.

I was knocked down by a car along Abuja-Keffi expressway in Mararaba, Nasarawa state. I was five years old. I suffered a compound fracture on my left leg, and I was bedridden for six months.

24.

A new friend asked me: "Are you a Muslim?" Because he heard me say some things about Islam. I've also been confused with being a Catholic because I recited the prayers.

With other folks, it's my ethnicity. When they hear me sing Fela Kuti or Aṣa, or just say any Yoruba phrase I am familiar with, they suppose I'm Yoruba.

A Lagosian argued with me when I told him I'm neither Muslim nor Hausa even though I hail from Nasarawa state. He was trying to genuinely affix an identity to my face, my hair, my accents, my dress.

And this is one thing about multiculturalism.

25.
Nobody is one thing.

26.
I heard people say autumn is a beautiful season in the UK; I saw it in pictures as well. And that was true. Being my first time in England, I stopped and took many pictures. Seeing the way leaves of many colours dropped to the ground, I said to myself: even dying leaves have colours—they are beautiful.

27.
That same night I read about Rimbaud, I wrote in my notebook:
May it happen that somebody sends to me a one-way ticket to Paris, the way Paul Verlaine sent a one-way ticket to Arthur Rimbaud. Poetry is funny.

28.
The most beautiful part of your body
is where it's headed
—Ocean Vuong

29.

I could head south or east, or just anywhere of my choice. But I have yet to receive a one-way ticket to Paris from anyone. In the end, nobody owes me tickets to places of my dream. Nobody owes me.

30.

There is a question always asked of travellers or just anyone: where would you love to visit? Or what's your dream city or place? Apparently, the answers we give fill buckets and run over. If it were a few months before this piece my answer would have been a yell of Florence, Italy. (I still love Florence and still desire and plan to visit, but it won't be my answer now—I have changed my mind).

31.

Think of mercury, think of the human mind.

32.

It still amazes me how our parents coped with the fluctuating career declarations we made those days as kids. My mother, I remember she twice advised me to be a teacher or focus on the arts. And I remember I said no.

Just like every kid I wanted to be everything. I wanted to be a medical doctor. I wanted to be a pastor. I wanted to be a singer. I just wanted to be everything. I don't remember wanting to be a writer, though—writing hadn't registered in my consciousness as a career path then. I also wanted to be a pilot; I wanted to fly.

33.

Two things I kept in mind if my dream—moving—to Kent was not going to work:
- Kill myself, or
- Disappear into total silence faraway from everyone forever.

That was how resolute I was in chasing this thing about creative writing. And that is how resolute I am in chasing poetry—the arts in general. I can travel any miles to experience poetry.

34.
If I die, I die.
—Esther 4:16 (MSG)

35.
The image of my father's body in his casket is still fresh in me, and I do not think it will ever fade.

36.
Words of my mum when I arrived home for dad's funeral: "Exactly. Just like your father; you look just like your father."

She hugged me and burst into tears as she gently stroked my hair. I was wearing my seven-month-old big Afro. "This is what your father likes, afro," she moaned.

37.
February 23, 2016, has now become the date I officially use as the day I decided to write fulltime. It was the day my friend, Saddiq M. Dzukogi and I were almost killed in an accident caused by a road safety officer in Minna.

Seeing my left arm dangling threw my mind out of my body. Somebody holding me by the side, Saddiq being attended to by someone else, I was in shock, I was screaming.

The x-ray confirmed it was a comminuted fracture. It could have been obituary: David is dead; Saddiq is dead.

38.
A fragile life: today you are here, tomorrow you are there; this minute you are happy, the next moment you are sad; in one swift sail you are where you wanted to be, and just in another swift sail you are stuck in a jam. One moment someone is breathing fine, the next moment that same person is no more.

I remember a scene from a beautiful Thursday afternoon in July in Abuja, Nigeria. I was in a moving bus; and though everything was fleeting, this sight I will not forget: a gliding bird ran into a black jeep, it fell right there on the road and was crushed to death. I thought I was the only one who noticed it but the sharp moan from other passengers in the bus consoled me; I turned and met the eyes of a man, we smiled at each other and shook our heads the way mourners do. I leaned into the glass window and said, even free birds die.

39.

Any time my mind goes back to scenes of accidents, any time my mind goes back to hospitals, beds and the sights I witnessed, any time I remember, I feel slightly exhausted. Call it post-traumatic anxiety, right? There is, however, a huge gratitude for surviving all these, for the help rendered by friends and strangers, and for my mother who cared for me while I was helplessly bedridden.

40.

I am far away from Nigeria now and thinking of my father from this little corner of England. It's cold out there. And I'm thinking of the things I remember about him:

- His hair, afro
- His travels, his safari jackets
- His newspaper, reading habits
- His very neat, cursive handwriting
- The way he answered greetings with 'hello, dear'
- The multitude of people he knew and associated with from all groups, classes and ages
- The multitude of people who came to witness his funeral

(People kept visiting our house months after dad had been buried: friends, colleagues, school mates, students he taught. One of those days, mum drew my attention to a new thought of hers. She said: "I now understand who your father was, why he did the things he did. I have no regrets for his life; there was a purpose to everything, I see it now.")

It's been four years since his death, and he would have been fifty-six. I'm also thinking of my mum and sister.

41.

I remember that cold December morning a few years back: my mother's prayers woke me. I overheard her praying for goodness

and guidance and success for all her children and friends. I
thought it was in my sleep or some dreamy experience, until I
went close to her door. Whether I like it or not, this is one habit
of my mum that I've missed these months—her prayers wake
you from your slumber.

42.
*Each
one we know
is in our blood.*
—Michael Ondaatje

43.
Genes.

44.
My sister was born in 1989, the year *Beasts of No Nation*, one of
Fela's classics was released. Elizabeth loves books. Her bookshelf
wasn't hers alone; it was also open to me. And just as I was very
close to her bookshelf, she and I had the tightest bond in the
house. Perhaps that's what books do: when we open them, they
never close ever after; they open new worlds inside us, and when
we find another being living the book worlds, we effortlessly
become family. Ironically though, I don't believe in the word
'family', or I'd rather say I am wary of the walls *family* erects. *I
hate walls.*

45.
But I believe in my sister the way she does me. I say this with a
reason: whoever gives you their hair to comb has some trust in
you—and you in them. My sister would give me her hair; I would
give her mine as well. Mum would give her hair to neighbours or
strangers to braid, like every other hair that needs to be made.

I also believe in books. I believe in poetry. I believe in art. I be-
lieve in dreadlocks and afro and braids; I believe in hair generally.
But these, especially, are not my mother's fancies; she believes in
other things—and I respect that. She doesn't believe in a male
body carrying a head full of hair or any kind of hairstyle that is
unchristian. So, what is Christian? That's one question mum and

I never had a common answer to. To let peace reign in the house, I would choose silence and never say a word.

Chatting with mum on WhatsApp, she asked, "when are you going to cut your hair?" She had seen a photo I shared online. We laughed and changed the subject of discussion.

I don't remember if she always insisted my father cut his afro; what I remember is, dad kept his hair the way he wanted. Sometimes I wonder if she ever remembers that she stroked my hair when I returned for dad's funeral. Maybe she does. Maybe the stroking wasn't about me or my hair, but about her and her husband, or something else. Mum is wild like that.

46.
"Speak with your sister," mum said. We were on the phone. After greetings, sister threw a question at me with her gentle voice. I wondered where that came from. I took a deep breath and couldn't find the right words to reply her. "When are you coming back?" she asked.

Shawna Kay Rodenberg

Prologue from *Kin*

2017

I am trying to sneak two ounces of primo marijuana that I have carried all the way from Evansville, Indiana, to Seco, Kentucky, past the producer of the *CBS Evening News* and into the double-wide trailer where my father anxiously waits for it. Two ounces is his minimum monthly preference, and we are nearing the end of the month. I can't see him, but I know he is cagey, because he is always cagey.

I am acting as a sort of guide for CBS, an ambassador to this region, the Appalachian Mountains of eastern Kentucky, often as inscrutable and inaccessible to outsiders as a war-torn third-world country. I have begrudgingly become a tour guide, a bridge, a translator, and a mediator. I have done this work in some capacity several times, always unpaid, for independent filmmakers, for NPR, and now for CBS.

This particular producer, a nervous, well-meaning blonde with doe eyes and the patrician bearing of a New England soccer mom, contacted me after she read an article I wrote about my job teaching English at a community college in eastern Kentucky. The piece detailed the experiences of some of my dual-credit high school students, who, after the foundation of their already run-down high school was irreparably damaged by nearby blasting, were crammed into a tiny middle school, where they remained four years later. The students, bright and full of promise, were fighting despair.

The producer flattered me and called my left-leaning article enlightening and moving. She asked if I had experienced any blowback in painting a negative picture of local politics, and I explained that the superintendent of that high school had insisted someone replace me—he didn't want me teaching his kids. She said that CBS was putting together a news segment on the proposition of school choice in Appalachia and asked if I would be willing to help. I had reservations for many reasons—my fear of public speaking, my worry that I might be somehow responsible for yet another unfair, stereotypical representation of the mountains and people I love—but I agreed, as I had before, because I believed school choice was just another way to undermine funding for Letcher County schools, and because, as my mom put it, "If you don't help them tell the story right, who will?"

A few days later the producer emailed me with a list of everything she'd need:

—an interview with me, somewhere related to my childhood, she thinks maybe at a diner

—B-roll of me in the country, walking on a back road

—photos from my childhood photos of my parents or grandparents in a one-room schoolhouse

—an interview with a passionate teacher who is against school choice but who voted for Trump

—interviews with students from families experiencing hardship, she specifies "father unemployed, drug issues, etc." (Here she adds that they will conduct these interviews in a sensitive way.)

—B-roll of beauty shots of rolling hills and winding streams, remnants of the mines, abandoned schools, churches, shots of various "hamlets" like Seco, shots of the local Walmart and Dollar Stores, signs of blight, and signage indicating this is Trump country.

I told her how much I disliked Mountain Dew–mouth and dirt-floor stereotypes. I explained that not only are those stories hopelessly incomplete and exploitative, they also widen the chasm between Appalachians and outsiders, the last thing we need. She assured me she understands. She uses the word *sensitive* a lot.

She wants to meet around ten, so I wake at three in the morning to make the six-and-a-half-hour drive to my hometown. I am used to the drive because it is my well-traveled commute to work and to visit my parents and my sister, but the producer, whose flight was canceled and who has had to drive the last leg of her journey, is already frazzled when she arrives late at the company store turned winery in Seco, where we are supposed to film my interview.

Immediately, we hit a snag. Despite his agreement to help them, the winery owner has gone to Tennessee, and his wife refuses to cross the street and unlock the door. An older, fearful woman, she insists that she cannot brave the cold because of a recent heart surgery. It is fifty degrees outside and sunny.

The producer is incredulous. She asks if that's really a thing, the heart surgery and the cold. I explain that most likely the couple has decided not to help with the story. She tells me that they've already had quite a day, because earlier that morning before I arrived, while the cameraman was trying to get some of the shots on their list, he encountered a gun-toting local who warned that "he better be careful where he decides to take pictures."

Over the course of the day, she tells me this story multiple times, and I can tell that she is as baffled by my lack of reaction as she is by the gun wielder's honest warning. I do not mention my father's arsenal or his gun safe, big as a coffin, or that he has carried a loaded gun in his hand, not a holster, when arguing with neighbors over property boundaries. I don't tell her that land, privacy, actually, is nearly all that's left to fight over, to defend, in Letcher County.

We spend most of the afternoon driving around Whitesburg, the county seat, the town where I went to high school, filming scenes that will make good television. The cameraman tells me he has not been able to locate a Trump sign and asks if I know where one might be. I explain that people in the region are disenfranchised, apathetic, that they don't care very much about politics, that the laughable voting turnout in the recent election illustrates this reality. He and the producer nod, but keep their eyes peeled.

The cameraman is a dick. He tells me at least three times that the camera he is using cost sixty thousand dollars. He flirts and praises me for being "smart enough to get out of this hellhole." I ask him not to say that, and he shrugs and asks me why. I explain that my family still lives here, and when the producer mentions talking to them, I tell her, unequivocally, no. She is so exhausted from her disrupted travel plans and the ordeal of the morning that she falls asleep in the back seat while asking me questions like, what do you think these people want?

We finally make our way to Seco, where I am filmed walking up and down Fletcher Hill, my family's mountain, the mountain where my grandfather mined coal, where my father was reared with great love and brutality, where I picked my grandmother's strawberries and my grandfather's roses, where I rode my pony, Sam, bareback and without a bridle, where I played for hours with my sister and our holler rat girlfriends. This is the mountain that filled my childhood with the rushing sounds of the creek below, the headwaters of the Kentucky River, and with the brutal grunts and thumps of our neighbor, Junior, beating his wife, Ruby, to a pulp. Here my sister and I wandered unsupervised for hours and chased away packs of mangy, biting dogs with the big stick I learned to carry everywhere.

It is also the mountain on which my family sought refuge after leaving The Body, an End Times wilderness community, cloistered in the woods of northern Minnesota, that my father joined when he was red-eyed and mad with fear, following his tour of duty in Vietnam. When I was only ten years old and we had nothing left in the world, when even he realized he had nowhere left to run, my grandfather gave him a piece of this mountain, and together they built the little house we lived in, the house my sister still lives in with her husband and her three kids.

Here on Fletcher Hill, the cameraman gives me stage directions like "point over there" and "tell us what that is." I am not a natural, and we have to reshoot several times. At one point, he gestures that he wants to tell me something, and I assume it is that I need to relax or take a deep breath.

Instead, he looks over his shoulder to make sure the rest of the crew is not within earshot and tells me that just between us he voted for Donald Trump. He says he worked for the Clintons and Hillary is a raging bitch, that Trump is what our country needs because he knows business. With his face in my face, he confesses this like it will change my mind, or perhaps like it is something I have secretly wished for. I fight the urge to wake the producer and tell her I found a Trump supporter for her news segment.

I ignore the cameraman's confession and change the subject. I ask him to please not include any footage of my sister's porch. She is busy running her three kids to school and practices, and I know she would prefer the cluttered tangle of dogs and plastic toys not be broadcast on national television. The cameraman tells me not to worry and squeezes my neck like he knows me.

The producer, awake again, says she'd like to treat me to a nice dinner in Pikeville where they are staying at the Hilton, more than an hour from the elementary school where they are filming, but worth the drive to avoid the shabby hotel selection in Letcher County. I can tell she is embarrassed to tell me that the hotel I recommended in Whitesburg wasn't nice enough, because she thinks I don't know the difference and doesn't want to hurt my feelings.

While they are busy loading the gear back into the rental car, I see my chance. I tell them I'm going to say hello to my parents quickly before we pack up and leave. I grab my purse from the car, jog up the hill, push my head inside my parents' front door, and shove the paper bag full of weed at my father, who has been watching from the window.

"Thank you. I love you," he says. His relief is palpable.

"Gotta go, Daddy. I've got CBS out here riding my ass."

He laughs, gives me a peck on the cheek, says he understands. He checks inside the bag, tells me he is all set. He asks if I know what variety of weed it is. I don't. He peeks outside the window and tells me not to take any shit from those people. I tell him I won't.

Later that night, after the awkward dinner is finished, after I have met Jim Axelrod and listened to the producer talk about the stress of ordering costly pilgrim costumes and gluten-free cupcakes from a distance for her daughters back in—and these are her words—*the best school district in Connecticut, arguably in the nation*, I return to Seco to spend the night.

It is early evening and the sun hovers above the crest of the mountain, but the trailer is dark, as it always is. The shades are drawn, and billowing clouds of pot smoke fill the air. My parents are watching Stephen Colbert, my father's favorite. My mom tells me there is bologna in the fridge, and I make a sandwich with white Sunbeam-brand sandwich bread, Miracle Whip—my mother hates real mayonnaise—and generous slabs of tomato pulled from the kitchen windowsill, still warm from the afternoon sun. I salt the sandwich heavily and put on a fresh pot of coffee, always Folgers at my parents' house. I notice that my dad has purchased my favorite hazelnut coffee creamer in preparation for my visit.

My mother's oxygen machine huffs and puffs in the corner. She is already wearing her nightgown, not because evening is falling, but because she wears her nightgown all the time, unless she has to leave the house. I can tell she has been worried about me, because she is twisting her hair, which is what she does when she has something on her mind.

I tell my parents how the day went and about the ridiculous question about what *these people* want. (My father's quick response: *Did you say to be left the hell alone?*) I tell them about the Trump-loving cameraman—they both voted for Obama and for Hillary Clinton—and about a second potentially violent encounter that happened while we were idling on Main Street in Whitesburg in the upscale rental car, sticking out like a sore thumb, trying to figure out the plan for the next day.

Someone in the car, I can't remember who, had shared a bad joke, and we were all laughing, punch-drunk, overtired from our long day, when a local man, out of his mind on some drug likely made in a Pepsi bottle in the back seat of a car parked at Walmart, heard us laughing and decided he must be the butt of the joke.

He leaned through the passenger's side window and tried to pick a fight with the cameraman, who shrunk back like a kid's wiener in a cold swimming pool, so I had to intervene. I switched into my thickest accent and assured him that "these people ain't from around here and they don't even know where they are—I swear to God they ain't laughin' at you," which calmed him down and left my carmates slack-jawed as he apologized, god-blessed me, and hurried away.

My parents heave with laughter. They are proud of me for remembering who and what I am. My father even says so, an occurrence rare as a solar eclipse, and I soak up his approval like the desperate eldest daughter I am and always have been. I am a terrible insomniac, but that night I sleep like a rock, dead to the living world. I dream of my own five children back home in Indiana, wading quietly in our creek, blue jeans rolled carefully into highwaters, skipping pocketfuls of smooth stones that hit the water five, ten, even twenty times in a row.

The next day, the day of my interview with Jim Axelrod, I am a nervous wreck, and my father has changed. This is not unusual, especially on the last day of a visit when he knows I am leaving soon. I have come to expect it and tell myself it's because he loves me and hates to see me go. "You're gonna wait until I'm dead to move back home," he said to me once, more of an observation than an accusation, like he just wanted me to know that he knew, almost like he was joking. I didn't say anything when he said it, but I didn't deny it either, and this is character-istic of our relationship; he dances around our painful history, trying to take away some of its power, and I hold the cards of my version so close to my chest that no one, not even he, can see them. I know from experience that the price of letting your ver-sion of a story exist anywhere outside your own head is that the moment you do it's no longer your version but public property, subject to scrutiny and denial, and impossible to control.

When it is almost time for me to leave, he tries to pick a

fight, with me, with Mom, with my sister, Misti, who has hiked up the hill for a quick visit before I leave. He coughs his nervous cough that sounds like a stifled scream, a cough the VA has simultaneously denied the existence of and operated on. Nostrils flaring, he paces from his bedroom to the kitchen counter and back to his recliner. He makes this circuit dozens of times, changing the channel, then changing it back to the news. His political commentary quickly switches to talk of the End Times.

Mom sits quietly, the intermittent bursts of oxygen in her nasal cannula the only sound coming from her corner of the couch. She is still in her nightgown. My parents are only sixty-four and sixty-seven years old, but they have talked about being old for as long as I can remember.

When I was ten, my mother's uterus prolapsed. She called me into the bathroom to show me the shiny pink protuberance slipping out of her and asked me *Shawna Kay, what is that?* I told her I had no idea. I asked, *Is it maybe your womb?* She said, *I bet you're right. I bet that's what it is.* She said, *You don't want to get old, Sissy. Don't ever get old.* I watched her push her uterus back inside with her fingers. She was only thirty and had a hysterectomy the following year. She has had three heart surgeries in the past seven years, including a cardiac bypass.

My father looks over at me, and I look away because I know what is coming. He will say something so mean that there's no way to prepare for it. When my husband joins me for these visits, my father enjoys his company and behaves better, but Dave was not able to travel with me this time, so the outburst is inevitable.

We all know it is coming and that it will be directed at me. Misti tries to distract him by cracking jokes. Mom offers to make him something to eat. She asks if he's fed his horse, Beauty. Misti asks if there is a Colbert episode we haven't seen.

But he's still looking at me. He calls my name.

"Shawna Kay."

"Yes, Daddy."

He pauses, looks at the TV intently, like he is deciding whether to say the awful, honest thing he has conjured. Then he looks back at me.

"Don't you wish you could leave all this behind and we could go back to The Body where we didn't have to worry about anything and everything was taken care of for us?"

Nausea rises in my throat. I choke, trying to think of something to say, words that might end the conversation. Nothing has changed except his tone, his words, but I feel stuck, stranded on the mountain, like he'll never let me leave.

When he says *all* this he means *everything*. He means my family, because how could I bring them along to The Body with me? He means my education, my job, and my house in Indiana, all of which he sees as obstacles between me and my real home. He means he wants me closer, as close as possible, where I can take better care of him and Mom and help them solve the problems of their daily lives. He wishes we could live like we used to, quite literally in the middle of nowhere, as far away from the world as possible, a place even more remote than Fletcher Hill, and that we would have only each other. He misses that time in our lives.

I am trying to think fast, to hold my face carefully.

Misti steps in. "Daddy, you know that there are hard things about every place. There is no such thing as a perfect place."

Silence settles, spreading from the corners of the room to the center. The oxygen machine sighs. The TV is loud now. In London, a man has driven his car over several pedestrians along Westminster Bridge, then run toward Parliament with a knife in his hand.

"People will do anything to each other, won't they," my father says. It is not a question.

Dirty Work

A hapless jack-of-all-trades. That's an apt description for many a writer, aspiring or otherwise. Grave-digger, cold-caller, magician's apprentice… I've performed all of these jobs—briefly and badly.

I've gratefully forgotten a lot of my early gigs. But I could never forget Aldermaston, the first person to employ me in a remotely literary capacity.

I don't know if Aldermaston was the man's given name or surname (I was never bored enough to ask) but I do know that fate drew the two of us together one spring morning, a pair of decades ago.

Like most young writers, my a.m. routine consisted of opening the newspaper—they still had newspapers in those days—and thumbing through the classifieds in search of a more practical occupation.

That particular morning, an all-caps advert instantly caught my eye.

WRITER WANTED

Writers aren't, as a general rule, wanted. I continued reading, eagerly.

Must have excellent spelling and grammar.
And be good at writing sex jokes.

Enthusiasm cooling, I nonetheless went on to the end.

Send sample jokes to
Winky's EROTIC Greeting Card Company.

I sighed and set the paper down. Miller being the obvious exception, sex jokes are hardly an auspicious beginning to a literary career.

I sighed and picked the paper back up. My rent was almost a month overdue.

As I typed out a series of lewd fruit puns—one of them involving blueberries, I'm almost certain—I heard footsteps coming down the hall.

I held my breath.

It wasn't the landlord, fortunately.

The footsteps faded—and I went back to work.

＊

Days later, the phone rang.

"Stop it!" said the voice on the line. A woman's voice.

"Stop what?" I asked.

I thought I heard laughter in the background.

"Aldermaston would like to ... chat with you."

"Who's Aldermaston?" I asked, after thinking a minute.

I couldn't make out the answer. Not through all that laughter.

I *did* **make out an address, which I hastily scribbled down.**

"Stop it!" said the voice again.

Then the phone went *click*.

＊

2020 Queen Street was in an unseemly part of the city—a twenty-minute walk, tops, from my apartment. It was a weathered brick building with a pig in the window, a plush pig, and a faded sign that read *Winky's EROTIC Greeting Card Company.*

"I could use a drink," said a man lying on the sidewalk. I tossed him a quarter, stepped over his torso, opened the door...

An unreasonably beautiful woman was sitting behind the counter.

She smiled when I told her "I'm here to see Aldermaston." Then pointed to a sofa.

I admired the office paintings while I waited. There were tasteful nudes—and tasteless ones, too. As I leaned forward to get a better look at one of the latter, a pair of double doors flew open and a grinning bald man bellowed:

"It's you!"

I looked behind me.

"Been expecting you!"

I looked again.

Writers aren't, as a general rule, expected. But the man meant *me*. He back-slapped me into his office—the only word on the door was ALDERMASTON, in gold letters—and into an armchair.

"Ever hear the one about the man with three avocados?" Aldermaston asked me, cutting the end off a cigar.

I hadn't. So he told me. It wasn't terribly funny, I didn't

think. I laughed and laughed.

Then he told me the one about the piccolo and the hump-back whale.

Aldermaston blew smoke rings until I recovered. Then he said:

"We haven't had material like that in years. Not until *you* came around. Compared to *these* clowns" (he gestured to a crazed heap of papers), "you're Shakespeare."

I grinned. A writer takes a compliment where he can.

A dozen unfunny puns later—there were numerous species of erotic bric-a-brac to look at, at least—Aldermaston got around to the remuneration: fifty bucks per joke, paid weekly. I could work from home, and mail in material whenever I wished.

As coolly as I could, I agreed. Fifty bucks was more than I'd made in my entire writing career to date.

After we shook hands, Aldermaston threw his head back and laughed.

I laughed, too. For some reason.

Then he back-slapped me back out the door.

※

Of course the Muse is unaffiliated with any financial institution. The impetus of money, in my experience, does nothing for the creative faculties. But it does get one's fingers moving.

I was reading a lot of Balzac in those days. Taking my cue from the famous Frenchman, I drew the curtains, downed vats of black coffee, and wrote, over the next seven days, more than I ever have before or after—a Victorian novel's worth of blue haikus and lustful limericks. I posted the best pages to Aldermaston then took an earned rest, zealously awaiting my paycheck.

Unfortunately, that first check didn't arrive on time.

It didn't arrive at all, actually.

Neither did the second one.

After three unprofitable weeks, I decided to deliver my next gag-batch in person, and make some mild inquiries—if only for the sake of my landlord's emotional health.

This time, the man on the sidewalk was fast asleep. I opened the door to Winky's as softly as possible…

As before, Aldermaston was thrilled to see me. He plucked the cigar from his lips and with his free hand snatched my manuscript.

He thumbed through the pages, laughing uproariously.

"You're a genius!" he said at last.

I'd never been called a genius before. I've never been called one since. I enjoyed the moment.

"I particularly like the one" (he flipped a page) "about the ostrich harem."

I was particularly fond of that one, too.

Though it wasn't the only elephant on the premises—on the shelf next to me, by way of a bookend, was a pair of amorous pachyderms—the remuneration question loomed large. So while my employer gnawed on his cigar, I cleared my throat and said:

"About my paycheck…"

"No worries," said Aldermaston, waving the words away. "I'll tally things up, pay you at the end of month. Throw in a little bonus for you, too. How's a thousand sound?"

I thought it sounded great. My landlord would be thrilled.

I was still smiling when I walked out the door.

"Spare change?" asked the man on the sidewalk, suddenly waking.

I was feeling generous, so I tossed him a quarter. My last one.

✳

The end of the month arrived promptly. The paycheck didn't.

Forget whiskey: a writer's best friend is the instinctive inkling that he's being ripped off. That misgiving, interjecting itself between every bawdy bon mot and double entendre, was beginning to murder my productivity. I couldn't write another dirty word until I cleared up money matters with Aldermaston. So I called the office.

"He's not here," said his secretary.

I was sure I heard whispering in the background.

"When will he be back?" I asked.

More whispering.

"Next Friday?" she guessed.

The woman didn't sound overly hopeful.

"Then tell him to expect me," I said, as portentously as possible. "On Friday."

For some reason, the secretary laughed. She had a good, long laugh, actually. Then she said, "Okay."

And the phone went *click*.

✳

Over the next week, to preserve my sanity—I wasn't making any money, anyways—I decided to write a short story.

The story was about a doomed author. The idea just came to me.

I stuffed the finished story into an envelope addressed to A Very Large Magazine (one might as well be delusionally ambitious) and walked it to the post office.

On the stroll home, I dreamed up a dozen-or-so ways to murder my so-called employer. Some of them were quite inventive.

I wasn't serious, of course.

I was only half-serious.

It was cathartic.

✳

Friday rolled around. To my surprise, I wasn't dreading the confrontation with my employer. I was actually looking forward to it. I'd rehearsed the whole scene, which was to start off with paper-scattering, progress to shattering bric-a-bracs, and end with me emerging from Aldermaston's office, sweating gloriously, check in hand.

I stormed down Queen Street that afternoon with more vigor than I'd felt in ages. I leaped over the man on the sidewalk— he seemed to be meditating—and was about to burst open the door when something caught my eye.

It was the Winky's sign.

The sign was *missing*.

So was the plush pig. In the latter's place was a demure placard with FOR LEASE printed on it.

I still tried the door, for some reason.

Locked, of course.

I wasn't sure what else to do, so I squinted through the window.

Except for a broom handle and what looked like a ruined blond wig, the place was bare.

"You could really use a drink," said the man on the sidewalk, tossing me a quarter.

He was right.

✳

I woke the next morning with a broken head (so it felt), in

serious need of cheering. So I checked the mailbox. The daily mail is, alas, the highlight of a writer's waking life.

The only thing in the box was a slim envelope bearing the return address of A Very Large Magazine.

Instead of the expected rejection slip, however, the envelope contained a *check*—a generous one. Magazines still sent generous checks in those days.

I couldn't believe my good fortune. Neither could my landlord.

Things kept improving for me, after that. I can't say the same for Aldermaston. Though I never saw my old employer in the flesh again, I did see him briefly on television. On the evening news...

An unreasonably large man was escorting him from the courthouse doors into the back of a cop car.

I never did hear what he'd been sentenced with. I've never been bored enough to look into it. A writer knows too much already.

Twenty-odd years on, I'll still think of Aldermaston from time to time. Whenever I do, I grimace inwardly. I struggle, somewhat, for breath. Then I laugh and laugh.

I have no idea why.

Tatiana Schlote-Bonne

Blackjack

You sit at a $5 minimum bet table to play heads-up with the dealer, but an old man sits to your right, his silver chest hair poking through the buttons of his Hawaiian shirt. He shakes $80 out of his wallet, checks his pockets, and drops another crumpled $5 onto the table. He bets $10. Chest Hair is dealt a 17 and you're dealt a 12.

The dealer shows a 3. Chest Hair stands. You hit your 12.

Chest Hair groans—he thinks you made the wrong play. He's one of those idiots who thinks the dealer will bust on a 3, but you know that 60% of the time the dealer has a 6-8 as their down card, and even if they do have a 10, they'll likely pull a 6 through 8 and make it to 20. The indisputable correct choice is to hit. You're dealt an 8. The dealer flips a 7, pulls a 5, and busts with a 9.

You and Chest Hair win.

After a few more wins, he turns to you and says, You're pretty good at this. Who taught you?

Read the books. Taught myself.

You pick at your nails, trying not to look at Chest Hair. Small talk with other players is distracting, and you especially don't want to talk with Chest Hair, who organizes his chips in $25 stacks and recounts them so often you know that he's thinking, *If I can make it back to $300, then I'll be even.* Now that he's following your plays, he will win, and soon he'll be betting it all on something stupid, like roulette. If people were just like you: controlled and meticulous, then gambling addiction wouldn't exist.

The dealer points at your San Diego hoodie. Long way from Iowa, he says. You visit there?

From there.

Oh, cool. I joined the Navy and trained in San Diego. Man, those guys were tough. They called me Child of the Corn.

You almost laugh.

The new shoe begins. Your hand is twenty. Chest Hair has a sixteen—the worst hand to be dealt in blackjack. Child of the Corn shows a ten. The right play is to hit the sixteen because it's already assumed you're going to lose so you must attempt to better your hand. *Hit it.* You rub your temples. *Just hit it!* You wish Chest Hair had been dealt the twenty and you the sixteen because you'd at least play it right.

Chest Hair's two brain cells finally make a connection, and he hits his sixteen, pulling a 3. You're dealt a pair of 8s. Your fingers splay. You're given another pair of 8s.

You sit up straight. This hand only comes around once a month. It's the full moon of blackjack hands. You can win so much money from this one play—but blackjack is so much more than that. It's the high. Your cheeks tighten into a grin, heart thrumming in your chest. The blackjack high is the best high you've ever known. Nothing else has made you forget the monotony of your dreadful existence consumed by working as a barista and loving your cat and fearing that your life will never extend beyond the four walls of your apartment.

Nothing else has made you feel like dying one minute and like an unstoppable goddess the next.

Four eights on the table. Child of the Corn deals a 3 on each. You double down—one makes it to 21 and the other to 19. You get a 10 on your other 8—stand. You get a 7 on the last one, hit the 15, and pull a 5—stand. Child of the Corn's showing a 10. He fumbles to flip his card. You chew your lip. *Come on, come on, be a 7.* You hold your breath.

It's a 7.

You grin, sliding the $120 stack of chips into your arms.

You have to go work in a couple hours, so you cash out your chips, but before you leave, you feed $80 into the Cat's Eye 9 Lives slot machine. You max bet at $5. The machine meows with each spin. The odds of winning a jackpot on a slot machine are astronomically low. But you have a strategy: you turn one-hundred dollars into three hundred at blackjack, then put your winnings on a slot machine, only ever risking the casino's money.

You don't win anything from the $80 so you put in another $80—it's still the casino's cash, and you still have the $200 blackjack winnings from the day before. You keep max betting. Tonight's your night. You were just dealt four 8's at blackjack—you're lucky. You're on a roll.

You lose that $80. You feed in another $40. It's the last of the money you'll spend on slots. Two cat food bowls click into place.

The last reel flashes red. It's a third food bowl! You win 10 free games.

You imagine winning the $50,000 jackpot, the freedom it'll bring you—paying off your car, finally buying that giant exercise wheel for your cat, forgetting about rent for a while, visiting a new city. The free games pay you $140. You print the voucher, eyeing the exit or high limit room.

You head for the high limit room, where real winnings happen. You once saw a woman win $64,000 in here and almost died from envy. You feed the voucher and $100 into Crazy Money. You play $20 spins. In fifteen seconds, you lose $240.

It's okay. You laugh a little. Tomorrow—or hell, *tonight!*– you'll return and win it all back on blackjack. You glow in the light of the slot machine, digging at the bottom of your purse, uncrumpling any dollars you can find. Chest Hair's probably at roulette losing every last penny, but not you. You're going to win it all back.

You're going to win so much, you'll never have to gamble again.

E.C. Salibian

Childhood Pets: A Treatise on Untimely Death

When we were children, our household pets all met an ill fate, and that ill fate was us.

My parents were not pet people. My father, for a time when I was very little, kept bird dogs. He drove them to the Moroccan countryside in the trunk of his Peugeot, into and out of which, unaware of animal rights or the chemical properties of carbon monoxide, they leapt with unbridled joy.

"Those dogs loved to hunt, just not for me," he recalled years later. Rather than retrieve, they snacked.

After we moved to America, Daddy stopped hunting and my mother refused to let him get another dog. But he always had a soft spot for them. When we visited friends, their hounds invariably would find their way to my father, rest their chins on his knee, and gaze up with soft eyes.

More than anything, I wanted a kitten. But cats, to my parents, were vermin that prowled the Middle East spreading disease.

"Tro-cho-ma!" my father would say when I asked for a kitty of my own. The word, I was meant to infer, stood for some terrible disease one contracted from petting cats. Years later I looked it up and discovered he was probably saying, in his Armenian accent, "trachoma," an eye disease of questionable connection to cats (a study is underway) but that could get you turned back at Ellis Island. To this day I don't know if he was pulling a fast one or if he really believed that if I adopted a kitten, we'd all go blind and get deported.

Cat forbidden, I turned my attention elsewhere. First came the brief but tragic tenure of Harry the Turtle. Harry was a Red Ear Slider, *trachemys scripta elegans*, a two-inch salmonella delivery system who today would scrabble over pond and pebble as a federal fugitive. In the 1970s, the U.S. government banned the sale of sliders Harry's size when thousands of little girls just like me grew ill after handling them, which I did regularly, or after putting them in their mouths, which by mutual agreement I did not. Unlike a kitten, it turns out, Harry really could have killed us all. Except I killed him first.

Harry came to us from the basement pet area of a Korvette department store, where I begged shamelessly until my mother forked out the required ninety-seven cents. Her capitulation might have been a strategic alternative to strangling me on the spot or to acquiring an even more objectionable creature from the order rodentia. Harry had a yellow-rimmed green shell etched on top in a black geometric pattern. His head, legs and pointy tail were green with yellow stripes. Two red strips ran along the side of his head toward his eyes, which were beady and peered at me expressing unfathomable reptilian thoughts. When Harry walked across my palm and onto my fingertips, perhaps wisely attempting a swift getaway, the scratch of his toenails on my skin was thrilling.

Red Ear Sliders can grow up to twelve inches long and live fifty years, with proper care, which was not to be Harry's lot. The pet data sheets of today discuss electrical heat sources, water filtration systems, an amazing array of habitat products and nutritional supplements. Mine was not a family given to such extravagances. Harry was provided a cobalt-blue Portuguese glass bowl with Rococo feet that had failed to sell at the gift shop we ran in Garden City. My mother helped settle Harry into his Rococo residence with a little dish of water and pebbles from the back yard. There he might have clung to life, however tenuously, but for my catching wind on educational TV of a phenomenon called "hibernation." *Did you know that animals like bears and turtles sleep for months at a time? Can you say hi-ber-na-tion?*

This new intelligence regarding Harry's metabolic imperatives posed a dilemma. How was he going to hibernate in his Portuguese bowl, next to the living room hi-fi, with the lights going constantly on and off? I devised a solution. Lifting Harry up gently, I wrapped around and around his flailing green body a giant roll of toilet paper. Then I lowered him gently back down.

What people noticed eventually was the smell. Then the white mound. Each family member reacted to the loss of Harry—and my explanation for his wadded state—in his or her own way. My father was heartbroken for me. He placed his hand tenderly on my head and tried not to laugh. My mother knew she shouldn't have bought herself that moment of Korvette peace, and promptly disposed of the remains. The Portuguese bowl moved to a shelf in the basement next to another failed amusement, a jack-in-the box whose demented painted face, and explosive appearances following tinkly music, had long filled me with terror.

The worst thing about the Harry debacle, aside from the stain of murder on my soul, was the ammunition it gave my older siblings. My brother, Ara, was nine years my senior, my sister, Anais, six. They were not pet people. To my knowledge, Ara never wanted even a hamster. Anais in the dim reaches of time had asked for a kitten, but was bought off easily with two stuffed facsimiles in a basket. These two were suckers neither for bright slithering things nor soft cuddly ones. And they brought to their relationship with baby sister the compassion of Mafia hit men. Learning of my unfortunate ministrations to Harry, Ara and Anais could hardly believe I had handed them so rich and inexhaustible a trove.

Indeed, some fifty years after the death of Harry, my sister and I recently were driving together to a county park when we passed the carcass of a roadkill deer.

"It must have needed to hibernate," she said, steering her Honda Fit past the remains.

The carnage did not end with Harry. Following the turtle came a sullen, songless canary, which expired clutching its empty water dish after being moved, prior to a dinner party, from its regular spot in the dining room to an upstairs bathroom, where I promptly forgot about it. Regarding Harry's death I had been regretful but not, to my recollection, seared with guilt. It was an honest mistake; how could anyone guess he wouldn't like his custom-built spa? I still feel bad about that canary, though.

I was learning some things about my parents. They were not exemplary pet-care supervisors. The willful invitation of disease carriers into the household was alien to them, a baffling American practice. However, when I wanted something, they had trouble saying no. My parents had wanted so much when they were children—new shoes, schoolbooks, sometimes even enough to eat— that they couldn't bear see me suffer. This gave me evil powers.

From turtles and birds—and an unspeakable interlude of tropical fish that supplemented their food flakes with one another—I graduated to mammals. For a time, we had Bilbo the beagle. We adopted him as a puppy, but my parents wouldn't dream of letting him sleep in my room. I set him up in the garage with a dog bed, warm blankets, and a ticking clock so he wouldn't feel alone. If they'd have let me sleep there with him, I would have.

I should have read more into that ticking clock. Bilbo turned out not to be like Snoopy at all. Numerous alarming characteristics emerged. Housebreaking did not go according to the instruction book. Outdoors, Bilbo was an even worse menace. Some genetic drive made him find every dead bird in the back yard and haul it into a pile under the elm tree, where he'd toss the rotting carcasses cheerfully up and down for hours at a time. It got so I couldn't go outside or even look out the dining room window. Then he started wrapping himself around my shin and pumping furiously. What was that all about?

My parents found Bilbo a nice new home with the local butcher. Having seen the contents of this butcher's freezer hanging skinned on metal hooks, I'd always assumed Bilbo's fate would not bear close inspection. But my sister last week told me that yes, one of her classmates really wanted the dog and her family adopted it. So maybe Bilbo made out better than I knew. I hope so.

After Bilbo ate the big bone, whether in the sky or across town remains unclear, I scaled the last bastions of my parents' resistance, opened the floodgates to *tro-cho-ma* itself. I brought home a kitten. As with its ornithological and reptilian antecedents, its life was brief.

My literary tastes had progressed beyond Tolkien and I'd entered my Classical period, enjoying the historical novels of Mary Renault and Robert Graves, and the dactylic hexameter of Homer (Lattimore translation). Thus I named the little tabby female "Agamemnon."

Like many a Homeric hero, she perished in the field. One morning I called and called her for breakfast but Agamemnon did not come. My mother looked vaguely uncomfortable but said nothing. Amazingly, it turned out my aunt had seen the cat dead by the road on her way to work and telephoned my mother, who perhaps hadn't had time to dispose of the remains, a task at which she had grown proficient. In any case, my mother said nothing as I went searching for my cat. I called in the front and back yards. I walked up and down the driveway. I checked to make sure she wasn't stuck in the garage. Finally, I headed down the street—and there found Agamemnon, lying very still as if asleep, but in a spot where she would never sleep. I wept over her as Achilles wept for Patroclus. Then I arose with the same grim fury.

Down in the basement, next to Harry's now-dusty Portuguese bowl and the psycho jack-in-the-box, sat a white box. Perhaps it once had held a coat or several sweaters. For the purpose I had in mind the box had a tragic flaw. Embossed on its lid in gold script were the words "Bonwit Teller," the name of a high-end purveyor of fashion and footwear. This was not how I wanted Agamemnon to enter eternity.

"It says 'Bonwit Teller!'" I sobbed to my mother, showing her the box I'd brought up from the basement.

"It's ok," she said.

I carried the box to the end of the street, crouched down and picked up my cat, who had stiffened into a board. Her head and limbs did not droop to gravity, but rather came up together in one awful slab. I dropped the Agamemnon slab into the box, slammed down the Bonwit Teller lid, and carried her to my chosen burial spot in the back yard under the crabapple tree. I'd anticipated the loveliness of yearly blossoms but not the intractability of the root system. It took me hours to dig deep enough, hacking around and through roots, tears blinding my vision. I refused comfort, I refused help. My mother stood at the dining room window wringing her hands.

For much of the time I've been writing this account, I've had a cat curled on my lap. Cats, when they manage to avoid vehicular manglement, make wonderful pets. They sincerely resist encasement in toilet paper. If you forget to provide food or water, they don't expire quietly in the corner, but rather tiptoe across your chest to sniff your cheek and then pat it, at first politely with claws sheathed and then not. I have visited Ellis Island and made it safely back home with no ocular or geopolitical consequences.

The cat on my lap is white with a grey smudge on top of her head. She likes to tuck her face into the crook of my elbow as I type. One of her many names is Cat Eight, *Gadu Oota*. Cat Seven is asleep on the radiator, cooking himself like the pot roast he resembles. Seven and Eight lack the wit to ask what happened to One through Six, which perhaps explains their easy sleep. If they did ask, though, I could tell them Five lived eighteen years and Six lived twenty. Through trial (theirs) and error (mine), I got better at caretaking.

We love as best we can. It's a terrible thing, to be responsible for another life. Sometimes we smother, sometimes we don't know how to set limits, sometimes strike the wrong balance between holding close and letting go. When comfort is most needed, words fail us. My parents never did figure out how to deal with my desire for pets. But they tried. Years later what strikes me is how they tried to let me be who I am even when I became someone whose choices they could not understand.

John Saul

Four Tasks, or What I Came Up With when Covid Took Over

I.

Some of the people and things I like a lot
Turkish rice puddings, trees, Manet, Seurat, cardigans, the
coast of Ecuador, blue tits, headphones, Mary Pickford, station
clocks, breakfast, Siberian tigers, the woman I am having an affair
with.

Some things I don't care for
Conservatories, hardback books, liquorice, cheap airlines, dra-
matised murder investigations, horse guards, stupidity, trumpets,
currants.

More of what I like
Coots building nests, tweezers, artwork on the sides of refuse
collection trucks, zydeco accordions, paramedics, level crossings,
canna plants, warm hearts, raspberries.

II.

Editorial greetings from the north and coming straight to the
point. Here are the headings about books. Good if you can
respond to most of them. Also I'm doing a piece on the subject
of writers who share a name with another writer. Do you have
any anecdotes about you and the other John Saul that you could
share? And how are you getting on with the ten-points business?
Remember?—Come up with ten points to send to someone you
love. It's a sort of exercise. To give you a guiding push when
you're trying to keep in touch with friends everywhere. Send
them ten points.

Editors, editors. The book that made me cry. The book I'd never
lend. The book this, the book that, and now an anecdote about
sharing a name, what can I say? Listen, Joe. This is for you,
editor Joe. The fiction I write and the fiction written by the US
author John Saul, said to be resident in the Seattle area, could
hardly be more different. This has most clearly emerged on the

Internet, notably in reactions to my novel *Seventeen*. Some (mainly US) buyers seemed to have leapt in rapture at finding a hitherto undiscovered text by their hero, the US author, only to discover to their chagrin, not to say ire, that the tale before them was not at all about abducting children, skin burning or crushing some animal's skull. When *Seventeen* was available online, reviewers gave it either five stars or one, never something inbetween. The one-star reviewers would trash my writing, either as being pretentious or on the lines of 'not up to his usual'. Of course it wasn't *his* at all. It didn't seem to occur to any of these disappointed buyers (although they had at least donated to a good charity, which is where the sales income went) that there might be a reason behind this—another author having the same name. *John Saul's Words Make Readers' Skin Crawl,* as one magazine article was headed, gives an idea of what readers can expect—from the US author. Had prospective readers of *Seventeen* taken a few seconds to check, and seen that what was coming was to do with all the strangenesses that made up Britishness, they might have realised they'd be in for something quite different, indeed for someone quite different.

Occasionally, Joe, a photo of myself becomes attached to a book title of Seattle John Saul or vice versa. Careless website presenters (probably algorithms) have even allowed our photos to appear alongside each other, the images ludicrously purporting to be of the same person.

I've been surprised that no one has accused me of using his name. But no one has been that bothered.

III.a

The book I am currently reading
Empireland by Sathnam Sanghera. Another call to face the complexities of history and for stupid British myths to get stuffed. A welcome call, but how many calls do there have to be.

The book that changed my life.
Keith Richards did fall off a library ladder looking for a book (Leonardo da Vinci's study of anatomy). He got three broken ribs and a cancelled tour. In my case, the book that changed my life, any life? People, events, luck, yes, but books?

The book I wish I'd written
I did once say in the *Guardian* that I wish I'd written *The Shipyard* by
Juan Carlos Onetti. The column had to start 'I wish I'd written...'
That was of course nonsense, I would have to have been Juan
Carlos Onetti to have written it, and why would I want to be, to be
anyone but me? I was just glad to have read and spread the news
about a fine book.

The last book that made me cry
(Scratches head.) Cry? Tearful? I get worried sometimes. Looking
way back, to the days of the Famous Five, I didn't worry for the
children but I was terrified something would happen to their parrot.

The book that changed my mind
About what?

The book ... this is like Desert Island Discs without the discs. The
idea of the headings with the books is to name some books. With
Desert Island Discs the discs must be named. There could be no
Desert Island Discs without *Strawberry Fields Forever*. No Beethoven
raging at the piano, no Dusty Springfield. The book I'd take with me
to the island is *Hopscotch* by Julio Cortázar. The pages of the Bible?
I'd find a use for them.

IV.a

The ten points. This is where you come in, Michelle.

1 *La télé existe, Michelle*. There is after all the television. *Ca c'est une
découverte*.

2 ... *La télé, chérie, j'avais toujours des problèmes avec*. Always, problems
with the telly. You say it helps to relax you. *Quelque personnes aiment
la télé parce que ça aide qu'ils peuvent se detendre*. Relax, me? On the telly,
there are all kinds of tricks going on, it's a box of sad tricks. So
there's a resistance, *une résistance!*, a hump to get over before I can
sit on the sofa for hours on end. But now, now I'm happy it's there,
some of the time.

3 ... The idea of these numbers is to find ten points, Michelle, as a
way to say things, now that our lives are porridge. One thing I can
say: I love you. Studies say love, friendship, are likely to fall apart

without contact, but this is not going to happen with us. I will be
there for you always, wherever *there* is. I miss you, so much.

4 ...
III.b

The last book that made me laugh
Erasure by Percival Everett. The bit with the parrot—hilarious.
And for laughs Samuel Beckett never fails. Whole books of his
amuse. He too saw a goldmine in parrots. His parrot Polly got
ejected from a funeral because it swore.

I must have parrots on my mind.

The book I couldn't finish
The wonderful *One Hundred Years of Solitude* went on and on, for
years. Like solitude itself: round and round and round.

The most underrated book
There are so many. *News from the Empire* by Fernando del Paso is
one—another empire from the one in *Empireland* but with the
same cruelties, inanities, denials of what happens when you have
an empire. *Benefits* by Zoe Fairbairns. Dag Solstad: *Novel 11, Book
18*. Almost everything by António Lobo Antunes and Laszlo
Krasznahorkai—now that I'm asked—the two truly majestic
fiction writers still alive. Another male and Irish author wrote the
quite splendid *The engine of owl-light*—only to go and discount its
merits, saying he thought only three people could have bought
copies of it. I'm one. And if I can flit about, and why not, ev-
erything can be edited out can't it, I mean the actor Toby Jones
acted in that film *Notting Hill* and he got edited out altogether.
So Krasznahorkai I can mention again because he made me
laugh too, no I can't remember which book, but he had a woman
fight for her place on a crowded train and I almost expected her
to have a parrot in her basket but well, she didn't. She just sat,
finally, a picture of indignance, so pissed off (or *pissed*, as North
Americans say) about people fighting for a seat, people like her,
what was wrong with them.

The most overrated
There are so many. Some authors are really a load of old Bolaño.
I am waiting, still waiting, employing enormous patience, for a

certain acclaimed unnamed male practitioner to write a properly good novel. His short fiction was wonderful.

The book I'm ashamed not to have read
Michelle, to quote your old monk Rabelais, still not dead after five hundred years: *Fais ce que voudras*—Do what you want. Go for it guys. Ashamed? Of what?

The book I'd like to be remembered for
Will I be there to care? Only for the matter of John Saul in Seattle. I wouldn't care to be remembered as someone I never was.

IV.b

4 ... to keep my mind going I read a little French each day. I'm discovering fine new words. *papier buvard:* the dictionary says that's *blotting paper.* Then there's *miroiter. dédale. patins a roulette.*

5 ... that makes *shimmer. labyrinth. roller skates.*

6 ... and go walking. The Thames ... *La Tamise ne me dit pas beaucoup.* I don't really get the Thames. *Il y a très peu sur l'eau, pas de bateaux. Cette fleuve est plutot un mystère, la Tamise.*

7 ... I'll tell you about this *perroquet*, Michelle. I heard this from Percival Everett, so you won't have heard it—his books don't get around much, they are the opposite of the virus, which drops in everywhere, anywhere there's air and people. The virus, cackling occasionally at the human antics, the silly little arguments, the scuffles about it.

8 ... *Le perroquet* is by itself at home. Just off the little hallway, its cage swings (it has been ruffling its feathers, shaking off dust). There's a knock on the door. Parrot: "Who is it?" Reply: "The plumber." The door doesn't open. Silence. Another knock on the door. "Who is it?" "The plumber." More silence. Louder knock. "Who is it?" Shout: "The plumber!" No opening of the door. Silence. Hefty banging on the door. "Who is it?" In rage: "The plumber!!" Nothing. The next banging is so wild, so heavy the door falls in, the man on top of it, a bag of what must be tools beside him. At the shock of the fall he has a heart attack and lies there, still, dead.

9. The people of the house arrive home, consternated. The front door is down, smashed. A body lies sprawled on top of it. One boot has come off.

10. "Who is it?" says one.
"The plumber," says the parrot.

William Woolfitt

B is for Boxes

Louise Nevelson was the daughter of Russian Jews who had fled the pogroms in Ukraine. In her forties, she walked the midnight streets of New York, Little Italy, Skid Row, gathering scrap wood from trash cans, scrap wood with nails sticking out. She said that she was giving the scraps "an ultimate life, a spiritual life that surpasses the life they were created for." She also gathered wooden vegetable boxes and wine crates. At dawn, in her studio, she dipped all the wood she had found into troughs of black paint.

Later, she would arrange the scraps in boxes and display them in art galleries. Later, she would stack the boxes full of scraps and make walls, and then installations, and monuments, and altars, and a chapel.

My younger son convinces my wife and me to gather sticks and daisy-like weeds with him wherever we go—the playground, the greenway, the field beside the church. Sometimes, he ignores the sliding board, collects fallen leaves instead. He loves to work with cardboard boxes from the grocery store, dog food boxes, diaper boxes. These he crayons, and climbs in, and builds with, and tears into pieces.

I want to give him my attention, be present to him, but I also want to start writing again. I try to think of a way forward. Later, while he naps, I will try to find some scrap—a detail, a sliver of memory, a chunk of text I might quote from—and to cobble from that a sentence or two. Maybe I'll puzzle together a box of words. Later, if I have enough of these, I will try to arrange them, stack them, fit them into an essay of many small parts, a segmented essay.

In her thirties, Louise had drawn figures, had sculpted with terra cotta and plaster—nudes, ducks, owls. Some sources say that she first thought of working with old wood a decade later, while she and her son Mike were searching the streets for firewood. Others say it was when he was serving in the war overseas. She said, "it was secret, they couldn't inform us, and for six months at a time I didn't hear from him. It threw me into a great state of despair." She said, "my work was black." She couldn't locate her son; she couldn't get other materials for art; she turned to old wood and black paint and boxes. Louise put some smaller boxes inside larger boxes, draped them with velvet that was thick as shadows. She imagined that people who saw the boxes would respond to the velvet, lift it up, pull it aside, make their own views.

When my younger son holds the phonics bus and presses a red plastic letter, it says, "ay, ah, ah, alligator, chomp!" At two, he's a self-taught reciter of the alphabet song; depending on his mood, he croons or chants or shrieks the names of the letters. "He likes to a-b-c," I tell my wife. I write an abecedarian poem (each line starting with a different letter of the alphabet), then I try an abecedarian essay. I realize that I like to a-b-c too. I'll try any song, any pattern, any magic word that lets me push back the gloom. When the video shows the two-legged light bulb marching down the street, my son dances and calls out the word *shine*. He asks me to play "This Little Light of Mine" again and again. I hear this on the news: at the Unite the Right rally in Charlottesville, Reverend Osagyefo Sekou led the counter-protestors in singing the same song. He says, "We weren't going to let the darkness have the last word."

1943, Nierendorf Gallery: the gallery owner agreed to show Louise's drawings, but was not impressed when he looked at her sculptures. He said, "There is nothing to them... refugees from a lumber yard."

That same year, Norlyst Gallery: Louise's first exhibition of sculptures she had made from found wood. She called it "The Clown as the Center of His World." With chair and bed and mirror pieces, she assembled circus characters: a wild bull with nodding head and swinging tail, a tightrope walker, trapeze artists, a dog, some seals. Not one sculpture was sold. She took them home and burned them.

At the discovery museum, my son goes to the fun factory on the roof, stands at the bubble tank and blows bubbles. He dips both hands into the sudsy liquid, then his forearms. I can see where this is going; I've seen him eat from a snow drift face-first, seen him lie down in a puddle, move his arms and legs back and forth. He believes in total immersion, sees chances for joy wherever he goes.

1958, the Grand Central Moderns Gallery: Louise installed *Moon Garden*. According to *Life* magazine, it was "composed of 116 boxes and circular shapes stacked or standing free. They are filled or covered with odds and ends of wood.... Everything is painted black." Louise sold seven of the boxes.

In Louise's studio, many cans of black paint. She said, "There is no [other] color that will give you the feeling of totality. Of peace. Of greatness. Of quietness. Of excitement." Here, a skinny scrap of wood that looks like a frail man, a wasted king. Here, a long box that suggests a casket. Louise paints them black, puts the king-scrap in the box. She could build him a crypt, build him a garden.

Louise won't lid, or shut off, or seal *Sky Cathedral*, which is a section of *Moon Garden*—her assemblage, her all-black wall of thirty-six crates fitted together like altar niches—one crate framing dowels like eggs in a juggler's hands, one crate a puzzle of lava spills, one crate a tumble of clouds, one crate a handful of bone shards. Each crate is a rectangular mouth, exhaling shadows instead of breath.

My son becomes engrossed in his dump truck, sandbox, and the rocks in our driveway—so of course he crows when he first sees Parksville Beach, of course he enthusiastically sets to work. Even though it isn't really a beach—just a crowded manmade shore jutting into the water a few miles past Ocoee Dam No. 1, just a small square of dirty sand trapped inside a concrete frame.

In an exhibition catalog, Louise wrote that she was searching for "a new seeing, a new image, a new insight. This search not only includes the object, but the in-between places—the dawns and the dusks, the objective world, the heavenly spheres, the places between the land and sea."

Maybe I should teach my son to pray this line from the Sarum Primer, 1527: "God be in my eyes and in my looking." Maybe this is what I need when my son wakes in the early morning, crying for his stuffed Elmo, a diaper change. Maybe this is what I need when I can't segment or a-b-c my way to a new essay, when I sit with a blank notebook, a blank screen—new eyes, dawn sight, in-between sight.

My son's first word was *more*. When he was very small, he loved to grab my wife's phone, to look at my laptop and see what I was working on.

1959, Museum of Modern Art: Louise makes *Dawn's Wedding Feast*—an all-white, abstracted installation of plinths and altars, a wedding cake, a chest, a mirror, a pillow, bride and groom and guests in the form of columns. Julia Bryan-Wilson, an art historian, said the feast looked like "a mad machine, a splayed open engine with its guts and gears exposed."

Daisy-like weeds grow all over the county where I live, wherever there's ditch, margin, scarp, their centers a yellow smudge, scruffy petals a dingy white— but my son christens them pink flowers, and so they are.

1961, the Martha Jackson Gallery: Louise had decided to do a gold show next. She made *Royal Tides*: she chose boxes, furniture legs, columns, round picture frames and toilet seats to suggest moon phases and the rays of the sun: she painted them gold.

While I stare at a scrap I've written, my son plays with his phonics bus. He presses a letter, and I'm distracted by the bus blaring, "ex, ks, ks, x-ray fish, glub, glub." Soon, we're watching a YouTube video, and I'm learning this: also known as the x-ray tetra, it's a small see-through fish found in the Amazon River. I type, delete, type again a question I'm trying to find the words for. Could we ever peer into each other until we see the sources of the light that comes through us?

Then my wife walks downstairs, and my son runs into the hall to greet her. In the half bath, she changes a bulb. "Want help," my son says. "I help you." He shuts and opens the door, shuts and opens it again. He makes dark, he makes light.

1971: Louise creates *Luminous Zag: Night*, one hundred and five all-black boxes containing knobs, baluster pieces, and serrated planks. Louise said, "it's only an assumption of the western world that [black] means death, for me it may mean finished, completeness, maybe eternity."

T is for Tributary

My great-grandfather lived in an attic apartment, in my aunt's house on Vermont Avenue. He tended the succulents on his windowsill, snake plant, aloe vera. I knew him, called him Pap like my mother did. He loved flowers, had raised peonies and hydrangeas. When he was fourteen, he'd started working as a miner for the Elk River Coal Company in Clay County, West Virginia, then was a miner in Marion County, and I have a flicker of him, a crumbling memory, zinnias and pink lozenges, the bright of him that imagination gives me—a flaring match, here and now gone again. He was an avid pipe smoker and boxing fan; he rapped the floor with his cane when Ali flattened Smokin' Joe.

Bear: [ber] *v.* as in bear a burden, a load, a weight, bear testimony, the sore backs and throbbing shoulders of laborers in 1915. Water boy, millworker, railroad hand, trackman, I try to hear the ballads they heard, the rush of rivers, the babble of shoals, the blue notes, the songs Pontine Nolan sang for the people who remember him. Although Nolan and Pap did not know each other, they lived at the same time, could have been the same age: Nolan who tore the trees apart for the making of furniture, Pap who tore into the earth's seams for the harvest of coal. One man full of splinters, one full of dirty dust.

Pontine Nolan lived in Chattanooga after he had come north, in a Black neighborhood, maybe Blue Goose Hollow, maybe a shotgun shack, or the bottom of Cameron Hill, or the shabby edge of the city, or in what one observer called "a forest of brick and iron smoke stacks," or near the Tennessee River. Nolan worked at the Loomis & Hart sawmill, might have cut boards for headboards, armoires, vanity tables that would be trimmed with mahogany and ivory.

Pap was white; Nolan was Black. I'd like to believe that Pap would have shared with Nolan a pan of biscuits, a jar of water, a table, a seat on the train. That Pap would have listened if Nolan had told him he had a hope, a worry, a dream. And I'd like to think that learning about one of them could add to what I may know about the other. I first read about Pontine Nolan in *Once I Too Had Wings*, a book made from the 1908-1918 journals of Emma Bell Miles ninety years after she died. Only three pages about him. Miles remembered Nolan singing the blues for her, telling her what he had seen in the red hills of Georgia before he moved away from there, the terror he had felt.

And when he wasn't at work? I imagine Pap cooling his feet in a shallow creek, Nolan fishing the Tennessee, pulling in a carp, a spotted sucker. They might have worn similar things: blue bib overalls, flannel or chambray shirt, undershirt, homemade drawers, sack coat, canvas cap, Rockford socks, hobnail shoes or rough stogy-boots.

Pap might have gone to the Grand Opera House, might have heard a quartet sing "Down by the old mill stream where I first met you. Pontine Nolan might have gone to the White Elephant, the Liberty Theater, might have heard Ma Rainey sing "Look what a hole I'm in."

Pap was born in Clay County in the village of Procious near the Elk River—or Pe-quo-ni, as the Lenape called it; according to some historians, *Pe-quo-ni* means "the walnut river." The Elk River is 172 miles long. In 1875, white men were greedy for the riches they could extract from the Elk watershed. Senator Frank Hereford said that it "runs through a country heavily timbered with pine, walnut, cherry, oak, poplar, maple, hemlock, and sycamore of the best quality." He said that "the cannel-coal of the Elk is inexhaustible."

The Tennessee River is 652 miles long. The Tanasi, the Cherokee called it; some historians say *Tanasi* means "meeting place;" others say it means "river of the great bend." Miles saw the river "swollen and muddy," fed by creeks of green water.

On December 31, 1915, Nolan and his friend Preacher Snooze visited a boardinghouse; they sang and played their guitars for Miles and some women who worked in the hosiery mill. Miles described Nolan as "bronze-colored, loud voiced;" later, she called his voice "velvety." Pontine Nolan sang, "Let me tell you my sad dream;" he sang fragments of songs. His wife was probably at a chicken stand. He had been running the saws; his left hand was injured, but he could still make music. Snooze was there, but Nolan must have talked more, or made a stronger impression on Miles: in her journal entry, Nolan was the main character; his songs and his stories about Georgia made the evening memorable for her. I read that Pontine Nolan went home at nine-fifteen p.m. After that, he's gone. Miles did not write about him again. I search the internet, but I find no other trace of him.

Georgia could be a bad place, Pontine Nolan told Miles and the women at the boardinghouse. Miles wrote Nolan's account in her journal: *Never had trouble with nobody there myself. I like the money; they pay off in gold. But having to get out and go to work at three in the morning with men who had Winchesters on their shoulders, and these amateur guns—Lord! You'd run on to dead people laying by the railroad. One time we saw a big nice box, went and looked in, and bless the holy Lamb, there laid a boy as big as Lonny. Every time I go around there, I hear about somebody being killed. They won't work a black mule by a white one down there.*

Maybe my great-grandmother told Pap there would be a better life for them, more peace, or a safer home for their children, if they moved to Marion County, if they started over someplace else. She had grown up on a mountain near Ivydale, near Booger Hole. Maybe she lived on Pilot Knob, or Velvet Knob, or Painter Knob. When she was fourteen, she and her younger sisters hid in the woods while their stepmother threw dinner plates, a woman fuming in hateful rage. According to *The West Virginia Encyclopedia* and several newspaper articles, Booger Hole was the murder capital of Clay County. Henry Hargis vanished, and the blood of a Jewish peddler was found under the hay in a barn, and the clockmaker's body was thrown into Rush's Creek, and in 1917 Preston Tanner was struck by a splitting maul and burned in his cabin, and Lacy Ann Boggs, age eighty-four, was shot while slicing apples for a pie after she told her neighbors that she knew where a body was buried. Lacy Ann and the others could have been Pap's neighbors, his kin.

Before that, my great-grandmother's uncle James was tied to a hemlock tree by Confederate bushwhackers, and then they shot him to death.

I imagine this again and again: on a raft, in a passenger car, I'm crouching or sitting and there in the creek, beside the tracks, I see an object but can't tell what it is, a thing obscured by the murk of the water, the speed of the train. A large rock, or a fallen tree, or broken concrete with rebar, or a wooden box. I don't want to think it could be a body. There's its shape, there's its shadow, there's its effect, I see how the thing I hope is only rock or fallen tree changes the flow and the speed of the creek, hear how it changes the air that whistles around the train.

Pontine Nolan sang whole songs and parts of songs that night in the parlor of the boardinghouse, and maybe Miles laughed, maybe she clapped her hands. Nolan sang "Pallet on the Floor," "Stagalee," "Home Sweet Home." He sang, "kiss my girl good bye," sang "come here honey." He rag-timed, he riffed, he tapped the floor.

In her notebook, my grandmother described what her mother cooked for a holiday meal: "Jar of green beans, mashed potatoes, gravy, pumpkin pie, cranberries, oyster dressing, chicken bought at the company store, penned up overnight and butchered by Dad." It was what Pap's labor could provide, his loads of lump coal, nut coal, egg coal, and slack coal, add to that what money my great-grandmother made from sewing dresses and pajamas and coats for neighbors, from taking in boarders. My grandmother remembered their cramped house on First Street, coal shed, privy; she remembered the bedroom she shared with five brothers and sisters, the folding beds. It was a time when "a few more dollars meant a lot."

Hammer, mill file, oilstone, gritted whetstone, animal fat: these might have been Nolan's tools.

Pick, shovel, auger, tamping-bar and needle, small hat lamp and can of oil, can of blasting powder: Pap's tools. Red liniment and bluestone rub for Nolan's sores, and for a cut hand that wouldn't close, for a lace of scars (some bruise-blue, some still red, enflamed), and slices, and nicks. For Pap's cough, make a tea from mullein roots, whiskey, horsemint, the bark of a black gum tree. For sore knees, tie a string soaked in turpentine.

In 2016, a thousand-year-flood destroyed homes in the communities of Procious, Bomont, and Camp Creek. The Elk overflowed its banks, rose to more than thirty feet. Some families lost everything, had to live in campers and tents on Walgrove Road and at Blue Creek.

Extant: [ek'-stənt] *adj.* as in still existing, not destroyed or lost, the several surviving journals of Emma Bell Miles given by her daughter to a university library, the paper easy to tear, the Mead spiral notebook, three subject, wide ruled, where my grandmother started to write down her memories of Pap and the coal camp where they had lived, so many blank pages, more than half of the notebook empty. In my kitchen, an offshoot of Pap's snake plant lives without much water or light. Miles called the Carolina Paroquet one of the "shadows from the past," thought the lost bird might still exist deep in the Everglades, "surrounded and protected by the silence."

There might be irises and yellowbells at Pap's cabin site in Procious, some dim trace in Booger Hole, flood debris or dried mud, trailhead or riverwalk, grassy circle or fifty-foot metal sculpture where Nolan's home might have stood in Blue Goose Hollow.

I imagine rivers that bend, noisy floods, eddies washing away the memories I cup in my hands. Nolan's back at Loomis & Hart manning the rip-saws, shriek and whine, metal biting wood, I can't hear him anymore. Mouth of the mine, Pap climbs aboard the mule-powered man-trip, fades from view.

I try again. Icy winter nights, they might do the same things, the distance between them diminishing. I see him look for sticks to burn, creep out while his wife snores, and shiver in the alley outside a hall, and press his ear to brick, and hear a rag, a ballad, a shout, hear a man sing about leaving town on a train.

Y is for Yucca

i.

Misnamed with the Taino word for cassava (a completely different plant) by Gerard and then Linnaeus, the yucca genus originates in the hot parts of the Americas. Including about fifty species, it's characterized by a tall woody stalk, a circle of stiff leaves, and creamy bell-shaped flowers. Yucca flourishes in the poorest soils, in the barrens and the badlands, on roadsides, in sand dunes.

In southern Appalachia, in graveyards and at the sites of former farmsteads and vanished cabins, untended plantings of y. filamentosa—with its clump of sword-shaped leaves and showy burst of pale flowers—green and ghost what has gone back to earth.

Y. filamentosa is sometimes called Adam's needle and thread because of the long threads raveling from its sharp-pointed leaves. According to the botanist and slave owner Stephen Elliott, "the leaves of this plant twisted and tied together are used for strings, ropes, and even cables for small boats. It appears to possess the strongest fibres of any vegetable whatever." Y. filamentosa is also called silk grass, or bear grass, or Confederate flax, or tie-plant, or meat hanger; its leaves were used by white Appalachians for stringing up hams in smokehouses. Or used by the Cherokee in poultices and salves. Also called everlasting, or ghost in the graveyard, for yucca's mass of white blossoms that seems to float above the ground.

In the deserts of California, y. brevifolia "bristles" and "stalk[s] drearily" and grows "shaggy with age," Mary Austin writes in *The Land of Little Rain.* Y. brevifolia dies slowly, Austin reports, and then "the ghostly hollow network of its woody skeleton, with hardly power to rot, makes the moonlight fearful." Night lizards and wood rats live inside its dry limbs after its death; ladder-backed woodpeckers and northern flickers build their nests in its empty trunk. Austin saw y. brevifolia in Death Valley and on the mesas. It was called tree yucca, and then supposedly some Mormon settlers thought it looked like Joshua of the Old Testament stretching out his arms to welcome them, and now its common name is Joshua tree.

Tallest of the yuccas, it's a drought tolerator, a night breather, and can live to be three hundred years old. And might be extinct by the end of the twenty-first century, or limited to a few Joshua trees hanging on in small refugia at higher elevations—extinct because of too much climate change, too much heating up and drying out, and not enough yucca moths to pollinate it, too many invasive species and too many wildfires, too many desperate rodents damaging its rough skin for sips of moisture.

I hope there's still time for us to learn a leathery gumption from the yuccas, a we-can-change-our-ways from bear grass, a you-might-survive from the Spanish bayonet that offers its tender daggers when we are hungry, its flower stalks for us to roast over a fire. Y. gloriosas and soap trees and our-lord's-candle, with their soft tips and seed capsules and saw-toothed leaves, teach me that some words should be guarded and others should be poured upon the ground. After wet winters, Joshuas can branch profusely, can flower and fruit. After too-hot summers, there is a wise one weeping for the water-hungry cities and the blasted mountains and the ice shelves breaking apart like windowpanes stomped by a boot. Maybe the wise one will play the fool and win on love by a cut of the card deck. Or maybe that's sap-head talk, the tomorrow-hope that spoonleaf spreads to Adam's needle and thread, the buzz that I drink up. When my lidded sun and my cloud of dust-where-a-mountain-stood shut out all but the slenderest thread, and when my skin grizzles beneath the blinding eye, and when my face is abraded by a blast of grit, oh let me take it in.

ii.

Flashy and pungent, yellow buckwheat favors ground where nothing else grows, its long thirsty roots reaching down through fissures in the olive-drab shale. Lena Artz might have dreamed about it, might have hoped she would find y. filamentosa, maybe even the rumored prairie violets. She went to the shale barrens. She may have first seen the barrens when she was a girl on her father's farm, and now she was forty-four, a teacher, a scientist, now she wanted to know again the leather-flower that grew there, and wavy-leaf aster, and the delights in primrose scent, in shades of orange and gold. She hiked up fire trails and followed old road-ruts, and she climbed the steep banks of Devonian shales, and she warily inched down the loose gray slates, down what she would describe as the "rugged and precipitous outcrops" not far from the Cow-pasture River. She meant to have a long and careful look at "the most barren parts of the shales" and the "crevices of the harder layers of rock." In 1935, Lena Artz was writing her thesis *Plants of the shale banks of the Massanutten Mountains*. When she went to the shales, she measured buckwheat roots, she collected specimens for the herbarium at the university. She found bluebells growing on cliff-edges, she found blazing stars, and bird's-foot violets, and wild bleeding heart.

Adam's needle and thread, y. filamentosa, and yellow buckwheat remind me of Jesus's parable of the sower, in which a reckless farmer goes out to plant a crop and scatters the seeds any which way. I imagine the stony ground and the hand-flung seeds and the unnamed fruit. Imagine springing up too fast, being scorched too soon, having no root. The rabbi saying that the seeds are like kingdom words, the good soil is like listening ears. When my son was three and not talking much, my wife and I tried to open the world to him whenever we walked or drove to his preschool, tried by naming for him *mailbox* and *cow*, *steeple* and *leaf* and *bucket truck, chicken truck, log truck*. We were flinging words, we were praying against stony ground.

iii.

The yucca giant-skipper—a yellow-banded, brown-winged butterfly—is thought to feed on mud instead of flowers; it makes its home wherever its favorite yuccas grow. In utility corridors. In scrub. In the serpentine barrens that the botanist and explorer William Bartram described in 1791: "chains of hills whose gravelly, dry, barren summits present detached piles of rocks." In the bone heaps that Bartram saw nearby: "white, gnawed bones of ancient buffaloe, elk and deer, indeterminably mixed with those of men, half-grown over with moss." See there, in gravel, in powdered bone, see Adam's needle and thread, y. filamentosa, and moundlily yucca, y. gloriosa, yielding their leaves to the skipper mothers' glued-on eggs. See the yuccas giving their roots to skipper caterpillars who feed, and expel silky tents, and tunnel like hungry miners through the yucca-crowns, the part where stem joins root. Before the skipper pupas can unwrap, and dry, and hurtle through the air, there is wind, or is it breath, or a word, lifting the yucca hairs, the skippers' just-hardened wings.

Abdulbaseet Yusuff

Quartz

I hold the man's gaze.
(Not in an intimate way, please. But hey, WikiHow says holding a
person's gaze is one way to exude confidence, and I want to appear
confident. Some other tips include looking good, smelling nice, and
a firm handshake, though I find this last bit of advice weird: a firm
handshake feels to me like an invitation to arm wrestling.)
Anyway, who is this man whose gaze I hold?

※

Let me start from the beginning.
It's a sunny Saturday morning. I'm walking through a rowdy
market in Gwagwalada. Sweaty bodies, barrow-pushing boys, col-
ored plastics, a parked Peugeot with a speaker fastened to its roof (a
pre-recorded ad for herbal medicine blaring from it), puddles from
an early Friday rain resisting the scorch, fruit shed – everything is
jumbled. The market has everything. Well, except a conscience.
That's suffocating for people like me with a bloated conscience.
My right thigh is keeping vigilance over the wallet in my pocket as I
meander through the maze of people. You know how markets are
full of straying hands, and how straying hands like pockets.
I'm here to get a new bottle of perfume. To be honest, I'm
not particular about fragrances. *Oud* seems to be the prescribed
fragrance in this city, but who the hell cares? You are allowed to
be nonconformist if you don't have money to splurge on luxury.
Before long, I reach a sort of jewelry shop where things like that are
sold. Mirrors, bangles, and all the glitter-glitter stuff that humans
love. No bling-blingz though.
The shop is at the tail end of the market. Inside it, the shop-
keeper is scooping fura into his mouth; the milk coated a slim part
of his mustache and made him look like a silly child. As soon I slide
the door open, he wipes his mouth with his sleeves and covers the
bowl with a hand fan. He then reaches out to pause the music pour-
ing from his phone – a criminally auto-tuned Hausa love song.
I spend minutes fsst-ing sprays on my wrist, bringing them to
my nostrils, until my wrists smelled so good they smelled bad.

Then, I settle for one that smelled like morning – but who am I kidding? It smelled classless, but fine. And I was fine with fine. There is something about being in lustrous company. Even the dullest things lay claim to sparkling. I proceed to look at other things. Necklaces, rings with fake, gaudy precious stones, watches etc.

Among these, one wristwatch catches my eye. I try it on and it looks great on my wrist. I could already imagine myself walking on the street, flaunting it, checking time for no darn reason. Because I still have a little change, I decide to try my luck. Even though I fear it is an expensive watch, I manage to steel myself. Switch off your conscience and haggle shamelessly like a savage, I say to myself. After all, the market has no conscience. Eat or be eaten. It is all capitalism, baby.

First rule to successful haggling: be an expert. If you are not an expert, perform expertise. I hold the watch limp in my hand like a seasoned watch collector, turned it this way and that way, like it had quality assurance messages that only I could see. The shop owner is losing his patience, his eyes constantly drifting to the bowl on his table.

Quartz is on the watch's glass. So I say, "Quartz."
"What?" the man asks.
"It has quartz," I repeat. Just trying small talk. Economic foreplay, so to speak.
He shrugs. "Is quartz not good?"
"No, no, I didn't say that."

I sit on a nearby stool in the self-assured manner of a successful haggler, someone with a degree in haggling from an Ivy League college, *magna cum laude*. I stare at the watch and when I lift my eyes, the man is watching me with bewilderment. Outside the glass doors of the shop, the world moves nonstop – unaware of the Haggling Olympics about to go down.

"How much does it go for?" I finally ask, holding his money-hungry gaze. This is that superficial gaze.
The man laughs. "How much do you think it goes for?"
Smart move. I know he is trying to gauge my level of expertise.
"How about you just tell me?" I say firmly. Firmer than I intend. The voice of conscience is trying to rear its fat head.
The man scratches his bald head in the absent-minded manner of people whose heads aren't really itching. Just a thing

of habit.

"Pay N1200" the man says, wiping his hands on his trousers. He starts to rearrange perfume bottles. The perfume bottles grumble because they are already arranged and need nobody's hands touching them without valid reason.

Not so expensive, I think. But a man's got to be savage in the market. I try to not think of his family; I try to not think of whether he makes any profit as I am wont to do in times like this.

"That's a lot," I say. "I'll give you N500"

Confetti explodes in my brain. If this were televised, cheers would have erupted across the city. I pat myself on the back. Over 50% cut. I feel my conscience frosting.

"Haba!" the man exclaims. "That's too low. Pay N1000."

We ping-pong offers until we finally settle at N700. I walk out of the shop feeling like a badass negotiator. But for restraint (which is a cool synonym for money), I would have put up a Better Call Saul kind of billboard in some part of town. Only it would have my name and picture instead of Saul Goodman's.

✸

Standalone, the narrated event has little value. But, if you place it side by side with the fact that two days later, I am sitting out with my aunt, a woman who knows what is what and how to do. If you place it side by side with the fact that a man hawking jewelry walks past us.

If you place it side by side with the fact that my aunt, in checking for new earrings for her daughter, finds the same watch I bought for N700.

If you place it side by side with the fact that she likes it too and asks for the price. If you place it side by side with the fact that the man's first asking price is N500.

If you place it side by side with the fact that my aunt haggles to N400, you would see why I think highly of myself. Even at my least considerate, I'm still the most considerate person I know. N100 worth of considerate, as this story shows.

Jane

In my first week of social work in the emergency room, I've picked up my patients' pain, and it burrows into my skin all the way home. Once I close the door, I kick my red clogs off, pull my pants down, throw off my shirt, unclip my bra, and fling my clothes in the corner next to my bed. No matter how naked I stand, the ache still finds hooks to hang onto, crevices to burrow into. I am hungry to climb into the bathtub and see if I can scrub their sorrows off of me.

Tonight, it is Jane who holds me captive, a prisoner in my own home. I can't seem to wash her words off my body. I can't seem to think her pain out of my head.

✳

"Who wants to see an abscess?" the doctor asks earlier.

"Sure, I've never seen one before." It's my third day at the hospital. I've never seen a lot of things.

It is a perfect half-dome. Violet and red and in some places, yellow-green. Then the opening, like the hungry mouth of a volcano. It is almost like any other wound I've ever seen, and it is fine. It is the sight of her vulva that strikes me down into the uncaring ground: some smooth skin, but mainly, little patches she has missed shaving. Shoddily done, like a last minute remembrance.

These little patches pain me. I once shaved in college, back when I believed that was what all men liked, and all those times I'd shaved, I never missed spots. I took my time; I was careful with the most sensitive part of my body. To see Jane's patches jerks me violently to the reality that she feels she has to sell her body for drugs, and I imagine her trying to groom herself but keeling over, dropping the razor, too high to be careful with herself. Too high to be gentle with herself.

✳

Tonight I practice Reiki on myself before I fall asleep. The bath has helped a little, but I am waging a war against a hurt that fights to kill, a hurt that isn't mine that I nonetheless carry like three lifetimes of responsibility. I lie on my back and place my hands over my third-eye, and teardrops roll down the side of my face like a battalion of foot soldiers, dripping salt into the nooks of my ears.

With my eyes closed, I see Jane's eyes. In the hospital bed, after we ask her why she no longer wants the doctor to drain her abscess, she squeezes her eyes shut as if to bully the tears back to where they came from. She bristles at the question, and between her clamming her eyes shut and opening them wide to blink away the tears, her crow's feet converge into a million tiny folds. *He was too rough. I don't like being treated like that.* As the shame of her life comes swelling to the surface, her face morphs from a lifeless gray to a bright red. Her pain seems boundless, an invisible sadness emanating from her hollowed center. There are two pink stains on the white blanket she swaddles herself in, artifacts of the abscess fluid the doctor managed to drain before she told him to stop. Before he was too rough.

I imagine that when she sells her body for drugs, when the men are rough with her, she doesn't ask them to stop. But now, she does. She can't tolerate even a sliver of rough.

☀

"How much fentanyl do you use?" my supervisor asks Jane. All the other patients in the emergency room tell us the truth—they have nothing to lose. Three bags a day, a bundle (ten to fourteen bags) every two days. But Jane doesn't want to tell us. When she is asked, she says only, *Too much.* We barely hear her—she whispers it muffled from under the face mask from under the blanket, like a secret she needs to keep hidden. Yet, she cannot hide. She is horribly visible in front of me, her shame blaring from inside. The diamond piercing on her left cheekbone glistens under the antiseptic hospital light. *Too much.*

My supervisor asks if Jane uses another drug, to which she answers, *No, not my thing. It was never my thing.* As if fentanyl is her thing. Fentanyl—not even like heroin, whose name sounds almost noble. Almost brave. Fentanyl—some modern, lab-created, Frankenstein abomination, the "y" at the end of the word slashing into the bottom of the line, interrupting the grace it could have had. It is ugly, and it is stupid. It is the only warm blanket that has ever protected Jane. The one stained with two pink drops of fluid doesn't do the job nearly as well.

✳

He was too rough. I don't like being treated like that.

"I'm sorry you feel that way," my supervisor says. I watch, like an apparition in the night—invisible, helpless. I don't know enough yet to do anything but watch. If nobody else were in the room, I would rest my hand on Jane's thin shoulder and remind her, "Nobody deserves to be treated rough. *You* don't deserve to be treated rough. You deserve kindness." But I just watch.

Aside from the "Hi" I say when my supervisor introduces me at the beginning, I don't know what to say, especially when we leave the room. *Hang in there? Take it easy? Feel better?* These things all seem spectacularly out of Jane's control. So I say nothing. I don't even pull the curtain closed for her when I walk out, despite that being her wish the last two times we saw her. Because what if she doesn't want it pulled shut now? I want to respect her wishes, not acquiesce to the mistake of assuming anything. I want to be gentle with her. I want this life to be gentle with her.

✳

He was too rough. I don't like being treated like that.

So the doctor prescribes her antibiotics. What good will that do when the abscess needs to be drained first? Even if the doctor drains her abscess, what could save her body when a torrent of fentanyl and shame are ripping through it? Jane tells us she'll come back—when he's not here. She wants another doctor. Someone who isn't rough with her.

✳

At the end of my third day, my third eye trembles. I am not yet accustomed to being so close to the dying, to the dead. To the living who are lunging after death, inches away from catching up to that sweet forever sleep.

I cry myself to sleep, unable to fight my tears back the way Jane did. I dream of gentleness.

Cyndie Zikmund

Feline Intuition

Easter Sunday morning my hand dug deep into the trash behind San Jose's Stevens Creek Hyundai, pushing around discarded lunch wrappers and spare parts with a twisted dry cleaner hanger. Sweat beaded above my upper lip and collected in the crease of my chin underneath an N95 pandemic mask. The odor of rotting garbage surrounded me. Instead of heading to the beach, I told my husband we had to stop and search for my good luck charm, a black rubber cat named Bendy Five Percent. I had mistakenly left the replica of my first pet when I emptied my car for trade.

For the past forty-seven years, Bendy Five Percent had ridden in my car wrapped around the rearview mirror, guarding the back bumper, channeling the protective spirit of my mother who had died a few months before I purchased the amulet. Christians have St. Christopher medals, Hindus have statues of Ganesh, metaphysical beliefs have Archangel Michael. I had Bendy Five Percent.

"I'm coming for you, Bendy Five Percent," I telepathed to her as we sped down Highway 280, twenty minutes from the dealership. I had noticed that Bendy Five Percent was missing from her perch above the rearview mirror when I checked for the charm, like a pilot measuring gauges before takeoff.

"Call them and see if they're open," I said to my sleepy husband. We'd left early to beat the crowds, heading to the coast, hoping to enjoy the unseasonably warm day.

"Google says they're closed," he said.

"Call them anyway, someone might be there," I said while remembering the day I had purchased Bendy Five Percent.

It was a few weeks after my mother had died in 1974. I was sixteen and had just gotten my Driver's License. I drove her seafoam green Toyota pickup into Helena, Montana, our closest town, and at the Ben Franklin Five and Dime, I bought the Bendy Five Percent and an orange rubber ostrich, commemorating passing the test. Sadly, the ostrich was a casualty of a car break-in a few years later, leaving Bendy Five Percent my only good luck charm.

"This is Cyndie Zikmund, I left something in the car I traded-in on Thursday. Is my old car still there?" I said over speaker phone. The stranger put us on hold and checked the back lot with nearly thirty used cars parked side by side. He returned and confirmed my old car was onsite. This announcement gave me hope.

The original Five Percent had been a sign of hope. When she was a kitten and I was away at Girl Scout Camp, she contracted feline distemper. The doctor told my mother that ninety-five percent of the cats who contract the disease perish. Refusing to let my first pet die on her watch, my mother nursed the cat back to health. Centuries old superstitions claimed that black cats were bad luck. They became a hallmark for spooky Halloween decorations. Five Percent's survival proved some black cats bring good luck and hers was twice as concentrated as regular, I reckoned.

Five Percent had been weaned from her mother early and suckled the bathroom rug in place of her mother's nipple. Eventually, she matured into my constant companion, accompanying me on long hikes in the pine forest behind our mobile home park. We had a special place overlooking a natural hot spring where I sang a made-up song about the soulmate I hoped to meet someday. She usually stood silently watching, but sometimes, if I was singing with more emotion, she'd run up one tree, then back down it and up another, expressing my want in her outbursts. Feline intuition has been attributed to their acute senses, allowing cats to feel changes sooner than their humans like health threats, changing weather patterns, or passionate verse.

My husband didn't question the change of plans. He knew the priority was to get Bendy Five Percent back before my car was sent to auction. We couldn't lose my spirit animal.

When I was a freshman in high school, I'd lost the original Five Percent to unknown causes. The following year, I lost my mother to bone cancer. I didn't have a father. He had died from heart failure during a hospital test when I was too young to understand the finality of death. Losses can pile up on a person, making them cling irrationally to things. Like the original Five Percent had turned our small rug into a binky, I was grasping for Bendy Five Percent with the desperation of a child who had lost her blankie.

Hyundai's holiday crew was sparse. While two salespeople chatted in a glass-walled office, a service attendant led me to their back

lot where the sun beat down on three rows of used cars. Before the
attendant could find the keys, I ran to the middle row and tried my
car's door – someone had forgotten to lock it. My hands felt around
the rearview mirror. I opened the center console, the glove com-
partment. I looked under the seats, in the back, along the door cup
holders. I could tell the attendant wanted this story to have a happy
ending by his dejected look when I came up empty. The second
security person arrived to help, though neither knew how best to
assist. I wasn't emotional, but I was a woman on a high mission.
My eyes scanned the area, thinking like Detective Columbo whose
reruns I'd been watching on Amazon Prime.

Where would a thief stash the goods? I thought, morphing into
crime solving mode even though no crime had been committed.

From having two purses previously stolen, I knew that garbage
cans were the best place to look for discarded hot property.

Then, for the first time that morning, I didn't feel crazy. The
other item that I had hung over my rearview mirror peeked out
from under the dry cleaner's advertisement. A blue wristband from
the last live concert I had attended before the pandemic, Halloween
2019, One Republic. This was too specific to belong to anyone else.

Bendy Five Percent had to be nearby.

Three cars were parked in the service bays, no mechanics were
working that day. I emptied the garbage can with the vigor of a gold
miner.

This wasn't the first time I had needed to search for Bendy
Five Percent. In 1985, I came out of my apartment in Berkeley and
discovered that my Datsun – with Bendy Five Percent attached to
the rearview mirror – had been stolen. I was attending engineering
school, and Bendy Five Percent had been with me for eleven years.
The police had given me little hope of getting the car back, saying
most stolen vehicles were sold for spare parts within twenty-four
hours. When they called to say they had found the Datsun aban-
doned in a parking lot, I knew the reason it had been spared –
Bendy Five Percent was finding her way back to me.

Carrying a toy in my car for almost fifty years, believing it
brought me good luck, might be considered overly sentimental, but
Bendy Five Percent's record speaks for itself. In all the time I'd had
my good luck charm, I'd never been rear-ended, nor had a high-
speed collision. There was the one time when an armored truck
abruptly changed lanes and pushed my Honda to the shoulder like

a stunned moth, but the dent was easily repaired, and no one was injured.

I counted. Bendy Five Percent and I had owned eight vehicles, lived in four states, graduated from five schools, and had dozens of bad first dates in our years together. She had been the most permanent being in my life.

Desperate situations call for bold action. I entered the service bays with a mix of excitement and reverence for the tools and equipment that sat silent on their one day off a week. It felt as if I were breaking and entering even though I had two service attendants watching my every move. I walked slowly to the back and a small room appeared to the right.

"I'm going into this office," I announced as if admitting to snooping would make it okay. The older attendant gave me a nod.

Three plastic shelves were stacked on a small metal desk. One had a white terry cloth rag – the kind Amazon sells in packs of twelve. Between a pair of sunglasses and a Bic pen rested Bendy Five Percent. She was formed in the reclining position as if she were napping before her next gig.

That's how cool she is.

The person who details used cars had chosen to keep her above all other forgotten objects. I grabbed her as if I were breaking her out of prison.

"We have a new car now. You're coming with me," I said.

I turned to the astonished service attendants and told them the highlights of Bendy Five Percent's illustrious life. They smiled, nodded, and laughed open-mouthed when they learned she'd already survived two robberies. It was going to be a Happy Easter in the Hyundai dealership's back parking lot after all.

I didn't know how much time had passed. It seemed like five minutes, but I think it was thirty. For half an hour, my husband and our two rescue pups had patiently waited in the new car, reading the driver's manual, and trying to program the GPS for the beach. I had long ago realized that my husband was the soulmate that the original Five Percent and I had imagined for myself during those long summer days of awkward adolescence, singing to the pinecones.

The detour to rescue my talisman had added a total of ninety minutes to our drive, but neither my husband nor our pups complained. We are a family that leaves no member behind.

POETRY

Zeina Azzam

A Grammar for Fleeing

You know, when an emigrant needs something to hold on to, a spider web looks like a wooden beam. —*Rafik Schami,* Damascus Nights

Hudood, the word for border,
looms in her mind's vocabulary
like a passive voice, a noun for longing.
Maybe the undulating line runs in water
or in sand, splays on the imagined cover
of a passport, map for a new home.
She has vowed to cross it, daughter on her hip,
two legs doggedly moving apace,
two legs suspended, bare.
She plans to learn the other side
like a foreign language:
first the stones as single utterances,
then the houses and hills, sentences.
The scenes will warm in the light of the sun.
Now it's dark and the little girl
is ensconced in her arms, eyes closed,
but a lulling breeze could spell betrayal
if they aren't careful. She reaches
between her breasts for the pendant
inscribed with *amal,* hope, rubs it
like a magic lamp. The din of conversation
starts to rise as light gathers at the horizon,
where the singular message of true East
has grounded her since childhood.
Lay low, look west, wait for the boat.
She understands the grammar for fleeing,
unspoken rules that decide how
the journey will end, when words
like *harb,* war, and *joo`,* hunger,
might ebb and not flow.
Her toddler wakes asking for water
while the sea responds with crashing waves.

Zeina Azzam

A Language for Colors

Asfar she would say
pointing at a yellow tulip.

And the color of grass?

Akhdar.

My young daughter had mastered
not only the colors
but also the throaty KH,
two letters in English
that equal one in Arabic.

I would tell her it's the same sound
as in khamseh, khubez, sabanekh—
five, bread, spinach

and my favorite name
Khaled, Immortal.

I once confessed to a friend wistfully
that I would not name my son Khaled
because Americans couldn't pronounce it.
Now I wonder about such wisdom:
even my eight-year-old
could constrict her throat muscles the right way
to say Khaled—

immortal like an ancient olive tree,
a flame that never abates,
a mother's love.

This spring, I saw a patch
of double hybrid tulips,
asfar tinged with akhdar,

and thought of my daughter's
satisfied grin at learning those words
thousands of miles away
from her grandparents' home
in Palestine.

Here we are, hybrid Americans
living between two languages
and speaking in colors,
splendid flowers in a distant field.

Christine Butterworth-McDermott

Spell for Attraction, Containing Belladonna

Your eyes are familiar: purple like the skin
of a fruit she's bitten—

In another life, this girl addressed you
and undressed you without hesitation

but in this one, she rocks her loneliness
until the Fates grant her some unwinding.

The spell says first she must dig

>   in the black
>   dirt,   pull up
>   the nightshade,
>   replace it

bread   salt   brandy

>   let the hole
>   devour
>   these gifts

then shovel the dirt back over, bury
that which she offers up.

The spell says she must trek
for home, moist ground mucking up

her shoes. The spell says she must
not speak on the way across the field.

She must not speak until the hearth
greets her. Then she may think how

both now must be joined. The spell says
to grind the leaves, boil them down,

drop that tea in the eyes.
The spell promises they will grow wide

and beautiful—bella donna—she will blink
the power of the root. The spell says

you will not be able to look away.

Christine Butterworth-McDermott

Lesson of Fire and Phoenix

What boils down beauty is the cauldron
of odious comparisons
and the flaming conviction
you failed to brew the right concoction
          (that erstwhile love spell turnstile).

But damn toil and trouble—if you walk
away somnambulant, you leave the burners on.

Don't be a slow learner of the physics of scorching.
Don't choose to simmer like some shy incarnate.
Doubledown willingly. Own it, go for broke!

Hold open the oven door and throw your own
fool self in, devising the very worst hell of heat.

Succumb to all those imagined
defeats: melt, spill over, explode—
then navigate char. Rise, bare-boned,
purified, out of smoke.

Christine Butterworth-McDermott

The Sugared Plum

According to tradition,
it's bad luck to refuse your kiss
under the mistletoe.

Six drupes means six times
the tip of your tongue should hover
in the innermost corner

of my mouth. And though I am
curious about the taste
your lips might bring,

I also wonder how many tainted
berries brought you to linger
here, with the likes of me.

How many presents have you
already unwrapped, how often
have your fingers folded back paper

—or choked up girls with ribbon?
I'd like to stand here—instead—
on the threshold of your potential

gifts, rather than sweat in stifling rooms,
heady on spice and wool,
tradition hanging down above us.

Maybe later you can pull me out
to where the crisp air cools this blush.
Maybe later, it will be enough

to stare together at houses that shine
like beacons sugared with snow.
And then, if you lay your hand

to my throat, then, under no eaves
or fabrication, it may be just
enough to close our eyes, to wait,

to hold still.

Robert Fanning

Snow and Roses

—Gerald A. Fanning
(5/19/29-4/22/2013)

Make it quick, my brother said, pressing his phone
to your cold ear. A priest was waiting beyond

the curtain. One hundred miles away, I stammered
Dad, I'm not sure if you can hear me. I love you.

After hanging up, I walked out of my office into the light
of early spring, crossed the parking lot, opened the heavy door

of the church I never visit. I do love the hush of empty
sanctuaries, the chatter and engines of the day

made mute, the votive flicker, the floor stained
with rainbow, the air a hint of incense and lingering prayer.

Kneeling in the first pew, I stared up at a wooden Christ,
at some gilded Latin phrase over the crucifix that meant

nothing to me. One you no doubt knew well. *Father,*
let me call you that now that you're gone. Here we are

still, on opposite shores, another sea of indecipherable
language between us. Listen, father statue, father stone,

the test is over and we failed. But maybe now we can trace
the letters, sound out the words in separate tongues,

translate distance into love. Teach it to me in your new dialect.
I need to learn what this means. I need to know this by heart.

Robert Fanning

Model Nation

—for Gabriel

As you speak, new worlds rise in your eyes.
A voice within your voice—do you hear it, too?—
could fill a whole sea with whale song. It sings
fathom and *league*, sings *launch* and *conquer*.
It is ocean wide now, this good force of your going.
Yet still, my heart fumbles to fasten some small rope
around the dock—and so love is—wishes for a way
to keep us here. Too late. That little boat you were,
giggling in the tub as I blew bubbles, is oceans away.
Sailboat, tugboat, yacht, steamer, freighter,
I've been watching from the dock and hear already
the growing ache and groan of giant chains clanking
an iron hull, the long horn of adulthood calling you
with its sweeping wall of mist and fog.
When you look back and see me wave, may I be
the ocean's shoulders ever rolling beneath you.
Please—know me not as a country fading
from view, but as one who carried with love
the great world you now carry in you.

Robert Fanning

On Crater Trail

—Craters of the Moon National Monument

The first steep ascent, you and I reach
the rim, a vista of black lava flow on one side

of us, a plunging, dormant crater on the other.
It sounds like glass, you say, nudging a porous

cinder nugget with your foot. Like two lone
astronauts, we stand in deep silence for a moment,

staring off into miles and millennia of a broken,
breakable earth. We hike over ridges, down

into craters, leap small ravines of fractured
magma, cinder's silty crunch under our soles.

I enter an ancient cavemouth, look inside.
Somewhere in there, millions of bats hang—secrets

the dusk will later open. As we walk, I fly
back through my life, sharing stories, stopping

when I worry I'm boring you. To my surprise,
you say, gently: *No, keep going, I'm really interested.*

How does anything grow here? In seeming desolation
life somehow thrives; everywhere tufts of spiky pale

flowers—thistle, aster and sagebrush dot the charred hills.
Beneath us, dusty sandstone shifts from ash to rust.

Only yesterday I'd said *on journeys like this we leave
old selves behind.* Yet, on ground scorched into rock

and ruin, it's tempting to see annihilation as event,
the making made, the being fixed, the eruption history,

the flow forever petrified. At the end of the trail, we sit
and you ask: *now can I share part of my life story*

with you? When a heart far wider than mine opens:
rift of blinding beauty, river of fire and blood,

of what was solid: fluid again. And I become
no longer your father, and you no longer my son.

Kate Hanson Foster

Anatomy of a Home

On every wall, knotted pine
bares lifelines.

Checks and splits flaw the wood
beams where fibers compress

into empty space. A daughter bites
her graham cracker into the shape

of a moon and laughs. A son fusses
over a puzzle on the floor—piece

by piece, bucks interlocking
on an unknown hill. They are waiting

for the first flakes of another storm,
the baby to wake from her nap.

Outside, bald flashes of wood
ache where ice fractured branches.

Cells harden beneath the crack
of bark, the way silica remains

liquid as it is super-cooled into glass.
A father is away at work—wind pulls

and stretches the tree roots.
A mother, the heartwood, alive

inside death, log on log into fire.

Kate Hanson Foster

She Was

She was mother. She was
body in house, dedicated

to bleach until shine
spilled across porcelain.

She was feminist—flame
struggling to break from candle.

She swallowed a pill
that removed herself from her-self.

She joined ordinary people
in the bottom-up insurgency.

She plucked delicate excesses;
untied God from her body

and let her skin spill
in the purple penitential light.

She was problematic
to the coddled American mind.

She had the eye of a woman looking
to leap from her own painting.

She was not old or wise,
and no longer pretty.

She was a waterless
blessing. An empty garden.

And when she fucked
she was man and woman,

crashing her-selves on herself,
glad to be crushed by her own redundancy.

She was suffering—
cinder flashing heat back into fire.

Kate Hanson Foster

Selva Oscura

I. Purgatorio

Should you decide that I might be saved, consider the ink
of my wicked pride—my white overexposed nakedness.

I am an unplaceable woman. A tired bitch
announced in heavy footfalls down the stairs.

The bird of my lover's heart sags on the vine like fruit
over-fattening between two worlds.

The cuckoo clock teases out time, with every door slap
my old dog throws a sigh from his dirty floor bed.

I want my dog to die. His rancid fur stains oil in the hardwood,
his knowing eyes beg me to let him perish.

I thought I understood love, but it is just a feral
need of the body, a tedious, aging thirst.

Chemicals flush through mazes—a regular sickness
reaching out, but my pen needs to make a name of it.

If Hell is fire then may heaven be a cool wet wind
at the car window for my dog's final drive.

In the middle of this dark wood, let leaves drop
into dumb air. Let me glitter between the two halves.

II. Paradiso

The ash of my dog is not what I expected.
There are shards of bone—fragments in the fragment of his
weight,

I let myself say the world has no meaning.
The words leak effortlessly, like blood rushing from a wound.

I thought myself more a woman than *lie down*
lie down. The man has needs, the man has chemicals too.

The children are each their own empyrean. It is enough to have
them, fleeting as it may be, like an unkindness of ravens, and
then none.

My dead dog was handed back like a bag of flour. I placed him
into
a small box on the shelf. I lie to the children and say *he's still here*.

Maybe we are no more than our human peaks. The heaven of us
lives
in the swells and stretches before the inevitable crack.

I stroke the cedar box of my dog's dust. Good
old boy. My purest friend. I do not feel you at all.

A child's hand fits into a mother's like two gears clinked together.
Two gears clink together and that is the still-point-poem before
the turn.

Emily Franklin

Gallery of Extinct Birds

No one told me I would reach
an age in which I seek out
birds, finding joy in gold dust
finches, ruby throated hummingbirds
nasty on the feeder, fighting with their own—
and that we would lean our bellies into the cold

kitchen counters watching them peck
or sip or eat or steal thistle seed
we put out for one kind of bird, but another
takes. Not the long gone great auk with
my grandfather's estuary eyes but those
still with us: jays and cardinals
crested like rival baseball teams,
kingfishers stoic in the eye but desperate
in the stomach, the way I crave coffee most
the night before, thinking ahead to morning
when I will go through the routine I have
made for myself, structured as a nest and just
as comforting, as these birds flit around me

as though they are my thoughts or my husband's
as though we found them in the yard after all
this time when of course they were there before
or were drawn in by the array of feeders, by suet
and seeds we set out for them, desperate

as we are now that our children are in and out
by foot or car or sheer emotional
distance which is, too, what the birds bring—
winging beauty and impermanence just by being
birds and I wish someone had explained this to me

that I would reach the age in which I notice birds,
in which instead of hearing their song, I am calling them home.

Emily Franklin

After Scattering Ashes in August

I am learning to gather seeds—garlic chives, marigolds
both vanilla and pylon orange, coneflowers proudly bald
after I pluck each slim black-tipped seed and keep them
labeled in an envelope to dry and I am reminded

of my grandmother who with her knees in the dirt told me
gardening is the truest form of hope which swells
my empty body as I gather these although she will not see
and would have looked at my penmanship and sighed

because she found hope & errors everywhere
which kept her present, focused as the animals that
prowled her garden & once took up residence
in the driver's seat of her car where sunflower seeds

had spilled, forming neat rows in the seat seams
as though she had planted them and because the animals—
chipmunks, maybe—seemed so comfortable she allowed
them run of them place until they'd raised their young

walking instead of driving which she told me was good
for her and for the animals who left without warning
and whose presence I think she missed, though she smiled
and began driving again, hopeful they would come back

each season as though they'd all made a pact—
and she would not urge them elsewhere if they promised
to clean up what she'd spilled and I am asking the same
of the dirt today, to hold what I'm taking and make it useful.

Pauletta Hansel

So Maybe It's True

poetry doesn't make you a better person,
and the news that can be found there
is like some gone week's Sunday Times
tossed in its clear green wrapper
beneath the neighbor's car.
The one who died
and no one came to find him,
and you didn't knock on his door
when his trashcan of carryout chicken and ribs
sat spilling its own kind of news.
Maybe.
But, oh, to live awhile as marrow
in someone else's bones,
to breathe her breath upon the mirror
held up to your life,
doesn't it make you want
to fling open whatever door you come to,
doesn't it make you want to try?

Pauletta Hansel

Things I Would Never Say in a Poem

I love you. I love you more. I love you to the moon and back without at least a whiff of rocket fuel and powdered Tang for the journey. And too, I would have said that Tang would never be in any poem of mine, but there it is. The way my dead mother a lifetime ago plopped the top from a jar of it onto a lidless orange teapot because it fit. The way my husband every morning of our marriage states the moreness of his love with such conviction we were five years in, at least, before it dawned on me the phrase had not originated with him. And dawn without a streak of orange scratched through blueblack sky? Not in my poem. This poem, though, has its own way of saying what it wants to, of taking any old thing and not even trying to make it new. It's not a competition. My husband says that too, and so I let him win. That's how much I love you, I say.

Pauletta Hansel

En/vy

The Old French,
        how well they understood
the danger
        of outside looking in:
                videre from *weid*, "to see,"
        at the green root
of all wisdom
        and wit, invidious or otherwise,
of twit and video,
        our kaleidoscopic view.

One of   the seven
        deadlies,
                the ten
        shall nots.

Dante's purgatorial eyes
wired shut.

Cain over Abel,
        the Towers of Babel
                        and Trump—only pride
more weights the soul.

The evil eye is cast,
        uneasy,
from the head
that wears the crown.

Jeff Hardin

Without One Plea

Sometimes half the day passes and I've still not found
a way in, an angle of inventiveness, so that the whole thing
doesn't feel like the dullest experiment with my dumb self
at the helm. Is there a reason why I'm here, an undisclosed
location, and not on a mountainside, say, in North Carolina
or Montana, and is there a reason I think to ask such questions
when, just as likely, I might have been content with looking
out a window early mornings over coffee, two more hours
of overtime the only thing I'm thinking. For some reason
I go back a lot to one day with my siblings running down
the aisles and through the pews of a country church,
some Saturday, I'm guessing, the four of us called back
from foster homes to visit grandparents, sneaking off
to push those wide doors open. Churches weren't locked
back then. We crawled beneath the pews in mock wars.
We opened hymn books and bellowed mocking voices
at the rafters. We passed collection plates to figments.
It's likely I'm the only one who carries forth this memory,
the wooden floors, the window's stain of light across
our faces. The oldest, I stayed awake to listen for
a mother's car returning not returning long into the night.
Weekends over, we went to different homes. Soon enough,
we settled into other selves, other voices, other rooms,
and grew to be the absence of each other's presence,
the presence of each other's absence. I hear their squeals
of glee being chased, the end of our time together already
beginning. Is there a reason why my brother, decades later,
stepped into the presence of a bus he didn't see or hear,
into a grave I've never seen and have no way of finding
now? I'm here, not there, wherever I am, whoever I am.
I'm him, not me, sometimes. I'm that collection plate
borne along above the absence of a congregation.
I lift my face and sing off key some ancient words I can't
remember to faces forty years have turned to figments too.
I like to think they mattered once and rose above that
holy place—no one home to tell us not to enter, not to leave.

Jeff Hardin

Leaning Toward Another

Some things I'm content to let go of, though
don't ask which things, or when, or why, since
even my trusted answers I can't completely
trust. After all, this morning a blue sky so easily
turned drab, and now the trees sway in a windy
gentleness that seems expectant, though trees lack
consciousness, of course; so what I see must be
my own need magnified. Maybe the rain will come.
Maybe this moment is a prophecy come true
about which I know nothing nor need to know.
I reach and tug loose an oak leaf, which might be
a prayer, though don't ask me what it seeks or praises;
don't ask me who this intercession has in mind;
don't ask *am I my brother's keeper* if you're not
prepared to hear. When one tree leans toward another,
I want to eavesdrop. I like to think they share
a brotherhood, though it's as clear to me as anyone
I'm speaking of myself. What if I am wrong, and
in the higher limbs are words we have to climb
to find and hear? What if I overturned a stone
and light shone forth? It's possible, even today,
the roots of my soul are entwined with another's.
I like to imagine a person speaking and his words,
like black skimmers, circling an inland pond.
I'm content to let an hour pass and trust the sky.
Some words come back having touched some image
far out we can't see from where we wait all morning.
How lovely the glide of their dipped wings

                                        steering away.

Marc Harshman

A Red Hen and a Small Woman

A red hen goes scratching inside its small house
        while hail gravels the roof
        and I watch a bent woman walk resolutely on
        into the racing fog and wonder where she's going.
Cows moan, horses nicker, the rooster crows once as if its neck's broken.
The famous quiet before descends, approaches complete stillness
        except for the slender trill of the random breeze.
Then the Oz scenes:
        the tin roof on the corncrib flaps and screams,
        dust wraiths flute into the black afternoon.
The farm sleeps on.
And in a corner of the canvas the sky begins to lift its blue eyelid.
Eventually, the storm rolls up its coven of loud children
        into its gray rug and goes off home.
Mother yells for us to come out of the storm cellar
        now the morbid fear of tornado's gone.
Grandfather smiles.
Myself, though, fixed at the window, hidden,
        am following that woman as she goes further
        on into something I think is longer and deeper
        and wider and more dreadful and wondrous
        than any of my mother's fearsome storms.
I crawl into Grandfather's lap.
When I begin telling him what I saw and what I think
        about who that small woman is and where she's gone
        and what might become of us all, he keeps smiling.
The sun shone, the crops showed solidarity and rose up, drought stayed away,
        as did locusts and frogs and other wild misfortunes.
The fog will come again.
The storm will rain with ice.
The chicken will scratch for kings and queens.
Then the small woman will come, doggedly walking,
        and grandfather will go on smiling, holding still,
        as will we all, when the weather decides it's had enough,

and we grow patient, at last, waiting and listening hard
to the thin sound of that hen scratching
for something a boy might plant
that takes him to the stars.

Marc Harshman

Two Roads

He went further down the road than intended.
Getting back took him around the bend
      and so much longer to get back.
She didn't wait.
Her anger, so long simmering, took her
      where it needed to go.
She took the bus, another road,
      and would let the eagle fly
      on Friday and Monday and forever's foreseeable future.
He looked over the horizon, could see
      the commotion only in past tense.
The birds no longer told him their secrets.
He'd have to figure it out himself.
Had he loved her?
And the un-struck match in that haystack?
So much came down to time,
      its ineffability, and how much of it
      he'd squandered or misunderstood.
He should've stood still, silent,
      counted slow towards serenity,
      not taken that walk,
      not slammed that door,
      not said what he said
      on the way to this walk.
Should have, could have, and now
      will she or won't she?
Like black petals on a green flower in a snowy field,
      like sullen birds roosting in the shadows,
      where there used to be trees
      and a woman that sang,
                    sang like this
    even as he persists
    on trying to find some way home.

Stephen Hundley

To Pete,
who crushed my dog's skull with a hammer

Let me walk with you
across our front yard,
    where the grass runs brown
    where the pool has killed it
        forever-dead. I know
        you hate that.
The look of it, a stain
from your porch.
    The dog's bark
    keeps you awake.
        We received
        your letter.
We are away. You hear
the howl and the cry.
    See how fur sheds
    in clouds this time of year
        like cotton rolling, sticking
        to the ground.
Take her from the kennel,
    dragged by the collar,
        and load her into your van.
Take her to the woods
    by the water tank.
        By the marsh and the nothing place
        I played as a boy.
What sort of thing uncoils
    in your belly
        when you do
        what you do?
When you drag her
by the tail now
    to the marsh and the crabs
        where do you think you are?

Stephen Hundley

But What About Forgiveness

What about living angels
& the Methodist women
selling pork dinner tickets
& nailing my written sins
to a plywood cross?

What about Offering It Up
to a famous chocolate bust
of John Wesley, foiled in gilt
like a Ferrero Rocher?

Say what about picking rocks
from a riverbed / holding
each until it's blood-warm
& nailing my whispered sins
to the water's deepest gouge?

What about coming home
to those first, sharp prayers
made on gas receipts & bits
of shale / & What about them
waiting / rattling serpentine
               in the toe box
              of my boot?

Does the Enoree River Remember Hans Einstein?

Albert Einstein's son Hans worked as a hydrologist on a river near Greenville, South Carolina. His research weir is still there in the river but reached only by canoe. —for Dan Richter

Ask the scientist and the geopoet
in a small green fiberglass canoe
pulling over deadfall from
two miles upstream
to reach this altar to the past.

Ask woody debris, carbon storage,
wildlife bridges, a deer stampede,
perplexed suburbanites lounging
on stream side.

Ask arrival by self-propulsion
to that hidden forgotten spot
on the river.

Ask Hans Einstein's lab
built in 1930s, a research weir
for measuring sediment
bed load in the river.

Ask Einstein's aged instrument
formed of Depression concrete.

Ask the thick river comb,
piano keys
the river plays for us.

Ask the formed shoots the current
drains through downstream
like a boulder garden.

Ask the scientist up to his knees drumming
on concrete with his paddle,
making wild river jazz.

Ask if an argument
can be made that sediment
is not something to understand.

Ask about eighty years measured
not in history but in floods and droughts.

Ask Einstein's very artifact—
approached by water on a late fall Sunday.

Ask Einstein's concrete
Ozymandias cast on gneiss,
slick with algae,
yet still not yielding.

Ask decades of floods.

Ask the jet taking off
and landing at the nearby airport.

Ask poison ivy and greenbriar.

Ask the sweetgum snapped
by high water somewhere
upstream and strung
like a bow in current.

Ask cedars on the far side,
the only green.

Ask, hence, the last of fall color.

Ask Gibbs Shoals downstream stretching
all the way to the Vietnamese Catholic church.

Ask the scientist's tippy canoe
still upright like a fallen leaf.

Ask the schema we've brought along, a ghost
of the service to science
Einstein performed.

Ask his fluvial data stored off-site
in the National Archives.

Ask the territory.

Ask the mystery, these slab
fingers laid parallel
with slots for some contraption.
To control the flow?
Ask a flight of doves above.

John Lane

The Worry-Oak

The storm is a retreating army, foraging
our hidden provisions. The worry-oak
roots are sodden oatmeal, not nourishing
ropes to climb to heaven, not the sinews
the worry-oak rides to eternity.
The roots snap in least wind
but we can't hear them.
Instead we watch the hula dance
above our rafters, thinking that is
the big show. We gauge the gale
of grievances weather pitches at
us, mortal and secure in this
thimble of human certainty we call
a home. That stabbing music?
Acorns tap dancing on the roof,
bound for a sodden yard where
squirrels would mire in our acres
if they would abandon their
huts of sticks high in the air.
They've made our mistake,
thinking they can sleep it out,
nestled among a compost of
insulting leaves, heir to what
remains every fall of a proud
forest, a rainbow so striking
that inside thumbtacks hold
the scene to our wall in places
where trees are now two by fours,
ghosts of the beasts that threaten
our surety. Dawn is hours away.
Rain pulls me from sheets made
a nest by wear, but rising is not
enough to quell the fear the worry
oak outside our window will
split our house in two, a sandwich
on the yard's cutting board. First light.
I stare up into the dilemma of limbs.

George Ella Lyon

Family Scripture

It's better not to know.
If you knew, how would you stand it?

It's better not to cry.
If you start, how would you stop?

It's better not to feel.
If you feel, you might tell.

It's better not to tell.
Secrets keep us safe

It's better not to ask.
If we answered, you'd be sorry.

All you need to know is
It's better not to know.

George Ella Lyon

Tom Thumb Wedding Photo, 1956

Just turned seven
I am singing
in an itchy turquoise sequined
evening gown
clutching a bouquet of rosebuds,
ham-scented by their sojourn
in the fridge.

I am not the bride
but the second singer
in this end-of-first-grade rite
and I love my song
Because you come to me
with naught save love
though I don't know
what kind of love that is.

I do know my Aunt Stokes
stitched me this dress,
Daddy brought home the roses,
and Mother baked the biscuit
that put the shine
on my patent leather shoes.

George Ella Lyon

In Passing

So
   my
      mother
              and I
      were in
   the
one
   depart
      ment
              store
      in my
   home
town
   and
      we met
              my
      general
   science
teacher
   and
      her
              daughter
      coming
   down
stairs
   as
      we
              were
      going
   up.
Up
   to
      where
              I
      used
   to
buy
   chubbies
      in

                    the
          kids'
      depart
ment
    and
          where
                    I
          now
      proudly
wore
    a
          nine
              which
          I
    hoped
would
    be
          a
                seven
          maybe
      even
a
    five
          before
                    I
          got
      married.
And
    Joy
          Rice,
                my
          former
      teacher
said,
    by
          way
              of
          hello,
    Isn't
life
    better
          than
                anything?

Tiffany Melanson

Visitation: Tomoka Correctional Institution

You won't admit it. The names alive are like the names / In graves.
— Terrance Hayes

My brother is lead-chipped metal,
pimp walk in blue prison jumpsuit.
He is dead black skin.

I am the smell of salt
on his neck. I peel the dead skin
from his body like a sunburn.

Brother unearths us from the grave
our father dug for our mothers. We are the soil
formed from their murdered bodies.

When we breathe again
our names are different than the ones given to us.
We speak for the first time.

No one in the prison is awake
to see us turn to seed in the palm
of each other's hands.

Tiffany Melanson

New Testament

for Carl

During my third visit to prison we play cards:
Skipbo, Uno, Rummy, Spades, Phase Ten.
My brother says, "Somebody took the instructions
out the boxes a long time ago. Ain't nothin' here sacred."

We make the rules up the way we did as children.
We shuffle the decades old decks, so soft they surrender
without a sound.

I've run out of dog-eared memories to reference in conversation,
so, I'm thankful for the aging cards in need of shuffling,
for our clumsy memory of the stated rules,
for your homeboy and his old lady sliding into the seats next to us,
for a commissary line so long, it skims the concrete walls
with twenty bodies before our turn, when I say,
"Order anything you want."

This is the visit you tell me about the twenty years
you kept our father's name on your waiting list, excluding
the names of others, before acknowledging
he would never show up.

Five hours later, I hunch over my phone in the prison parking lot
to look up the instructions to every game we played.
On the back of the commissary receipt I write the scripture
we'll follow during all future visits:

Use a standard deck of cards (no Jokers).
Make a tally of the running score.
Put down your sets and runs.
The game continues until a player lays down
all the cards in his hand.

Tiffany Melanson

Color Theory

When I visit my brother in prison
every body is black or brown except
the men with guns.

I read once in an article on color theory
black is not a color, it absorbs
the visible spectrum and reflects nothing.
A black object may look black,
but still reflect light.

Black is the absence of color.

In the workshop the white men ask me,
*What's the point of all the references
to race in your poems? Aren't you more
than just black?*

Black's existence as a color depends
on the object it is transmitted through.

Black is a color dependent on how the receiver
takes in information about color.

Black is only a color when the color agents
are tangible objects.

Like the weight of a boy's body
against asphalt, left in the street to burn
his blackness into white light.

Like the body of the author of this poem.

Like the smell of metal on my brother's hands
as he reaches to touch my face
for the first time in twenty-five-years.

Tiffany Melanson

Hurricane Season

I.

That day the hurricane's breath licked Florida's
thick back, the wind as hard as our father's
hands against our swollen legs as we lied
to save us. *Did you take it? Tell the truth.*
I didn't know yet that no apology
could fix not having said the right words
to begin with. I was five. Should we have
understood already which objects belonged
to us and which did not? My brother and I
sat in our father's studio for hours after
watching him sleep off the whiskey, lacing
our small bodies into a tapestry of shame
the color of a fresh bruise. *Remember this*
he said to me as the lights shuttered off.

II.

He said to me when the lights shuttered off,
Stay quiet. Lightening flickered and sparked
against the ash gray sky. In the narrow hallway
we lit and re-lit the shrinking wick
of a dozen small candles long enough
to see before losing sight again.
Did I know this would be the last time
I'd see my brother as himself before our father
took him away? Would I remember this?
I was thirteen. For hours, alone
together in the dark we appeared
and disappeared to each other.
I finally understood what objects
belonged to me and which did not.

III.

I learned my children belonged to me and they did not
the day the shutters split and shattered against the house

until the wind slowed to nothing but breath.
Will the lights come back on? I'm scared.
Wind had skinned the curtains back to window
and bones. *Are you listening to me*
anymore? The air was a wet blanket of ash
through the window's broken teeth. I was afraid
to open the hallway door to see the damage.
My children asked me again,
Will the lights come back on? I was thirty-three.
I didn't know. I tried to remember
what my brother had taught me.
I told them, *I'll open the door*
knowing if the roof had caved in I would dig
a hole through the earth big enough to save them.

Jim Minick

Good Dirt

Already I have tasted fire.
Tongue to tongue,
I have licked
its heat and flame,
smelled hair
singed in my nose.

Already I have heard
the pop of skin
after it blistered.
Such pain I did not know
until the nerves went numb
from the bright explosion.

Let me tell you:
Fire's deepest secret
is a heart that has no color,
and in that heart,
the rumble and roar
disappear.

When I die,
the tongues will lick me again,
only more fully
and only after my spirit
has already leapt.

Ashes from bone
make good dirt.

Jim Minick

Stress Test

A phone call at the start
to slap me from sleep. Or

does it begin before,
when a gas explosion

scorched my arm and face?
Or before that with cells

colliding like flint and
steel to spark and grow? What

nucleus of stress em-
bedded in Y and X

to grow into that al-
most obliterating

pitch dark passage of birth?
Or did this stress begin

generations back with
blood of running and blood stopped?

Anyway, the call: *We need
more tests*, the voice explains,

so, of course, I say yes.
Next day I wait alone

with Gideon's black book
and *Wheel of Fortune* loud.

Then Nurse punctures skin to
plunge liquid into vein.

Nuclear isotopes,
she explains. *To get a*

better picture. We watch
the tiny Chernobyls

disappear. *They'll be gone*
in sixty hours, if you

drink lots of water. I
drink three cups and want more.

Next I lie to watch a space-
craft hover over chest

beaming my heart across
the galaxy of this room.

Don't move, Nurse warns before
she leaves. So I stifle

each cough, ignore all itches.
The machine hums and clicks.

Minutes become eons
until finally it stops.

I breathe and scratch and cough
and think of the four *s's*

in *stress test,* hissing snakes
of steam *ssss-ing* from valves.

No nuclear explosions,
yet. So I return to wait

in a place invented
by stress: cement compressed

to pounds per inch; glass from sand
burned clear; wood, wind-shaken,

rings curling a dark heart—
all must pass. Or else.

This is why I am here:
Once last month when I tried

to rest, my heart fluttered
like a wren and then slammed

the bone bars of my chest
for just a moment—

before it calmed, unlike
the panic in my head.

At last, Doc appears
while Nurse connects

electrodes and I tread
the rolling mill. *Your heart*

looks good, Doc says, then adds,
So far. Soon I'm huffing,

staring at a heart poster.
I ask how the blood moves.

Doc says, *This is the world's*
best pump, proud like he made it.

Man-made pumps are only
a third as good. He taps.

Oxygen-depleted blood
comes in here. His pen maps

blood from heart to lungs to
heart to brain. *A closed system,*

nothing better. I'm sweating
now and holding tight, steep

ground whirring under foot.
Yet I get no closer

to that heart. I breathe hard,
watch the monitor with Doc.

This looks good, he nods. *Yours
went up real smooth, no hitch.*

I'm going to slow you down.
Soon I walk on flat ground.

The whirring dies. No more
hurry to go nowhere.

You're fine, Doc smiles. *No need
to invade this time.*

*A little arrythmia,
a hiccup of the heart.*

At home, I hike the woods
to heave ax over and

over, my body a pump
that *thunks* each round of oak,

riving the heart to reveal
a salvation of sorts

and the slow truth of fire.

Theresa Monteiro

Some Advice

If a learned man scans
the work of your mind and finds
the meter lacking (unrefined?)
put a wolf in your poem.
Because a wolf is not a symbol,
it's a mammal, a carnivore.
Like rusty train wrecks (in which
steel cargo cars lie crumpled
in a field beside aloof cattle) or
someone else's suffering, it's hard
to look away from a wolf.
Make him surprisingly thin
through the hips and thick around
the forelegs and chest. He is just
steps from the shadows
of old conifer trees, bare trunked near
the ground for having shaded each other
out of flourishing. There should be
a little snow on the ground, a veneer,
with sharp grasses poking through, little
spears of the earth around his paws.
The ambiguity of not knowing
if we are headed toward winter
or spring keeps the reader's eye
moving from line to line because
who can relax when a wolf,
(eyes much smaller than
legend would have it, much closer together
on his triangle face, and more focused
than the eyes of a loyal horse or family dog)
is present? When he turns toward
your reader, make sure it's only
his head that rotates—his body
still oriented toward a grassy valley, mountains

just beyond—where they meet, invoke
the blue-green color
of a bruise, healing.

Theresa Monteiro

All That is Broken

Here are some things a person can fix:
A flat tire, though, sometimes
the tire's not fixed, just
replaced; a bad haircut,
but, if it must be fixed
now, the one solution is to
take away more. Waiting
for new growth is not fixing,
it's patience. A wooden spindle
cracked in half when
a chair's knocked over in
a fit of anger, can be smothered
in wood glue and
clamped with a vice. Sometimes
you need new parts, sometimes
you need mercy. See the shepherd
boy in Germanic-looking shorts and
funny hat cast in porcelain? He has that
dreamy look figurines like to take,
an ornamental gaze, a self-indulgent gaze
of unnamed sorrow. The real boy leaping
from cushion to flowered cushion,
arms in the shape of an airplane,
will knock the figure
from the shadow box
(a ping of fissured porcelain
on a pinewood floor)
and having looked at nothing sorrowful
in all his life, will afterwards,
feel ashamed. And will afterwards
apply himself to fixing:
chairs and tchotchkes,
bicycle chains, lawn mowers, picture frames—
but wondering, always, how
to fix the whole world?

Theresa Monteiro

Suburban Hymn

Stuck in my craw:
To say, *I praise you*, is not
to praise. It rattles
hollow—one penny in a tin can bank.
The can in an empty room sounds
its echoing clang, the clang
diminishing, the way
a cry for help falls deeper
into canyons in cowboy movies—
the half-life of sound, shrinking. But the sound
of flattery (which has volume)
is not praise. Praise the world
by making lists?
-An old hand, veiny, along a banister in half-light
-A honeybee landing on a curved branch of catmint, bobbing
-Clean fire on a cold night
No.
Say praise and mean *tell the truth*.
Say praise but mean, *I don't deserve what is here*.
What is here is the penny—
its small, raised face so
serious and precise.
Who decided the least worthy
coin should be the loveliest color?
Who invented the tin can bank, soft
beans swapped for
copper-joy of small value?
It rattles, not hollow, but makes
solid sounds like pangs (of hunger, regret)
and a baby laughs at the sound,
a deep, flowering laugh, growing
louder as it spreads. She laughs
at the penny sound, at how
silly all the small things are.

Robert Morgan

Bone Song

To make music from a bone
that's hollowed out and cut with stops
is a kind of resurrection.
The skeleton with flesh long gone
and bleached to startling whiteness has
both lightness and the strength to hold
with knowing hands, to kiss the ports,
as death becomes a melody
of breath and fingering, to sculpt
the air itself with color, time,
to call up spirits out of earth
and prove time is a miracle,
a stream the music sails beyond
in relic from the common ground.

Robert Morgan

Cairn

What is the human need to set
one stone on stone, the loose rocks brought
to this particular place and stacked?
The scattered stones will call until
they're found and chosen to lie flat,
with slate on slate like pages of
some rough account, memorial to
the source from which the pieces broke,
a cenotaph or elegy
that's held by force of gravity,
as sign connecting here with
the horizon, approximate
to human form, to show resistance
to erosion's sprawl, with strength
among the scree of fragments, as
a monument to stand above
the natural wash and wear of all,
to honor the imagined whole.

Robert Morgan

The Clouds Today

A universe of billowing
and cosmic conflagrations, stacked
so high they seem to topple
down miles and miles on top of us.
To look this high creates a sense
of falling helplessly away.
Titanic cliffs of vapor dwarf
the hills and humble fields below,
more monumental than the heads
and features on Mount Rushmore. But
the undersides of clouds are smoothed
and flattened by the surface winds,
though higher up the currents twist
and boil in all directions at
the different elevations with
a kind of wildness sculpted by
the knife of turbulence, so far
above the local air we breathe,
in heaven's mad complexity.

Lisa Parker

Smoke, Salt, Sweet
Manhattan, September 28, 2001

Burnt metal still stings the nostrils
weeks later, drifts on perverse winds,
settling into flag stripes, sometimes random pieces
of paper, still charred or rain-wrinkled and stuck
to building sides, all the still-upright things
that gather and hold.

But for all the shattered and shuttered things,
wooden crates at the Fairway Market
still line the storefront and I touch dusky apricots,
sunny lemons and purple eggplants,
red and yellow peppers, bin after box after crate
of cucumbers, kale, and radish,
brown and red onions still sloughing skin onto Yukons
and Idahos beneath them.

I walk to O'Donnell's pub and Robin
has a corner table at the window
where we can watch the sidewalks
and sky over mugs of black
and tan that sweat the wood grain,
small plates of aged gouda, pocked and nutty,
an applewood-smoked gruyere and deeply orange
Vermont cheddar, a fuchsia stripe of Portofino red,
crooked and imperfect.
We watch the silenced tv in the corner, its banner
still scrolling estimates of casualties, something
about a dirty bomb radius but I am intent
on the soppressata and wild boar salami delivered to us,
brick red and fatty speckled, it is
pungent as any wild thing left to its own devices,
and Robin says *I'll bet this is what it tastes like*
to wander the woods rooting for acorns and hickories.
I don't tell her those boars

would trample her and eat everything
but her belt buckle.

The next plate, a perfectly symmetrical circle
of prosciutto-wrapped melon, ebony pools
at the edges, a balsamic reduction
to dredge the sweet, salty bites through.
Peter Jennings' face appears in the background,
then a random person showing how to seal a window
with duct tape in case of another anthrax attack.
We watch his mouth move, a familiar muted thing, until
we've had enough and walk the few blocks where
the bread and sugared air is a path, a reprieve,
the tiny Italian café where there are no TVs, just
the orderly crowd, everyone leaning into glass cases,
Neopolitans and glazed fruit tortas rearranged and replaced,
pistachio biscottis, pignolatas, lemon and orange crocettes,
the frozen cases of bright pink gelatos and chicory brown spumoni.
We settle on a chocolate amaretto cake, admire the dusting
of confectioner's sugar and raspberry glaze,
slow ourselves in our final bites,
linger over the plate, push tines into last crumbs,
watch the sidewalks and sky, the locals
who hold each other's elbows
as they speak.

Lisa Parker

Hillbilly Transplant: Seed and Scatter

The prayer plant you gave me is dying.
On the windowsill overlooking 71st Street it wilts
even now with this light Spring rain.
If I was a diviner, this would be the sign
that says *Run, girl*.

First was the prayer plant – early in love,
when we were still mango and pepino dulce,
heart-shaped chirimoya and blood orange filled to bursting,
sweet sticky things that lingered on skin and tongue.
Still midday smiles at thoughts of night, Peruvian flutes
and flamenco guitar in the background, our bodies
moving dark over light.

First was the prayer plant – before the table
you grabbed at a parking lot auction in Alphabet City,
or the handmade candle, cornflower blue
and lavender, big as the Inca Cola bottle mold,
before the pin from Lima I suspect was really
for someone else, the one you put in a leather pouch
you made from old boots, laced with sinew,
my initials burned onto that tight brown skin
with a heated paperclip.

First was the prayer plant - a cutting
from the wooden planter perched
on your radiator, a birthday gift
you set down inside a terra cotta pot,
worked the soil as you rehomed it,
covered the excised roots over,
pushed until nothing moved, explained
in both languages as you pressed my body,
soil still on your hands, how those soft oval leaves
turn upward, *abierto*, at night, back down again
with sun break, sultry murmur
against neck and collarbone.

First was the prayer plant – before nights
of too much rum and pisco, late arrivals,
your late-night reconnaissance
trolling online for a younger body while mine,
all 30 years of it, still hummed in your bed,
love-drunk and willfully blind to ever-refilling glasses
of vodka-heavy chicha morada, to anything

beyond the sight of you cooking rice in clay pots
you brought back from your hometown in Cusco,
the classical guitar against your bare chest reclined on the sofa,
oil canvasses you painted that covered the bedroom walls –
gitanos and toreros, my favorite behind the bed, a flamenco dancer,
crimson and cobalt skirts painted mid-arc, arms
above her head, eyes closed, her perfect gypsy body
poised in sweaty ascension.

First was the prayer plant- and last,
last was the rain-soaked midnight walk
from 98th and Broadway to the subway, that final
humiliation of being put out
not with a fury or a passion
but with an assault of indifference, a disinterest
no artist's canvas could unmar.

I should bring the plant back inside.
It did nothing to me, after all.
But there is something cleansing in the dropping,
one by one, of these leaves, their pale green and fuchsia
slapped against the marble sill by this surging rain.

Linda Parsons

The Light around Trees in Morning

So much light, I think it's caught fire,
the paperbark maple self-immolating—
but it's only the coppery scrolls' silhouette
facing east. Someone once important
to me planted this tree, led friends to this
very spot as if it was the only blaze,
the only crown in the garden.

Importance ebbs in time, keeping its own
mystery, and we're left on our knees,
in cinders, smoldering ash, as I was,
turning to what's more important—
clover in the iris, overrun with thyme
and chocolate mint, the scrawl
of minor serpents to read and expel.

A woman alone makes good headway
in the weeds, my corona aflame, unscrolling
like seraphims' swords at the entrance
of nothing and everything Edenic. Sometimes
I think light comes only when we're bowed
too low to notice our leaves and limbs
burnished by morning, our bodies
in spontaneous combustion.

Linda Parsons

From a Distance

Mother died last night, / Mother who never dies.
—Louise Glück, Faithful and Virtuous Night

The third day, before morning coffee,
lyrics came and filled me with knowing.
Your last cent spent on Earth left me broke
not with your going, but with years hot
to the tongue. Lyrics stirred release
at long last in spirit's rising: From a distance,
there is harmony, sent to me this third day
of mourning/not mourning. For all we know,

God is watching us, a gardener toeing
stones from the mouth that never echoed
the why of our turning, unknowing.
Our spent garden prickly and dry
then as now, but for your message
from a distance this third day from dying.
My cup warm not with old dregs rising,
a certain peace left on the tongue, undying.

Linda Parsons

Come Home

Tonight the gloaming is a shadowbox
of corridors, time-dimmed like the Sunday
School room of ancient ladies my grandmother
called Miss in formality: Miss Rose Davis,
Miss Rose Harris. The ancient world mapped
those yellowed walls—Paul's travels
through Antioch in Syria, Macedonia, Athens,
Corinth. Paul the tentmaker mending
the knotted nets, converted in a flash
to a fisher of men.

Cicadas starting late this summer, not yet
a blast like Paul's fiery Damascus moment—
more like my grandmother singing
from the Broadman, her vibrato rising
and settling around me, already asleep
in her lap. Take me, take me, mememe,
they rapture in high fidelity, their invitation
in the half-light: Ye who are weary,
come home.

Nearing seventy, my own gloaming,
I watch only for the soft tent of night
to fall. Insect voices I wait for all year
call from the canopy, primitive and unnamable.
The portals of home always lit, always open,
map where I've tripped and was pardoned
beyond reason, blasted deaf and blind
by mercy. Take me, I call, me,
and they open wider still.

Daniel Romo

Faster and Noticeably More Furious

I admit it's been a while since I watched a film
in the franchise, so I know I've missed a lot in

between sagas: births and deaths and resurrections,
street racing evolving to makeshift space missions.

I understand, firsthand, our lives all have sequels
in which plot twists occur, even though in a sense

we write our own scripts. But in which movie
did gearheads turn murderers? When did guns

become an addition to stick shifts? Somewhere in
the series, what began as friends sipping Coronas in

an Echo Park backyard segued into semi-automatics
used for self-defense in a Central American jungle.

Somewhere in my own story, I stopped to consider
the necessity of shots fired and the placement of

bullets and realized the only true target audience
is yourself. So how does the Toretto bloodline,

a map of open byways and highways, not speak to
every nerve in Dom's body pleading with him that

the finish line is only as sweet as the muscle car that
brought you there, and that the message isn't really

to go big, but to simply go home. We are taught to
keep our foot on the pedal and not let up, but in that

way are unable to savor the gust of air from the
checkered flag. Instead, we slide our hands across

our foreheads to wipe off the sweat from cleaving a
machete through the fronds of our own Amazon as if
violence is our only way out.

Daniel Romo

9th Inning

The singer and the actor have reunited after a two-decade
hiatus in which rappers and athletes and divorces have

interrupted the moments in between their first kiss and
most recent spotting in the club as if their newest merger

is an advertisement for indecisiveness and mid-life crisis
and makes me wonder if there is an expiration date on

loneliness, because to jump from person to person is not
a lost art, but an art in loss. And when the barista told me

she'd never be part of a marriage again because of all the
paperwork that accompanies the end of one, I pondered

if her half-empty coffee cup outlook would always be
worth the cost of never even considering a refill. My

favorite baseball team's closer continues to blow saves
and his manger continues to send him out at the end

of games which in non-baseball vernacular translates to
your boyfriend still hasn't proposed, and you want to believe the

next month is when he'll finally take your hints to heart. But what
we are willing to accept for ourselves and what we want is

the equivalent of dropping to a knee locked in limbo,
either having the strength to return to a standing position

or allowing our body to just fall face-first into the earth.
Sometimes we need to be the one to walk out of the

dugout towards the pitcher's mound, take the ball away
and say, "Kenley. Thanks… but you're done."

Moriel Rothman-Zecher

Memorial Sonnet

There was this dog on a train through the Czech Republic,
his head the size of a watermelon. He was loosed, and spit
flapped from his jowls. In the panic, the man checking tickets
forgot to ask if I was a Jew. I reached for the dog, all went quiet.
Citizens of Europe, bear witness, I felt the clamminess of his mouth
as he bit off half my pointer finger, like we agreed beforehand,
and leapt through a window, carrying part of me further south.
They got him on the coast, tranquilizers. He slumped into sand,
then they used a machine gun. They returned my finger's part,
along with his head in a plastic bag, warned me via chat to forget
the whole story. There was something to that, for when I started
to write this, I felt the scabbed-over flesh on my finger grow wet
and taut. They burst through, tiny whelps, tongues dripping drool.
Safe at last, I fell into grass, blood and spit on its tips like jewels.

Moriel Rothman-Zecher

Copyright

*"Sitting in the studio when they called to let me know
my song had made No. 1 in the USA."* —Max Martin

Everyone wrote "Footsteps," or so they
Claim, is the thing, except that actually
I did.

It came to me one night in a dream,
I mean, in a chatroom in my dream.

Crazy, right? Another user had just
DMed me some very unsettling images,
and He followed

Up with the poem. I know I won't get any credit,
This being Scandinavia and all, with its stringent

Regulations about who gets to write
Pop songs, but still, Lars and Sven

Do owe me a debt of gratitude for the time I gave them
Aubrey Graham's email, which they claimed
"to have lost?"

They asked me, the only living yid in Stockholm,
Knowing I had the login info to the Database.

Every time I looked down into the sand, in the
Weeks after letting the infamous father-son duo
into Drake's inbox like that,

I saw just one set of footsteps, which told me
I was being carried by the Lord, even though
I was suffering, you know?

Leona Sevick

Scorpling

She caught you just
as you emerged
from her operculum,
elevating abdomen,
arranging legs.

Gently she placed you
on her back,
watched over
your fragile body
with twelve sets of eyes,
held her breath
in book lungs as you
molted and hardened.

On days you'd climb down,
explore
until hungering
brought you back to her,
she'd lose sight of herself,
regret nights she craved
her life of solitude.

You'd return
until the day you didn't.

Rooted in the words *to cut*
                    is your name.

Did your mother's mad
loving, her venom,
make you stronger
than you would have been
otherwise?

Boy, I've told you
how we begin
is not always
how we end.

Leona Sevick

Familiar

In this fairytale cottage tucked into
an electric green mountain, circled by

snakes and every kind of biting thing,
she waits for him. The floors swept clean, cupboards

stocked with all that he loves, she clears spaces
for him to work, to heal. Cooking now, her

mind's knowing hands finger whole chickens, rub
pimpled flesh clean in warm running water,

handle wings like the folded arms of babes—
the slippery, delicate chest recalling

nighttime baths. She chops crone-knuckled ginger,
onions, a fistful of flat-leafed parsley

and drops them into steaming cauldrons slick
with dumplings. Slitting fat eye roasts, she stabs

them with garlic, baptizes with chenin
blanc. Squash she juliennes into lovely

legs. A sparkling brut sweats in a bucket
as she remakes the bed, folds hospital

corners, plumps the pillows, imagines hands,
manly and once proud, cup her breasts, caress

her waist then beckon her to straddle him,
to rock her hips gently then not gently.

Her fingers count out days ahead. Are there
enough to bring him back to what he was?

In this sort of fairytale there are no
demons, no cannibal witches to aid.

There is only this familiar scene: a
good woman setting right what is broken.

Darius Stewart

HIV Blues

Read me a poem about loss I say.
Are you on the mend? I say.

I shake my head no.
I need a poem to ease my anxiety I say.

Why are you anxious I say.
I've lost the compilation of all my favorite sad songs I say.

Have you ever tried listening to opera in foreign languages I say.
All opera is in foreign languages I say.

No, all good opera is in foreign languages I say.
But not to those who understand opera I say.

You mean those born in the country of the language I say.
No, those who understand out of the greatest miseries survives
the greatest beauty I say.

You mean the music and the singing I say.
I mean everything I say.

Darius Stewart

On the Bus
for Kasim

Riding from Knoxville to the Appalachian forests,
I'm hunched in the corner of my seat,
next to a man who seems to be unraveling,
striving for composure in the way
despondent men do: mouth agape
& drooling, eyes sunken as if his face
intends to make a cave of its own flesh.
He moans like there's some creation
struggling to be born, as if
he is reincarnating himself,
as if doing so will allow him a second
chance to avoid mistakes he made
in his past life. & I cannot help but feel
pity for him, as I recall another bus ride,
the number 10 that wound its way around
the heart of Knoxville, & you were there beside me,
breathing softly, I remember, so softly I felt
the machinery of the inner ears churning
to process the sounds you were making.
I asked what's the matter, & you hesitated.
So I persisted in the same way I did
when I urged you to make the long, cold walk
from your apartment to mine, to tell you
I tested negative when you were not
in the mood to celebrate as I had, only hours earlier,
with champagne & a lobster tail. & recalling
that moment, I realized why your breath
seemed to whisper. So I wept. Embarrassed.
Which coaxed more tears as I tried to learn compassion.
You said the virus had not taken its toll.
I was relieved. Or was it our years of friendship
that made me unafraid to touch,
to wrap my arms around,
to shoulder your grief.

But where is that compassion now?
This man is resting his bleached head on my shoulder.
For a moment I think it's yours.
But he mumbles about forsythia, four-leaf clovers.
& I'm frightened because I will love you
with the same passion that I wonder if anyone will clamor
to pay respects to this half-living man.
I push him against the window.
Scoot farther to the edge of my seat, shuddering
when I hear his head
knocking against a pane of glass.

Darius Stewart

Existing in the MRI machine after a seizure due to delirium tremens

is like deplaning in a slow single file
conveyer belt of sluggish passengers still wired
into their sleep modes since it's four in the morning
everyone shifting through the narrow aisle
gathering their wits their luggage but not
the human decency to maneuver with purpose
as Houdini once did to escape a straightjacket
padlocked inside a great tank of water
but turtling along as if shackled in ankle-cuffs
chains around their waists connecting more chains
in cross-sections of heavy metallic links
the length of their bodies
escorted on either side by guards
trundling in their own lackadaisical fashion
securing these passengers-turned-captives
beneath the arms & down the long corridor
they schlepp to the execution chamber
shuffling while meantime your head aches in peril
the kind of pain that must be like a blown-out tire
& no spare & the driver wracking his head
against the steering wheel until he groans
with regret for not spending a little extra
for a measly donut & now he's stranded on the side of the road
with passersby carrying on the usual business of apathy
or else there isn't enough time to stop & offer assistance
as they are needed at the airport to collect their friends & relatives
whisk them home unaware they're in no hurry so early
in the morning to be "collected" weary as they are
as it's been from Seattle to Portland to Atlanta to Knoxville
one insufferable layover & no booze to keep you starry-eyed
like a child's propitious discovery of the well-kept secret
hideaway where the candy is kept
& he'll sort through all the options of how
to make his belly ache as you would indulging a liquor
cabinet's inventory to reacquaint yourself with a reliquary of spirits
you've been long without but still

jubilant as though you've happened upon
the most desirable of sundries
no more collateral damage
of days ransacking a room for even a milliliter
titled into the bottom of an errant bottle &
later crawling the floor with a lampshade around your ankles
purring like a walrus
all of this a sign of the wretched past & presently
a celebration akin to the serendipitous unearthing
of a chest of jewels buried among the ruins of a derelict field
if only the drink that brings back your soul will assuage this aching
that refers itself throughout your body
the way a clot transfers itself from the leg to the left ventricle
if it wants to kill a man if it wants
to commit itself to healing
the suffering you endure
when there isn't a swill of liquor to be had
when a kink in the machinery reduces you to shivers
if you don't soon taste the elixir to calm
your beating heart coding the S.O.S.
as you slope toward the revelation
you're inside the belly of a ravenous beast

Darius Stewart

Poem to a Son

Finally I'm trying to forget
the impossibility I will ever father

a son.
Then remembering I'm trying

to forget, I remember
the forgetting & am heartbroken,

lying in bed, twilight slicing
horizontal lines

into my flesh,
as if the arced moon intends to remind me

I'm prisoner to a grave fault.
& if the stretch of night would give itself

over to my grief, I would wrench
the crescent—stardust, helixes of galaxies,

isotopes, invisible matter—
from its smug, overbearing suspension.

But how will I feel in the morning, when
I overhear the old couple next door arguing

because the perfume of her gladiolas has become
so overwhelming, & he complains

of allergies? But later they make up
as there's something to be said

about the long-coupled. They remind me
we must find shameless happiness

wherever it may be—in woodpiles
they spend stacking together, preparing

for winter. In the screech
of a raccoon chasing ghosts up cedars.

Even in the old house of my boyhood,
where the neighbors have a son.

A boy
I've seen only in the dim corner of his room,

back against window, tucked playing.
Some nights I've watched him

as his father stoops over the hill of his back,
gliding hands along the ridges of spine.

I watch the child lean into the cupped palm,
his father scratching the fine hairs of his head,

& I imagine joy welling inside a boy
with a face like mine.

Ben Weakley

The Wooden Elephants of Herat

I type Afghanistan into a search engine
that spits out words connected to places
and I get more places: *Kandahar, Khowst,*
Gardez, Herat.
                 I never deployed to Herat.
But Herat is where a woodcarver cut
scraps of walnut into two elephants
I brought home from the war to give my son.
For eight years they roamed his room as he played
in the ivory carpet of his imagination
until the tusks, tiny as matchsticks, fell out.

He is ten now. He does not remember teething
on my dog tags or holding my sweat-stained
patrol cap in the Fort Knox gym the night I came home.
He does not remember stopping
to salute the flag when the trumpet played retreat
on post. He no longer plays with elephants,
and now I pack them into a cardboard box
with faded uniforms and dusty boots—
relics we're unable to throw out
but no longer want to display.

Ben Weakley

Field Dressing

The silent doe stiffened in her bed of leaves,
where moments ago she fell, panting.

Her last breath rattled.
Life passed from nutbrown eyes
into damp January morning.

The snow wrapped us in a womb of silence.

My frost-tipped fingers wrapped tight
around the stained handle of a buck-knife,
the curved edge trembling.

Warm against my back, my father's hand.
Soft against my ear, my father's voice—

Careful, son. Cut gently.
We eat what we kill.
We honor the animal.

We honor the dead who give us life.

Boys like me are not made with words enough for this.

Ben Weakley

When we were boys

every grandfather contained stories
from *The War*, told in whispers from other rooms.

Their trophies preserved eternities
fixed between the quick and the dead.

Framed inside a shadow box on the wall,
my best friend's grandfather kept

a utility sleeve and brass casings
from two Japanese bullets that sailed

close enough to rip the fabric but miss
his young muscle and bone.

Another friend's grandfather trudged
across Burmese jungles and swamps

picking off Japanese officers,
disappearing into mist.

Long after the war, he wouldn't lie
down in a hammock—in his dreams

the emperor's soldiers still crawled
into camp, buried their knives

into his buddies' sleeping bodies.
His wife painted her kitchen red orange

like the rising sun. The old man
refused to speak to her

until she buried the enemy's shade
beneath a hue of muddy harvest gold.

These were the ancestors we worshipped
in backyards when we played war,

when we stormed beaches with sticks and hunted
hidden enemies deep inside the caves

of our imaginations, before we understood
what must be survived before coming home.

Beth Weinstock

On Troy Hill above Pittsburgh

Outside the chapel of Saint Anthony,
in the descent of an April afternoon,

the crossed branches—last summer's skeleton—
scrape for entry, for permission, at the stained windows.

The door is heavy, and I move inside,
stopping short with heavy breath to adapt

to silence, to the rich and worried velvet
of the nave. The wind so vocal

the shimmy of light from altar votives
seems to dance at its command.

I count three steps
between each Station of the Cross,

where above me the pained faces
of the painted traitors hoist the Jew

mutely into the air. On the south wall,
in a tiny reliquary, rests a fiber of Mary's veil,

and underneath, the skull
of another saint (maybe Matthias), wreathed

by bone chips from 12 apostles. A tooth
from St Anthony himself, and 22 splinters shaved

from the wooden crucifix. Such gravity.
Such affection. Such adoration

metered out to pieces
of the whole. What wouldn't I sacrifice

to certify my loss as this authentic?
Darkly, the way I chose again and again

to fall in love with the parts of this earth,
not without friends and dinners and light laughter,

and not without the red-hot charging ahead
into the smoky allure of desire, but nevertheless

always with the helpless sense
that all could be lost.

I envy their certainty—
that on the same day the righteous die,

we must insist that fragments are saved.
As if I could have taken a chisel

to the edge of my son's iliac bone
and closed a fraction of him—a relic—

within the door of a small glass amulet.
As if culling parts, like the priest

who scurried these slivers across the Atlantic,
could signal *this is eternity*,

moreso than a pleading symmetry
of grandiose arches, and moreso

than the ascendancy of gold flutes
toward the sky. As if

I could wander into the museum shop
next door, open ten to three most Sundays,

and ask the lady to show me how
to claim his lock of hair

and leftover marrow
alive.

Beth Weinstock

The Poet Starts a Rough Draft of Her Obituary

A marvelous orchestration it was, or colossal failure.
All those days, the waiting for the right words
or the right mirror, or at least
the right waiting room. All those days

in glittering conversation with the wrong gods.
How to know then how much was ending,
when for so long I came in hot
and unrehearsed and the walls of this house

gathered round like curious medical students.
When my nervous system could barely rouse
without hearing the voices
of the children sing, or the breathy gossip of curtains,

swinging in the window wells. How did my newborn
poems always suspect when I'd gone
and fallen in love (here she goes again),
and my sheepish fantasies that followed;

why hadn't I shouted in their tender ears
to grow up, come to terms with what
was wrestled? Every weekend,
I sensed disappointment

when they had nothing to do and nowhere
to go, sitting on my bed in little black dresses,
clutching their evening bags.
It's the same way I'd used the mulberry silks

of Vogue magazine as wallpaper,
and called it adolescence; the same way
I stayed plastered
to the front page of the New York Times,

and thought myself worldly. A marvelous
orchestration it was! How I could gloss things up
here or slow them down there, and how
the repetition of words could be

a salve, a weird expensive ointment, and how
the repetition of words could be-
come nothing but lines at the corners
of my eyes. How gentle now, this softening.

This lure and ruin, this desk and home
where I love deeply all the animals
that trail behind me, the ones that breathe
and jerk in their dreams at my feet.

Where the cracked clock ticks
in a tattered blanket to help the puppy sleep,
and where these days I never find time
to get a shot off, but still… don't you ever feel

illuminated from within, like a Christmas village
in fake snow? Soon enough, I'll hold
the clenched-up remains in my hand,
(unpolished, unpublished) and have to let go.

Whatever is lost in the large and ardent translation
of a life cannot be durable, yet I am buried
by the near-syncopal thought that I once
imagined a life should be so…

linear? I know, I might've built it differently,
the house and the radius of lines that led
to the house. But here I sit
in blue-ticked and stained overalls,

and how dare I forsake the mess
of my dogged architecture; feral, a child
who nestles her madness—her creations—
into well-behaved rows.

Dana Wildsmith

Prayer

And if I am a Christian, I am the least of all.

Well, that's
for sure. I love these words in Romans:
neither death nor life,
nor angels nor demons, not as a verse
affirming my faith, but
because they sound like Poe: *Neither*
angels in heaven above,

nor demons down under the sea...
Also, I am convinced
that hell's not a place, but a journey,
heaven's not earned, but spent,

and *prayer* is just another name for song.
Demons dither when
I pray unceasingly through song.
I am persuaded that when

I die, the best of me will drone
eternally in tune
with gratitude for every song
I've ever sung.

Dana Wildsmith

Door

I'd rather have a door that I could shut
to keep my morning space unoccupied, but
with someone always on the other side to meet
me there halfway between my wants and needs
mid-day when I've exhausted those first thoughts
that first light always brings like little beings caught
between another world and mine. I want
to bide my time in pondering but can't.
I never can. By noon, I need relief
from what's inside, or what's outside needs me.

And that's what doors are for. A door provides
an easy out when mystery collides
with what my mind can translate into words,
or should. When whispers only I have heard
beguile me most, an open door will end
the spell and save me for the world again.

Cynthia Young

But My Sister Said All Poets Are Liars…

just because,
when we took a walk one day,
me in a woolen sweater, her in a sleeveless cotton top,
someone threw a boulder out an open window
from a Highrise. My sister said
it was a pebble,
but I saw it grow from pebble to rock,
a piece of black coal like the ones the Coal Man
would bring in his truck once a month
to feed our furnace just when we thought
we would freeze to death like orphans,
our fingernails long as Cruella Deville's,
but icicles like those hanging from eaves.
But wait! That rock grew from coal to stone,
and kept growing, like the big ones
in the Ocoee River, boulders you could use
to cross the river like I saw the Cherokees do,
ghostlike echoes imprinted in air if I stared long enough…

My sister said "Stop! You were too young to remember
The Coal Man, and you were never cold, because I
remember heat; and when did you stand on the edge of any river
and how do you know exactly what tribe crossed where?
How could you create a ghost story from a boulder,
and a coal story from a pebble?
How could you say our parents didn't provide?

And then she walked away, so she didn't see the boulder bury me,
Push me through concrete to molten lava until I was on the other side,
where I rested in the graveyard of once-upon-a-time imaginings,
poetic images
my sister said she couldn't
close her eyes to see.

Cynthia Young

I Was Raised to Be Invisible

I was raised to hide
from the Boogeyman,
to not go with strange men
even if they were called "Uncle";
to walk away from love after the first slap,
the first "Baby I didn't mean it, but
it was your fault."

I was raised to be a good daughter,
to not take up too much air,
to do what I was told without talking back,
and so I sat in that barber's chair for "a facial",
and I, hungry for perfection, let him
put his hands on my teenage face
covered with perceived imperfections
all distorted in the bathroom mirror.
But I didn't want his hands to roam down
to my breasts, barely budding.

But I was also raised with Black girl magic,
with the power to leave that chair,
to run from the boogeyman,
to be strong enough to tell,
to raise my voice,
to scream.

FICTION

Noah Alvarez

Uncle Tito

Uncle Tito had been living with us for the past two months. I thought it was the coolest thing in the world having him at the house. But Mom and Jerry didn't want him to move in at first. They said it would be like taking care of another kid because of how sick he was. He had lost his house, his car, and his pride. So Mom gave in.

In October I made the freshman basketball team. On the night of our first game, I rode to the gym in the backseat of the Volvo. Jerry drove and Uncle Tito sat shotgun. On the way to the game Jerry had to drop Uncle Tito off at the Y for a meeting. If Uncle Tito missed one meeting he was done. It was Jerry's rule.

Uncle Tito wore a wife-beater under his cigarette-scented flannel and a gold Jesus-piece around his neck. He carried a plastic water cup in his hand. He could never keep his hands still. He wore his sunglasses everywhere, even at night and indoors.

Uncle Tito drummed his fingers on his thighs. He was self-conscious of people looking at his hands when they shook, so he always kept them moving. Jerry leaned forward over the steering wheel and tried to ignore him.

Why are you so jumpy over there Tito, said Jerry. You didn't mistake the Grey Goose for water did you?

Very funny Jerry, said Uncle Tito.

Uncle Tito smiled and tried to brush it off, but he'd been working hard to try and stay sober, and Jerry knew how to get under his skin.

Uncle Tito looked at me in the rearview.

You excited for your first game, squirt?

He doesn't like it when you call him that, said Jerry.

He doesn't like it when you call him that, mocked Uncle Tito. I tried not to laugh but I couldn't help it. Uncle Tito smiled and Jerry looked back at me disapproving.

I've known the boy longer than you have, said Uncle Tito. I've been watching him play since he started back in the third grade. I can name every team he's played for. I can't even remember the last time I saw you at a game, Jerry.

I forget that you don't know what it's like to have a job, said Jerry. Or responsibilities.

I'm excited, I said. I wish one of you guys could come watch.

I know buddy, said Jerry. I'd be at every game if I didn't have to work. Your mother is proud.

I don't think he likes being called buddy, said Uncle Tito.

Jerry tightened his grip on the steering wheel. We pulled up to the curb in front of the Y.

This is your stop, said Jerry. Don't stumble in there now.

Uncle Tito ignored Jerry. He unbuckled his seatbelt and turned to me. He lowered his glasses and looked at me with his yellow-tinted eyes.

Lights out tonight kid, he said.

Uncle Tito winked and jumped out of the car. He closed the door and I climbed to the front. He waved at us as we drove by. I waved back and Jerry floored the gas.

Prick, Jerry mumbled.

I think it's awesome having Uncle Tito around, I said. He's been doing really good with us.

Don't expect it to last, said Jerry.

✳

I got home from school the next day and Uncle Tito had moved the futon from against the wall to right in front of the TV. Our house only had two bedrooms and one bath. The living room had become his room and the futon had become his bed.

Uncle Tito was smoking a cigarette and taking big gulps of his water. He was watching a Celtics game that he had recorded the night before. He never watched basketball for pleasure. He was constantly studying each game with unbreakable focus.

I was on the way to my room when he called for me.

Hey big head! Come sit down. I want to show you something from this game.

I went in the living room and sat down next to him. The smoke was unbearable and he kept taking drags.

You can learn so much from these guys, he said.

Uncle Tito had gone to the same high school I went to, and back in the eighties he was the star point guard. He was only five-foot-ten and a hundred and fifty pounds, but he led the state in scoring, assists and steals three years in a row. He was named the state's Mr. Basketball his senior year.

He was on his way to a full ride to Fresno State before he tore his ACL in the state semi's his senior year. After the injury, he lost all the speed and agility that made him a star, and Fresno State lost interest. He played half a year of ball for a junior college in Illinois but he had to drop out because he flunked all of his classes.

Uncle Tito put his arm around me and pointed to the screen.

You're a good shooter kid, but you're letting too many opportunities slip away because you're not attacking the basket. Look here.

He paused the game.

Look at the ball-handler here. He doesn't do anything special. Just a quick one-two dribble to get his defender off balance. Then he drives to the basket. Easy lay-up.

You haven't been to any of my games this year, I said.

But I've watched every single one. They come on public access. If I'm at a meeting, I record them and watch them after. Look.

Uncle Tito switched to a recording of my last game and we watched the first few minutes.

Man, he said. When you dribble up the court, your hair bounces on your head just like mine did.

I was about to ask him something when Mom stormed in the house. Uncle Tito tried to ash the cigarette before she came in the living room. She stood in the doorway with her hands on her hips.

Goddamnit Tito! she yelled. I told you a million times not in the house! Jerry is looking for any reason to throw your stupid ass out. And in front of your nephew?

She came and snatched the cigarette from his hand. I don't understand why you always have to act like a jackass, she said.

Mom turned to me and cocked her head.

To your room, now, she said. You have homework. And you, she turned to Uncle Tito. Get your lazy ass up and help with the groceries.

We both stood up, a little ashamed, and followed our orders. Before I went to my room, Uncle Tito patted me on the back.

We'll watch it after dinner tonight, he said.

I closed the door to my room, too excited to start my homework.

＊

One night Uncle Tito's meeting got cancelled. That same night we had a game against our rivals, Alderson Catholic. Mom agreed to take Uncle Tito to the game with me since she had a babysitting gig and couldn't stay to watch.

In the car Uncle Tito didn't shake as much. He rubbed his hands together and said things like, It's going to be a good one tonight. He acted like he was going to suit up himself.

Do you have your water cup? Mom asked Uncle Tito.

Yes.

I'm just making sure. And you know the school is a smoke free zone, right? No smoking outside the gym door.

It's a two-hour game. You don't think I can make it two hours without smoking?

I'm just reminding you Tito.

Mom pulled up to the gym entrance.

I'll be back around nine-thirty to pick you guys up, she said. She rubbed her hand on my knee. Good luck, honey.

The boy doesn't need luck, said Uncle Tito.

We walked to the big glass doors. Uncle Tito was behind me rubbing my shoulders. When we went through the doors into the foyer Uncle Tito looked up at the high ceiling. The lights were bright and he looked out of place in his old school.

It feels different, he said. He stood in the middle of the foyer.

The gym is this way Uncle Tito.

He continued behind me but kept looking around, up at the ceiling and over his shoulder.

On the wall just before the gym doors was The Wall of Excellence. It was a glass-display of the school's best sports teams and athletes over the years. There were pictures of the old football team before it was disbanded in ninety-four, and there were pictures of the current state quarterfinalist in tennis, Sarah Hash. But no section was as coveted as the basketball area.

Our school had never won a championship in anything, but the basketball team was the closest we ever came. Uncle Tito stopped in front of the display and pulled his sunglasses down. An official game ball sat in a case with two jerseys hung above it on either side, one white and one navy blue. Both had the number 6.

My fucking jerseys, said Uncle Tito. He sounded surprised and upset at the same time.

It's the only number no one is allowed to wear, I said.

Uncle Tito looked around the display case and spotted a wooden plaque with gold lettering. Above the words was a picture of a young man with sharp cheekbones and curly hair who posed like a soldier in his jersey. Uncle Tito nearly dropped his water cup.

This plaque is a symbol of recognition to Tatum "Tito" Petrola School and State leader in points, assists and steals.
Tatum is a first team all-state selection, as well as an academic all-state member.

I watched him study the picture and the words under it. I felt proud to be standing next to him and his plaque. My friends loved to remind me that was my uncle in the picture. But Uncle Tito didn't even smirk at it. He threw his sunglasses back on his face and continued to the gym.

They need to take that shit down, he said. My records were broken seven years ago.

✳

After the game, we sat on the curb outside and waited for Mom to pick us up. Uncle Tito was trying to think of something encouraging to say.

It is what it is kid, he said.

We lost by thirty-four, I said pitifully.

Yea. The team sucked tonight. But you had twenty points tonight, so you didn't suck, right? Man, I swear you're getting better.

I was past the point of frustration. I was tired and the sweat on my body had dried and made me cold.

Behind us the doors flew open. The three referees who called our game came out, all of them talking. Two of them went to the right towards the parking lot. The third, a tall, skinny guy, walked towards us. He was parked in the student parking lot on the other side. As he passed us him and Uncle Tito made eye contact. He stopped and a smile spread across his face.

Son of a bitch, he said. It's Tito Petrola! You're Tito Petrola! He put his hands on his head in disbelief. I knew that was you up in the bleachers man!

Do I know you? said Uncle Tito.

I played for Hillsborough back in the day man. I was, like, a sophomore when you were a senior. You dropped forty points on us in the playoffs! No one could guard you man!

Oh yea, I remember that.

I can't believe you're sitting in front of me. Everyone used to talk about you. You're the best player this state's ever seen. Man!

Uncle Tito folded his hands to keep them from shaking. He didn't look all the way up at the man.

Then the man pointed at me, like he hadn't noticed me the whole time.

Wow, and now your son's out here playing ball too, he said.

I waited for Uncle Tito to correct him but he didn't. Instead, he just smirked.

Tito, your boy's a spitting image of you. He turned to me and pointed to Tito. Hey kid, when your old man was your age, no one he played against could stop him. Every shot he put up found the net.

The man felt around for his keys in his pocket and turned his truck on with them. He drove a new, white Ford and he started to walk backwards towards it.

Tito fucking Petrola, he said. Man. Make sure you come to the next game and say what's up.

He turned around and kept walking.

Tito Petrola, I heard him say again. Then he got in his truck and pulled off.

Uncle Tito didn't speak. We sat there like the encounter hadn't happened. He tried to clear the phlegm from his throat but couldn't. Then he lowered his head and threw up between his legs. It was mostly bile mixed with a few chunks of the pasta we'd had for dinner. I stood up and backed away.

I'm fine, he said. He waved his hand in the air to confirm it. I just need a damn cigarette. Where the hell is your mom?

A few minutes later the Volvo pulled up. It was too dark for Mom to see the vomit on the ground.

Don't tell her a damn thing, said Uncle Tito before we opened the doors. He got in the back seat.

You're taking the back Tito? said Mom.

The boy played hard. He deserves it. But he doesn't want to talk about it.

Tough night, huh? she asked me.

I said he doesn't want to talk about it.

All right, all right, damn, said Mom. Are you feeling ok Tito?

Tito didn't respond. He was upset but I couldn't tell if it was about basketball or that guy bugging him, or if maybe he was actually sick. But I didn't think about it too much. He would feel better tomorrow.

❋

Uncle Tito didn't let me mope around after the game. He told me to quit being soft and put in the extra work to make sure a game like that never happened again. Every day we didn't have practice I was putting up shots in the backyard. Uncle Tito would smoke and watch me.

Shoulders squared, he would say over and over. Elbow in. Come on now.

One day I struggled with my shot and Uncle Tito yelled these things over and over. I put the ball down and held my hands on top of my head to breathe.

You're exhausted, he said. That's why you're not shooting consistently.

Hey Uncle Tito, how come you never shoot hoops anymore?

Uncle Tito crossed his arms and thought about it.

Well, he said, I just don't anymore, I guess. I don't know. I'd probably throw my back out if I tried.

I picked up the ball and held it towards him.

I bet you still got it.

Not anymore, kid. Haven't touched a ball in years.

Come on Uncle Tito. How are you going to coach me if you can't lead by example?

Don't get smart, kid.

Just a shot or two and I'll leave you alone. Deal?

Uncle Tito hesitated but he finally took a deep breath and stood. He popped his neck to the left and right and clapped for the ball. I passed it to him. He came to where I was and put the ball down to stretch his arms across his chest and both of his shoulders popped. He picked the ball back up and spun it on the tip of his middle finger and let it spin like it was a muscle on his body he was flexing. Then he tossed it from his finger and caught it in his hands and put his forehead to it as if in prayer.

Prepare to be disappointed, he said.

His beer gut hung from the bottom of his shirt and his

shoulders were slumped forward. He moved like he was thirty years older than he was. He barely bent his knees and his feet barely left the ground but the shot he put up was graceful when it left his fingertips. His elbow extended smoothly and the flick of his wrist was like a cherry on a sunday.

The ball spiraled high in the air and dropped through the hoop and splashed against the net like water. The rim did not rattle.

Well, he said, I guess I still got it. Let me see it again.

I passed him the ball and he put up another shot. Nothing but net. I kept grabbing his rebounds for him and he kept putting them up. Out of forty shots he only missed two. I noticed Mom watching us from the kitchen window. Normally at this time in the evening she'd call us in for chores or dinner. But tonight she just smiled and let us play.

Me and Uncle Tito started a game of H.O.R.S.E but we only got to O before it was too dark to see the ball. I kicked my shoes off on the patio and looked over at Uncle Tito. I hadn't realized how exhausted he was from putting up all those shots. He struggled to get each breath out of his throat. He was bent down with his hands on his knees. I took his arm and put it around my back and helped him into the house onto the futon.

Jerry was on the recliner reading something on his phone.

Jesus Christ, he said, flaring his nostrils. Would it kill you to hop in the shower real quick before dinner?

Suck a fat one, Jerry.

Will you two shut up? Mom yelled from the kitchen. I'm not dealing with your all's bullshit tonight.

Jerry stood up and walked to the kitchen. He mumbled something under his breath before he was out of the room. Uncle Tito was still panting on the futon and didn't notice. Or he was too tired to respond.

✳

After dinner I lay in my room and skimmed through a book I had to read for a book report. It was eleven at night and I was already supposed to be asleep but I kept hearing what sounded like a cat pushing out a hairball. I put the book down and creeped over to the door and cracked it open. I realized it was Uncle Tito dry heaving.

Just lay down, I heard Mom say in a weak voice. Uncle Tito

moaned and the springs in the futon squeaked under his weight.

It was just a game of H.O.R.S.E, said Uncle Tito. Is that all it's going to take to kill me?

It's just a headache, said Mom. You're exercising again and you're tired. That's a good thing. That can be your success story for your meeting tomorrow.

Mom started to hum something. She got quieter and quieter and then stopped. He must have fallen asleep. I heard her walk to her room. Before she opened her door I could hear her sniffle. I thought she was going to cry. She went in her room and quietly shut the door.

✳

When the weather got cold everyone's mood got worse. Jerry started working six days a week and Uncle Tito started going to the doctor, which meant Mom had to drop her baby-sitting gig to keep up with his appointments and meetings.

One day I found blood in the toilet. When I asked Mom about it she didn't say who it was. But Uncle Tito's skin was turning yellow and he couldn't keep his food down, so I put two and two together.

Uncle Tito and Jerry didn't go back and forth like they used to. Instead Mom would give Jerry that mean look to make him do something that showed he at least pretended to care about Uncle Tito. He would refill his water cup or get him a dinner plate or a barf bag. Uncle Tito didn't even crack jokes. They weren't cordial but they dealt with each other, like there was some cold understanding between them.

He stopped wearing his sunglasses and he only got up from the futon to go to the bathroom. He kept a plastic bag with him just in case he got the spins. He only watched Wheel of Fortune and other boring game shows on TV but he never actually paid attention to what was going on. It was like Uncle Tito was never actually there anymore. He even stopped talking to me about basketball.

One night I sat next to him while he was watching Wheel of Fortune. His skin smelled rotted and he looked lost staring at the TV.

Is there any way you could come to our game tomorrow night? I asked. If we win we make the freshman team playoffs.

I have to go to the doctor's office tomorrow, he said. He

didn't bother to turn from the TV to answer.

Oh.

If you haven't noticed, I can't really go anywhere anymore.

I just thought that maybe-

Let me shoot it straight with you kid, he said. He bent over to look in the kitchen. Mom had her headphones in while she cooked.

It's time for you to understand what's going on. I'm going to need a new liver if I ever want to be normal again.

But I thought you stopped drinking?

I did. I've been sober for eight months now. The thing is, the damage has already been done. I went twenty-six years drinking every single day and I didn't stop soon enough to save myself. I'm lucky I bought myself a few extra months by quitting when I did.

I sat there with my mouth open trying to think of something to say.

Just don't make a big deal about it, he said. It's my own fault.

Dinner's ready! Mom called from the kitchen.

I'll make you a plate, I said to Uncle Tito. He patted my shoulder.

You're a good kid, he said. Sometimes I wish you were my own.

I went in the kitchen and got him a small bowl of chili. I handed it to him and went for mine.

Why are you moping around? Mom asked.

I didn't answer. I took my chili to my room and let it go cold on my dresser.

❋

The next night was the biggest game of my life but I had no motivation to play. I walked home from the bus stop and dreaded putting on my jersey or shooting a ball or seeing Uncle Tito. I resented him for not being able to come to the game.

I got home and took a nap and then ate dinner. At six-thirty I got my gear together and went out to the car. Mom sat behind the wheel with the engine running. I didn't notice Uncle Tito was sitting in the back until I got in the passenger seat.

I was surprised to see him. He had on one of his navy blue high school jerseys over his hoodie and his sunglasses. He smiled at me when I got in the car. It was the happiest I had seen him in weeks. There were a hundred things I wanted to ask him about from the day before but none of them were worth mentioning now, as if those problems just didn't exist anymore.

You're letting me sit up front? I said.

Why not? Special treatment for the star player, right?

Mom took off and Uncle Tito put his hands on my shoulders and squeezed.

I thought you said you weren't watching the game, I said.

It's the biggest game of the year. Just cause I can't be there in person doesn't mean I'm not watching.

I had spent the whole night prior making myself understand that Uncle Tito was too sick to focus on basketball right now, which made me hate the thought of basketball. Now that I knew he was watching tonight's game I was ecstatic. And then I felt the pressure to win. I started to tense up in the front seat.

We pulled into the school parking lot. Uncle Tito reached behind his neck and unhooked his Jesus-piece. He held it delicately in the air and looked at it for a moment. Then he handed it to me.

I guess it's time I hand it down to its heir, he said.

I stared at it and watched it glisten. He kept dangling it.

Take it before I change my mind, he said.

I took it and hooked it around my neck.

It was your grandad's. He gave it to me before he passed away my senior year. It used to be my good luck charm.

I ran my fingers down the gold chain. I couldn't believe I was actually wearing it.

He looks just like you, Mom said.

Before I got too carried away Uncle Tito gave me a noogie.

You're going to be late, dummy, he said. He lightly pushed me towards the door and I got out. Uncle Tito got out and went around to the front.

Remember, channel four, I said.

I know what channel smart ass, he said. He got in and Mom blew me a kiss and they drove away. I fingered the cross on my chest the whole way inside.

※

The gym was so empty that it would have made the game feel less significant any other night. That's how freshman games were. There were maybe three pairs of parents in the stands and a group of potheads sitting in the far corner. But it felt like the whole world was watching me from home. I could see Uncle Tito leaning forward on the futon blowing into his fists, Mom begging him to lean back and relax.

The boys on Denton Valley were as big as trees. Their arms were the size of my head and any of them could have passed for seniors. The whistle blew and our center didn't bother jumping for the tip. We immediately retreated to defense.

Their center was a fourteen-year-old who was six-foot-seven. As soon as he touched the ball he bullied our center in the post, backed him in and put up an easy layup. He put up ten straight points just like that before we could get one of our own.

I was trying to get my teammates involved the first quarter but every shot they put up clanked off the side of the rim. They made a few bad passes that went out of bounds and Denton Valley's point guard got a couple of steals and that's how the first quarter ended. I walked to the bench ahead of my teammates and pouted.

I heard Uncle Tito in my head. Quit acting like that, he said. If you don't want to lose then take control of the game.

I gave my teammates fists bumps on the bench and tried to act optimistic about the second quarter. Our big man set some screens for me and I hit a couple of threes. We stole the ball a few times for some fast-break layups. But we didn't have anyone big enough to stop their lumberjacks in the post. They put up points effortlessly. Before the halftime buzzer sounded their center caught an inbound pass and dunked the ball with both hands and made the frame of the backboard rattle. I had scored fifteen points so far and felt better until I looked up at the scoreboard. We only had fifteen points to their thirty-one.

We sat in the locker room at halftime with our heads down like the game was already lost. Our coach let us sit in silence and stared at us, disappointed. He shook his head and told us how sorry we were.

I could see Uncle Tito pacing around the living room cussing at the TV, calling us soft and pitiful. Our coach wasn't going to say anything useful and Uncle Tito expected me to do something. So I took control of the room.

What the hell's gotten into us? I yelled. I looked at my teammates with my fists clenched. My voice echoed around the locker room.

Why are we scared to shoot the fucking ball? It doesn't matter how big they are. They're too fat and slow to keep up with us. We should be running circles around them!

My teammates sat wide-eyed and some of them straightened up. Some of them nodded their heads at what I was saying.

We can't be scared to lose. If we play scared to lose we'll miss out on every opportunity we have to win. If they hit us, that's fine. We'll take the foul shots. I'll even score every fucking point if I have to. But I need all of you to give me everything you've got. Do you understand?

My teammates didn't say anything but I felt a spark in the room. They stood up and circled around me. I could feel the urgency to win. I fingered the cross on my chest and put my hand up to break it down.

Family on three! I yelled. One. Two. Three!

✳

We came out like a different team in the third quarter. I hit three straight threes and my teammates knocked down a few more. Finally, Denton Valley was getting tired and they started to miss. We took advantage of every rebound and scored on fastbreaks. We cut their lead down to six with three minutes to go in the third.

On defense I lost my man on a screen and I got stuck guarding big boy. He could have picked me up and tossed me across the court like a tennis ball if he wanted to. He pushed me back with his shoulder and demanded the ball down low.

He got the ball and dribbled a couple of times. I tried to go for it but my arms couldn't reach around his waist. He put his head down again and pushed me off-balance. Then he pushed again to get to his spot under the basket, but instead of trying to push back I stepped to the side and let gravity take care of him. Without the resistance he expected he fell forward with all of his weight. There was a loud thump on the hardwood and he lay there with his hands over his face. I could see Uncle Tito standing in the living room with his arms crossed, nodding his head. He had told me the most important thing you can do is play smarter, not harder.

The big man was sent to the locker room with a concussion and all of Denton Valley's momentum left with him. The fourth quarter came around and by then it was a different game. I hit another four three pointers and my teammates kept coming up with steals that led to easy buckets. Denton Valley was exhausted and we were playing like the game had just started. We outscored them twenty-four to zero in the fourth quarter. The clock ticked down and when the buzzer sounded I looked up at the scoreboard.

Fifty-five to forty. We were in the playoffs.

✳

We celebrated on the sideline, giving each other hugs and chanting Playoffs before the ref made us line up to shake hands with Denton Valley. They looked angry and on the verge of tears when we passed them. Afterwards I looked to my right and saw Jerry standing on the court, away from the other parents. I walked up to him, and even though he wasn't smiling I was excited to see him.

What are you doing here? I asked him.

I'm here to pick you up.

Did you watch the game? We're going to the playoffs!

I haven't been here for long. We need to go to the car.

I'm supposed to go to the locker room first. We always meet in the locker room after the game.

We don't have time kid. Get your bag and let's go.

He sounded frustrated and I was anxious following him to the parking lot. He didn't look at me or anyone else when we walked outside. He kept his head down and we got in the car.

What's the matter? I said. Where are we going?

We have to get to the hospital, he said. He sped out of the parking lot and ran a red light as we left the neighborhood.

Are Mom and Uncle Tito there?

Yes.

Is Uncle Tito alright?

Jerry thought about it. His hesitation told me everything I needed to know. He kept his eyes on the road and sighed.

I don't think so buddy.

I looked out the window and didn't ask anything else. I didn't care about Jerry or the game we won or my new necklace. Even though the buildings and people were blurs as we drove by and we ran stop signs and another red light, it didn't feel like we were going fast enough.

Brett Biebel

Minnesota Miracle Man

7AM in the dead of summer, and Jesse's got these ropes all wrapped and bundled on his neighbor's porch. "Listen, Al," he says, "Thought you might drive me out to that memorial down 63 and tie me up on one of them crosses they got. Overlooking the highway."

Al's shirtless and in gym shorts. Behind him, his daughter is pouring Trix is what it looks like. A shitload of it. She acts guilty, but neither Al nor Jesse cares one bit. Al says, "Hon, take a note for your mother. I'll be back when I can," and the girl nods and then pours some more, and off the two of them go, looking a little tilted. Not quite devilish, though not exactly straight neither.

When they get there, Jesse picks the cross on the left. The left as you face them, and Al does as he's told. Right arm, left arm, ankles. Jesse's down to his boxers. He's hanging outstretched and grinning like an idiot. Not a cloud in the sky. "Go on now," says Jesse, "Get the fuck out of here."

"And come back what? Around 3 o'clock?"

"Hell no. You get gone and stay gone, and if I die out here, it was never your problem anyhow."

Al shrugs. "No one's gonna stop, you know," and Jesse probably agrees, but he decides he wants to give them the chance.

"Good Samaritans," he says. "When I was thirsty and shit. Give 'em a shot at redemption, and we all deserve a little, or isn't that what you think?"

Al's hands go up. "Whatever you say, man," and then he's in the car and blasting his way back toward town. Jesse watches him go and looks at a couple hawks, an oriole perched on the mile marker. He closes his eyes and breathes. There are mosquitoes. Gnats too. Spiders and crickets and even ticks, but they all seem to have enough sense to leave the poor man alone. It's hard to tell if Jesse's grateful for this, or if it was all supposed to be part of the experience, and he won't be up there for long in the end, a few hours maybe. A trucker will stop before noon, and the next time it'll be this lady biker, and then an actual horse and buggy, and the Amish man driving it, or maybe he's Mennonite, he'll be called Jeremiah, and they'll ride in silence for a while, down a gravel road that leads to the quarry. "What is it you're trying to prove?" he'll ask, and Jesse will laugh because the answer is nothing. But, someday soon, if he keeps at it, Al will be right. No one will come. Families will pass and wonder. Scratch their heads. Hope he's a mannequin. They'll hear their kids shouting from the backseats of hybrids and brand-new sedans, crossovers with crumbs piling up in the crevices, and still they'll just drive on by, knowing it's for their own safety, and you never know with people do you? This is what they'll tell themselves, is how crazy they can be. Waiting. Just lying (in a manner of speaking) in wait. Jesse will understand on some level, of course, though maybe he'll resent them. Maybe he already does. Maybe, and he won't know this for sure, at least not until it happens, but it might be one of those big political projects, and they're experiments, really. Confirmation bias. The ultimate test of assumptions, and the hope is that, one day, his every expectation will find itself so gloriously fulfilled.

Brett Biebel

In the Offing

V an Allen works for the Minnesota Highway Patrol, and
when he's on the late shift, he'll find dead animals every-
where. Racoons and shit. The stuff people hit and maybe don't
even realize, or else they're drunk and worried it's a person, and
so they just keep on going. Forget what happened. Maybe it'll
disappear. What he does is call this buddy of his from Crosby,
and the guy's tall and wears glasses and has some weird fucking
obsession with hieromancy, and they'll look at these rodents and
birds mostly and try to find the sacred organs. The lungs, the
heart, the liver especially. The buddy hires himself out some-
times, but that's mainly just for show, and he always relishes these
late-night calls from Van Allen. Can't fucking wait to hit the pave-
ment at 3AM and considers it his true vocation, and he never
makes prophecies per se. It's more like checking for harmony.
Bringing human attitude into congruence with divine whim, and
it's all a matter of accretion, they decide. Patterns. Large enough
samples. One night, they figure they'll be out on 371, and some
hawk or skunk will throw everything into focus, and they'll sit
there and have a cigar, and "You reckon what I reckon?" Van
Allen will say, and the buddy will take his glasses off. He'll pinch
his nose.

"Sure does seem like anger to me," he'll say, and Van Allen
will wonder if they really needed all this data, all this death, just
to get there, and maybe he'll even put it out there real direct, as
in like, "Hey, Jesus, Dell, just what the fuck was this whole thing
about anyway?" and Dell will shrug. He won't know any more
than anyone else, but he'll spit on the ground and stuff some
feathers into his pocket and tell whoever's listening that maybe
there is no point, and that's the issue with oracles, isn't it.

"Sometimes you show up, and you're already twelve years too
late."

Lauren Davis

Into the Sun

We awake and the sun is on us and our arms are not around each other. There's a field. The high grass is dry, dying. My hands are earth-stained. The wind—absent. The land lacks cattle, gnats, birdsong.

Where are we? he asks, though his lips do not move.

My hand is over my eyes. I spot a wire fence in the distance, and beyond it, a hedge of leafless trees. The fence curves around the horizon—north, east, south. To the west of us, there's a slight hill. The sky is empty.

How did we get here? he asks, though his mouth does not open.

It is unexceptional, this countryside. My palms are on the ground. I am trying to steady myself.

Jonathan, I say.

What? he says. When he speaks, his voice echoes.

There is no sound.

Before we woke here, Jonathan had been on the Pacific Coast Trail. I had asked to go with him, but he told me he needed to do it alone, going on and on about growing into himself, wanting to fully become the man he was meant to be so that he could do right by me, and I had told him he was everything, yet my protests did not matter.

I have to, he had said.

At least let me go with you, I had said.

You cannot know what it means to love you, he'd said, and he pulled me into his arms and his hands were warm and swallowed my waist and I grew soft and sleepy and he kissed the crown of my head.

The night before he left, his mother texted me.

I don't like this, she wrote.

I don't like this, either, I wrote back.

I stayed by the phone, tried to distract myself with work and writing and the TV. He had just proposed a few months ago, at sunset on a mountain. The ring palladium, blue-stoned, too large for my finger, but I put a bit of tape around the band. I rubbed the ring like a rosary.

He'd trained for a couple of weeks, going on long climbs in the morning and the evening. His gear looked professional, expensive, never really broken in.

We stretch our legs, our arms. We wander towards the fence some yards out. But when we are within a few feet of it, we cannot near it. We are no closer to it, no matter how much we walk. The land seems to stretch and contract, like water finding a shape. Or a rubber band, a snake that coils, strikes.

Jonathan narrows his eyes. He tries to run towards the fence. He gains a few feet, and then the fence moves away from us. Or we move away from it.

Are we on drugs? he says.

I'm not on drugs. Are you on drugs? I say.

No. Are we asleep? he says.

I don't know, I say. *Try to wake up.*

How do I do that? he says. *Come here. Hold my mouth shut.*

Seriously? I say.

Just do it, he says.

He sucks in air, and I hold my palm over him. The seconds slow, and then he struggles away from me, wheezing.

We need to wake up, he says.

He gasps for breath.

Should we try the other direction? I say.

He puts his palm on the small of my back.

Yes, he says.

This time the horizon allows us to come closer to it, and the hill reveals its slight incline, dotted with white flowers and dandelions.

I've failed you, he says.

What do you mean? I say.

The whole point of that hike was to make sure I knew how to be strong for you. Now we're stuck in whatever this.

We are tired, and we fall back asleep in the weeds, though I do not dream.

The sun won't set here. When we wake, we're hot to the touch.

We travel about a mile until we spot a cliff, and beyond it— nothing but sky. The cliff reaches as far as we can see, from east to west. In both directions, the fence meets the edge.

Where do we go now? I say.

We build a bridge, he says.

There is no other side to build to, I say. Of course he knows this. I try to say it kindly.

He steps towards the edge, and the edge moves away from him. He sits, puts his hands over his face. He stays still for a long time. I turn from him, towards the fence. I sprint towards it. The fence moves away from me. I creep towards it. It creeps away.

He says, *Remember that first weekend I slept over? We stayed in bed, ate ice cream. Your cat wasn't sure about things. In the morning when I woke up, he was sitting on my chest, watching me.*

I kiss his forehead.

We could just jump off the cliff and see what happens, he says, his smile strained.

It won't let us, I say.

What if we close our eyes? he says.

Maybe another day, I say.

There are no days here, he says.

Why do you think we're here? he asks.

I'm not sure if he expects an answer. I don't give him one.

Maybe it's my fault, he says.

What do you mean? I say.

I did something, maybe, he says.

What did you do? I say.

I don't know. I was on the trail. It had been three days. You know this. Then I went into the trees to change my clothes. They had gotten damp. They were uncomfortable. I left my pack next to the trail. I was trying to be decent.

He sighs, rubs his eyes.

I looked up and a moose was staring at me, he says. *It frightened me, it was so huge. When it turned and left, I finally relaxed. I hadn't realized I had stopped breathing. I tried to find the trail again, I guess I got turned around, got lost. The forest was so dense, and my compass wouldn't work. I didn't know it could swallow you like that.*

I'm here, too, though, I say. *I'm stuck here with you.*

Then what happened? he says.

I had been lying on the couch, writing a story in my notebook. I had set the scene. A field. A fence. A cliff. Then the phone rang. When I answered, the policewoman told me another hiker had spotted an orange backpack in the woods. Inside was

Jonathan's ID. The hiker called for him, and waited, but he never appeared.

Have you heard from Jonathan? the policewoman said.

He called me two days ago, I said. *But not since.*

We are opening a missing person's report on him, she said.

I would love to see a pigeon. Just a single spider. Or a small, pathetic cloud. To feel a breeze. To have the choice, if I desired, to plummet.

Help me dig, he says.

Dig what? I say.

We can try to dig ourselves out of here, he says.

We only have our hands, I say.

The soil is soft. Help me, he says.

The first layer of dirt, giving easily, is not unlike powder. Then there is grit, which cuts into our skin. Our knuckles turn red, bloody. Then we feel a hard surface, unforgiving.

What is that? Rock? Jonathan says.

I spit into the hole, wash off the dirt. We hit thick glass. It has a gentle arch, like a large fish bowl.

Help me, I say.

We look down together, our heads touching.

I see myself beneath us. I am lying on my couch. My eyes are closed. Across my chest is an open notebook. The pen has fallen to the floor.

Wake up, I say to the body of me that sleeps. I pound on the glass.

What is this? Is that really you? Jonathan says.

I ignore him.

Wake up, I say again.

I look peaceful there. My cat walks through the room. Overhead, the sun stays steady in her place. The earth does not move.

Life Jacket

Holly walks out on the movable platform that spans the tank. Before they were led from the staging room to the tank, the team running the research had explained the deal. The Engineering Department has a contract to test different styles of life jackets—or PFDs, as they called them—"Personal Flotation Devices." They need people of varying sizes, weights, and body composition to complete their results. Holly can't picture where this process might be shelved. What's the "Safety" section?

When she told the techs she was from New Jersey, near Asbury Park, they were thrilled. It's 1980; *The River* has just been released and it turns out they're all Springsteen fans. One of them, Ned, asked her if people from Asbury Park were all really "leaving town" and she'd looked at him with confusion. "Independence Day," he prodded. "Like, pinball, the ocean, The Stone Fucking Pony! Is it all, like, empty now?" She shook her head and looked down the hall at the wave tank, still and dark below its railing. He started singing "The Ties That Bind" as he untangled the large, colorful pile of jackets.

The platform bridges the water about two thirds of the way down from the wave generator. The tank is a long, narrow pool, about twenty feet across but fifty yards long. It is one of the oldest wave tanks in the country, was built to study naval architecture, not bodies in water. Holly had gone to school here for four years without knowing it existed. She thinks: *Naval Science—V.* She doesn't recall what floor. It's not a section that ever got shelved much.

She is paired with a body builder named Russell, who strikes Holly as not just built, but over-built. Everything about him—unhurried movement, shaved head, short sentences—signals exaggerated efficiency. Like he's broken some code and is demonstrating his expertise. He tells Holly he is a business major. Naturally, Holly thinks. And then: *HG—Finance. Somewhere in the basement.*

Holly must seem totally inefficient to him. She is not overweight, precisely, but rounded. Her rust-colored hair is pulled back in a messy braid that almost reaches her waist. Wisps fly out of every link of it, like the long spiny hairs that mark the segments of a wooly caterpillar. The only thing that is similar is that she doesn't talk much either. Russell acts like her reticence is an affront, while his is a game plan. Last year Holly would have immediately decided she didn't like him. Today he barely registers.

So here she is on the platform, about to climb down a ladder, fully clothed, not in the best shape after a long northern winter, into the cold water. Russell of the efficient body composition stands beside her, looking like he should be posing in an ad for people who test PFDs. The air reeks of chlorine. Holly starts to doubt her decision to take this temp job. But the library hadn't worked out, and her rent is due.

When not fanboying about Springsteen, Ned had lectured them about "Archimedes Principle" as they were getting ready in the staging room. Holly doubts that she needed to know the details of buoyancy and displacement in order to follow directions, but they're getting paid by the hour. She learned about the forces on a body—the density of weight pulling downward, the buoyancy of fluids pushing up. It seemed simple, complete in itself. She thought *Physics—QC, Floor 1A in the old building. Right by the Reference Room. No, don't think about the Reference Room.*

Holly climbs down the ladder ahead of Russell. His "ladies first" rankles her, how he covers his reluctance with feigned chivalry. The water is colder than she'd expected. She has to tread hard to stay surfaced as her clothes and shoes soak up the weight of it. Muddy April light seeps through windows high up one tiled wall of the tank. Nearer to Holly, the other wall has a slim pool deck running its length, with a metal safety railing and doors opening to the corridor. Russell descends after her and moves toward the window side. Their eyes meet, and for a second they share a nervous camaraderie at the strangeness of this—floating, fully clothed, in this cold, murky tank, like subjects in some weird science experiment, which, Holly supposes, is what this is, even if in the service of some corporation's bottom line, not the advancement of pure knowledge.

Knowledge—wasn't that what the grad library was all about? Holly's first job after graduating had been shelving books there. A world-class institution, and every book was placed where it needed to be by the people in the Stacks Department—almost all women, and almost all over-educated for this job. Some had been there for five or ten years. A few were plotting their way out, but most were just glad to get the benefits and be around books, even if at something just above minimum wage. Holly had felt like she fit right in when she needed that home the most.

With no warning, the machinery switches on. Holly and Russell, following instructions, turn away from the platform to face the far end of the tank. Small parallel wedges begin to glide toward them. One of the researchers throws the first PFDs at her and Russell. She catches hers and struggles to put it on, still treading as the waves begin to reach her. It is orange and plumy with complicated white straps. Another researcher looks at his stopwatch, timing how long it takes to put them on. Russell finishes first. He says, "Hah, it's like being on 'Beat the Clock,'" which Holly thinks is ridiculous. It's not a competition; there are no prizes. Then: *PN Television—right in the middle of Literature. One of the highest floors in the newer wing.*

So many floors in the Library, millions of books, all needing to be put into order. Order—that's what Holly needed. Books and papers in piles all over her apartment. Her untidy braid. Food rotting in bowls at the back of her fridge. A botched post-graduation break-up. It was a job, even if an unskilled one—the only type available in this recession. Reagan has been on TV telling the rust-belt unemployed to vote with their feet. A hallmate's family had done so—moving from Midland, Michigan, to Midland, Texas, where the jobs supposedly were. Last she heard they were living in their car. No wonder the midwestern Ned had romanticized her home by the ocean. No wonder he assumed everyone was leaving there, too, but in a Springsteen kind of way, which automatically made it cooler.

She thought she'd learn to embrace order. She thought she'd learn to figure out why she'd graduated into such a shit job. Such a pale post-college life. Walking around campus, seeing all the undergrads doing undergrad things, she felt invisible. Signing a lease to stay in town after graduation had seemed a good thing when her boyfriend Peter suggested moving in together, and then a bad thing when he'd flunked his spring classes, been suspended, and moved back to his home in the Upper Peninsula, and finally just a thing to deal with, lease in hand, rent due. One of her co-workers in the library, a wannabe law student saving for tuition, studying for the LSATs while she was supposed to be shelving books, suggested she sue him to cover his half. Mostly Holly felt like she'd dodged a bullet. And Alice the co-worker, that was something else not to think about.

Sometimes, walking through town, one of those perfect college towns that always make the top ten lists of perfect college towns, she suspected she was invisible. And there she last week, searching university kiosks for notices of temporary jobs, to replace the library job. This one paid four bucks an hour, well over minimum wage. A few days of that would help make the rent.

After getting her jacket fastened, she turns to face the lines of waves that march toward her like a procession of long glass prisms breaking against her neck and shoulders. She has been told not to lift her head or move at all—just float levelly, let the life jacket do its work. Her task is to count how many swells cover her mouth as they pass by. The techs send different level waves—six inches, one foot, one and a half—as she bobs and counts, bobs and counts.

This goes on with each device. Some aren't like the usual life vests at all; one version is simply an inflated tube she wraps under her arms. One is a coat with flotation sleeves she labors to get her arms into. It doesn't work at all and she's happy to take a break after that struggle. She becomes less and less conscious of Russell floating a few yards aware from her. She has stopped noticing much of anything besides how cold she is.

After they've run through the drill several times, she and Russell climb up the ladder and out of the tank to the staging room filled with space heaters, hot chocolate, blankets, towels. Steam pours off her drenched clothes. She stinks of chlorine. Water puddles beneath her, squelching out of her sneakers and clothes. When they head out again for the next round, Russell is dragging and she asks him if he's okay. "Fine," he says, "I'm fine."

Halfway through the first morning, everything stops. Something is drifting by as she floats—a large, dead goldfish. Its edges are frayed. Eyes smeared; tail missing. She quickly swims to the ladder and hoists herself out.

"What the hell!"

"Damn," Ned, says, "thought we got all of those."

"All? There are more?" Russell, still in the tank, looks positively ill but insists it's no big deal. "It's just dead. Heh—we're swimming in fish stew."

Ned tucks his longish blond hair behind his ears, nodding in appreciation.

"Oh, yeah. Sorry about that. The engineers who use this tank to test boat hulls keep goldfish. You know, like pets. When we threw in chlorine to clean the water for you testers, it killed them. Anyway, we tried to fish them all out," he chuckles a second at his own joke, "but once or twice a day one of them floats up that we didn't see."

He gets a net and pulls it out. It must have been dead a few days and almost falls apart before Ned can collect it.

Biology, QH. Still in the older, north building. Is there a more precise class for "dead things"? Holly starts to feel queasy. Seasick from the waves, the idea of the dead fish, maybe. But she needs the work. She treads and counts and bobs and counts for the rest of the day.

Death. That could be shelved in so many places.

By the last break, Holly is exhausted. Russell looks worse. Huddled across from her wrapped in several blankets that hang close enough to the space heater that they, and he, would be in danger of catching fire if everything wasn't damp, he is shivering and has taken on a blueish tinge. He pulls in breaths of air like each one is weighted with an anchor.

"Are you okay?"

He shakes his head. "I don't feel so good."

She offers to make him another cup of hot chocolate. It's powdered mix in envelopes, and the water in the electric kettle the techs left with them is barely lukewarm. He shakes his head.

"This guy I roomed with," he croaks out.

"What?"

"His older brother had a heart attack. Died last year." He stops to take a long, ragged breath. "Twenty-seven."

"Wait. Russell, you think you're dying?"

He shakes his head through his shivers. "I dunno. I don't feel good."

"Okay, Russell, you're not going to die. It was probably the cold water, shocked you." He's scared and she feels bad about having judged him when they met this morning. He is shivering violently. Holly's mind watches his symptoms and then shelves them in the medical section—the R shelves. Mentally she takes the elevator and wheels the cart of sorted books to the right floor. At the same time, she bolts to the door and calls out to the techs who have disappeared, coordinating the information from the latest set of tests in whatever room the building's mainframe computer is housed.

Finally her calls get their attention, and when they run in and see Russell huddled over and shivering, three of them race back out to find a phone, while Ned stays in the room with them. "Stay with us, buddy," he says to Russell, whose breathing gets more and more ragged.

While they wait for the ambulance, Russell rallies somewhat. He's able to walk out with the medics. They say it was probably an asthma attack from the chlorine and that he'd panicked. They'll take him to Health Services to check him out.

Holly watches from the far corner of the room, shivering.

When she began in the Stacks Department, it was deep winter. The sun would not be up yet when she got to work. The library was deserted except for the workers. She would go to the sign-up sheet to choose her location for the first hour. The early task was always the same—choose a floor or section of the library to clean up all the errant books and put them back where they belonged. She usually chose the Reference Room. She liked its empty resonance, long and cavernous as a cathedral nave, tall stained-glass windows at either end. Narrow tables crossed the room, a line of chairs on either side and banker's lamps in the middle, their green shades adding a veneer of importance to the space. She checked them for encyclopedias, atlases, journals, and other stray books, and piled them on her cart. Then she made the rounds of the room, depositing those that belonged there back on their home shelves.

Some days she'd pause, and open the volume in her hands— *The Atlas of South American Rivers*, or Volume D of *The Encyclopedia of Chemical History*. It didn't matter which it was, or if it was a topic that interested her. The more obscure the better. She'd read the unfamiliar place names and the tales of solutions to solutions, running her finger down the page like she was rereading facts she knew by heart, checking to make sure the book got it right.

Few of her coworkers had any sense of where to go next. They stayed where they felt safe. Where they fit. Alice the law school aspirant was the only one thinking about a future. She shelved and studied, and at night she waited tables to save for tuition. It took a while for anyone to notice that she didn't eat.

Holly was the one who found her, passed out in a far corner of the Reference Room, slumped near her book cart as if she'd sat for a minute, then put her head down to rest. She must have come in really early to beat Holly to sign-ups. Except her name hadn't been on the sheet; otherwise Holly would have gone somewhere else. Alice's skin was damp, and book dust stuck to her cheek where it touched the ground. She was in a corner of generic encyclopedias—no specific topic at all. She was barely breathing. The baggy t-shirt and oversize cardigan she wore, which normally billowed around her, draped across her still body like a parachute after a bad jump, the skydiver outlined against the ground. Her thin limbs drawn starkly under the material.

And then she wasn't breathing and Holly couldn't make her start. She'd pumped and yelled and pumped and screamed for help. They'd worked on her in the ambulance, in the ER, not wanting to let such a young woman go. But Alice had gone.

The next morning, Holly started to enter the library, but couldn't force herself to climb the stairs to the front doors. She tried again the day after, standing on the wide front steps, the winter-brown grass and paved plaza of the Diag spread out behind her, while a well-known local figure, the kind people find colorful or annoying or both, stood on a concrete bench at the far side, loudly intoning the Greek alphabet, as he did almost every day.

"Alpha" rang out, as it had many times when Holly had sat in classrooms in the surrounding buildings, and she put her foot on the first step. "Beta" and she paused. Another step with "Gamma" and then with "Delta." But by "Zeta" she was frozen, and by "Epsilon" she'd turned and was on her way home.

Greek, her mind says. *PA. The beginning of the Language Stacks.* She never went back.

And here she has found herself, in the Engineering Building. Treading. The techs announce that they're done for the day, with Russell gone. They'll call for a substitute for tomorrow. Ned asks Holly if she'll be back. She thinks about her rent. The empty shelves in her refrigerator. She thinks about Russell's phlegmy breaths. And the oily sheen in the water around the dead fish. The space between heartbeats; the space after Alice's last one, within which Holly is still suspended.

She thinks: the floors of the library need new names, new subjects, new areas of collected knowledge: places to shelve hunger. Pain. Anger. Incandescence. Blankness. Time. Or end of it. And maybe, also, a new physics: the mass of witness. The guilt of buoyancy. The density of loss.

She says, yes, of course she'll be back. Knowing she'll be floating tomorrow, and the next day if she's lucky, if the contract money stretches that far, if there are enough jackets that need testing.

Treading and counting, as each small swell breaks across her face, the lines marching down the tank like the long tables laddering the length of the Reference Room. She'll be watching for killed fish, poisoned so that she could play at testing survival. Struggling to keep her nose and mouth above water, as her jeans and shoes fill with water. Heavier and heavier, she'll kick against gravity, the flawed composition of bodies.

Monic Ductan

Two for a Dollar

I'm already running late for work when I turn to lock my front door and I see that my terrier, Ralph, is holding his empty food saucer in his mouth, looking up at me with big brown eyes.

"Shit," I say, remembering that I forgot to buy dog food yesterday. "C'mon," I say to Ralph. He follows me down the stairs and we skirt the side of the house. Mama lives on the first floor of the house, and she also owns the bakery around the corner where I work. She's always busy in the mornings, and I just know she's already at the bakery, taking on all the responsibilities herself. An octopus in the kitchen, she somehow has enough arms and hands to make donuts, brew coffee, and shape biscuit dough at the same time.

Ralph and I hurry over to the next block, where we jog up to the bakery's back door. I tell him to wait outside while I get the dog food for him. Mama keeps some in a little bag beside the bakery's kitchen sink. She does this because one time when I was running really late, I'd left the back door of the bakery open and Ralph came in, somehow climbed up on the counter, and was face-first in a tray of chocolate donuts by the time I came back from the restroom.

Inside the bakery, the counter is dusted with flour. Dozens of glazed donuts lay on the cooling racks. Mama stands in front of four trays of pastry dough. She ladles an apple and sugar confection into each piece of flat dough. Afterward, she will repeat the process with the peach and sugar confection on the other counter behind her. The apple and peach turnovers are among our best-sellers.

Mama is a brown-skin Black lady with a thick mop of hair that always sits on top of her head in a bun. In the bakery, she wears a hair net, no jewelry and no nail polish. Her apron is dusted with flour and so are her hands. If you could see the way her eyes widen and brighten as she bakes, you'd think she was beautiful.

"Sorry I'm late, Mama," I say, going over and planting a kiss on her hairnet.

This is eclipse day. People will be tailgating on the square and we want to have plenty of food to offer them. It will be a long day for us, since the solar eclipse is set for the afternoon and we plan to stay open past our regular noon closing time.

"Don't you think we need another rack or two?" I ask.

"Other racks are already done, Lolly," she says, gesturing with her head to the other side of the curtain. I pull the curtain aside and gasp when I see the three full rolling racks loaded down with turnovers, sausage and eggs biscuits, bacon and egg biscuits, and both glazed and chocolate donuts.

I hope we can sell it all. On days when we have a few extra donuts, we stick a *2 for $1* sign on the door and people always clean us out.

"Luke says folks are planning to camp out in front of the library. We leave our front door open and let everybody get a whiff of these turnovers, and that'll bring 'em in!"

I smile. Mama always talks about what will bring customers in. For nearly a year, she's considered serving lunch, but Patty's serves lunch and dinner and draws a big crowd. Best fried fish po' boy around. Plus, Mama likes closing at noon each day so that she has time to work on her other business: sewing and alterations. I helped her design her own website and everything. We hand out her cards at the bakery, and with prom season coming up she's already been hired to make three gowns by the end of the month. I think Mama is the smartest woman in the world. She always finds a way to make money.

A scratching sound comes from out in the dining room. I go to the dining room doorway and see Ralph. He has one paw against the glass of the front door. When he catches my eye, he starts wagging his tail. He drags his tongue across his lips and pants. The empty food bowl sits beside him.

"Hang on," I tell him, holding up one finger.

In the kitchen, I grab the bag of dog food and take it out to the sidewalk to fill Ralph's dish. As he wolfs down the meal, I look around the square. It isn't six a.m. yet, and though we open at six our business doesn't get too heavy until six-thirty when the first shift at the auto plant stops by for their coffee and biscuits on their way to work.

I walk Ralph back to the house, fill up his water dish, and put my leftovers from last night's dinner in a dish for him.

Back at the bakery, I tuck my braided hair into a hairnet, wash my hands, and tie on my apron. I'm starting the coffeemaker when the bell above the front door dings. I pinch myself for leaving the door unlocked. "We aren't open just yet," I say, turning to face the door.

It's Jenny Broadnax. She's our part-time employee. She doesn't typically work on Tuesdays, but Mama probably thought we needed the help. Jenny comes straight over to me. She's a white girl who always has loads of energy, and her bouncy ponytail matches her chipper mood. "Lolly," she says, "Todd and I are engaged." She pauses a moment, awaiting a response.

"Congrats," I mumble and then remember to smile.

Jenny holds her hand out and I step closer to see the small diamond ring.

I nod. "Pretty."

She gestures for me to sit at the table across from her.

I start to make some excuse, but then realize I can listen to Jenny brag and laugh behind her back later with my friend Deidre.

I drop my rag on the counter and sit with her.

"He asked me last night. I'm so excited," she says. Her eyes look off into space, as though remembering. "You know, his family has forty acres out in Wilson County…"

She seems to work her boyfriend's family history into nearly every conversation. The fact is, her boyfriend works at the same shit factory where my boyfriend works, regardless of forty acres and a mule or whatever else his family owns.

"Don't you wish you had a ring?" she asks.

"Not really," I say.

She leans forward and smiles.

A few customers roll in, and we have to get up to tend to them. By nine o'clock, our morning rush is over. Most customers take their goodies to go, but ever since Mama put in free wi-fi, some patrons come in with their laptops and tablets. I brew more coffee and occasionally nod at Jenny, who has come over to the counter to continue talking about her boyfriend, er, *fiancé*. I can't decide if I'd rather stand around in the kitchen or if I'd rather stay here and be annoyed by Jenny. When I tune into the conversation again, she's talking about what a good father Todd would make. She's probably right. Todd doesn't seem to have much going on in his life, and I could see him dropping everything to teach a kid how to fish or ride a bike.

I excuse myself from Jenny and yell into Mama's office that I'm taking a break.

I go out to the sidewalk, holding my breath that Jenny won't follow. As the door shuts behind me, Jenny is saying, "Hey, Miss Henri. I got a ring last night..." and I imagine her holding out her tiny diamond again.

Luke's headed my way, and he nearly walks right past me without speaking until he sees me looking at him and gives me a half-hearted nod. Luke is the Black man who's been seeing Mama for a few months. He played high school football, but his body type doesn't match that of the others who played with him. The other former football players are wide-shouldered and pot-bellied. The white ones usually ride around in pickups with American flag bumper stickers. The Black ones have the pickups but don't flaunt any stickers. Luke doesn't fit either type. He's long and lean, more like a basketballer than a footballer. Long bundles of veins rope their way up his sinewy arms.

He goes into the bakery and I stand for a moment on the sidewalk. The morning air feels so good on my face and neck after being in the warm restaurant.

Later, I start two pots of regular coffee and another of decaf and begin to wipe down the counters while they percolate. Luke's laughter rolls through the kitchen.

"Did you think about what I asked you?" he says, his voice turning serious.

Mama says something in a low voice, and I move closer to the doorway.

"It don't matter," Luke says. "She's gotta move out sometime. You can't have her living with you forever."

My heart beats a little faster. I don't live *with* Mama. I live in the apartment upstairs from her place. Besides, she and I get along well. No way would she put me out. I wait for her to tell him that. She'll be polite about it, of course, but she'll tell him.

"You know how rough she's had it. Ethan left her with me and hasn't looked back."

Luke comes back, sharp and angry, "That ain't none of your problem, Henri," he says, calling Mama by her nickname. "Didn't you say she's dead weight? She's twenty-something years old. Let her find a job somewhere else."

"She's hardly been on time a single day since she started working here, and you think she can keep a real job? The girl will need a keeper her whole life."

One of them, probably Luke, gives a frustrated sigh.

The bell above the front door rings, and I force myself to smile as I turn toward our next customer. Jenny is out in the dining area, showing off that dang ring to two older ladies. Thank god she didn't hear Mama and Luke shit-talking me.

Struggling to block Mama's words from my mind, I greet Amanda Southerland.

"Coffee this morning, ma'am?" I ask, taking a paper cup from the stack by the coffee machines.

The next two hours are pretty busy. I take the orders and run the register while Jenny bags and pours and runs her mouth to the customers.

Mama's words keep coming back to me: *Think she can keep a real job? Will need a keeper her whole life.*

At lunchtime we have a lull in customers, and I'm washing a coffee carafe when Mama steps into the kitchen doorway with a big smile on her face and asks me if I'd be okay while she walks down to the bank to take Luke a snack. She waves a white sack toward me, and I know it's loaded down with pastries and biscuits. I roll my eyes.

"What's wrong?" she asks.

"I heard y'all talking this morning," I say, my voice sounding cowardly and pitiful, not at all like I intended.

She stares at me, as if she can't remember dissing me.

"Do you not want me living there?" I ask.

She comes farther into the kitchen and stands at the other end of the big, metal sink.

"I didn't say I didn't want you," she says, putting the white sack down on the sink's ledge.

But she still hasn't said that she *does* **want me.**

My father, Ethan, was the king of short-term relationships. He stayed with a string of women between my middle and high school years, and then he stayed with Henrietta Longhorn, the woman I now call "mama." Henri was smart, owned her own successful bakery, and, most importantly to adolescent me, she knew all the tricks of female-dom. She wore makeup, had her hair

professionally done twice a month, and even showed me how to
walk in high heels, all of which were things my real mother would
never have taught me, even if she had stuck around. My mother
was a factory worker who wore steel-toe boots and hairnets and
always smelled of wood and tobacco, not the soft magnolia scent of
Henrietta. My stern mother rarely spoke. Henrietta listened when I
complained about girls at school and was so excited to hear about
my first date that she flicked off the TV and hustled to the doorway
as soon as the boy dropped me off.

In short, I loved Henrietta. *Mama.*

"Lolly," Mama coos my name and puts a hand on my shoulder.
She's come to my end of the sink and tries to coax me in for a hug.

I resist her, thinking of the night Daddy left us. He told her
he was going to Texas to work in the oil fields. He threw a bunch
of clothes in a suitcase and half-zipped it, his jeans and underwear
nearly falling out as he stood in the doorway. A bolt of lightning
lit the sky behind his head right as he turned and looked at Mama
and me. Daddy was a light-skinned Black man with hazel eyes and
tobacco-stained teeth.

"Say goodbye and get in the car, Lolly," he told me.

Going with him would mean hours on the road to Texas. Once
we got there, he'd take up with some other woman, someone like
my real mother, a hard-edged woman with sore feet and some
exhausting job. The choice was easy. I shook my head at him. "No,"
I croaked out.

He repeated his order for me to get into the car, which remind-
ed me that I was an afterthought. He'd not given me so much as
twenty minutes to fill a suitcase or to say goodbye to her. He wanted
me to follow him with just the clothes on my back.

"No," I said, more forcefully that time.

He stared at me, and then he turned and went out into the
carport.

"You'll be back," Mama called to him as he slammed the car
door. But after six years, we still haven't seen him.

I look at her now, standing so close to me at the sink counter.
I wish I could make a dramatic exit like my father. I can't, though.
I've not saved any of what I've earned at the bakery. My checking
account was overdrawn again last month. Now, I have a little over a
hundred dollars, just enough to buy Ralph's food and some supplies
before the next payday.

"If you can't say you want me there, I'll leave," I say.

She drops her eyes to the sink, and I read sadness on her face. Or is it pity? She doesn't speak, and so I do: "You want *him*? You don't think I can live there if he moves in? Are you done with me?"

She shakes her head. "Lolly, I'm not done with you. I just think you could be doing more. When you started this job, you said it was temporary. I always thought you'd wind up doing something else. Teaching school or maybe getting a bookkeeping job or something."

I roll my eyes. Luke works in some accounting office at the bank. For a second, I picture myself working alongside him. No way in hell.

"You don't even like working here," Mama says.

"Yes," I said and then pause before claiming, "I do."

Except I hate the early mornings. And I hate the way certain customers talk down to me.

"I'll start looking for a place," I tell her. She doesn't protest, and that bothers me.

I turn my back to Mama and walk toward the lobby, and then I turn back to look at her. "You shoulda told me. I shouldn't've had to hear it from Luke."

I go back into the dining room to wipe down the tables, but they are already sparkling clean and still wet. Jenny must've sanitized them right before she clocked out for the day.

A minute later, Mama walks past me and out the door and moves down the street toward the bank. For a second, I want to grab her arm before she disappears, turn her around and yell at her. Mama hates confrontation. When Daddy used to get into a fussing mood, she'd cry and lock herself in their bedroom

I go out to the sidewalk to look around. People have already lined up along the railroad tracks. I look for my friend Deidre, who works down at the bank, but I don't see her anywhere. I wish my boyfriend Mac were here, but he doesn't get off shift until later. If I have a type, Mac would be it. Every man I've dated is a tall and broad-shouldered Black man who wears ball caps and has ugly hands and feet. One previous man I dated had an ugly black burn scar from his job as a fry cook, and another had a few mashed toes from a forklift accident. Mac has sweaty feet and thick toenails.

I imagine telling Mac about Jenney's engagement.

"Is this a hint from you?" he'll ask.

He asks me that a lot. We've been seeing each other nearly a year and whenever I stop to admire a ring advertised on TV or want to drive to look at a new subdivision, he asks if I'm hinting for a ring. He'd surely buy me one, too.

I go to the kitchen to wash down some dishes. When Mama returns, I report that business is dead and I think we should close up shop.

"It's barely after one. Let's give it another hour or two," she says.

I feel like quitting right here and now. I could move in with Mac. Life with him wouldn't be so bad. Foot powder and a mani/pedi every month would fix him right up.

"I haven't had a real break this morning," I say. "I'm going out." I'm out of there and moving down the sidewalk before she can even protest.

Minutes later, I'm sitting alone under the terrace's shelter at the town library. Most of the other townspeople have gathered farther up the street around the hill where the courthouse sits.

Henri's Bakery is a red brick building, like most of the shops on Main. A sign outside the door says HENRI'S in orange neon lights. A man comes out the door of the bakery carrying two coffee cups. Five more people enter. I imagine Mama in there rushing around, filling cups and scooping up turnovers. "Screw her," I mumble. If she can go see Luke for half an hour every morning, then I can sit here another fifteen minutes.

People come and go from Henri's. The line spills out onto the sidewalk. At one point Mama peeks her head out the front door and looks left and right, but I duck my head and turn away.

The sky darkens faster than I anticipated, not like a regular dusk where the sky changes so gradually. The streetlights come on. A little girl stands on her father's toes as he waltzes her up and down the street. She wears her hair in cornrows, a style I wore at that age. It makes me feel warm in the belly to see a daddy and daughter love each other so much. I never danced with my daddy.

I take the eclipse viewer glasses from my apron pocket and put them on. Everyone in town seems to be looking up at that sky. Darker and darker it grows. The final image is a simple ring encircled by light. So *pretty*, the people gasp, pointing. To me, though, it's a letdown. All that talk and camping out on the square just to see a circle of light?

The sky begins to lighten. Mac stands out on the sidewalk in front of the bakery, waiting for me. I don't want a thing to do with that place, but I do wish I could squeeze Mac. Most nights when he's off shift, he stays over with me. We drink cheap coffee and eat salty snacks as we sit on the little porch that overhangs Mama's roof. He's a foreman at the plant and seems content with it. Lived here his whole life and never wonders what it would be like to leave. I want to see other places. Once, I coaxed him into driving to Atlanta one weekend, just to *see* it. He drove, hunched over the steering wheel through all that traffic on the interstate, never once complaining because he knew the trip was what I wanted. When I finally do leave this town, I'll miss Mac.

I take the long way home, walking slowly around the businesses on the south end of Main Street—the electric company, the old ice cream shop with its neon sign that sits higher than any other.

Ralph greets me at my front door. I pick him up and take him into the bedroom. There are lots of pictures of Ralph, Mama, Mac and me together. I go to the dresser and look at the one of us at the park the weekend I turned twenty-two. It was the single happiest day I can remember. Even the weather was perfect.

I take Ralph to the bed and pet his fur as I lie on my side. He starts to bark as someone comes up the stairs outside. I shush Ralph, but he goes to the door and I hear him scratching his paw against the wood as Mac knocks and hollers for me.

I flip over onto my back and stare at the ceiling. He's such a good man. Something *is* wrong with me. I'm angry. Bitter. And something else, something I can't name.

Finally, I hear Mac's retreating footsteps growing fainter as he descends the stairs. I go to the front window with Ralph at my heels to watch Mac as he walks back toward Main Street. Above Mac's head, black birds fly over the trees near Bushy Creek. Once, I saw a black bird flying alone, away from the flock, moving toward the highway as though escaping something. Flying away.

June Gervais

excerpt from **Jobs for Girls with Artistic Flair**

July 1, 1985
Blue Claw, Long Island, New York

How freeing it would be—how useful, how illuminating—if a fortune-teller should walk through the door of Mulley's Tattoo. Who else could Gina consult? For three days she'd been pacing the docks behind the shop, as if she'd catch some brilliant idea swimming in the river, just fish it out of those rainbow wriggles of oil slick. An hour ago, Dominic had said *Enough*, and he was the shop owner, the ten-years-older brother. He summoned her back inside to the shop's waiting area, where he'd set up his Olympia portable typewriter on the coffee table. *You're not wasting your life here. Time to make a plan.*

From the age of fifteen, Gina had done all her homework in this very room, while drifters and eccentrics told their stories over the staccato buzz of Dominic Mulley's tattoo machine. This was the one place on Earth where she belonged. She'd memorized every design on the flash posters, their stock eagles and ships and arrowed hearts. She'd painted that mural over the couch, the centerpiece to all their flash: a muscled mermaid leaning against an anchor, holding an artist's palette, as if she had just lettered the boldface MULLEY'S on the wall.

As of last Saturday, though, Gina was a high school graduate; she still had a nasty sunburn as a memento of the ceremony. Now began some other life.

Step one, Dominic had said. *Write a résumé.*

Résumés meant interviews meant jobs where you had to look people in the eye, and that was never easy for her like it was for Dominic. She always said the wrong thing, or the right thing in a strange way, and had to escape sometimes to the bathroom because breathing felt like sucking air through a cotton filter. It had happened when she worked at the bait shop, the movie theater, the housekeeping service, and the card store, and wherever she worked next, it would happen again.

Here she sat, though, miserably clacking out her name on the

Olympia, one percussive letter at a time. If she were a typewriter key, which one would she be? The ampersand, with its crossed arms? No—a left parenthesis. The scrawny bend of her body, the shy hunch to her shoulders—

"Hey, chickie." A customer, a biker with a blond horseshoe mustache, was snapping his fingers at her. He was getting a tattoo of a blue devil from Mackie, one of the guys who worked for Dominic. "You work here?"

"She's the lackey," Mackie said, pausing to dip his needle back into a little paper cup of ink. Sweat glazed his bald head; his arms swelled out of the sleeves of his T-shirt.

"I help my brother run the shop." In truth, Gina wasn't allowed to run anything but the vacuum. She turned her attention back to the typewriter. *Hard worker seeking position as* · · · **what? Leave it blank for now.** *Strengths include*—

"What I'm asking is, you do tattoos? Say I wanted some art-work down here." Gina glanced over to see the biker moving his hand to his fly, giving her a sly look. She rolled her eyes. Dudes always made that joke like they were the first one to think of it.

Focus on the typewriter. *Strengths include attention to*—

"She can't tattoo," Mackie said. "And if you're that commit-ted to decorating your dick"—he hocked a load of phlegm and bent to spit it in the trash—"I charge a hundred-dollar handling fee."

"Dammit," Gina said. She'd meant to type *detail*, and now she'd accidentally typed *dick*. She pulled the carriage release lever and yanked the paper out.

"So what are you, the secretary?" the biker said.

"I'm looking for a job."

The biker scratched his mustache. "Thought you said you help run the shop."

"I don't take a salary." She liked saying it that way. Classed it up.

"So what kind of job are you looking for?"

And that was the question, precisely—the reason she needed a fortune teller. She could not envision this new life she was supposed to create much less the next step toward it, which made these orders from Dominic—*Just picture yourself in five years*—im-possible. The best she could do was list all the futures she didn't want:

Not anything that required a degree. College was a foreign land with an impossible price tag.

Not any of her after-school jobs—the kind you got because you wanted to stock the neglected pantry with more than spaghetti and ketchup. The kind you quit or were fired from within a few weeks, because whenever someone talked to you, you gaped at them like a fish.

Not her mother's jobs: bartender by night, receptionist at a glass-and-mirror company by day. Not anything, in fact, that would resemble her mother's life, or keep her in that house any longer than she had to be.

But also not anything that took her away from Blue Claw, because that would mean leaving Dominic. Clearly he needed her just as much as she needed him, but in some act of pointless martyrdom, he kept harping on her to get out of their hometown and *strike out on your own.*

This is not a real list. This is just a pile of nots. You're making this difficult, Dominic had said. *Just write down your skills.*

My primary skills, she'd replied, *are doing your grunt work, managing Mom, and drawing weird pictures.* This only made him scrawl out his own list—

JOBS FOR GIRLS WITH ARTISTIC FLAIR

—and stick it next to the typewriter before stalking out of the shop on some errand.

"Hey," the biker said. "Did you fall asleep over there? I said what kind of job?"

Gina rubbed her face with both hands. "I am considering"— she picked up Dominic's list—"floral design. Window dressing. Seamstress. Candy making."

"Gina," Mackie snapped. "Less dit-dit-dit. More type-type-type." He turned to run his needle in water.

"You want to come work for me? I restore elite vehicles. I just did a Lambo for Judas Priest's drummer." This was clearly Gina's cue to be dazzled. Did anyone actually imagine impressing a woman that way? If Gina were trying to get a girl's attention she would do something legitimately sexy. Like ask the girl what she loved doing, what made her lose track of time. And then listen to the answer. Or perhaps knead a loaf of bread dough, in a casual and quietly confident way, while asking the girl what sort of sandwiches she liked and making occasional meaningful eye contact. In her dream world, she could pull that off.

Gina got up and turned the typewriter, so she was facing away from the biker, toward the front window. Just as she got settled, a Dodge Tradesman van pulled up to the curb, and out climbed one of the largest human beings Gina had ever seen.

Elise Gregory

Lupine

Her brother, Anders, threw a party for his college friends, most who'd never set foot on a farm. They wouldn't know the back end of a cow 'til it kicked. That afternoon it'd looked like an REI fair with all the colored, nylon tents. Geirolf muttered in Norwegian while he ran the second milking of the day. She couldn't tell what he said, but his pinched brows meant it wasn't good. But then he was always pinched these days. Anders no longer talked much with her since his return in May. Used to be they'd feed the calves together. Catching up with his friends, she guessed.

He'd used the pile of buckthorn and sumac behind the barn for a bonfire, close to the ten-foot corn stalks, rows that stretched to the bluffs. She watched the smoke grow heavier from her second story window and guessed they were burning wood pallets. Smelled like it. No longer the fresh green but chemical in the air. She climbed down the oak beside her window to get a closer view of all the mess. The wide limbs, familiar and where she usually sat. But tonight was about escaping her room which felt warm and too small when she could hear all those voices outside.

The barn made a secretive spot. Dark forms laughed and passed bottles then laughed harder. Some pairs kissed on the square bales her brother had set out. The night was still, and the smoke stood up in the air like a mast.

Most of the kids were out of towners, though she thought she could make out the thick body of the Peterson boy. And was that Hiran? Manny? She looked for Anders but couldn't find him among all the bodies. People she thought she knew, then they turned, and it was just the look of them in the shadows that tricked her into thinking they were familiar.

Years back, she, Anders, and Henrick stacked cedar and white pine limbs they'd trimmed on their land. They used a long-handled saw to cut the lowest branches, most with needles that trembled and dropped with the first cut. Sap swelled and ran down the silver trunks. Their arms were covered with sap. Needles knitted in their hair as they heaped branches into a huge, haphazard teepee. Then

Anders squirted it all with kerosene.

The eruption was so sudden and so hot it burned off her eyebrows, eyelashes, and bangs. She'd shrieked and fell underneath Anders's weight as he smothered his own shirt into her burning face. The heft of him was such a comfort that she didn't cry.

For months after, Anders and Henrick called her hedgehog while the hairs grew back spiky and stiff. If she could find Anders now, she'd razz him about almost setting her on fire before she turned thirteen. With the flickering light she caught him with some girl, faces locked lip on lip. Beer cans nearly sideways. She knew better to interrupt him and gazed back into the flames.

She could have stayed happy seeing the fire climb and the shadowy figures beside. Then a guy wobbled into her.

"Hey, didn't see you there," he slurred, zipping up his shorts. "Are you Anne?"

"Nope."

"Who are you then, I can't see too well now that I'm away from the fire."

Her eyes had already adjusted to the dark, and the moon was out. She could see the boy's chin length hair and sharp jaw. He wasn't much taller than she was, though his chest and shoulders were wide like many of the wrestlers in this area.

"Lupine," she said and stuck out her hand, feeling immediately like a little girl.

The boy grasped her palm and opened it to his mouth, touching his tongue to the middle. It reminded her of the goat kids over at Terra's place where she'd been milking mornings—an animal act. It shook her. Not enough to let go. She prided herself on being a farm girl. And this was her brother's college friend. An outsider. Besides, Anders wasn't beside her.

She wanted to see where he would lead. The possibility of danger interesting. She liked the necessary labor of feeding calves, milking goats, but it was solitary work. Without public school she felt even more alone when Anders left. This wasn't her brother. She knew this absolutely and knew he wanted something from her. For once, she wanted to be seen.

"Lupine, I like it," he said into her hand. "Hey Lupine, did you see all this corn. It's like a black hole."

"Where are you from?" she asked knowing he couldn't be

from the Midwest.

"Boston, and look what I brought with me." He pulled out a flask. It flickered in the firelight and so did his eyes.

What intensity, she thought. And here, she'd only stolen sips of warm PBR from her brother's stash. She took the warm metal. His lips were wet with the stuff. She imagined she was pressing against his mouth as she swigged. She threw her head back, and the liquor burned her throat.

"Whoa, that was a mean drink."

She coughed, "You didn't say your name."

"Gus. So Lupine, do you want to go to the fire or explore the corn?"

She could have told him she explored the corn all the time in full sun, but she felt the liquor ignite her cheeks.

The corn was something different at night. If animals used it as cover during the day, all sorts of nocturnal critters were doing the same thing at night. She'd rather not run into a coyote or badger. But the danger excited her. This night when no one seemed to know her. Instead of telling him it was a dumb idea she asked for another drink. It burned less than the first.

"I'll follow you," he said.

His heat was closer and hotter than anyone she'd known. It was hard to tell if it was the alcohol or Gus who had her heart racing. She looked for a wider row. All symmetrical except for one or two long openings. She turned back to see the fire grow and leap higher—wondered if Anders had added wood. She smiled.

Gus, thinking she smiled at him, grinned and grabbed her. He probed her mouth with his tongue. His mouth was slick and hot and tasted slightly like the flask and something muskier. It made her lose her breath. She wasn't quite sure she liked it and pushed back on his chest. He held her and grinned into her face with a doggedness she'd never seen in a man. Not that any man had ever looked at her. His spit was still on her lips. She didn't know quite how to wipe it off without him seeing. She shoved at him again and then turned into the corn, finding a slightly larger row so they could move more freely.

Leaves still flicked against her pajama pants. Webs caught her cheeks and hair. She wished she'd made him go first, irritated at herself for not speaking up. Then his hand went to her shoulders just below her neck. It traced down. She stopped. With his other hand, he squeezed her hip.

"You wanna stop here?" he asked.

She did, even though she thought it was silly to be inside such a narrow space. She would have led him to the upper barn where the air was sweet. But she was curious now after his kiss. She stood still and let him turn her. He kissed her eyes, ears, and left wet streaks down her neck, making her legs tremble. What was she doing? She wasn't sure how to use her hands at all, laying them like blocks of wood on his shoulders as he moved down her, kissing the whole way.

She let him lift her shirt and tug down her pajama pants. She stood in her underwear and long hair while he kept kissing. Every place he didn't touch felt cold and very naked. She should be embarrassed. When she thought of other people, she felt colder, like they were turning from her one by one. But she liked the kissing: how it coiled inside her—a snake ready to strike. When he said she was lovely, she couldn't quite believe him since the stalks blocked the moon. Still, it was a nice offering, and she allowed him to pull at her panties. He threw off his own shirt and shorts and boxers. She could only half see his skin glowing in the fractured moonlight. He wanted her hands on him. His chest. His hips. She could tell as he took her hands in his— moved them to each place. His body hot in comparison to hers.

It didn't seem odd to her since she'd witnessed so many animals breed, though there was hardly such preparation. Really, she never followed the squeamishness of her mother, Gin, who'd seemed frightened of tampons and Lupine's bleeding. But, it was awkward in that small space. He tried lifting her to his hips. The leaves and stalks were knives against their skin. He wanted her to turn around and kneel, but she wouldn't. That was too far. She wouldn't have her first time without someone's face beside hers, and she liked the kissing. The pushing she could do without except for that coil in her belly.

Kissing her mouth, he stood her back on the uneven dirt. She felt relief to have her bare feet in the soil even though it was cold. Her head spun from the drinking. Or him. She wasn't sure. He took her hand and pressed it back on him, pulling her hand back and forth until she understood what he wanted her to do. She felt detached from her body and his then. The darkness helped her and so did the thought of the bonfire that her brother had made.

As Gus helped her dress, she hid her face behind her hair even though she knew he couldn't really see. He put his mouth to her hair-covered ear and said, "Thank you. You're beautiful," which made her feel both pleasure and the need to cry. They tripped their way to the fire.

He fed her more alcohol. It helped her with any tinge of shame. They toppled over one another on the hay bales. His arm slung across her shoulders, hand squeezing a breast.

The fire lit up Anders's face across the way. She shrugged Gus's hand off. With her fingers she combed her hair over her face, hiding from Anders. But he'd already seen them. He was beside her fast. Even with the firelight his face looked dark. She knew she was in trouble.

"Shit, Lupine. You're supposed to be in bed."

"Hey man," mumbled Gus and pulled her onto his lap.

"Fuck you, Gus. This is my kid sister."

Anders hauled Lupine to her feet. Up to the house he dragged her.

"Hey, I can walk," she said. But he didn't respond. Maybe he didn't hear, she thought. And she said again, "Hey, let me walk, will ya?"

They were unsteady on the stairs. When he shushed her, she could smell smoke and alcohol on his breath. He stunk and she guessed she did too. She could feel his fingers digging into her upper arms. Still, she thought he might talk with her like he used to nights before he left for school.

Instead, he growled as he shoved her inside her room, "Stay away."

"Why?" She stood grounded in her bedroom doorway.

He tried pushing her inside again then harshly whispered, "Gin needs to have a talk with you is why. This isn't up to me."

"She doesn't talk."

She wanted him to come in and sit on the old rocker. Legs hanging over one side.

"That's not my problem."

"You're the only one besides Grandpa Etzel who talked."

His face wobbled close in front of her round and glowing, "Listen, Lupine, I'm drunk. Now is not the time to have a little fuck-chat with you. I'll talk to you tomorrow."

He snuck back out to the fire, his friends, and booze. She wondered what exactly she was supposed to stay away from: Her brother? Men? Drink? What really had she done? The ceiling swirled in front of her. It took time to release the images of her brother and Gus.

Over the past year, she'd tried texting her brother then joined Facebook just so she could see him post selfies that had nothing to do with her, farming, or family. It hurt to see his superimposed smile, arm around a stranger whose face was just as large and fuzzy from drink. She missed him.

Anders never did talk about the bonfire even though she waited on the straw bales beside the charred remains of pallets. The nails glowed in the afternoon sun as she waited for him to come sit beside her. She heard the calves bellow. She watched all the colorful tents stuffed inside packs. Ander's friends, all strangers to her, packed up their cars. A parade of out-of-state license plates. Maybe she saw Gus climbing into a Volvo with another girl, Lupine wasn't sure, and anyway he wasn't looking for her. She sat and watched the corn bend and sway. The cows tromped back inside for evening milking. And Anders never came for her.

Destination Unknown

At dusk, lights came on in the town the river ran through. The river, now dark, carried with it the lights like starlights, and cajeput flowers that had fallen from the riverbank floated white on the water.

He bought from a ferry peddler sweet rice cooked with mung bean, packed in a banana leaf, and black coffee in a styrofoam cup. He ate while the riverboat waited for passengers to board. Then he took off the cloth cover of the birdcage, set the cage on his thighs and began feeding the myna with leftover sweet rice.

"You like sweet rice or you like papaya," he said, watching the bird peck a yellow bean from his palm.

"Papaya," the bird said, bobbing its head twice. "Yummy yummy."

"What'd Ly give you?"

"Papaya." The bird purred deeply.

"Where's Ly?"

The bird looked around, then bobbed its head repeatedly.

"Call Ly," he said. "Call her." He watched the bird as it fluffed its feathers then called out, long, clear, Ly Ly Ly Ly. Then it cocked its head and watched him intensely.

The new passengers were coming on board, a woman and a young girl, who sat down on the bench seat across from him. He smiled at them and the bird bobbed its head and croaked, "Hello guest!"

The girl's face beamed. "A talking bird!" she said.

She bent forward and looked at the bird. It tilted its black-crowned head, studying her. "What's your name?" the bird squawked.

The girl broke out laughing, her hand covering her mouth. She had an eyetooth that made her smile charming. "He can really talk," she said to him.

"Yeah. He can mimic all kinds of sounds."

Just then another riverboat was passing by out in the broad water, its motor chugging steadily. The myna looked around,

346

shifting on its thin legs and making some deep-throated sounds.

"He heard the boat I think," the girl said.

"Yeah. He can neigh like a horse, meow like a cat." Stroking the bird on its breast with his finger, he said, "What the cat say?"

"Meow," the myna let out a crystal-clear cat's sound.

"Oh my," the girl said.

"What's your name?" he asked her.

"Kim."

He glanced up at the woman who had been watching them. She wore an indigo blue headscarf, sitting with a carry-on bag on her lap. "Where're you folks going?" he asked her.

"The Plain of Reeds."

"Oh. It must be in the flood season now."

"It already was when we left last week. And where're you going?"

"The Plain." He lied.

"Oh really? Visiting?"

"No. I live there." He knew nothing of the Mekong Delta.

"Well, neighbor, you must've been away then. We had early flood this year. What d'you do there?"

"I have a fishing boat." After lying the second time he looked down at the myna and then at the little girl. "Kim, you want to feed him? Here. Just give him bits of this." He put some sweet rice in the girl's palm. "Let him pick from your hand what he wants to eat, bean or rice. There."

The girl gently touched the bird's head with her finger. The bird pecked a yellow bean from her palm, tossed its head back to down the food and sang, "Thank you, Ly, thank you."

The girl laughed. "Oh, you're so sweet." Then she looked at him. "Who's Ly?"

"My lover. I mean my girlfriend." He caught the woman smiling as she adjusted her headscarf.

"The same, isn't it?" she said to him.

"What is?"

"Lover and girlfriend."

"You have a lover?" the little girl said, all perked up.

"Yeah. She's his favorite person. He knows her well."

"Where is she?"

He thought for a moment and the woman said, "Your lover." He glanced at the woman and then at the girl. "She's home."

"When are you going to marry her?" the girl said.

"Shhhh," the woman said.

"I'll ask her to marry me when I get home," he said, smiling.

The girl's face beamed. "You should, I think. Will she say yes?"

"Yeah. I know she will." He picked up his cup of coffee and let the myna drink from it. "She's carrying our child."

"You mean she's pregnant?"

"Yeah."

The woman dipped her head toward him. "Are you serious?"

"She told me yesterday."

"Then I think you ought to marry her. Soon."

"That's what I'm planning for."

The little girl stroked the myna's back as it dipped its beak in the coffee. Then she said, "Is she a nice girl?"

"She's beautiful."

"What does she look like?"

"Well."

The woman giggled. "Don't mind her."

He shrugged. "First time I saw her, she was coming down the road one night on this beautiful white horse. I could hardly breathe while I stood in front of her. I knew I would never be the same again without knowing her."

"Oh." The little girl's mouth fell open. "I always love horses. I wish one day I have a horse of my own."

"They are beautiful. I have a quarter horse myself. She has a stallion. We'd ride around together sometimes late in the night."

"Can she still ride?" the girl asked, raising her eyebrows.

"Of course. Why?"

"She's pregnant."

The woman laughed and patted her daughter on the head.

"Sure she still can ride," he said.

"Can he stay on her horse's head while she rides?" The girl touched the myna's beak with her finger. "I saw mynas standing on buffalos' backs."

"Yeah. I'll tell her. We'll try that next time we ride out."

The riverboat sounded its whistle. The girl sat back on the bench seat, looking at him as he put the cloth cover on the cage.

"What're you doing that for?" she asked. "How can he breathe?"

"Just so he keeps quiet and won't bother other people with his talking."

"Can I hold the cage, please?"

"Sure, Kim." He leaned forward and placed the birdcage in her lap. She wrapped her arms around it, her eyes gone soft and dreamy.

It was evening now and the river was quiet. The water was dark red as blood where it ran into seaward tributaries. In the cabin, lights had gone out and the passengers were sleeping. The girl slept, her head resting on her mother's shoulder, the birdcage in her lap secured by her arms around it. Sometimes in the night it began to rain as the riverboat passed a town and its lights beyond the wooded bank blinked like diamond dust. He woke hearing the sound of rain and, in its empty cadence, thought he heard her voice. He imagined the sea almond trees around the servant quarter standing solemn, dripping rainwater from their lacquered leathery leaves, the fruits ripened and red, and if it rained early in the evening the resident bats would not come out. That was where he had stayed and worked for her husband, who was twice her age, sexually impotent, even before he married her. He was also suffering incipient throat cancer. The night she spent in his room, she said to him in a toneless voice, "Recently, my husband has asked me to do something for him. If I do it, it might help save him from dying." She went into a silence and he didn't want to break it nor volunteer his voice. Then she said, "He wants me to have a child. That his impending misfortune could be avoided if we have a child to raise as his descendant. He said the severity of one's own evil karma might be assuaged by receiving an auspicious birth of a child into one's life."

He'd often thought of the consequence of their act in that room, driven by her own choice to have a child for her husband. The thought of seeing her carry a child had troubled him, how painful it would be should it become a reality. Then one evening after dinner, having gone back to his room and sat down on the bed and taken off his shirt, ready for a night bath, he heard a knock on the door. He flung the shirt over his shoulder as he opened the door. On the dark veranda she was standing, arms folded on her chest, back turned toward him, gazing at the grove of sea almond trees.

"Hi," he called out to her.

She turned around. "Can I come in," she said, barely loud enough for him to hear.

He stepped back to let her in and closed the door. In the cage hung from a ceiling hook, the myna croaked, "Hello guest!"

"Hello there," she said, touching the cage as the bird tilted its head to regard her. Then she spoke without looking at him, "He must be speaking very well by now. Am I right?"

"What he likes to do is birdcalls. He's alone by himself most of the time so he picks up anything he hears from outside."

"Poor little one."

He draped the cage with his shirt and then brought the only chair he had and placed it in the center of the room under the naked light bulb in the ceiling. Then, after she sat down, he stood around, his hands jammed in his pants pockets, and then slowly sat down on the edge of his narrow bed. She was still in her business suit, single-breasted navy-blue gabardine and cuffed pants legs, and the air had a scent of her perfume, which he remembered well.

"I hope you've been fine," she said, her hands clasped in her lap.

"I have no complaint. How've you been?"

"Okay." She nodded then brushed back a strand of hair that had slipped down on her forehead. "I found out yesterday that I'm pregnant."

Something very cold went through him and he shivered in his bare torso. He simply nodded.

"I've thought I was at one point," she said, holding in her breath and then slowly exhaling. "But I wasn't positive of it till yesterday when our physician confirmed it."

He wondered if their personal doctor knew, too, of the truth of her pregnancy. He felt overwhelmed. She ran her fingers through her hair. Her jacket sleeves stopped just at the wrists, where they revealed the white cuffs of her shirt. She lowered her gaze at his bare torso and then looked up into his eyes.

"I want to tell you something," she said, "and I want you to be ready for it."

"Tell me."

"You can't stay here any longer."

He slumped and then immediately straightened his back. "I

hear you," he said.

"You rarely ask questions, I notice."

"I don't think my questions would change anything."

"You don't even want to know the reason, do you?"

He fixed his gaze on her face. The hollow in him was so desolate he saw her face like just another face. Then he saw in those almond-shaped eyes the sorrow he had sought words for. He knew he loved her. More than ever. He nodded. "Yeah. I want to know."

"He won't tolerate your presence around here when I tell him. The father of my unborn child."

Again he nodded. Then words came to him. "I think I know how he would've felt."

"Do you? And do you know how I feel?"

He crimped his lips. "I wish I knew."

"I must live with the guilt that I've put you through all this."

"Is that all?"

She pursed her lips like she was stuck with thoughts. Then she let out a deep sigh.

"You have no feeling for me?" he said.

"What do you think?" Her voice was nearly inaudible. "Must I speak it?"

"That's what I thought," he said, hearing the muted pain in her voice.

She looked down at the linoleum floor, sighed, and looked back up at him. "You must leave tomorrow morning. Your foreman will drive you into town. Once I tell my husband tonight, he would want you out of here."

"I can leave any time. I'm more worried about you."

"I can take care of myself. May I ask where you'll be headed to?"

"I don't know." He smiled. "I wish I knew."

"Is that the truth?"

"I never lie. At least that's what we have in common."

"Only that much?" Her eyes were half closed with the familiar softness he knew well.

He drew a deep breath. "Sometimes," he said, "what isn't said says a lot more."

After she left, he took a bath then went to the barn and saddled the quarter horse. Her stallion wasn't in its stall. He led

the horse out of the stable and down the gravel walk to the gate.
As he opened the gate, standing in the cold silver illumination the
lamps cast about him, he looked up toward the second-floor
veranda where the railing etched quietly in white against the
night. Her husband in the wheelchair wasn't there.

Night dew had wet the sand, and the water in the pond by
the parsnip field looked pale in the moonlight. Toads croaked,
their throaty calls echoing in the swale. He stood the horse and
gazed at the field. Gone now were the breathtaking yellow flow-
ers that dotted the field like myriad butterflies fluttering. Now
the stalks, slender and broken, had browned, and the stubbled
field was sterile looking. The horse lowered its head to nip at the
stalks. Paperlike seeds lay scattered on the ground, and in the
stalks fireflies blinked and the field seemed to be speaking to any
soul that understood its soundless voice.

He rode along the dirt path toward the lighthouse and up
the slope, cresting it under the peaceful creamy moonlight that
bathed the sea, the dunes. In the breeze the whistling pines
smelled of dried cones now lying like well-worn rocks among
a mat of rusty red needles. When they shed and had paved the
ground thickly, hamlet children would come and rake them and
bag them for firewood. The air then reeked of a pleasant odor.

He rode down the slope through a patch of goat's foot vine,
the horse snorting heavily, kicking up sand as they crossed a long,
long tract carpeted with evening primrose flowering pink and
white, and among them dune sunflowers rose tall and yellow as
the moon. Sea breeze brought their heady scents so thick he had
to breathe through his mouth to clear his head.

Wolf spiders were coming out of their burrows in the sand
where the horse stood grazing. He watched them push out the
tiny pebbles they plugged their holes with against floodwater. He
turned the horse back, heeled it hard and it took off like a crazed
horse. He was riding hard until he saw farther up the shore her
white horse standing on the watermark the waves left, and up
on the sand she was sitting, her knees drawn up to her chin, her
hands hugging her knees.

When he reined up he couldn't hear his own breathing for
the heavy snorting of his horse. He got down.

"Hi," he said as he took off his sandals and stood holding
them in his hands.

"Hi," she said, lowering her head to rest her chin on her knees. She was barefoot in her tight blue jeans. The breeze fluttered the loose sleeves of her white shirt.

"I thought you'd never come out this way again," he said, standing in one place as his horse found its friend and now stood side by side with the stallion.

"I thought so too about you."

"Well, looks like we have to say goodbye one more time."

"One more time, yes." She didn't brush back the stray hair the breeze left tangled on her face.

"I kinda wished that you'd be out here. But, well, I also wished that you wouldn't."

That drew a faint smile from her. "Why?"

"I don't know why. Maybe it'd be very hard to say goodbye again."

"I imagine so." Then she gazed up at him. "Why don't you sit down with me?"

He placed his sand-coated sandals between his feet, sitting with his arms cradling his knees next to her. The breeze brought an herbal fragrance from her hair and suddenly he felt lightheaded.

"How's the little guy doing," he asked without looking at her. The autistic boy was the son of her husband and his now deceased wife. After his wife died and before the man remarried her, twenty-five years his junior, some sickness has left him sexually powerless.

"He's fine," she said. "I don't know what to tell him when he notices that you're gone."

"How could you tell that he could tell?"

"I just know."

"You want me to give him the myna?"

"No. If there's someone you want to give it to, it's me." She smiled a gentle smile.

"Then it's yours. It can say your name very clearly. It said where's Ly now after you left tonight."

"No, keep it. I don't want it to remind me of something that'd haunt me thinking about it."

He gazed out toward the distant mud flats, dark and shimmering. The blind man wasn't in sight. The first time he knew about the blind man, he was riding on the beach with her and she raised her arm and pointed toward a small human figure, slumped and pale in the moonlight, working on a sand flat halfway between them and the bonfire. The figure moved a hand net along the wet sand, a basket hoisted on the hip. "See that person?" she said. "He's blind."

"I see him."

"He's from the hamlet. Born blind. He picks clams and fish, those dropped by fishing nets when they haul them out of the boats in the late afternoon."

"I guess he never needs no light on the beach to do what he does."

"No. Just have to be aware of the tide cycle and the moon cycle. You don't want to be swept away by high tide when you're out here by yourself at night. He told me every night he goes out and away from the hamlet as far as he could, till his ears could no longer pick up any sound, human and dogs, from the hamlet. He did get lost sometimes though. Told me when that happened he had to rely on his nose to smell the wind, even use his tongue to test the wind to find his way back."

Now she caught him gazing and said, "What's out there?"

"I guess I wouldn't see him again before I leave tonight."

"Who?"

"The blind man."

"It'd be late when he's out there during high tide."

"Sometimes I caught fish out that way and just threw them back in the water 'cause he wasn't there." Then he shook his head. "His is a different world."

She broke her gaze with a nod of her head. "Ours too."

"You and me?"

"Your world and mine."

"You know what I often wish for?"

"You're a man of few words so I'd be delighted to hear."

"That when I met you, you're just an ordinary girl from a poor home like me."

"What made you think that would work out for you and me?"

"You'd have nothing to give up for."

"You've never said you love me."

He looked into her eyes, gentle and demure, and in that moment he saw the graceful softness that had melted his heart once and again. "I love you," he said. "But it's never easy for me to say it."

She leaned her forehead against his and, her eyes closed,

touched his face with her hand. "Do you regret that you met me?"

"No." He tried to smile. "I learned from you to like surprises."

"Did you really?"

"Do you regret it?"

She shook her head and put her finger on his lips. Her face felt cold against his and the fragrance of her hair brought him the very name of sorrow.

✳

He woke twice when the boat docked to let off passengers and pick up new ones. Night riders who came on board as quietly as thieves, their clothes rustling, some carrying nothing while others lugging with them merchandise wares. Once, past midnight, the boat docked and ferry peddlers sang out their food choices from the landing. The woman woke, looking around in the faint reflection of lights from the food stalls.

"Where are we?" she asked him.

"I don't know." He craned his neck looking out toward the pier. "Aren't you hungry?"

"No. I brought food with me. Would you like some?"

"No, thanks. If I eat now, I'd stay awake for a while."

"You mean you want to save your stomach for what she has for you at home."

"Well."

"Does she know you'd be home soon?"

"Yeah."

"Aren't you excited?"

"I am. I mean, knowing she's home waiting."

"You forgot the little one inside her, too."

"Oh yeah."

"You can't go anywhere long enough without thinking of them."

"You tell me. You been there before."

"Yes. I've been there before." She lay her cheek on her daughter's head and smiled. After a while she said, "Where are you exactly on the Plain?"

"Where?" He cocked his head to one side. "You know where the canal ends into the Plain?"

"Hmm. I think I know where."

"I'm somewhere around there."

"Maybe someday I'll take my daughter there to visit you. She loves horses."

"Sure." He looked back out to the landing and the woman, at his silence, didn't inquire further of his whereabouts. Then he said to her, "When will we arrive there?"

"By early morning. I thought you knew that."

"Well, not exactly. This is my first time away from home."

"You can't wait to get home to see her again, can you?"

"Yeah."

"I'm happy for you."

"Thanks."

Soon the riverboat was moving again. He slept and then woke to see the velvety black of the night glowing with myriad tiny lights, yellow and green, that the fireflies made in the trees that lined the banks. He watched those stars until the boat left them behind. In his sleep he smelled the strong smells of horses and heard the sound of waves and, waking again, saw that it was getting gray in the sky and that the banks were yellow with riverhemp in bloom. Among them were gnarled trunks, like black giants, of the mangrove trees. It was drizzling and the wind came up from the land and he could smell the fragrance of cajeput flowers and soon he saw them, tiny and white, crowding the riverbank, the cajeput trunks wetly black like buffalo horns. The Plain now came into view, flat, immense and steely gray, without boundaries, brimming with floodwater. Past clumps of bushwillows with the tops of their bushes above the water, he heard moorhens calling, and rain now falling and popping like packets of broken needles on the surface of the water, the wind damp, and in that grayness a heron rising to air.

The riverboat found the ferry landing in the rain. The woman woke her daughter up.

"We're here, sweetie," she said to the girl.

The girl rubbed her eyes and looked toward the landing. "Is daddy there waiting for us?"

"He'll be there." She picked up the birdcage from her daughter's lap and gave it to him. "Well, we're getting off here. Yours the next stop, I guess."

"Yeah."

The girl pulled the cloth just to peek at the myna. "Hello baby," she said.

"Hello," the myna said.

"He never sleeps, does he?" she asked him.

"He does."

"I'll miss him, I know I will."

As they stood up, the woman with the carry-on bag now in hand, he said to them, "Wait."

They looked down at him. He took the girl's hands and put the birdcage in them. "Kim," he said, "you take him home with you now, okay?"

"Oh my," she said.

The woman smiled, shaking her head. "You're spoiling her now."

"Teach him something new every day," he said to the girl.

"Will he forget what you've taught him?"

"He won't. He's a very smart bird."

"Would he say Thank you, Ly, when I feed him?"

"You tell him your name. That's all you do, hear?"

"Will he love me like he loves her?"

"I'm sure he will. He needs affection. Like us."

"Thank you so much."

He sat back, hands on his thighs. "You all have a good day now."

"You'll be home soon yourself," the woman said, tapping him on the shoulder.

"Yeah," he said, smiling at her, "home, yeah."

After they departed from the boat, he leaned his head against the sash and gazed across the water. Farther up he could see a huge mangrove tree, gnarled and shaggy, rising out of the water like an ancient landmark. Beyond it, a house, still a small dark shape on the low, gray horizon. Beyond that, the final destination of an unnamed landing where the riverboat would stop.

He heard the little girl calling out to her father on the landing and then the myna's croaking voice, "Hello guest."

The rain was coming down hard. It was the rainy season again.

Charotte LeBarron

The Beige House

We couldn't sit on the sofa in the house growing up. My mother didn't allow it. The probability of spill, scratch, or rip was not entirely remote, so the couch remained shrouded in a plastic cover.

Whenever guests visited, we peeled off the stuffy case, plopping nervously onto the unyielding cushions. I watched her pretend not to watch the guests. Coiled fingers on glasses of potent red wine. Hummus dollops teetering on crumbling pita chips. Sometimes, I bet myself how many minutes would elapse before she moved the party to the patio.

The sofa was beige and antique. My mother described its hue as "cream" which was something she never ate. She was a creature of skim milk, cauliflower, and yellow quinoa. Bland things that didn't inspire anything, least of all an appetite.

Truth be told, the whole house was beige. There were pale, scratchy carpets that the cleaning lady vacuumed every Thursday morning. Hand-made lace doilies—no longer quite white—perched beneath a pewter dish of tiny shells and fine sand. The grand piano was paramount, its varnished, ebony surface and gleaming white keys imposing and somehow celestial.

Back then, I incessantly compared our colorless dwelling to the rambling farmhouse of my best friend Melody. It had old creaky floors and a massive painting of a red rooster in the kitchen. Fluffy black cats skulked atop armchairs, shedding on the bold Afghan blankets from tag sales. The fridge was stuffed with plump organic raspberries, misshapen eggs from the chicken coop, and broccoli so fresh you had to scrub in earnest to remove the soil.

Melody's mom taught yoga. She had a belly-button ring, tattoos, and a half-arm full of jangling metal bracelets. On warm nights she smoked pot with her boyfriend on the back porch.

At the farm, I dabbled in tempeh, oil paint, and downward dogs. Melody's mom told me to read Roxanne Gay and gave me a battered pamphlet of Buddhist sutras. I devoured them under the covers in my bed back home, clinging to the precious sliver of robustness that emerged when I left the beige house behind.

One summer, Melody's mom told the kids they could each paint their room any color. Melody chose a vibrant tangerine. She let me make a mural on top of it.

"Paint me some naked women," she said. "Like Michelangelo."

Melody frequently talked in the same sexually frank way as her mother, voicing things that should have felt crass, but always seemed brave. We already knew she liked girls, although she hadn't announced it yet. I sketched two women the color of inky midnight, locked in an ambiguous embrace. I drizzled glitter across the breasts, thighs, lips, and necks like clusters of cosmic laugh-lines. It dribbled between their toes into a single, sparkling puddle like blood. The wall was the first time I painted for anyone besides myself and the first time I saw tears jam up in the reddening corners of Melody's eyes.

"This thing is massive," she told me, and it was.

❋

That summer I was a "lady's helper." I found the job in mid-June from an advertisement in the newspaper. This felt quaint, and, at $20 an hour, paid far better than scooping ice cream.

The lady was named Carmella. On my first day, she opened the door to the foyer, clad in a gray velour sweatsuit. Her hair was generously streaked with silver, its tendrils threatening to topple from a precariously wound bun.

Donning a mild, appraising look she welcomed me in, handing off a piece of cardstock with several tasks written in tidy cursive.

"I'm headed to the studio," she said, gesturing vaguely, the little amber bead on her dainty silver bracelet, sliding up her forearm like a dribble of warm honey.

"Ok," I said shyly, masking my desire to stare. "I guess I'll get started on this list."

Her gaze lingered on the petunia hanging in the window, the neat shelves of sensible heels near the door, and the blade of grass wedged in the crook of my flip flop. Up close I could see little nicks in the pads of her fingers, eyes crinkled with sage bemusement, and the nearly imperceptible way her lips arched up at the corners. I wanted our eyes to meet. I knew, instinctually, that being seen by her would be unnerving and fantastic—a

scrutinization of blemishes and beauty marks resulting in micro-
scopic clarity.

"There's lemonade in the refrigerator, dear," she called over
her shoulder, her departure imbued with the same detached kind-
ness. "Please, make yourself at home."

It was overcast and muggy. The interior of the house
matched the vague wisps of clouds meandering across a
brooding sky. Everything was gray. Stainless steel appliances.
Stone countertops. Metal window frames. Gradients from
paper to soot cultivated by someone who understood but
largely eschewed color. In each room there was a single burst
of vibrancy. An orange pewter jug. A turquoise door handle. A
magenta bowl of fruit.

I polished the spoons and scrubbed the rim of the toilet.
On the bathroom counter was a pail full of shards of glass. The
slivers of blue chinaware, beer bottle, and translucent vase felt
sensical, if inexplicable.

When I finished, I poured myself a cup of lemonade and
meandered to the yard.

Behind the row of rose bushes was a shed with a massive
bay window, its frame painted a dusky purple. A stone walkway
twined towards a clawfoot bathtub packed with a hodgepodge of
dilapidated glassware. I spotted hunks of dinner platter, a win-
dowpane with a hole through the center, and a chartreuse vase
missing its bottom.

Bizarrely, I wanted to cradle each fragile, broken thing in my
palms, letting ragged history leech into my fingers. I lusted for
rummaging, but touching the glass felt like reading a diary, so I
retreated to a lawn chair and savored the lemonade.

The drink was cold, zesty, and whimsically yellow. I popped
off my shoes and let my toes sink into the verdant, manicured
lawn, feeling suddenly childlike. In the beige house growing up,
lemonade—like all sugary beverages—was sequestered to birthday
parties and fantasies.

Once, I asked my mother why we couldn't buy lemonade
mix.

"To be candid, Evangeline," she said, with a wry, uncharac-
teristically sheepish grin, "I fear I'd drink the whole thing in one
sitting."

"Because you like it?" I'd asked. We were in the Stop & Shop snack aisle. I swung my ruffled socks and tennis sneakers over the edge of the shopping cart.

"I love it," she said, shocking me. The list of things my mother loved was short. That day, she bought the lemonade and two do-nuts—chocolate frosted with rainbow sprinkles. We ate them on a bench in the sun and she didn't even remind me to wipe the sugar from my lips.

✳

When I told Melody about Carmella's gray-scale house, she seemed as intrigued by it as me.

We were in my room burning incense near an open window so my mother wouldn't smell it. Melody splayed in the armchair, her messenger bag tossed nearby, overflowing with notebooks and lip gloss. She twiddled a menage of scrunchies around her wrist.

"Do you think she's some sort of artist?" she asked.

"I'm not sure," I said.

I'd googled Carmella, of course. Apparently, she was the for-mer wife of some Wall Street big-wig. Apparently, they'd met when she was his secretary. Apparently, his new secretary was his new wife although Carmella had managed to retain one of their three homes.

"You could be an artist, you know," Melody mused absently. "I mean, look at some of this stuff."

She gestured at the beige wall over my bed which was covered in postcard-sized paintings.

Sunflowers with little colored buttons as their centers. A mermaid encompassed in crushed jingle shells. A still-life of the wayward, twining pea plants at the farmhouse.

There wasn't any order or motif to the paintings. I'd hung them crookedly with double-rolled tape because my mother wouldn't let me put nails in the wall. Sometimes they slipped onto my bedspread, and I'd come home to my creation staring up at me like an eye. When I walked past gallery windows downtown, there was an order to the artist's work. A collection of seascape water-colors. An assemblage of abstract color blocks. My work seemed convoluted and incoherent, like fleeting thoughts brushing the edges of something important.

"I think my art may just be a mess," I told Melody.

She glanced up at my favorite part of the wall: the zone where I kept portraits. There was a depiction of Melody emerging from the center of a rose, done entirely in red brush strokes. I'd painted my mother at the piano. Wholly black and white. It was hazy and dream-like except for her pen-etched hands, strikingly clear as they navigated the keys.

Once, years ago, Melody asked me why I never painted myself. I told her I didn't do self-portraits, but this was a lie. Whenever I sketched Evangeline Webber, the colors swirled like paint-water being swept down a drain until I discarded the dizzying murk in a wastebasket.

Usually, if I deprecated my art, Melody told me to, "Stop being ludicrous." This time, she just stared me straight in the face.

"Isn't that the point?"

❋

Melody didn't detest men, but she didn't find them particularly useful either. We were united in this cynicism, which a therapist would probably say resulted from having absent fathers. Hers was some sort of drifter, from what I'd gathered. Melody's mom told me once—with neither wistfulness nor animosity—that she "loved him until she didn't."

Melody's dad called her occasionally and once he sent a ukulele on her birthday. Sometimes, outside on the porch at the farmhouse, she strummed it while she relayed anecdotes, blending from light and upbeat to twangy and dramatic like a movie soundtrack.

I didn't even know my father's name.

"Why don't you just ask your mom about him?" Melody wondered once.

The truth was, I had asked. Years ago, at breakfast. My mother didn't respond. Instead, she took the vacuum out of the closet and wordlessly scoured the floors until I left for school.

"I don't need a dad anyways," I told Melody, "I have my art. I have friends."

The plurality of friends was a lie and we both knew it. In elementary school I was painfully prim and unnervingly quiet. Every morning my mother yanked a brush through my curls until my skull ached so she could painstakingly plait long, ornate braids. She put me on the bus with an old-fashioned tin lunch-box full of crunchy, dressing-less vegetables and multigrain crackers. I spent the entirety of recess swinging, mainly because it saved me from asking other kids to play. When I pumped my rail-thin calves and soared up towards the metal beam and cloud-adorned skies, it rendered the four-square, hopscotch, and jump-rope below to mundanity.

Melody showed up in fifth grade. Her hair was blue then, like always. Sometimes, when she walked down the hall, she hummed to herself. When school had the annual spelling bee, we were the last two kids left standing. In the end, she could spell "eudemonic," and I couldn't.

That day at recess, Melody sat down on the swing next to me.

"Hi," she said, brushing the tips of her toes back and forth across the woodchips and peering at me through the metal rungs of the swing's chain.

"Hi," I said. And then we just swung.

When I got home from school I looked up "eudemonic" in the Merriam-Webster on the bookshelf in the beige house. It meant "conducive to happiness" which I only half understood until the next day when Melody swung with me again, the two of us careening skyward and giddily giggling like a pair of rare birds.

✳

Once, after a shift at my old ice cream shop job, one of the boys I worked with asked if I wanted to go get high behind the elementary school. I told him I didn't smoke, but he said that was fine, and so we ended up on the swings where he fiddled with a lighter and some Zig-Zags. When he finished, he told me I was "pretty damn pretty" and my mind whirled with secondhand smoke and the inconceivable notion that I could be wanted. When I told Melody, I expected her to be thrilled on my behalf.

Instead, she closed her eyes.

It was barely more than a blink and something only I, who'd attuned to her motions and expressions during the years elapsing between preschool and freshman year, would notice. Her eyelids lingered closed for just a second too long, like a veil between me and the pain that I suddenly suspected was flicking across her pupils. I imagined them rolling around beneath the thin flaps of skin, itching to pop back out of the dark, pink sanctuary, or maybe, longing to stay in. When she opened her eyes, remnants of unspoken truths lingered in the two blue orbs, flecked with harsh light and reality.

✳

The next time I was slotted to clean for Carmella, she didn't meet me in the foyer. Instead, I found a stout piece of notebook paper on a table near the door. I was to harvest parsley from the garden and organize a storage closet. The fridge had lemonade again. It was raining.

The garden was tucked away behind a picket fence and well-pruned rose bushes. Chives wavered in the breeze, pert basil leaves stood at attention, and mint sprouted from every crevice like hair in an ear.

The purple shed was a few yards away. I watched portly raindrops lollygag down its windows, suddenly sure that this was the studio Carmella mentioned. I clamored towards the building, shamelessly peering between its half-drawn curtains.

She sat on a metal chair, eyes closed. Her crookedly buttoned suit jacket was the color of a storm, and her fingernails an egregious, hollering red. A colossal, polished, diamond ring dangled between her breasts on a silver chain.

The skin on Carmella's cheekbones looked taut, like invisible strings tugged it towards youth. Her spine arched, impeccably erect, her fibers and fluidities coagulated into semi-solid form. In her lap was a piggy bank. She stroked the glass on the pig's glistening tummy and chiseled ears, cradling it like an infant.

I was viewing a ritual not yet meant for me, perhaps never meant for anyone besides her. I'd caught her in some deep, private, potentially art-adjacent act that I desperately wanted to ask her about. I ached to know all of it—what provoked the sparks of brightness and the shades of gray in her home. Whether she was tempering restraint with vibrancy or subduing the vividness.

But then, her head bowed, curling over the glass pig like a gooseneck lamp. Her shoulders quaked and the wind picked up, the thin pane between us burgeoning into an impermeable wall. As whirling air swept away thorny dignity, a tear trickled down her well-powdered cheekbone. Worried that more would follow, I looked down and headed home.

❋

My mother's love of entertaining was real, but in constant conflict with her lust for control. Parties at our house were typically satisfying, but seldom fun, like solving a tough geometry proof or re-arranging your sock drawer by color. My mother was aware of and unbothered by this differentiation, as were her friends, most of whom worked at the university too.

Her PhD was in classical music. When she wasn't composing

or doing research, my mother taught piano lab to freshmen and advanced theory to music majors. She detested the freshmen, most of whom were only in the course to fulfill a core requirement. At one dinner party in the beige house she imitated them on our baby grand, slamming her thumbs up and down the keys like a plodding elephant. The academics roared. Most of them hated teaching talentless underclassmen too.

I wondered, on occasion, whether a college degree would make my mother appreciate my art. This was a frivolous musing because I already knew its answer. In her eyes, the best, and perhaps only, way to elevate my work from infantile scribbling to a verifiable passion would be a degree followed by other manifestations of prestige.

I worried that regimented study would tarnish the rawness I both bemoaned and treasured. Although I suspected I'd enjoy art school, I feverishly clung to my iconoclasm. I needed it, to render her achievement anything less than engulfing.

Sometimes, when nobody was around, my mother played for real. Her fingers flitted up and down the swath of black and white, notes swelling to fill the living room. Every bar of music screamed for openness, lilting skyward like wayward red balloons. I almost expected the beige walls to blow clear off, floating away like her.

My mother didn't make mistakes. She didn't sing. Her demeanor was dream-like yet clear, as if the notes absolved her of some gargantuan weight. I often wondered what it was.

※

The last time Melody came to dinner was some evening in July. I seldom invited friends to our home, so my mother was elated. That night, she made pork chops with white rice, canned green beans, and applesauce from a jar.

My mother knew Melody was vegetarian, but didn't see this as a sufficient reason to discard routine.

"I wish there was a dog I could sneak bites to under the table," Melody griped, grinning at the comedic impossibility of a dog in the beige house.

"The rice tastes better if you mix it with the applesauce," I told her as recompense.

The relationship between Melody and my mother tended towards terse. Melody's disdain for established metrics of worth was a rare challenge to my mother who relished rules and titles and was surrounded by others who relished rules and titles. I could have told Melody that to earn my mother's warmth she'd have to feign interest in prestigious institutions and accolades, just like I could have told my mother that the way to win Melody's approval was to disparage capitalism and offer a reasonable breadth of sustainable milk substitutes. Each wanted the other's respect, but neither could conceive of admitting it. The result was a slab of pork congealing on a china platter and a strip of blue hair, swinging like a dare.

"How's school these days girls?" my mother asked, gingerly slicing off the fatty rim of a chop.

"Abysmal," I volunteered.

"Delightful," said Melody with a cough-syrup sweet smile.

My mother sniffed, pointedly angling herself away from me. "What sort of things are you studying?"

"Geometric proofs. *To Kill a Mockingbird*. In health we're labeling diagrams of penises. Art is the best subject, of course," said Melody.

"Of course," said my mother, eyebrows arched mildly.

"Evangeline's been doing some neat paintings, you know," said Melody, "Mrs. Kreueller says she's the best in our class."

I sawed off a hunk of pork and slid it through a well of applesauce.

"Did she?" said my mother.

"Yes," said Melody, "Not that any of us are surprised by that." Her washed-out blue-jean eyes met my mothers' in challenge.

My mother laid fork and knife in an "X" across her plate. "Evangeline didn't like the arts much as a child," she mused aloud, twirling her wrist in circles through the air as if it longed for something to grip. She reached over and pinched my arm like a plush toy, fingers lotion-tinged and cold. "I tried to teach you the piano for years. I'm not sure I ever encountered someone with less interest."

I fiddled with the napkin in my lap, wringing its slack into rigid twists.

"There's more than one type of art, you know," Melody piped up.

"Obviously," my mother's eyebrows shot even further up her already crinkled forehead and her lips drew into a thin, stoic line.

"There's also art outside of 'the arts,'" I said.

"Meaning?"

"It doesn't have to be regimented and institutional to have worth."

"Obviously," said my mother, "But we can't discard our metrics of assessing value either. Justin Bieber isn't equivalent to Mozart. Graffiti isn't the same as Monet."

It was the fight I longed for, but never had the gall to begin. Heat radiated from Melody. She trembled slightly, like water about to boil.

"They're not the same, but can't they both be valid?" I said, swaddling myself in the shawl of Melody's energy and meeting my mother's gaze.

"One is objectively superior." My mother brushed a stray hair off her temple.

"Based on what?"

"Standards of artistic value."

Flames burgeoned within my cheeks. I vehemently wanted my mother to flush crimson, but she remained the non-descript hue of a skin-colored crayon.

"Created by who? Old, white men who suck?" I hurled the dagger at her relevancy with abandon. My mother fancied herself a fellow critic of the patriarchal paradigm. I knew well the slick satisfaction that flicked across her face when her wit triumphed over that of a man.

She paused, put down her knife, then looked me dead in the eyes. "Better they than the talentless."

I shriveled, needlessly swiping a napkin at the corner of my lips. Silverware clattered against ceramic dishware. The plates were scraped bare and the noise hollow.

＊

The piano faced the window in the living room, and though she pulled the lace drapes shut, the light still dappled through, tap-dancing atop the varnished lid. Some days, during lessons, I wanted to hop up onto the piano and shake every bit of me, gyrating, jigging, flailing, flopping.

Others, I ached to lie stomach-down on the carpet and watch oscillating flecks of sun, wishing I found the keys as tantalizing as the light.

Her hands were on mine like two shaggy guide dogs. She

always said I had piano fingers. It was a waste, really, with my long, elegant hands that I didn't have more interest. When she said "interest," I heard aptitude, because the truth was, I tried.

One week before lessons, I painted a pair of Ked sneakers, covering them in yellow, crooked-grinned, smiley faces.

"Look what I made, Ma," I said, because this was back when I still believed we might both be kindred artists who'd learn each other's languages.

"Won't the paint just wash off in the rain?" She listened to Greig's *Concerto in A Minor* and graded freshmen's labeling of treble clef notes.

I looked down at the shoes. The yellow smileys still smiled, but they looked less happy. Like when someone's voice says, "Good for you," but their eyes say something else.

The next time it rained, I wore the shoes through puddles, letting the paint trickle off. In the dun-colored stream, my toes pruned and bloated. The smiles turned garish, sodden with something harsh.

✳

The last time Melody came to dinner at the beige house was the last time because she walked out the door and said, "You know, Dr. Webber, it really wouldn't kill you to give Evangeline the respect she deserves."

"That's rich coming from a child who's so obviously been raised in a household devoid of respect," said my mother.

There was a low seething hiss. If we were a pot, the lid blew off, its contents—steam, half-cooked spaghetti, and years of pent up everything—spewing onto the doorstep.

I yelled.

Melody yelled.

My mother yelled.

Our angst puddled in a heap like vomit.

The door to the beige house slammed and the wooden "Welcome to Our Home" sign fell onto the stoop.

Somehow, I was inside Melody's Subaru, cheek pressed to the glass, picking at threads on the hole in the knee of my pants.

We sped away from the silhouette of my mother's face in the living room window, gaunt behind the lace drapes. I watched in the rearview until she and the house receded into cream-tinged tininess, a speck of beige on a vast, dusky night.

✳

When I woke it was early—too early for the sun. I was in Melody's bed and so was she. She rolled over and blinked at me.

"Hi," she said.

"Hi," I said.

"Well, that sucked."

"Yeah."

We were quiet for a moment. I moved my leg and the sheets rustled like billowing wheat.

"You know I love you, right?" she whispered. "Yes, of course," I didn't hesitate. Of course Melody loved me. And, of course she'd want to tell me now when she might be the only one who did.

I was grateful for her then. We were something rarer and more precious than blood. We'd chosen each other, knit our spirits together. We were sisters without the passively inherited genetic code, our link forged consciously in knots.

The clock by the bed ticked. Melody's brow furrowed. Her fingers clenched the feather pillow, nail beds raw and beet-colored. Breath caught in her throat like she was about to speak, but instead she gnawed her thumb and stared at me. I wondered what she saw.

She inhaled, sucking words into her larynx like starving captives fingering the key to their rusty chains. It wasn't light enough to see the mural, but I imagined the glitter-blood drizzling down onto our foreheads, drop by agonizing drop.

"No," she said, her voice collapsing into a whisper. "Like, I love you."

And then her lips were on mine and my mouth made a little "o" in surprise, and it was gentle, and kind, and everything that I wanted to want.

Except I didn't.

"Oh," I said.

Something like hot tar roiled in the back of my throat. If I didn't leave now, it would spurt through my holes—teeth and ears and seams at the corners of my eyes. If I didn't leave now, I might never return. And so, confused and blindsided, I went.

Her shouting was plaintive. My name. Come back. Bare feet mashing into the gravel driveway. Bleeding. Running. Breathing.

When we first met, Melody hated shoes. In the summer she'd cast off her dirty flip flops to run up creek beds and climb trees.

Her feet were filthy and calloused and I envied their toughness. I was the soft one with pale, dainty skin susceptible to sun rays and mosquito bites. I was a fledgling mammalian critter lying face-up on a rock in the sun, squishy and ripe for impaling. I didn't know then, that tough things can be maimed, and soft things can wield the knife.

I ran until I felt light—like an empty husk or an effervescent speck of suds. My feet didn't hurt, because I had none, my essence reduced to the colossal, elephantine thudding of the heart barricaded in my ribs.

I ran until I was on the other side of town. The side with large, austere houses. At the top of the steps, I rang the doorbell. When nobody answered, I rang it again and again until it opened and Carmella peered out at me, her eyes like twirling cyclones.

She took in the weeds between my toes, salt-smudged cheekbones, and woeful bedhead.

"I employ you, right?"

"Yes." I tucked my hair behind an ear, shuffled the bloody feet, unsure whether she was joking.

"You don't look like you're here to work," she said, cracking a concern-tinged smile.

"I'm here to prune the herbs," I said, reddening at the brash untruth. The reality was, I didn't know why I was there except that the gray house was neither the farmhouse nor the beige house, but some enigmatic third place, removed from the dichotomy.

"Let's get you a glass of lemonade," she said, opening the door wide.

We walked through the foyer to the kitchen, and she poured two glasses from the pitcher, dropping ice cubes into the little glass cups with a clink.

"Ah lemonade," she said. "It's sweet and tart and frivolous. It doesn't have nutritional worth or get you drunk. It's purely for fun. I rather think it solves everything."

"I wish that were true," I said, after a slurp.

"Why do you think it isn't?"

We sat at the breakfast island. The sun peeked through the clouds and a breeze rustled the shards of hanging glass.

"My best friend is in love with me. I don't think lemonade can solve that."

Carmella paused. I waited for her to ask if I was in love with the friend that loved me. I wondered whether she'd been in love with the man who was once her husband. I wondered whether she had a friend.

Instead, she pulled a little vial of pills out of her pocket and shook two into her palm. She put one after another on her tongue, then took a swig of lemonade.

"What are those?" I asked.

"They say I feel too much." She closed her eyes.

"Do you ever think they're right?" I asked.

"Sometimes," she said. "Sometimes it's all so fucking gray."

We were silent for a moment.

"Today is pretty fucking gray," I said, surprising myself.

"Gray depressing or gray confusing?"

"What?"

"Is it one gray extending in all directions, as far as you can see? Or are there so many grays you don't know where any of them stop and start?"

I thought for a moment.

"Both."

She stood up, wrapping a cardigan around slender shoulders, "Follow me."

And so I did, down the steps, across the yard, and into the shed. Carmella unearthed artifacts from the bathtub outside, piling rose-tinted wine glasses, miniature flowerpots, and fragments of mirror at our feet.

"What are they for?" I asked, as my hand shot out and brushed the rim of a scalloped butter dish.

Carmella didn't answer. She picked up a pewter figurine of a Victorian woman with an impossibly tiny waist and held it over her head, looking up at it in reverence like an idol.

Then, she threw it at the ground.

It wasn't a slip off a cliff, but a jump. A nosedive.

"Help me," she said, gesturing to the butter dish. And so I did.

Christmas ornaments. Beauty compacts. Lambs from a nativity scene. We hucked them at the patio's floor with rampant, rabid, fervor, breathing deeply and grunting like men. Something shattered. Many things shattered. Little by little, then all at once, pain billowing over me in waves.

When there was nothing left but a pile of jagged glass, we

fell back onto the lawn chairs.

"What was that for?" I asked, again.

"I make art," said Carmella, "Mosaics mostly. I'm drawn to broken things." She pushed a button on the wall and the roof of the shed fell open like a blooming flower. As rivulets of light streamed in, she gestured to our feet.

Under the heap of ruined glass peeked the edges of a giant sun, made of rainbow shards embedded in the concrete. It seemed ludicrous that I hadn't noticed before the rays extending on either side of us like arms poised for a hug. It was every color, but when the sun glinted down on it, the bits and chunks of disparate objects converged into strands of pure, nameless brightness.

"It's beautiful," I breathed.

"It's complex," said Carmella, "Which I've always found more worthwhile."

✳

I crept back into the beige house and didn't leave. Two weeks of tiptoeing and praying I wouldn't run into her while pouring a bowl of cereal or brushing my teeth. In a sense, it wasn't such a change; we'd lived as waifs for many years, connected only by wisps of longing and echoes of agitation.

At night I dreamed of the cream-colored wallpaper, oatmeal-scented hand soap, and blonde wood of my bedroom loor. Beige was a hulking creature with gaping, cavernous mouths set on devouring me. While I dozed, the creases of its papery fingers brushed the soles of my feet and its weak, shallow voice breathed in my ear. When I woke up, I realized it didn't have a face.

I stopped sleeping. At night I slunk down the stairs and sat morosely beside the window in the living room. I tossed newspapers over the carpet and set up my easel. The first night, I stared at the barren, moon-lit canvas. My mind was flat and deflated, abandoned by the creativity that usually coursed through its gelatinous tissues.

On the bed of crumpled newspapers, I quivered. Words were never a worthy vessel for capturing the magnitude of it all, but my hands had always understood the innate shapes and hues.

I opened the local paper. *"Citing safety concerns, coalition of mothers forms to advocate for a new playground at the elementary school,"* said the headline. The accompanying photo was of our swing-set.

I held the words in my palm, stroking ink and complexity.

Then, I brandished a pair of scissors and chopped them up, snipping apart the phrase until disparate letters remained. I glued them to the canvas and the moon twinkled a grin. The scent of ink and sound of snips carried me towards an unknowable shape, albeit one that felt rooted in my essence.

For nights, I delved into the frenzy of letters, swishing oil paints atop them with bold, deliberate strokes. While I worked, I drank coffee, liberally pouring in packets of cream and Splenda from a stash I kept beneath my bed. It was sweet—too sweet. I guzzled it anyway.

Finally, my mother caught me. I felt her before I saw her, peering over the staircase to determine whether the precarious position of the coffee cup or the paint palette alarmed her more. I waited for a tirade of disciplinary actions. Instead, she just watched me swirl the blue with the red into a rich queenly purple, flicking it adeptly across the canvas.

"What do the letters say?" she asked, finally.

"What?" I looked up, mock-surprised by her presence.

"What are you spelling with the letters?"

In my hand I had a "Q" an "R" and an "X." Big, Times New Roman style—from a headline.

"Nothing, Mom, they're not spelling anything."

She didn't speak for a long time. Just watched me paint. I could feel her anxiety palpitating through the air of the already stuffy living room.

"I don't get it," she said, softly, finally.

"You never get it."

"But I'm here," she said.

I looked at my mother and she looked at me. In her silk nightgown, eye mask propped on her forehead, she was small and earnest.

"I know," I said, and it was true. She was here. She'd always been here.

"And I want to get it."

I was floating, morphing. Shrinking into a child then ballooning into the vast, indescribable thing I'd always been.

Wordlessly, she slipped down the staircase and perched on the piano bench, drawing her spine straight and touching her fingers to the keys. I dunked my paintbrush in red and let it hover over the page.

And then, we made art.

Her hands crafted magnificent melodies. Mine bequeathed color to a fragment of imagination. Both trembled with the rigor of smashing open the beige walls.

✳

I slogged up the dusty farmhouse driveway, encumbered by canvases. A black cat twined around my ankles like a hug as I fingered the house key I'd had since middle school. Its teeth were starkly jagged, like they'd moved farther apart and sharpened. I shoved it deeper into the fabric of my pocket, suddenly uncertain that it would still fit the lock. An almost-ripe raspberry dangled from a bush near the porch steps. I plucked and ate it, the tart unreadiness exhilarating, or perhaps unnerving.

Propping my paintings against the screen door, I drank them in. On canvas, Melody's expression swirled and churned, transformed in each painting by a different fancy or anguish—smiling, smirking, somber. Reducing her plethoric dimensions to just one face would be a travesty, and so I'd made many, outlining her bones in red and her hair in blue. The substance in between was tiny newsprint letters. They didn't spell anything, but I hoped she could read them anyway.

For so long, Melody was hopelessly entangled in my creations. She wasn't just their subject, or their benefactor, but a tenet of their formation. It was she who christened my scribblings and snippets and splatters. She said, as if it was the most obvious thing on earth: They're art. You're an artist.

If a thing is nameless, does it even exist?

Without Melody there wouldn't be a mural or a postcard wall or this collection of her likeness. My art wouldn't be seen, but rather stowed—in a below-the-bed shoebox, or my mind. Everything hinged on the tiny, precious, paramount visibility. Without it, there might be art, but not this art. There might be me, but not this me.

A window on the second floor creaked open, and ukulele strumming flooded the driveway, sweet and a little morose. I knew she'd climbed out the window and onto the porch roof.

I looked at the paintings again. They really were lovely, a monument to her. They said what I wished I could holler, lips craning towards the mildewed roof and cloud-speckled skies. *I love you, M.* Because I couldn't bring myself to espouse a sentiment so woefully detached yet tantalizingly akin to the one she craved, I'd made her the art.

Why, then, did it feel like an unnuanced memorial?

The ukulele stopped and the stairs wheezed a familiar creak.

It hit me quietly, like a whisper or a breeze: the paintings were just a pedestal. The altars we each tended for the other were the problem. They were alluring, sure, but too tidily reverent. Too narrowly fawning to accommodate the gnawing, agonizing, fascinating disarray.

There was a paper in my pocket. I pulled it out, unfurling my hand, kneeling, and flattening the crinkles on her steps. Two eyes, two nostrils, two earlobes. A muddle of curls, bold cheekbones, the oft-detested chin dimple. The drawing was rough, scrawled in charcoal and watercolor, but the shape, while malleable, was defined.

The door opened.

I handed Melody the paper. Surrounded by her face, we stared down at mine, her fingers tracing and my eyes following the uncertain lines, post-folding crease, and muted, barely perceptible hues. The painting was incomplete and technically inferior. It wasn't whole yet, and maybe it never would be, but I hadn't tossed it away either.

The return to her orbit was achingly exquisite. Dripping with complexity and trembling with messiness, the moment, like us, defied categorization.

And wasn't that the point?

Christopher Linforth

littlerocksensaterwantsmore84

翠菲:

Ihope this time you will respond to my comment. Your latest video transcends your last. The way you appear on screen, your thin body cloaked in black silk, your face calm, lips bright and red. You clutch a closed hand fan. You look at me and spread the fan in a smooth motion. Pictorial courtesans appear across the paper leaves. Arced along the edge sits a calligraphic message I cannot fully translate: something about touching the world from a home computer? Then you glide the fan through the air, still looking my way. I appreciate that. It starts the euphoric glow inside of me. You tap your fingernails on the fan, a lovely clacking, and then wave it once more in midair. The short video ends. Perhaps twenty or thirty seconds in total. I know you link to a website where I can purchase a longer video. But I do not wish to buy you or your love. We already have an intimate connection. Money would soil what we have. Please, 翠菲, respond. Since my previous comment, a few days ago, I now have more freedom in how I live my life. My girlfriend is gone, and we can be together. I am unsure of where you are in China, though googling your name indicates that you could be in Hong Kong or Macao. Here in Little Rock, I sometimes see women like you in the mall or jogging through Riverfront Park. Sometimes I see women like you in downtown restaurants. They play with their food: forks gently curling glistening spaghetti or teeth tugging on bread rolls. It's all so tender, heartbreaking. I almost approached a young woman tonguing her ice cream the other day, but I thought you might disapprove. And I felt guilty. We have so much, 翠菲, and still more to experience. I have made copies of all your ASMR playlists. I am glad you do not talk in your videos (that would be pandering to the whisper community!); I appreciate the video clips of you crinkling sheets of paper and running your wettened fingertip around the lip of a crystal glass tumbler. I try to ignore the endless likes and the baffling dislikes and the thousands of views. It should be just one: mine. Recently, though, I am unsure that is enough. I want to watch you in person. I can book a flight, just tell me to where. Or you can visit me. I can show you the Clinton Library (all those pages waiting to be turned!) and the Sculpture Garden (your nails tapping on all the stone and metal!). You can stay at my studio apartment. I will set out Jell-O and luxuriant moisturizer and Bristol paper with soft lead pencils and, of course, a hand fan. And you can re-create my favorite videos. I will watch you, in a mirror if you'd prefer. Just be near me, touch the world around you, show me what it can be.

Christopher Linforth

Comedown

Nathaniel: And here I am coming down from those edibles you sold me. Except that these CBD candies are in fact Flintstones Gummies. And the euphoria I felt earlier was actually my bowels contracting coupled with a rising sense of nausea radiating through my body. In my still-very-hungover state, I did wonder—if only for a moment—why the edibles were caveman- and dinosaur-shaped. But I needed to de-stress after last night, and I ate at least a dozen shortly after buying them from you. I had little choice. Jess ended it yesterday. And the subsequent Maker's Mark and smokes hadn't helped very much. In truth, after getting wasted, I'd had a wretched dream about drowning in a river, heavy stones in my pockets sinking me Virginia Woolf style, and I saw Jess on the far riverbank laughing as I slowly went under. Sometime in the night I woke up very cold, feverish, shivering from sweat. At first I thought I was wet from the river. In front of me stood a fading image of Jess watching me drown. It took a moment to piece together the dull gray space of my studio apartment. Eventually, I rose and went to the kitchen area. I warmed myself with a cup of reheated coffee then texted you about the edibles. I still have your reply: *It's fucking late. 20 for $100. No discounts. No layaway. No fucking around. You still owe me $10 for that LSD tab. So $110. Venmo me. Outside Canal Bar in 15.* As you took almost an hour to arrive, I considered asking for a discount or maybe getting something harder. Maybe doxepin or amitriptyline. But I wanted to chill, ease myself into the coming morning. My ragged cough had made smoking weed a painful experience, especially after already dispatching a pack of Marlboro Lights. So when you appeared, chatting on your phone to some girl, I was ready to fuck you over, steal the edibles. But I'm a nice guy, Columbia-educated, with parents who teach at a liberal arts college in Connecticut. I grew up on the consumption of empathy-inducing literature. My developed Theory of Mind stemmed from exposure to Tolstoy and Austen and Keats and Achebe and Sei Shōnagon. Or so my parents always told me. Anyway I was too tired and sick to rob you, so I paid you that damn $110, and I snatched the baggie without ever closely examining the contents. I popped the first of the gummies on the Uber ride home. I enjoyed the soft gelatin texture, and had another, even offering the driver one. "You'll enjoy it. It'll take the edge off," I said. He refused, so I ate his. When I got back to my studio in Crown Heights, I turned on the TV and found the infomercial channel. I muted the sound and watched two fiftyish women, pancaked in makeup, sell Helenite jewelry. Their pudgy fingers pointed to oversaturated green pendants and earrings and teardrop rings. Then the infomercial cut to footage of the Mount St. Helens eruption and a plume of dark volcanic dust rising into the sky. I watched that channel for hours, reliving the eruption over and over. I felt nothing, no pleasure, no sense of despair. My mind had cleared. It was just me and this superficially shiny gemstone. Then in the creep of morning light the gummy over-dose took effect. And so here I am in my bathroom. I've been so eternally constipated, sitting here on the toilet while writing this text. The intensity of the pain is worsening—now a crescendo of sharp, stabbing pains in my gut. Nathaniel, I've been cursing your name, threatening to make you reenact *2 Girls 1 Cup* by yourself, and I'd film it and then send it to your friends for them to make reaction videos. Then I'd upload them to YouTube and Vimeo and Dailymotion and share the videos with your parents, even your Peace Corp sister over in Lesotho. Then I'd send Jess a special copy of the original video, with a plinky piano soundtrack and janky credit sequence, and ask her to experience the pain of another—the dream, my dream, that drowning in the freezing dark water.

Nathan Alling Long

Leave

It's an old, familiar secret that any good lover knows: to make a person value something, take it away.

That's what I did, with myself: I moved out of the house Jalea and I had been renting the past three years, and I drove across the US to Tennessee, where I found a one-room cabin on ten acres, with hand-pumped well and an old wood stove.

It was quiet. I woke and ate and slept on my own schedule. There was no longer arguments about money or dishes, or how many signs of affection each of us needed.

But of course, I came to see that whatever I took from Jalea, I also took away from myself. After a few months, I would sit in my cabin, on the farm I'd always dreamed of owning, and think of her, imagine her walking down the lane, admiring the garden I'd plant-ed, then making dinner for her on the wood stove and us lying on a blanket in the clearing, staring up at the stars once it grew dark, feeling alive, full of a wonder I felt we'd lost back in San Diego.

But Jalea didn't come, though she did call, and I'd get her mes-sages when I walked out of the hollow I was living in and climbed the hill, where there was reception. I'd walk along the dirt road, the gravel underfoot, listening to her voice from 2,000 miles way, recorded somewhere and now sent through the small metal box pressed to my ear and think, this is the connection you now have to her.

And once I'd listened to the message, I'd walk some more, to the spot on the hill where the reception was best, thinking of what I'd say if I got a hold of her.

Sometimes there would just be her voice again, recorded, asking me to leave a message, with the distinctive laugh, as though she were embarrassed or found it funny to be saying the phrase everyone says on their recording:

Please leave me a message.

I'd heard the phrase so often, my mind began to hear it differ-ently, like this: Please leave me. (A message.)

I wondered even if this was her way of secretly telling me what she wanted.

And I had left, though I was still calling her, still trying to connect, from the gravel road at the top of that hill in Tennessee. I'd leave her my own message, upbeat, sunny, describing the day, how the wind was blowing through the tupelos, how I'd found a turtle in the garden who became the garden's mascot, how a heavy summer rain had brought down trees and dug a pool in the creek deep enough now to swim in.

Sometimes, as I talked into the metal box I pressed to my face, I imagined we were having a conversation, which, reduced to its core, its binary essence, said:

Please leave me, please leave me. (A message.)

Look what I have, look what I have.

Other times, Jalea would pick up the phone, we'd talk for a long while, and I didn't think about what it all meant, except that I felt the longing still, in her and in me. It felt like all we were saying:

I miss you.

I miss you, too.

Sometimes we even said those exact words.

The summer passed like that. The bean plants shot up, then their long pods dropped down. The garlic grew like thick grass, then browned and curled over. There were sweaty humid days so full of mosquitos and no-see'ums all I could do was sit in the creek pool and swat at horseflies or lay in bed by the cabin window trying to read some old damp paperback I'd started and abandoned years ago, when my life was too busy for it. I couldn't even imagine working outside or climbing the long hill to check my messages, to try and talk to Jalea. I even stopped imagining her being here. What was there to show off? Who would want to stay in this sweltering heat?

Then a thunderstorm came in late August. I ran out into clearing naked, arms stretched, feet spinning in the unmowed grass, the grey-green sky another world cracked open like old porcine by bolts of lightning. I laughed as gullies of rain washed over my feet. I went to the garden and picked the cherry tomatoes that had fallen in the down pour, and ate them one by one, laughing as the cold rain beat against my skin.

After, I dried off, put on clothes and shoes and marched up the hill with my phone, passing the leaves and sticks as they tumbled down in a current of water in the ditch beside the road. The sun was breaking through the heavy white clouds as I reached the spot where I could get reception. I stood looking out over the valley, steam rising off the tops of the tupelo trees.

In what had been a week without talking, there was just one message from Jalea. "Call me" she said.

I did, but I sensed it was not a good sign. I feared hearing "Please leave me..." one more time, but Jalea picked up just before the last ring, though at first she didn't say anything.

"Jalea?"

"Yes," she said. "You called. I thought you wouldn't."

"It's been hot," I said, which suddenly didn't seem like a good excuse, although I couldn't think of how to convey just how hot and humid the days had been.

"You weren't just avoiding me?" she asked.

"No," I said, though a part of me felt excited by her words. There was a sorrow in them, a hurt that suggested longing. "I'm sorry," I added. Then, "You wanted me to call?"

"I did," she said, but remained silent.

The steam of the trees seemed to pulse in the sunlight. I looked West at the endless blanket of green that, even with an electronic signal, seemed impossible to cross.

"I'm seeing someone else," Jalea finally said. Though she had never been with anyone else before, her words felt like an old, familiar story.

"I see," I said, although what I saw and what she had said had nothing to do with each other. I kept walking up the hill through the steaming heat.

"How does that make you feel?" Jalea finally asked.

I wondered if she wanted me to say that it made me sad, that it made me want her more. But I couldn't tell her that; I wouldn't give her that. All I could do was offer her less, in the hopes that she'd return to me.

"Will you say something?" she asked after a long silence.

I had reached the top of the hill. The sky was clear now and the reception was good. Still, I said nothing. Not a word, I thought. Not a word. It was the only thing I could give.

Zero Sum Game

A is for admiration, which is what you want from him more than anything. To inspire wonder is your goal, but you get the sense you're failing miserably.

B is for beautiful, which is what he calls you, cradling your face between his hands, trailing his fingers up your legs. Lately, he throws it out in an offhanded way like 'hey, beautiful' when you walk by him at a party you attend together where he spends the majority of the night huddled in a corner talking with a woman whose lithe body is barely covered by a flowery romper, which is somehow the style of the summer. She's like some kind of oversized baby, you think as you watch them. Some kind of hot, giant baby.

C is for cunt, a word he likes to use a lot when you have sex which embarrasses you but you don't say anything because God forbid you come off as overly-sensitive. He doesn't refer to you as a cunt or anything like that, but the first time he says 'this cunt is mine' you have to press your face in the mattress to stifle your laughter.

D is for desperate, which is how you're feeling these days.

E is for the embarrassment you know he sometimes feels because he is twenty-one years older than you. E is for explaining, which he does a lot about work, food, travel, clothing. When you call him a mansplainer he sulks for a few minutes and then explains why he isn't one.

F is for fickle, which you both are to a fault. Each time you meet you're not sure who he'll be or who you'll try to be—for him, yourself, whomever is watching.

G is for generous, which he is with his money, his things, both of which he has a lot. The trip to St. Kitts, the earrings, the Vespa he buys you so you can zip from campus to his place instead of walking. That he hasn't yet noticed you never pierced your ears, too afraid of needles of any sort even now, is disconcerting. But you push it to the back of your head, like you push the earrings to the back of your dresser drawer.

H is for husband, which he once was to a woman named Laura.

I is for indignant which is how you feel so much of the time and which you do next to nothing about.

J is for Jess, the name of his seven-year-old daughter whom you met once while working as a babysitter at a dinner party.

K is for what you text him when he tells you he can't bring you to a conference in San Francisco after all.

L is for lust and lost. You feel both every time you see him and one feeling only compounds the other.

M is for marriage which he says is a mistake he'll never make again.

N is for no, which is what you first say when he asks you to dinner.

O is for omission. When you tell the story of how you met at a dinner party, for example, you omit the fact that you'd been hired to watch the children so the adults could eat and get drunk without interruption.

P is for pedo, which is what your friends call him.

Q is for questionable, which is how you would, if pressed, characterize most of your actions since you've met him.

R is for renegade, which is what he calls himself sometimes, and which you try to omit from your memory. When he calls himself a renegade for starting his own law firm at thirty, you refrain from telling him that makes him about as far from a renegade as he can get.

S is for sex which is what this is all about, really, but you're fine with that.

T is for telling yourself what you need to tell yourself.

U is for understood. Which is how you felt at the beginning, when he talked with you about books and writing and art and listened to what you had to say.

V is for vacillate, which is what you do all day every day.

W is for wobbly, which is how you feel now. Wavering and wishy washy when you used to be so sure of who you were.

X is for an unknown variable in an algebraic equation. X is what your relationship feels like—abstract, changing, a placeholder.

Y for yes which is what he says, without hesitation, when you tell him we should take a break.

Z is for zero which doesn't mean nothing even if it's simpler to think it does. Whatever it was you had with him wasn't nothing. Afterall, the absence of something is a thing in and of itself.

Dance, Rockette

The cottage was only a rental for the month of August, so it wasn't up to Eve to keep the garden alive, but it had been hotter than usual for a couple of days and the blue hydrangeas that flanked the front door were drooping tragically in the late afternoon sun. She got the hose and sprayed them down, then went around back and watered the roses. The children were out on the lawn playing a game with their babysitter, Mattie, who was the seventeen-year-old daughter of friends in the city. If she'd had her druthers, they'd have gone someplace livelier than Connecticut, but her husband, Rick, had fond memories of growing up in Old Lyme, and it was an easy commute from the city. For the past three weeks he'd been spending long weekends out here, arriving by train late on Thursdays and going back to Manhattan Monday mornings, but starting today he would be staying all week. It was the last week, the end of summer.

She went inside and upstairs to her bedroom, where she put on a peach-and-white-flowered blouse and a pair of slim white pants. Orange sandals and her strand of south sea pearls, gold earrings in the shape of scallop shells; as she brushed her dark hair, she noticed a rime of gray roots that would necessitate a trip to the salon as soon as she got back to the city. She assessed her appearance in the mirror. Chic or dumpy? A little of both. Almost immediately after her fiftieth birthday, or so it seemed, her bright-eyed prettiness had faded, but she couldn't complain; she'd had her day.

She drove over the bridge that spanned the Connecticut River, wide here where it met Long Island Sound, the marshlands emerald, the water slate gray, the cloudless horizon glowing pink. She turned into the train station lot and parked facing the platform so Rick would see her when he disembarked. Rummaging in her purse, she got out of the car and lit a cigarette. The kids would go crazy if they knew she occasionally smoked, but Rick didn't care. She inhaled deeply. She had five minutes to herself. Rick might have bought a few beers at Grand Central to drink on the trip, in which case he'd be blurry when he got off the train. But he'd been looking forward to this evening at the Rosses' all week— Ben Ross was his old high school pal—so perhaps he'd remained sober this evening in anticipation of a better drink.

The train was announced and after a few minutes arrived. Rick was the second passenger out. Eve waved and watched him come down the ramp. He'd loosened his tie but looked otherwise tidy.

"Right on time," she said as she ground out her cigarette with her heel.

"I thought we were going straight to the party," he said.

"We are," she said.

"But you need to change," he said.

She looked down at herself. "This is what I'm wearing."

"Do you think it's dressy enough?"

"What did you expect, a tiara?" She knew what he was thinking. Ben Ross had invented some small but necessary technological widget that had made him wealthy, and while she and Rick were well-off enough to live in a three-bedroom on the Upper East Side, Rick had struggled along the way, moving firms twice before finally making partner. Renting the cottage for a whole month had been a bit of a stretch. Eve guessed Ben's good fortune had gotten under Rick's skin. He and Ben had been playing tennis at Ben's club every Saturday morning, riding there together in Ben's sleek black Ferrari. "I think I look nice," she said. "I'm wearing the earrings you gave me."

"I didn't say you don't look nice," he said as he got into the driver's seat. Eve handed him the keys. "But I think Ben and his wife might be expecting us to be dressier."

"It's better to be underdressed than overdressed," Eve said.

He started the car and drove out of the lot. "I think it's better to be just right."

"Okay, Goldilocks. Do you want to go home so I can change?"

"We're already late," he said.

"Better to be late than early."

"What's with you tonight?"

"Nothing. What's with you?" He didn't answer. She looked out at the river. Mattie was bored, the kids were bored, she was bored. The pleasures of Old Lyme had long been exhausted. They were all looking forward to going home. She wondered if Rick had found whatever he'd been looking for by returning to the halcyon scene of his youth. But Rick was a simple guy, meat and potatoes, not given to self-reflection.

＊

The Rosses' house was reached by a narrow road that wound through a forest of oaks. Nothing had been done in the way of landscaping, and the road was unpaved and bumpy. A branch scraped the side of the car; rocks flew up from beneath the tires. A deer flitted past. There was a sudden odor of skunk. Finally, the road widened, and a stone cottage appeared.

"How sweet," Eve said. It had a charming, rose-covered trellis.

"That's not their house," Rick said. "That's the caretaker's cottage." *Of course it is,* Eve thought. Rick drove on for a few more minutes until they reached a white-pebbled drive that led to a three-story, gray-shingled house. Four cars were parked on the edge of the drive. Rick pulled up behind the last one. "That's the house," he said unnecessarily.

"Well, that is some house," Eve said. She'd never seen a house with a widow's walk before. But the house wasn't old, the widow's walk was an affectation: no one had ever used it to scout for homecoming vessels. A flight of steps took them up to a deep porch that was furnished with a row of wicker rockers like the veranda of a seaside hotel.

Rick knocked on the side of the screen door. "Hello!" he called into an empty front hall.

"Hang on!" came a woman's voice, and then the woman herself. She wore what appeared to be a knee-length, very tight, pink-and-white-striped T-shirt, her pelvic bones popping out like knobs, and a pair of pink high-heeled sandals that looked impossible to walk in. Her hair was long and thick and reddish blond, cascading down her back. Diamond earrings in the shape of chandeliers swung fetchingly from her ears. "Well, don't just stand there, come in!" she said. "I'm Helene, Ben's wife."

His first wife? Eve wondered. Surely not, she was too young. "We're Eve and Rick," she said.

"Oh, I know," said Helene. "Come on, follow me. We're all out back."

They went through a large living room that was furnished almost entirely in white—*no pets or children,* was Eve's first thought—and out onto a flagstone terrace. A glass-topped table was set for eight, with a tiny vase containing a pink rose at each place. Candles in crystal cylinders stood in a line down the center of the table. The silverware appeared to really be silver, sparking in the last light.

"What a beautiful view of the river!" Eve said.

"We're on a bluff," Helene said. She pointed to where a flight of wooden steps began. "Those steps over there go down to our dock."

"You have a boat," Rick said as if he already knew it.

"Yes, but we hardly ever use it. There are so many other things to do."

Such as? Eve wondered. She would enjoy a boat ride. Maybe Ben would take her on one if she asked him. He stood on the lawn with a woman and three men who all had drinks in their hands.

"Buddy!" he called and came over to Rick.

"I don't want to rush anyone," Helene said. "But Gladys says dinner is ready." Now Eve could see she wasn't so young after all. Forty-five at least. Obviously, she'd had work done on her face: her skin stretched taut over her cheekbones and sharp little nose, her forehead was smooth, her lips artificially plump. Her breasts were the size and shape of cantaloupes, revealed by the deep scoop of her neckline. Ben was a big guy with a considerable belly. Helene was painfully thin. She waved her arm as if to corral her guests. "Everyone, come on!"

The man and the woman were husband and wife, and the two men lived together. Tad and Gina and Timothy and Pete. Tad and Gina were Helene's "oldest friends in the whole wide world." Timothy and Pete were merely neighbors.

"Ben and Rick went to Old Lyme High together," Helene said. She sat at the head of the table, Ben at the other end. Eve was sandwiched between Timothy and Tad. The table was meant to hold six, but they were eight. Eve would have thought she and Rick were the odd ones out if they hadn't been invited last week.

"Rick was cool," Ben said. "I was a loser."

"Now Ben is cool," Rick said.

"And you're the loser?" Pete said.

"I'm an attorney," Rick said. He picked up the empty wine glass by his plate and looked at it with disappointment.

"No, I mean, obviously I'm joking," Pete said.

Timothy turned to Eve. "You live in Manhattan? And what do you do?"

"I take care of our children," Eve said. "A boy and a girl."

"I would have thought your children would be grown up," Gina said. "Ours are, more or less." Like Eve, she wore linen slacks and a casual blouse. *So there*, **Eve thought**, *I'm not underdressed.*

"I came late to motherhood," she said. "I was thirty-eight when I had my first."

Pete looked at her over the top of his eyeglasses. "You must have done something before coming late to motherhood."

Eve paused. *I really can't stand you*, she thought. "I was a Rockette," she said. Rick stared at her.

"No way!" Gina said. "Wow!"

"You never told me that," Ben said to Rick.

"It's ancient history," Eve said. "I don't talk about it much. It's hard on your body as you can imagine. I had to stay in tip-top shape all the time. And the constant rehearsals and spectaculars—well, let's just say the glamour faded after a while, though I wouldn't trade the experience for the world, and of course I keep up with the girls. I ended up quitting when I was thirty and becoming a flight attendant. Rick and I met on a flight to Hong Kong. It was lust at first sight. Ever heard of the mile-high club? We conceived our first child in an airplane lavatory." There was a long silence. Ben cleared his throat. This was the most fun she'd had in a month.

"Gotcha," she said finally. "I worked in public relations. I can't do a high kick to save my life, and I've never even been to Hong Kong."

Pete and Tad screamed with laughter.

"You had me going!" Gina said.

Ben shook his head in admiration. "You could make a living as an actress."

Eve twinkled in the light of their attention. "Oh, now. Do I really seem like the mile-high type?"

"Never mind a Rockette," Pete said.

※

Dinner was served by a maid who wore a black dress and frilly white apron. Eve thought the costume was Ben and Helene's idea of a joke; she'd never seen anything like it in real life. Rick sat next to Helene, who ignored him in favor of Pete. At the other end of the table, Ben held forth about politics. Eve worried that Rick wasn't having a good time, but Ben was his friend and he'd wanted to come, so it was on him if he wasn't having fun. She was happy enough eating grilled tuna and chocolate mousse in a little porcelain cup while exchanging wry remarks with Timothy, who was as nice as Pete was not. Tad talked about himself. Gina flirted with Ben. Pete and Helene were as thick as thieves.

When the mousse cups were cleared and the coffee finished, Helene produced a joint. "I got this from an economics major at U Conn," she said as she lit up. "Lovely boy. Making money hand over fist. He's got everything you could want: cocaine, pills, whatever."

She took a toke and passed the joint to Rick. He looked at it as if he'd never seen such a thing, then took a little puff. When it came around to Eve, she almost said no. She hadn't smoked pot in decades.

"Oh well, okay," she said. She took the joint. The smoke rasped her throat. She held it in her lungs for a few seconds and coughed as she exhaled.

Timothy applauded her. "That's the way, Rockette!"

"I don't know what possessed me to say that," Eve said. "My kids love the Rockettes. We always go to the *Christmas Spectacular*. They dress up like toy soldiers, it's cute."

"Your kids dress up as toy soldiers?" Gina said. She took a toke and waved the smoke away from her face.

"No, the Rockettes do," Eve said.

"Oh God, you're not going to talk about your children, are you?" Pete said.

"She's not," Gina said. "I asked a question. People do have kids, Pete. They refer to them sometimes in conversation."

"Sadly," Pete said. "'Never work with children or animals.' Do you know who said that?"

"W. C. Fields," Eve said. All of a sudden she was as stoned as she'd ever been. Pete's head appeared to shrink. She looked at Helene, who was taking a second toke. "What's in that stuff?"

"Marijuana," Helene said.

"That's right, W. C. Fields!" Pete said. "You should go on *Jeopardy!*"

"I knew someone who was on *Jeopardy!*" Gina said. "A girl I went to college with. The funny thing is, she didn't even seem that smart."

"Let's go into the living room," Helene said. She got up and stumbled on the flagstones. "Watch out, everyone!" She giggled.

The light in the living room was rosy and mellow. Eve sat down in a deep, snowy couch and lit a cigarette.

"Feel free," Helene said. "Go right ahead."

"Can I bum one?" Gina said. Eve handed her the pack. "To tell you the truth, I can see you as a Rockette. Those long legs of yours."

"Dance, Rockette!" Pete said. "Show us a high kick!"

"You know what kind of dancing I love?" Eve said. "Swing dancing."

"Oh, I love swing too!" Timothy said. Eve squinted at him. His voice echoed as if from a cave. "Ben, find something on Spotify we can dance to."

Ben lumbered out of the room. In a minute, "Boogie Woogie Bugle Boy" came through invisible speakers. Eve snapped her fingers in time to the music. She was a good dancer, but Rick would never oblige her, and perhaps he was right not to: he danced with a bumbling lack of focus that made him impossible to follow. He sat on the opposite couch drinking a snifter of something tawny. She looked at him. *Home soon,* he mouthed. Or maybe he said it aloud.

"Come on!" Timothy said and pulled her up off the couch. He took her into his arms with surprising strength and assurance, leading her over Helene's carpet. It had been years since she'd danced even a foxtrot; it took her a moment to catch the rhythm and move as one with Timothy. She felt the flexibility of youth return to her limbs as she ducked under his arm and twirled out again. He pulled her to him and they rocked vigorously back and forth.

"He's in the army now," he sang. "Ta dah, ta dah, ta dah."

"I think I better stop," Eve said after a few minutes. "I'm dizzy from all this twirling."

"Helene!" Timothy called. "Take Eve's place."

"I don't know how," Helene said.

"I do," Gina said. She got up and joined him. Eve was released.

"Bathroom?" she said to Helene.

"Through there, first door on your left."

She sat on the toilet, and with her elbows on her thighs she rested her head in her hands. If she closed her eyes, the world stopped whirling. Most "good times" weren't particularly fun, she decided: fun was for children and simpletons. After a while she exchanged the toilet for the floor and lay on the cool tiles like a starfish. The ceiling was painted with vines and fronds and colorful birds, a genteel Connecticut jungle, as if Helene and Ben expected people to lie on the floor all the time and wanted to give them something to look at. The smell of gardenias or jasmine came from a scented candle. She thought she could stay here all night.

There was a knock on the door. Helene peeked in.

"I thought you looked green around the gills," she said. She extended her hand and helped Eve up. "I guess the pot disagreed with you. And you drank an awful lot of wine."

"Oh, I'm sorry," Eve said. "I didn't mean to."

"Nobody does," Helene said. "Gladys has a habit of topping off people's glasses, so you never know how much you've had. I've told her not to time and again. She's as dumb as a box of hammers."

"She looked pretty silly in that maid's costume," Eve said.

"I know, right?" Helene said. "Ben insisted. He thinks it's classy." She laughed shortly. "He doesn't have the first idea what classy is."

They went out to the living room. Eve gingerly sat down. Helene brought her a glass of water. Pete and Timothy were slow dancing to "April in Paris" like teenagers in love.

"Where is Rick?" Eve said. No one answered. She went upstairs and looked in all the guest rooms, three of them, empty and spotless. Lingering in the vast master bathroom, she examined Helene's army of face creams and potions, dabbed perfume on the insides of her wrists. The bathtub was reached by two marble steps; the shower was the kind that shot jets of water from the walls. She checked out the contents of the medicine cabinet: Klonopin, Vicodin, codeine; Sensodyne, Advil, Certain Dri. She took a Klonopin, put it back, and swallowed two Advil instead.

"Does anyone know where Rick went?" she said when she came back downstairs.

"Home, probably," Tad said. He sat next to Helene, smoking

another joint. "I saw him go out of the room with a pretty glum look on his face."

Eve went to the front hall and looked through the screen door. Their car was still in the driveway. She walked out to see if Rick was sitting inside it, which he might have been if he was feeling sulky enough. Cupping her mouth with her hands, she called his name. Nothing. The pulsing scream of late summer crickets and the fainter sound of "April in Paris."

*

Lit only by the moon, the steps were rickety and steep. Eve hung on to the single railing with both hands and crept down to the river. She knew Rick was down there, she could feel it, though he didn't answer when she called. She was afraid he'd fallen and was lying unconscious on the beach or had drowned in the placid water. She reached the dock and walked out to where Ben's boat was tied up at the end. It was a speedboat, sleek as Ben's Ferrari. Rick was sitting behind the wheel.

"Jesus, Rick. I nearly broke my neck on those stairs. What are you doing?"

"I was thinking about going for a ride," he said. He held up a tiny replica of a buoy with a key dangling from one end. "I found it on a hook inside the front door."

"Get out of there and let's go home."

"Join me." He patted the seat beside him.

"Just for a minute," she said. She took off her sandals and climbed over the side of the boat. Rick's face in the moonlight was dead white. "I guess you weren't having fun."

"No, but you were. 'Dance, Rockette!'" he said in a fair imitation of Pete's nasal voice.

"I embarrassed you, is that it?"

"Yes. No."

"Which?"

"I want this," he said.

"This boat?"

"This boat, this house, this everything. I'll never have anything like it. There's no way in the world."

Eve was silent. Water lapped against the boat's hull. A village winked on the opposite shore. Rick sighed.

"I loved high school. You know that; I've told you about it. Ben is right, I was cool. I was the goddamn prom king, the captain of the football team. I was the cliché."

"You enjoyed yourself," Eve said. "Not everybody can say that about high school."

"I think those years were the best of my life."

"You don't love these years?" she said. "Being married to me, raising our kids?"

"I like these years fine," he said.

"But they're not what you imagined for yourself."

He shrugged. "Don't most people imagine something better for themselves than what they end up getting?"

"Not me," Eve said. "I love you; I love my children. I have enough, and I feel lucky." It was true, more or less. She was mostly content. She started to get up. Rick could fuck off.

"Wait." He grabbed her arm. "Go for a ride with me."

"You can't run off with Ben's boat."

"Why can't I? I'll return it. He's too stoned to notice."

She sat down again. She was still pretty stoned herself. She put her fingers to the outer edges of her eyes and felt two nests of deeply etched lines. Rick was still handsome, not a strand of gray in his hair, the prom king forevermore. "Do you think Helene is beautiful? Do you want her as well?"

"I don't want her," Rick said.

He untied the line and turned the key in the ignition. Slowly, he reversed the boat until it was clear of the dock. As he gunned the motor and the engine roared, Eve felt a ghost of a thrill. The river ahead was undisturbed, a sheet of black glass to be shattered.

That One Morning, The Whiskered Auklet

I took the Top of the World Highway till it turned into the Taylor Highway till it turned into Chicken, an Alaskan town of about fifteen people; Dad was one of them. Two campgrounds pulsed with floaters in the summers. Round cedar planters filled with butterfly weeds, catchfly, and marigold sat outside the liquor store. Me and the town dog, Captain, a three-legged mutt they'd found at the airport, sat at a picnic table. RVs started pulling in, all white, all filthy. The Chickenites milled about, starting their mornings with cut-rate spirits.

There was Chuck Baker who shot guns at people's cars if they parked on or too close to his property. He was always certain someone was going to come along and steal his generator. He had welded the body of a frost-blue 1967 GMC K1500 onto the treads of a salvaged army tank and parked it out to rust by the mouth of his land. The previous summer, a traveler who had tried to sit in it was mysteriously shot in the knee.

There was Astrid Lindberg, a Swedish woman in her early 40s, known for her Aryan beauty and shooting a grizzly dead two winters prior. In the saloon was a framed photo of her perched behind it, grinning, while it bled onto the surrounding snow. There was Trish Powell and her brother Jimmy Powell, who were suspected to be incestuous. And Doug Freeman, a retired marine engineer who had money but had gone off the deep end. There was Linda Washington who ran the post office and was never charged for coffee. And, of course, Vicki Cormier, who Dad called "the town bicycle."

That wasn't everybody but it was damn near close. Dad staggered among them, approaching me on his way to the liquor store, nursing a hangover.

"Brit," he said. "No breakfast?"

"I had some," I said.

"I must've been out like a light." He passed me to enter the store. "Need anything?"

"I'll take some Gordon's, I guess."

"You got it." He walked up behind Doug, slapped him on the shoulder, and said, "You're shaking more than an epileptic at the disco."

"Don't I know it, bud," said Doug as they went inside.

An RV pulled up with two young guys in the front seat and my heart stopped being one solid thing and popped into beads and wild clots. The one driving was so-so, maybe looked a little older. But the other one resembled a cheapened movie star, rugged and alive, with an elbow out the window and a crooked grin like Marcus Mumford's.

"Hey!" I called out.

They didn't hear me and carried on to Goldpanner, an RV Park down the road. Dad came out and handed me my gin. He was a young 38, had me when he was eighteen, and seemed to have never grown up.

"See you at the bar, Wally!" Doug called out, passing us.

"Catch you on the flip," said Dad.

Entering Chicken, a conspicuous metal sculpture of a chicken, "Eggee," stood next to a tattered wayfinding sign, which listed names of other towns around the world, (i.e., Hen, Israel; Rooster Rock, Oregon; Chicken Scratch, North Carolina; Cock-adoodle, Australia). An explorable dredge sat with its gigantic arm; weeds came up like plumes from its base. Sparrows' nests huddled in its high-up crannies.

The whole town consisted of Chicken Mercantile Emporium, Chicken Liquor Store, Chicken Creek Saloon, and Chicken Creek Café, all composed of the same dark wood, sitting in a quaint row. The mail came by plane on Tuesdays and Fridays, so long as the weather was right. I was born in Chicken, but mom moved us to Buckeye when I was one. She'd wanted to be closer to grandma, who was supposedly dying, but turned out to be fine. Dad stayed in Chicken. He couldn't trade in Garganeys, Northern fulmars, American coots, and Pied-billed grebes for Penduline tits, Curve-billed thrashers, and Yellow-eyed juncos. For cash, he whittled wooden chickens and they sold them at the mercantile. I went to Alaska every summer to stay with him.

He watched me bend to see the RV drive toward the park.

"You see something you like?" he asked.

"Don't know," I said.

"Are we going watching tomorrow?" he asked.

Dad was a birdwatcher. He'd gotten me into it, had bought me a bird book and everything. Mom had become a sixth-grade teacher and was getting married to a new man. Dad didn't like to talk about that.

"I'll be free," I said.

"Sounds good, kiddo."

That night at the saloon, Jimmy Powell was hand-rolling cigarettes. Vicki was tending bar and dancing around in a tee shirt from the mercantile, which she had cut into a tank top. It didn't reach the waistband of her acid wash jeans, and under the blue neon bar sign, I could make out every stretchmark.

Two self-proclaimed "documentarians" leaned over the bar to "interview" her. They were filming bits and pieces on a 2008 Motorola Razr flip phone, and called themselves Phil and Steve, two Floridian bachelors cracking jokes about the outhouses.

Upon seeing Vicki, one of them said, "Oy vey! Muy bien!" and the other said, "You come here often?" before falling into unearned throes of laughter.

In the winters, Dad and Vicki shacked up together, usually at her house, which was farther away. She had a messy, burning way of talking, and a rasping laugh which seemed to smoke from her mouth, disappearing and turning to nothing. She was all about men. She would have married Dad, surely, but he described himself as a "free agent"; every summer, he screwed what blew through town.

"What can I get you boys?" she asked the tourists.

Vicki had a nineteen-year-old daughter who went to college in Montana. Whenever she came up in conversation, Vicki would say, "That girl's a mystery." I hadn't gone to college. What was I gonna do? Try for nursing school? Be a nanny? I didn't have plans beyond watching birds with Dad in Chicken all summer, then be a bridesmaid in mom's "spiritual" Labor Day wedding.

The hot guys I'd seen pull up in the RV walked into the bar, both sweaty and dressed in plaid short-sleeve shirts. I didn't hesitate.

"Find any gold?" I shouted to them over the noise.

"About two ounces!" the hotter one yelled.

"That's worth, like, five hundred bucks," I said. "Buy me a drink!"

His name was Dylan. He and his friend, Stevie, had driven

over from the suburbs of Seattle. He kissed me softly on the neck, as if it were my cheek. Within five minutes, we were making out in the corner by the pool table. The "documentarians" tried to film us, and in turn, Dylan called out, "Fuck your mother!" His beard stank of cigarettes and his teeth weren't brushed, but he was striking. For all I knew, he was on a poster in an idiot girl's room.

Back on the barstools, he asked me, "Where are you from?"

"Here," I said.

"Bullshit," he said, and leaned over to Stevie to say, "Brittany's from here."

"Yeah, I was born here. My dad lives down the road."

"Big house?" asked Dylan.

"No."

"Big enough for us?"

"Not really."

"Damn," he said, smiling. "I'm pretty sick of the RV."

I got back to Dad's house alone, which was a one-bedroom cabin down the road modeled after the post office. He put an air mattress in the living room in the summers for me to sleep on. When I got inside, I could hear he had brought somebody home.

By the sound of it, he had her up against the wall, and over the wooden thumps was the cannonade of skin clapping skin and mammal girl cries. She sounded young. The fridge had been left hanging open, so I closed it.

I eased onto the air mattress on the living room floor and waited for it to stop. After a short while, she came out of the bedroom in a green crocheted bra and a denim mini skirt, which she was pulling back down over her tail on her way to the bathroom. She was just as delicate and young as she had sounded, no more than a year or two older than me.

She noticed me on her way back to the bedroom, put her hand over her heart and said, "Oh, hi."

"Hey," I said.

She went back into the bedroom and closed the door. There was a fly caught in the white lampshade, exhausting itself, throwing its body so hard against the parchment that its noise could be mistaken for a fat moth or small bat. Against the growls of the wind and distant drunks, this was the sound I fell asleep to.

I woke up to her laughter. They were still in the bedroom, getting it on. I rolled over and pulled the pillow over my head.

They came out a little while later and Dad made breakfast for us. Her name was Trina, and she had dry, long hair like sand: sea-ish blonde and holding the lasting efforts of the sun.

Dad flopped eggs onto plates in yellow curds. His scramblers always came out the same. Trina carried her plate around, eating as she walked. The bare bottoms of her feet rubbed back and forth on the vinyl. I could hear her callouses, like sheets of sandpaper. She said she was from Yountville, a little town in California, where she still lived with her brother and a couple of roommates.

"What kind of birds you got out there?" asked Dad. "Meadowlarks? Scrub jays?"

"I don't know," she said. "We've got lots of things."

"Much to learn!" he said.

I watched her turn on the balls of her feet in a sort of mild, distracted ballet. Her fork went sliding down the blue of her plate and she caught it.

"Probably not as many as you've got out here," she said.

"Oh, don't say that," said Dad. "They're everywhere and they're special everywhere."

This, too, was how he felt about girls.

Trina went back to her RV and me and Dad went out to watch birds. I carried the bird book, which I didn't need, since he was there.

"So, your mom," he said, "she happy?"

We'd walked far enough out that we couldn't see the tourists panning for gold in the creek. We'd made it to the blonde grass way off the mud of the road.

"Yeah, Brian's great," I said.

"He's *great*?"

"I mean, yeah, they're happy," I said.

"When's the wedding?"

"I thought you said you didn't wanna know."

"I did? I said that?" he asked. I didn't say anything. "Shh, take a look at her," he said, pointing up at a brown bird with a white chest, which had perched in a Black Spruce.

"What is it?" I asked.

"Yellow-billed—" he said, "yellow-billed cuckoo. There must be rain coming."

"They like the rain?"

"They predict it."

His mouth was slightly open and outlined by his thin Balbo beard. I liked watching him watch the birds more than I liked watching them myself. He could appreciate them in a way I couldn't, seemingly in a way *nobody* **could.** He was in his purest form, his holiest, grandest self.

"So, your mom," he said again, "she's good."

"Yeah, she's good."

"Just checking, just checking." A full minute passed, and he said under his breath, "Brian." Then he lowered his binoculars and said, "Let's keep going."

He stood under Tundra bean-geese, Surf scoters, Eurasian coots, and Eastern whip-poor-wills, stepping in silence, then in wind, then in darkness around the silt and gravel. I could see him under Red-breasted mergansers and Trumpeter swans.

Hungry, me and Dad made our way to the MacLeries', the only married couple in town. They were our neighbors by about a mile. Upma MacLerie, a woman from Delhi, was always cooking. We arrived as if invited, and she had out metal bowls of curry, Aloo Gobi, and Chole Bhature in a row on their loud plastic tablecloth, which was painted with apples and cherries.

Upma's husband, Scott, was a quiet vegetarian who spooned potatoes and cauliflower into the pockets of homemade naan and moaned through his mustache like he was getting the full experience. She fried peas and carrots into rice for him and looked at him with enviable love. She could have turned me into a proper wife if she taught me to fry paneer and bake chickpea flatbread. She moved over the table in a tie-dye tee shirt, serving us with joy. The curries steamed so profoundly that I believed their bright colors would fade. The smell of hot tomatoes got in my hair and came through my sweat. They had all the windows open, and the house filled with mosquitos; me and Dad slapped our arms and legs, cursing. He said that cooking with fenugreek was why Indian people smelled. He said this under his breath at every dinner at the MacLeries'.

"You going to the bar later?" he asked me.

"I was planning on it," I said.

"I might catch you there," he said. "Trina said something about going."

Upma drank scotch straight from the bottle as we talked.

"Fenugreek," Dad whispered toward my shoulder.

"See any birdies today?" asked Scott.

"Oh, beauties," said Dad.

"You should start taking pictures," said Scott. "You could compile them into a book."

"You're shaking like—"

"Like a leaf?" asked Scott.

"Like a chick on a washing machine," said Dad.

"I'm due for a drink."

Upma set the scotch down in front of Scott. He pretended not to notice it for a few moments, continuing to eat. When he thought we had moved on or looked away, he picked it up and took a drink. He was one of the only ones left with any shame.

At the bar, me and Dylan were scooting our stools closer together. He was calling me pretty and I didn't believe him, but his breath was hot on my neck, and it felt like everybody was looking at us. For once I felt like one of those girls getting handed stargazer lilies or her hand held on a blue carousel.

"I'm not gonna miss you when you leave," I said.

"Bitch," he said, laughing.

I looked around for Dad, but he never showed up. The two local Bobs—Bob Patterson and Bob Landry—were working the bar but only serving draft beer, no matter what anybody ordered. Everyone had to check their weapons at the door, which scared the peace-and-love tourists who all seemed to think that guns were just a widespread myth.

"People around here are pretty hardcore," said Dylan.

"You think I'm hardcore?" I asked.

"I don't know yet," he said, and went for my neck. Into it, he asked, "Can we go to your place?"

"I think my dad's there," I said.

"Well, Stevie's getting sick in the RV," he said. "I should probably head back. Maybe I'll see you tomorrow?"

Just as the Yellow-billed cuckoo had predicted, the rain came down in sheets. It seemed to become a welcome, adventurous part of the tourists' camping excursions, as they stood under it in wide stances, beaming up at the thunder. The locals stood in the bar, looking out.

"You think they've ever seen rain before?" Bob Landry asked Bob Patterson.

"In California? Probably not," Bob replied.

Back at Dad's, it seemed he had company again, but not Trina. I could hear the carnal wailing of a familiar voice—a woman's—and then an unfamiliar man's voice said, "Is someone here?" The bedroom door opened and there was Dad, Vicki Cormier, and a young, bearded floater, all messed up and half-dressed.

"Brit—" Dad said, but I turned and went back out the front door toward town.

Even over the rain, I could make out the sounds of animals, each of them less frightened than me, until I reached the Gold-panner RV Park. I looked for Washington license plates, found them, and saw Dylan's hat hanging from the rearview mirror. I knocked. He came out, confused.

"Brittany," he said. "What's up? What are you doing here?"

"I missed you," I said.

"Well, sure," he said. "Stevie's kinda knocked out. Maybe we should stick to tomorrow."

"Couple of minutes? I'm wet."

Dylan laughed, then his smile faded, and he stepped to the side to let me in.

"She's a 2007," he said about the RV.

I couldn't tell by his tone whether he thought this was new or old. The beige velveteen driver's seat was piled with roadmaps and magazines. It was humid from the rain, which sounded even louder than it had outside. The pine overhead cabinets looked down on reduced ceramic countertops and a faded palm leaf couch. The hallway led us by a breakfast nook with matching palm leaf benches, a black microwave and upwards of thirty beer cans.

Across from the bathroom door was a single bunk, which had nothing but a rumpled top sheet. Dylan motioned to it for me to sit.

"Want a beer?"

"Okay," I said. "This is your only bed? Does Stevie sleep on the couch?"

"Oh, there's a queen back there. Stevie's not feeling good."

I glanced around the corner and could see Stevie's leg sticking out on a big, striped bed on the floor.

"Can he hear us?" I asked.

"Hey, Brittany!" Stevie called out.

Dylan handed me a beer. I sat on the bunk, ducking my head and scooting back against the wall with my knees to my chest.

"So, you missed me? You wanted to see me?" Dylan scooched in beside me, folding himself into the space.

I leaned in and kissed him. He grabbed my breasts, then took my shirt up over my head. I heard Stevie vomit into a plastic bag, which crinkled under the weight of beer. I unhooked my bra, and it came off between us.

"Nice," said Dylan.

My skin was cold and damp; my clothes had soaked through. It felt as though the rain had paled and bloated me. He got to my shorts and underwear, then I was crouched there naked, feeling part cavewoman and part alien, like I was on an exam table. He fumbled with his jeans and put his dick through the zipper.

"Are you not wearing boxers or anything?" I asked.

He got on top of me, somehow, as if in urgency, he had expanded the space of the bunk, and he fucked me all wrong and very selfishly. I went along with making girlish noises, as this was expected. He finished on my midsection. His dick turned back into a mere penis, and I asked him if I could pee.

"I don't know, can you?" I should have laughed but I didn't have anything left.

I heard Stevie adjust in bed; he was essentially in the room with us. The toilet had a fuzzy, brown cover and I couldn't find the flusher. The RV toilet paper crumbled on my stomach when I used it to wipe off. I could hear Stevie say, "Dude, nice."

When I came out, Dylan was laying on the bunk, taking up the whole thing. I was still naked. He'd tucked his penis back in and was fully clothed. I grabbed my shirt and underwear and sat on the edge of the bunk.

"Are you sleeping over?" he asked through a yawn.

"I probably should, huh?"

"What?"

"I probably should," I said. "The rain."

I crawled into the bunk and he reluctantly pressed his body up against the wall, facing away from me.

I barely slept and Dylan didn't seem to either; still, we didn't talk. As soon as it was light out, I put my shorts on and, not wanting to put my bra on in front of Stevie who was eating Cheez-Its in the breakfast nook, I tucked it under the bunk.

"Heading out?" asked Dylan. "See you later."

"Yeah, maybe at the bar," I said.

"We'll probably get breakfast in a little."

I made my way through town, which had dried in the light, and sputtered with early risers, walking around with monogramed JanSports and Velcro Tevas. I could hear the Mountain bluebirds and Eurasian collared doves. My head hurt but the air smelled good. It was still cool out and I wondered what my face looked like, how I smelled.

I got back to Dad's and he wasn't there. I paced in the kitchen, which was too quiet. He had a TV that wouldn't turn on. I took a quick shower in the moldy tub, shook a spider from the hardened towel and threw on one of his sweatshirts from the mercantile, which read: I GOT LAID IN CHICKEN.

I lit the stovetop to heat the pan, sprayed some PAM, cracked two eggs right into it, and pushed them around with a rubber spatula. I overcooked them a little, as not to overthink their preparedness, and as I shook the saltshaker, heard Dad coming up the road.

This time, again, he was with Trina, who carried a digital camera and a purple insulated lunch bag. She was just as beachy, but taller than I had remembered. She hung off of Dad like a Raggedy Ann, tugging on his arm, giddy as though she had discovered him. They came in the house on my first bite.

"Where'd you go last night, Brit?" asked Dad.

"Goldpanner," I said.

"You know somebody parked there?" he asked.

"Mhmm," I said.

"That's where we're parked," said Trina.

"Where were you?" I asked.

"Had to show this one a bird or two before she skips town on me," said Dad, and kissed her temple.

I felt as if I'd cry. Then—someone kill me—I did.

"You went birdwatching?" I asked, quietly at first, through a cracking voice. "You took her?"

"Brit?" Dad took a step toward me, as if testing the floor.

"You went watching?" I asked again.

I felt the tears running down my face already, and my throat closed, then a desperate breath opened it, forced its way through, followed by the sobs, the definite sobs.

"Oh, shit," said Trina, "I'm sorry."

"What's wrong, honey?" Dad asked.

I threw my plate on the floor, but it didn't break on account of being plastic. The eggs splattered in tired jams on the base of the counter and the floor.

"Stay the hell away from me!" I screamed, and felt my finger pointing, which was embarrassing—humiliating—and only intensified the tantrum.

"All right, now," Dad said. "Breathe, Brittany, breathe."

"Shut...the fuck...up!" I said, hyperventilating.

"I didn't know it was, like, your special thing," Trina whispered to Dad, like I wasn't there.

"Don't make it sound so lame!" I yelled.

"Let's make more eggs," said Dad, gently, "or a gin."

I ripped out of the house, barefoot on the dirt and rocks, which hurt almost like burns: a quick, chasing pain. I was running toward town when I saw a Whiskered auklet on a mound. I approached it and it didn't move. It was sitting upright and blinking lethargically, certainly alive, but must have been hurt or sick as these birds were only ever out at night; even then, they were hard to make out with their little, black bodies and short wings.

She had a beak like a candy corn in color and size, and her delicate white whiskers sprouted sideways from her brow with the drama of a feathered headdress. She had silver, moonish eyes and white stripes down her face.

Dad would've lost his shit. He would've nursed her back to health. I'd seen him do it before, many times. He would have put a dishcloth in an empty tissue box and dribbled pear juice on a plastic spoon; he always got them to drink even by saying quiet, kind things: "Come on now, baby. I know you like pears." I picked up a rock about the size of my palm.

In needless violence and bewildering anger, I bludgeoned her. I bonked her good on the head; it appeared she had instantly died, but I hit her a second time, opening her wing, chest and shoulder, and could feel the softness of her meat. There was some blood but not much and I threw the murder rock as hard as I could off to the side, but all of a sudden wasn't strong, and it landed close by with a soft thud.

I stared down at her trusting, black body and her dead head and the canyon I'd created in her chest and sobbed again, this time in horror. Her webbed feet pointed up toward the sky and looked slightly too large for her body; if she were a woman, she would've been a size ten.

I ran from the scene so that I wouldn't be caught with her, and slowed down when I reached town, eyes still red, breath un-caught, feet still bare. I remembered what Dylan said about breakfast and burst into the café. He and Stevie sat over cheese omelets and coffee at a table by the door.

"Hey, Brittany," said Dylan. He didn't sound excited, but I sat down.

"Sounded like you had a good time last night," said Stevie.

"Are you okay?" Dylan asked.

"Yeah, just forgot my shoes," I said.

"Yeah, but are you crying?"

"I was thinking," I said, "maybe I could come with you guys."

Dylan and Stevie looked at each other. Stevie shrugged as if to say, "this one's on you," and got back to his omelet.

"What do you mean?" asked Dylan. "Are you serious?"

"Yeah, I mean, I've just been having a lot of fun with you and was thinking—"

"We're actually leaving today," he said.

"Oh, that's fine. I mean, that works for me."

"Like, right after this," he said.

"I don't even need to pack," I said. "Isn't that what you guys do mostly? Just live off the world or whatever?"

"I just don't think it's gonna work out," said Dylan. "We're not passing back through here. It's super out of the way and there's not much to do."

"Oh, you wouldn't need to drop me back off or anything."

"I'm really sorry, dude," he said. "I don't really feel *that* way if you get what I mean."

I nodded, looked around the café to see that all the other tables were listening, and stormed out. Right before the door closed, I heard Stevie call out, "But thanks for the bra!"

I had to pass her body on the way home. I had hoped that she would have been picked up and buried or simply floated away, but she hadn't moved. I put my hand up to shield my face as I walked by the mound, kicking the murder rock farther away, as if I could smack the pink off it.

Dad was home, saying sorry, spared of the dead auklet for now. Trina was sitting on the couch, not reading the room, flipping through my bird book over Riesling.

Dad belonged under turkey vultures and Marbled godwits. He belonged under Brown-headed cowbirds and Western ospreys. I got to be born under white pelicans and scarlet tanagers. There was nothing—just all the prairie warblers, all the upland sandpipers, flycatchers.

Liam O'Brien

I'll Bid My Heart Be Still

Our grandfather, the world traveler, spent very little time in the country where we lived. He worked as an antiques appraiser, specializing in fine string instruments. *Is this a real Guarneri? No, but are you a real Heifetz?* The two weeks after his death were the longest time in fifty years that he had spent in the place he formally called home. This was West Virginia, our awful state. We joked, at his wake, that he had done well to avoid it. Grandpa Sam, Traveling Man.

Still, I was fond of Falling Waters, where his house was. No one else in the family lived there; most of us worked in Martinsburg, and lived there or just outside it. When I was twenty-four, Grandpa Sam had commissioned me to stay in his place and keep an eye on it while he spent a year as a lecturer in Vienna—the real Vienna, not the West Virginia one. He thought of me, I guess, because I was the one musician among his progeny. He'd given me my first full-size viola—sold it, actually, to my parents, to be paid in installments over a couple years of lessons. *No art without a measure of sacrifice.* He liked that I kept playing, even if I'd never be a professional or an expert like him. His house in Falling Waters, small and empty, was a good place to practice music. Rebecca Clarke's "Passacaglia" and "I'll Bid My Heart Be Still"—I played those dry. I've barely touched them since.

I was not good, that year in Falling Waters. Not all my time was devoted to the viola. In fact, I spent much of it trying to meet men (and often succeeding). I suppose in the olden days I would have waited by the fishing holes or in the bathroom of the public library, tensing myself up for an exchange of glances that might mean pleasure and might mean trouble. We have other tools now. Still, the principle is pretty much the same. It's not smart to meet a man in his car, or go to his house before you speak to him in public. We do it anyway. I did that year, at least. I'm still alive.

Returning to Sam's house after ten years, as I told my boyfriend on the phone the night we arrived, was not exactly like stepping out of a time machine. The house had deteriorated. Nobody else had been hired to keep an eye on it. I guess Sam decided he didn't care. I arrived with my cousin Carrie and her husband, sitting in the back with their year-old daughter. Macy was clutching my finger at intervals, using it to wave my hand around and then dropping it. Building up her muscles, I gathered.

We hauled ourselves out of the car into a sea of cousins. There are sixteen of us, and most were there already, crunching around on the gravel and taking pictures of each other and the house. It looked terrible. The deck was full of wormholes, slick from the dripping dogwood tree that overhung it. The tree had embedded itself into the roof, which didn't look like it would last—half the tiles were gone, exposing the tin underneath. All I could smell was dogwood flowers, which have always struck me as rotten even when new. When I walked around to the back, I saw that the covered porch had fallen down. Beams and scraps of screen leaned against the back wall like a kid's fort. I knelt to look in, remembering the hammock that had hung in there and the things I had done in it.

"Sully!" someone said, and when I turned around my cousin Mike was coming in for a hug like the fullback he used to be.

"Mike!" I managed to say, crushed into him. Here he was, the only cousin who had made it out of West Virginia. Smart boy with a football scholarship.

"Why would you *ever* come back here?" I asked, when he'd let go of me. He slapped me.

"Don't say that. I hate the negative thinking."

"Oh," I said. The slap had hurt, probably more than he'd intended. I stood there, looking him over. He was thinner than I would have expected. His posture was still good. I used to wonder what went on in the locker rooms and showers with jocks like Mike. The picture of someone sucking his cock popped up, and I grinned, then reversed it, since he couldn't see into my head. Sometimes it's nice to have a dirty mind.

We walked back around the house together. Mike was telling me about his family, how much they loved Philadelphia, how there was this great church they were going to. I said, truthfully, that I was glad to hear it; I always imagined that I'd get religion myself someday, one that would take me. Mike laughed. That rotten dogwood smell hit again, and then I saw the kid.

It was the way he was standing. You can't really tell by looking at someone, right—but sometimes you can. He had most of his weight on one leg, and the other touching the ground in front, sort of ballet-style. His thumbs were in his pockets, head tilted back to look up at Talia, my youngest cousin. His hair was cut close, but I could see that it would curl and float if allowed, dark-blond. I could picture him in a club, five years on, looking out at all the passing men whose performance of indifference would be amplified just for him.

"Hey," Mike said, "You haven't seen Kelly since she was a baby. And have you even met Shay?"

"No," I said. "I definitely haven't."

Mike introduced me to Kelly, a tall dark fifteen-year-old who looked just like him. She said, "You're the musician," with cocktail-party poise.

"Sure," I said.

"Are you going to play at the funeral?"

"I guess so. If we don't run out of time."

She was bored with me and I was bored with her. Mike was tackling another cousin. We exchanged smiles. We drifted. I took the chance to get my stuff out of the car and made my way up to the front door, bruising fleshy white petals with my shoes.

So, escaping like that, I didn't meet Shay until dinner. We cousins cooked together in Sam's rundown kitchen. Hotel pans of macaroni and cheese, salad in huge aluminum bowls from Carrie's restaurant in Martinsburg. Our parents, Sam's five children, set themselves up in the living room on old plaid furniture and got the bar going.

"Hello, dad," I said when I saw my father with a tumbler of Scotch and something. "I see you found the good stuff."

"He stocked a bar well, if he didn't do anything else for this place."

We hugged. We stopped doing that for a while, when I was younger and angrier. Then both of us gave in a little. I liked feeling the loose, warm skin of his neck against my cheek. Dad was small and fine-boned, and was beginning to look more and more like a cat as he got older. Alert, springy, those green eyes. He said, "You want a drink." I admitted it and he built me what he was having. We went to the dinner table matching like that.

There were actually three dinner tables: kitchen, dining room, and the big coffee table in the living room for the kids to squat around. Dad and I sat down in the dining room together, but eventually Talia came in to ask me if I minded joining her at the kids' table, since there weren't quite enough chairs out here for all the "original crew," as she put it.

"I always thought you two were immature," Dad said. Talia made as if she was going to bite him, and he laughed.

When we joined them, the kids were having a roaring discussion about whether or not it was disgusting to put ketchup on macaroni. The twins, Grace and Amelie, were liberal with the big glass bottle. They offered it generously to us as we sat down.

"No thanks," Talia said. "But I love you anway."

Shay was across from me. He ate quietly, but paused sometimes to smile at what another kid was saying. At one point, he tried to suggest something, but his "And then—and then—" got covered up each time by louder voices. I looked over at him and raised my eyebrows.

"Then what?" I said.

He shrugged. It didn't seem to matter. But he smiled at me.

"I'm Sully," I said. "I'm your, I guess, your second cousin?"

"Okay," he said.

I didn't talk the rest of dinner, but the kids had plenty of conversation on their own. Talia joined in too. Towards the end, one little boy started crying and his father had to come take him up to bed. Pretty soon they were all going to bed.

"Cocktails once we blow the all-clear," Mike said. But instead I went up to Sam's study, where I was assigned to sleep on the leather chaise-lounge, and called Anthony.

"One of the next generation is gay," I told him when he picked up.

"Oh really?" I heard his big hot voice laughing, then coughing. "Hello to you too!"

"Hi," I said. "I'm telling you the important stuff. I am not alone here. Finally."

"I still don't believe none of your cousins are gay. There are too many."

"Neither do I, but that's as far as I get. This kid, on the other hand. I know."

Anthony was silent. He got it. His sister was a lesbian, so it was something different; but he understood. Just to be with family, and look at one of them, and *know*—it had never happened to me before.

"How are you doing?" I asked.

"I'm just fine. Just fine. Doctor tomorrow."

I was sorry I wouldn't be there for that. I always went with him. My Anthony.

"Let me know," I said.

"I will." He paused, then asked, "This kid—how old?"

"I don't know. I'm guessing twelve, thirteen."

Anthony whistled.

"Young," he said. "You better look after him."

"I'm going to try."

We said good night, I love you, be safe, I love you, good night. I brushed my teeth in the little hall bathroom. Passing the master bedroom, I could hear a whole slumber party of kids stirring in their sleeping bags.

The funeral was the next day. We all woke up, stiff from sleeping on couches or the floor, and put on our black. Our aunt Carol had gone out for dozens of bagels and gallons of orange juice. Getting into our cars, we brushed sesame and poppy seeds off our clothes onto the grass. The children were very loud that morning. There was more than one tantrum. But something about the funeral home cut it all off; we were as silent, entering the chapel, as a bereft family should be.

The brief service was given by a minister who, surprisingly enough, had actually known Sam. He made some jokes—Return of the Native, and so on. A couple of people were crying. My father was one of them, so I kept my arm around him as long as I could. But I had to get out my viola, and hand over the sheet music to the funeral home's accompanist.

It was "I'll Bid My Heart Be Still" that I played. It was still in my fingers, though stiff. The chapel was overheated, but my hands were so cold. They get this way, and can't be warmed by rubbing or hot water. What happened to me, as I stood up there and heard the first notes of the introduction? They rise, and the viola answers by falling. My whole family was in front of me, all dimmed, all looking alike. I was trembling.

Rebecca Clarke's piece comes from an old song, in which the singer mourns for a dead lover. The man who is gone and will not return—he was behind me, coffined, and I played for him even though he was not my beloved, even though I never properly knew him. The song reaches a high point of grief towards the end. When I first played it, I had loved that point. This time, I reached it and found it filled with people—men. Gone lovers. Anthony. I opened my eyes and mouth, working to breathe and to play. I made it to the end.

Playing the viola takes the place of crying. Afterwards is the same: the shock of being naked, the world too bright around, the working of cords in my throat. I got back to my seat and concentrated on putting my instrument away quietly. The rest of the service, even the lowering of the coffin, went by very fast.

The wake began as soon as we made it back to the house. Mike opened his trunk to reveal a box of bottles to rival Sam's own bar, and we all went inside.

"Wake *up*, wake *up*," someone said. The kids sat with us, and we went slowly from silence to the high, fierce party noise that any wake struggles for. Nobody sent the kids to bed. I saw Kelly drinking whiskey, but said nothing. Late in the evening, someone opened all the windows. In came the dogwood smell, stronger than ever, and I went for the bathroom to hold my head against the jade-green toilet.

When I came out of there, the one person waiting in the hall was Shay. Maybe he'd had a drink too—his face, in the dark, was very pink.

"Shay," I said, one hand on the door still.

"Hi," he said. "I need to." He gestured.

"Sure," I said, and made way. But I waited with my back against the wall, and when he came out again he gave me a doubtful look.

"Hi," I said. "Listen." It built up in me, the necessity of saying this. I had to, or I wouldn't, later. "If you ever need to talk about anything, please, I want you to know, you can call me."

I should have put my number on a scrap of paper. I hadn't thought that far. He looked at me, and I saw that I had scared him. Then he said, "Okay," and turned back to the living room.

Carrie and I left late the next day, the last car in the driveway except my dad's. I hugged him before we went, and he said, "Careful, I'm fragile."

"Yeah," I said, and kissed his cheek.

I had slept through Mike's departure with his family. On

their way now, up through the Allegheny Mountains and back to Philadelphia. In Carrie's car, I rested my head on my viola case.

"Ready for home," I said. Macy went for my finger, put it in her mouth, then shook my hand again.

"Home's ready for you," Carrie said. "How's Anthony?"

I hadn't heard from him, hadn't called last night. No news, best news?

"He's fine," I said. "He's wonderful."

"You're lucky," Carrie's husband said. I couldn't recall him saying one word, that whole trip. "We're all lucky, if we get someone who sticks around."

O'er the Ramparts

It's dusk when the doorbell plays a tinny series of bells that remind Kent of some classical music he can't name. It's the first time he's heard the doorbell, and whoever rang it is the first visitor at his new place.

"Hey, Tobe," Kent says from the cramped, unpacked galley-kitchen, "want to get that?"

Toby pauses his video game—a month-early birthday gift that Kent couldn't afford but knew would both probably piss off Stephanie *and* win him some soon-to-be-single dad points—and goes to the door. Kent is cleaning up their dinner, a Gigantor Prime Cut from Minsky's, half of which went untouched. He's angling the pizza box into the nearly empty fridge when Toby calls out.

"Dad, some guy," he says and pauses. "Jeff…says he lives across the street. Wants to talk to you."

Kent wads the paper plates and napkins and stuffs them and the plastic cups in the open trash bag on the floor and turns the corner out of the kitchen. A man in jeans and a black t-shirt stands on his slab porch in the dusky light. A haze of sulphury smoke hangs over the neighborhood. Pops and sizzles and booms fill the air around them. The man has tattoos up and down both arms, and his blonde hair is slicked back like a 1950s greaser.

When Kent steps past Toby and opens the storm door, the man's smile surprises him. It's wide and bright. "Hi," he says, extending his hand. "I'm Jeff."

Kent notices the man's unusually long fingernails on his right hand. Kent squeezes hard, overcompensating, a habit he's developed in his job as an admissions counselor at the applied technology skills branch of a local community college. The school offers a number of technical degrees: diesel repair, HVAC, auto body, construction. The students are nearly always men, many in their 30s and 40s, who've come to learn a new technical trade after being laid off or phased out of their jobs in the changing economy. Problem is, at least for Kent, these men often have difficulty filling out the online application, securing high school transcripts, and producing writing samples. Because the degree programs are associate's degrees, the students in the technical programs have to be placed in the appropriate composition and math classes. Convincing them the value of those classes is the hardest part of his job. He never forgets to point out, though, that all they need is a D and they can move on.

"Kent," he says. "What can I do for you?"

"Like I was just telling your boy, I'm from just over there." He jerks his thumb toward one of the identical duplexes that line both sides of the street. The only things that distinguished them are the vehicles in the driveways and the level of lawn maintenance. "I know you just moved in, but I wanted to let you know about the neighborhood fireworks show."

"Fireworks? *Cool*," Toby says, and Kent looks at him, incredulous.

"I know," Jeff says. "Pretty badass, right?"

"I had to drag you to the fireworks stand earlier. You said—" Kent starts, but Toby just shrugs. Up until this year, a day or two before the Fourth they'd hit three or four stands and load up on fireworks of every type: small stuff like snakes, smoke bombs, tanks, sparklers, and firecrackers; and bigger stuff, like parachute bottle rockets, roman candles, fountains, and shells. He always spent way too much money, but as much as Toby loved it, he never regretted it. He'd been banking on their shooting off fireworks together tonight being something special, something symbolic to show Toby that though he'd moved out, they were all going to be okay. It didn't seem to interest Toby this year, so Kent just bought a couple cellophane-wrapped variety packs of small nightworks.

"It's set to start in like an hour, over in the field," Jeff says, pointing to the field where their street ends in a cul-de-sac. The realtor told Kent she suspected the developer ran into financing issues. "Davis—the guy drives the jacked-up Ford down the way—has been putting it on for like six years now."

Though Kent had only been here for three days, he knows exactly who Jeff is talking about. Davis is the same guy who, at 7:30 that morning, was blasting some 80s pop mix that heavily featured Duran Duran while working on his truck.

"He's a good dude," Jeff says and sort of nods at both Kent and Toby as if waiting for them to agree. "Anyway, the reason I stopped by was to invite you, of course, but also to ask...you know what? Fuck it. Oops—sorry!" he says and slaps his hand over his mouth. "I mean, never mind."

"Ask what?" Kent says.

Jeff lets out a breath and his lips pop quietly. "It was my year to collect donations from everyone to help offset Davis's costs—we try to get folks to chip in five or ten bucks—and I didn't even want to ask since you just moved in, but the HOA chick said...you know what? Just forget I said anything. I mean, I know how it is."

"What's that mean, you 'know how it is'?"

"It's just," Jeff says and then looks from Kent to Toby back to Kent. "I mean, I *get* it man."

Kent doesn't look away from Jeff, though it takes everything he has. He hates that his situation is so obvious, and even more that Jeff is taking pity on him. If Toby hadn't been there, he's not sure what he would have said.

"Anyway, so a sort of new thing this year. Davis asked me to plug in and do a kind of Hendrix at Woodstock National Anthem-type-deal," he says, leaning back and striking an air guitar pose. "Should be pretty sweet."

"You play guitar?" Toby asks.

"Since I was probably—how old are you?"

"Twelve," Toby says, "or, I'll be twelve next month."

"I was about that age, yeah. I play guitar for a living actually, if you can believe it."

"Cool," Toby says, the word dripping with admiration. "Mom said I could get one for my birthday, and once everything gets back to normal, I could start taking lessons."

"*Normal?*" Kent says, but Toby's not paying attention.

"Tell you what, next time you visit your dad, bring your axe and I can show you a few licks. We can jam," he says and gives Kent a wink.

"Thanks!" Toby says.

"Hey, if your dad doesn't mind," Jeff says, and looks at Kent but doesn't wait for him to respond, "my boy, he's about your age, is out running around with some friends, and I'm sure they'd be happy if you joined them." Before Kent or Toby can reply, Jeff turns and sticks his pinkie fingers in his mouth and cuts loose a whistle that gets his son's attention a few houses away. He waves the boy over.

When he approaches his father's side, he smiles and says, "Hi." He looks like a perfectly normal kid, and not one from the band of pre-teen hooligans Kent's seen roving the neighborhood the last two evenings.

Jeff lays his arm over his son's shoulders. "Junior, this is Mr. Kent and his son..."

"Toby," Toby says.

"Right, Toby. You think Toby could hang out with you all? His dad just moved in."

"Sure!" the boy says, "C'mon!"

"Let me get my shoes," Toby says and sprints to the living room. He stumbles putting on his shoes and hustles out the door.

"But what about your new game?" Kent says. "You were gonna show me something?"

"It's okay. I can do that in the morning before Mom picks me up." Kent hears Junior introduce himself and watches the two shake hands.

"Come check in with me before the fireworks," Kent calls out, but Toby and the boy are already running across the yard and out of earshot.

"Don't worry, Junior's a good kid. I don't let him play with any of the little fucks who live here full time."

"He doesn't live with you?"

"Every other weekend, a month during the summer. His mom and I divorced a few years back. I don't want to say you get used to it, but..." Jeff says and offers a tight-lipped smile. "I saw your ex drop off your boy yesterday afternoon."

"Not my—we're separated."

Jeff looks at Kent and then around him into the house. "Okay," he says, and raises his hands, surrendering.

Kent takes a breath. "She's filed," he admits. "I just haven't signed the acknowledgment yet." And, without even thinking, he tells Jeff something he hasn't anyone else. "One morning after Toby got on the school bus, she told me she didn't want to be married to me anymore. Right there in the kitchen."

"Shit man. *Damn*," Jeff says. "Well, welcome to the least exclusive club in the world."

✳

As soon as Jeff leaves, Kent goes straight to the fridge and grabs two beers from the dwindling twelve pack. He cracks one and takes a long swallow. Though he gave off a pretty clear us-single-dads-gotta-stick-together vibe, Kent imagines he could become friends with a guy like Jeff, if he can set aside his envy. It isn't that he's a musician—though he has to admit it's pretty cool—it's that he is doing it, living the life he wants. Kent feels the same around the men he helps enroll at the community college. Though these men are often facing a forced career change, at least they are doing something to advance themselves. They're learning or refining a skill or trade and then applying it out in the world, building or fixing things. On his better days Kent understands he's a necessary cog in that wheel, but usually he sees himself like the guy in the circus whose job it is to hold the hoops highly trained animals jump through. Kent somehow cobbled together eight semesters worth of college in fits and starts and restarts over the course of a dozen or so years while working to help raise Toby and support Stephanie while she got her bachelor's and then master's in Social Work, and the best real job he could land with his General Studies degree and resume full of shitty part-time jobs was as an entry-level admission's counselor at community college. It isn't as if Kent sacrificed some ambition; he was too busy trying to scrape together money and finish school to have really dreamed about some future career. He liked history classes and had even briefly entertained thoughts of being a history teacher, but he knew there was no way he would've been able to do all the education classes, to say nothing of the student teaching.

Kent paces the rooms of his new place, looking at the paltry scatter of boxes. He thought his old house—his old life—had been so full of stuff, but when he packed, nothing seemed to belong to him. Everything was Anna's, or no…it was more like the things they'd accumulated over the years—lamps, pictures, end tables, books, CDs—belonged to the *house*, like they couldn't be separated. All Kent really wanted was for none of this to be happening, but since he couldn't fix that, all he took besides his clothes were the spare bedroom mattress, the old kitchen table that had been shoved in the corner of the basement and piled high with junk, and some of his tools from the garage. He could pretend that he's adopting a kind of Spartan lifestyle, and it might fool some people, but in truth, Kent just doesn't care. The relative emptiness of his new place suits him.

He finishes his beer, shaking the remains at the bottom of the can before placing it on a box marked "bedroom." He pops the second one and crosses the small living room and sits on his Goodwill-new couch. Toby's console rests on the beat-up coffee table, the game on what looks like the home screen. He picks it up but doesn't know what to do; he was never really into video games, but like most people his age, he had an original Nintendo as a kid. His only frame of reference is the two buttons and the plus-shaped directional control, but this has two joysticks and so many buttons he feels like he needs another hand, or at least a few extra fingers to make it work. He pushes buttons, and one must work because the text on the screen asks, "Join battle?" He pushes buttons again until one works again, and he is moved into a kind of lobby where a timer counts down until the "battle" begins. In the two minutes he waits, he drinks most of his second beer. When the countdown ends, his character, a muscled blond guy in sleeveless fatigues and, inexplicably, a scarf, is dropped out of the sky from some kind of flying bus. Nothing about this makes any sense to Kent, but he likes how it feels watching his character glide over the land. He figures out he can control his flight with one of the joysticks, and he wishes he could just keep floating over the surreal yet weirdly realistic topography. Dramatic mountains and cliffs dominate the horizon, and uninhabited forests, waterways, and a fully modern town dots the island below. When his character lands, an overly large pickaxe appears in his hand. No one else is around him, so he has time to mess with the buttons and figure out the basic controls for moving his character. He knows from the little Toby has told him that the object of the game is to find weapons and kill everyone. He discovers quickly that he can smash and break just about anything he strikes with his pickaxe, and he has an overwhelming urge to run wild, destroying whatever is in front of him. But it's all so immersive—even on the small handheld screen—that without even realizing it, he's fully absorbed in the world of the game.

Aside from the thumping techno pop, Kent finds it strangely tranquil walking his character along the river. Boulders and cliffs emerge from the hillside above him, and though he doesn't know where the river leads, he's happy to follow it. They weren't ever really an outdoorsy family, but there is something about this that makes Kent wish they had been. He imagines playing the game with Toby and having a younger version of his blonde character exploring this world alongside him. Sure, Toby'd probably want to destroy and kill, but that'd be okay with Kent so long as they could do it together. He even fantasizes scenarios where he kills some other character to save Toby, or somehow sacrifices himself to allow Toby the chance to win the battle. Though he couldn't afford this console—there was a nervous moment at Best Buy when he inserted his credit card into the machine and it took longer than normal to process—he starts thinking of ways to swing dropping another three-hundred and fifty bucks on a second one so he can play with Toby while he's at his mom's. He makes a mental note to cut back on beer for a month or two and see if he can skimp a little on groceries and maybe dig through some of his old shit to see what he might sell. He has some comic books and baseball cards from when he was a kid, and even a crate of his dad's old LPs. There has to be a little money there.

The river rounds a bend, and when his avatar climbs over several car-sized boulders, he's met with a gorge and a roaring waterfall like something from *National Geographic*. Kent feels a touch of vertigo. He marvels at the level of detail. Things still have a surreal, almost cartoony look, but there is a sense of harmony Kent feels at the abyss, and though he isn't usually an emotional guy, he knows if he let himself, he could cry. Again, he wishes Toby were here, either on the couch or in the game, to experience this. He takes a deep breath, grabs his beer from the coffee table, and brings the can to his lips. But on the screen, he hears a single shot and flinches, spilling the last of the beer on his shirt. His avatar throws up his hands and falls backward before dissolving into a blue vapor. Though there is no blood or gore, Kent experiences the shot viscerally, a pain deep in his gut. The view fades to black, and he flips the console onto the cushion next to him.

On his way to the fridge for another beer, Kent notices the two paper sacks of fireworks he bought earlier sitting by the door. "Fireworks," he says, "jesus…"

He grabs the sacks and is about to stuff them in the trash, but he stops. He imagines Toby coming to the kitchen for breakfast tomorrow morning, seeing the fireworks in the trash, and, head hanging, apologizing for not shooting them off with him. Kent's stomach tightens at the thought. He won't have his son feeling guilty for growing up. It occurs to him how stupid it was to try to force it, that it was just nostalgia, and that he should've known better. He gets the last two beers from the fridge, and then takes the fireworks and a lighter outside.

It's now dark, but the ambient light from open garage doors make it so that Kent can see most of the neighborhood has gathered in a half circle of lawn chairs and blankets at the end of the street, near the undeveloped field. A flashlight beam bounces around, and Kent assumes this is Davis finishing setting up the fireworks. A few small children run in circles, sparklers ablaze, the sulphury air thicker even than before. Though there are still small-scale pops and the occasional rat-a-tat-tat of firecracker strings, most of that has been replaced by the deep percussive booms of larger fireworks being shot off all over town. Two houses down, Jeff has pulled a giant amp to the mouth of his garage. A white guitar hangs from his shoulder as he tunes up and tinkers with his settings.

Kent takes his bags of fireworks to the end of his driveway and looks for Toby, but he can't find him in the crowd. Kids are still out running around, but in the darkness, he can't really tell them apart. Kent tears the cellophane from each pack, wadding and stuffing it and the thin cardboard backing into the bags, and lines up the fireworks on the curb. He doesn't allow himself much time to consider how pathetic this looks compared to what is about to happen at the end of the street. He opens a beer and looks again to where Jeff is finishing setting up. He raises his beer toward Jeff, and Jeff returns a devil horns salute.

Kent takes the lighter from his pocket, sparks it, and starts lighting wicks. He gets four lit before the first one, a silver fountain, begins hissing and showering sparks, and he has to back away. The second in line is another kind of fountain, but this one shoots crackling balls of red sparks eight or ten feet into the air. Kent swallows a mouthful of beer and notices that many of his neighbors have turned in their chairs and are staring at him. He raises his beer to them, too. "God bless America," he shouts. "Whoo-hoo!" But no one waves back.

Kent goes to the other end of his line of fireworks and lights as many fuses as he can before the first one ignites. He dances and whoops and hollers around the showering sparks and strobing, multi-colored crackling balls. "Fuck yeah!" he shouts. He's a little drunk, but not so much that he doesn't realize he's making an ass out of himself. Even more people are watching him, and Kent knows Toby'll be embarrassed. Embarrassment a kid is supposed to feel about his father, not guilt.

While everyone watches Kent, Jeff's guitar squeals a long drone of feedback which, after several seconds, bleeds into the opening notes of "The Star-Spangled Banner." Kent shouts along. "Oh-ohh, sa-ay can you seeeeee!" People look from Kent to Jeff and back, unsure where to focus their attention: at the guitar player ripping into the national anthem or at the crazy asshole singing and dancing around the puny fireworks spurting in his driveway.

A deep *thwonk* sounds, and a second later, above them bursts a blue pyrotechnic that Kent feels deep in his chest. Some in the crowd flinch at the boom. He wonders if there has been some missed signal or timing thing between Jeff and Davis. Things are out of sync, but he sings on: "By the dawn's earl-lee liiight!" At the next *thwonk*, people crane their necks skyward, ready this time and no longer focused on Kent's singing or Jeff's guitar playing, and in the flash of red from the burst, Kent sees Toby—he's sure it's his son—across the street, standing a few feet away from the group of boys, watching him. Kent stops and waves; he can't help himself. The next shells explode, briefly overwhelming Jeff's wailing guitar, irradiating them all in silver and then gold. Just as the light fades and before the next shell bursts, though he can't be sure, he thinks he sees his son raise his arm to wave back.

Ron Rash

Lucas

Lucas was on guard duty, posted near the river that separated the two armies. It was cold, colder than it had ever been back in Watauga County. This cold did more than seep into his skin. It encased fingers and feet in iron and froze hot food before he could sit down and eat. It made his chattering teeth feel like glass about to break. No layering of wool and cotton beneath the pile-lined parka allayed it. Lucas kept waiting for the cold to lift. It was already March but this place observed no calendar. The river was still frozen over. Lucas envisioned ice all the way to the bottom—no current, fish stalled as if mounted. This river had a name but Lucas wouldn't allow it to lodge in his memory. Since stepping onto the pier in Pusan, his goal had been to forget, not remember.

At Fort Polk he'd heard all manner of stories about what awaited him in Korea. Much of it was bullshit: the NK ate rats and snakes raw, could see in the dark like cats. But some stories were true, including how they would crawl into a campsite, slit a soldier's throat, then slither back into the night. Or if you were on the opposite side of a river, they'd swim across to kill only one man, even when they might have killed three or four. They were leaving a message: *We're saving you for next time.*

Though the river was frozen, Lucas knew that didn't matter. Two nights earlier, an NK had decapitated another unit's sentry. Crawled over the ice to do it, though several men believed he'd crossed over on skates. Lucas scanned the flat soundless snowscape before him. At least the moon was full tonight. A hunter's moon, they called it back home. It silvered the crystals atop the river. If not wary of an enemy's knife, Lucas would have taken time to marvel at such shimmering beauty, let it, though nothing else, deepen into memory. But even this moment had to be blocked. Lucas wanted Korea to be a house entered and then left, the door locked and the key thrown overboard to rust away in the Pacific Ocean's depths. He would be back with Naomi and their child, creating good memories. But Lucas had to survive.

Last week, for the first time, his unit had been in a fight. Aubert, a Cajun from Louisiana, had been shot in the knee. It was a nasty wound, and the medic said he'd need a cane the rest of his life. That was fine, Aubert had answered. He'd be back with his wife and children. He'd be warm, and he'd be alive. Aubert was right. Getting home was what mattered.

Lucas did not allow his eyes to leave the river, all the while listening for the rub of cloth on the ice, the scrape of finger-nails. Most nights the wind howled across this hard country, but tonight it didn't even shiver the willows lining the bank. There was a rare, disquieting silence. The rest of the unit was encamped thirty yards behind him, the trees muffling snores and dream mutterings. Only when men awoke with a shout or scream, which happened every night, did Lucas hear them. But no such noises came from the opposite shore. Did the enemy ever sleep? Perhaps all they did was wait until you did. The silence was palpable as the cold. On winter nights back home, he might hear a dog howl or an owl hoot. But not here, as if no animal could exist in this place. Lucas wished he could smoke, at least feel some warmth inside if not outward. But the flare of a match, even the orange glow of a cigarette tip, could bead a rifle. He reached for the pack of gum in his pocket, then remembered he'd given it to a child in the village they'd passed two days ago. All the while, he listened hard, wanting to hear at least a breeze, then looked heavenward. Though the moon was startlingly bright, he could not find a single star. Lucas had the sensation that both armies had quietly withdrawn, leaving him alone beside this frozen river.

He let the M1 dangle in the crook of his arm and clutched the hood tighter. He bared his gloved wrist to check his watch, found comfort in the second hand's slow but steady circling, the tick of passing time. Only a few minutes and Murphy would replace him. As cold as he was, the enemy across the river was colder. Lucas had seen what their dead wore, the tan jacket with, at most, a sweater underneath. The jacket's material was as soft and pliable as the quilts that had covered him on winter nights in North Carolina. He could see how some G.I. s believed the enemy was covered with hair from the neck down. How else to survive wearing so little?

On the edge of Lucas's vision a shadow shifted. After hours of guard duty, a soldier easily imagined things, could even halluci-nate. Wind became whispers, shadows flesh. Lucas waited, heard nothing. He pushed the safety forward and stepped into a stand of willows that lined the right bank. A darkened figure lunged, a knife blade tearing through Lucas's overcoat, the tip raking his rib cage. Lucas grabbed the man's arm, dropping the M1 as both men fell to the ground, Lucas rolling on top. He reached out, felt his rifle's barrel and grasped it, only then realizing he'd forgotten to fix the bayonet. Lucas let the barrel go, but as his hand found the stock, then the trigger, the NK clasped his waist. They tumbled off the bank and onto the ice. It did not break and the landing knocked them apart. The M1 slipped free and skittered out of reach.

The man wore no coat, only a sweater. If a hat or cap, it had been knocked off. He was shorter than Lucas but had the square-shouldered build of a wrestler. His hand still gripped the knife. Both men were panting, their breaths whitening the air between them. Once their breathing steadied, they listened, but both banks were silent. Lucas jerked off his gloves and pulled the bayonet from its scabbard. Neither man tried to stand. They crawled closer, stabbing at each other, but the ice allowed little force in their thrusts, Lucas even less so because of the parka. Then the other man crouched and sprang forward. His knife blade glanced Lucas's neck, drawing blood. The NK's free hand slipped and he fell face first, rising onto his knees as Lucas's bayonet slashed his cheek, the man's molars glinting white before the gash closed. One hand on the ice for balance, each stabbed and slashed, everything slow and unrelenting as in a nightmare. The two soldiers came together, arms entangled as they rolled onto their sides, each pinning the other's right arm. Midriver, they broke apart, each gasping for breath, each knowing a shout would bring fire from both shores. The man's hair was long for a soldier's and he had to sweep it from his face. Their eyes met in acknowledgement. The fight would be settled as it had begun.

They could see each other clearly now, the moon stage-lighting their struggle. Dark smears marked their path across the ice. Most of the blood was Lucas's. To have a chance, he'd need the parka off. The blood on his left hand had frozen, sealing the fingers together. Lucas rubbed his thumb over them and blood flaked off. Their white breaths plumed slower. The mole on the North Korean's chin, a bit of wool unraveling on his sweater seemed charged with significance. Both men still on their knees, Lucas stared deep into the other man's eyes, hoping to distract him as he eased the coat off, but then the NK lunged, not to stab but to knock Lucas off balance. Lucas's right forearm caught in the coat sleeve and as he struggled to free the arm he heard a crackle.

The other man was on top now. Lucas raised his left arm in defense. The blade raked across his wrist. Another stab sent the blade into Lucas's left shoulder and his arm went limp. Briefly, world and time saturated into a luminous amber. Another stab tore Lucas's parka and peeled more flesh from his ribs. The world expanded and contracted like a heart. He twisted sideways and rolled, managed at least to get the forearm back through the parka's sleeve. As he got back on his knees, the ice crackled again, louder. Lucas looked at his right hand and found it empty. As he searched for the bayonet, the North Korean raised his knife overhead and lunged. Lucas dodged the thrust and the blade tip pierced the ice. As the other soldier pried free his knife, Lucas retrieved the bayonet. They kneeled before each other, almost reverent as their breaths merged beneath a gibbet moon and sprawl of stars. The North Korean moved first. Attempting to rise into a crouch, he fell and the ice buckled. Half submerged but still wielding the knife, the man sought purchase. He got both elbows on the ice before Lucas crawled forward and shoved him under. When the head bobbed up, Lucas grabbed a fistful of hair and shoved harder and this time the head did not resurface. The ice beneath Lucas began to fracture.

He held his breath and splayed his arms and legs. His heart hammered against the frozen river, as if seeking entry to its own annihilation. Lucas used his elbow to drag himself onto firmer ice. He heard a tick, then another, and turned his head. The sound came from yards past where'd they'd fought. Lucas heard it again and knew its source was not on the river but beneath it. The tick came again. Then the knife blade sprouted from the ice. In the moonlight it gleamed like a silver flame.

As Lucas crawled toward shore, he glanced back and when the blade did not disappear, he continued crawling. The ice was thick now and he moved quicker. But for the first time he was scared. Even this close to the bank, an enemy rifle might be aimed at him, a finger on the trigger. He thought he heard a whisper. Then Murphy was helping him up the bank.

Lucas would tell the story of that night only once, on an evening in 1970 when his son announced he was enlisting. He thought it might dissuade the boy, but it hadn't. Lucas had never told it again, though the story would tell itself in his dreams. Sometimes the knife belonged to the North Korean, other times to Lucas. Yet always both their hands were knit together around the handle, frozen there forever.

The Deep Tangle

*"[T]here was something of the women molded into the great,
stalwart frame of Hollingsworth; nor was he ashamed of it;
as men often are of what is best in them."*
— Nathaniel Hawthorne, The Blithedale Romance

The thing most people remember about Jane Gwen is her lush and copious laugh. Some might fixate on her cascade of chestnut hair or the long legs beneath the wispy sarong she wears in the field—easier for periodic bug checks. Really, Gwen! A force of nature—a gale force Gwen, we used to joke. Turbulent, sea swelling. But her laugh. How to describe? I'll try by describing one quintessential evening in Key West. It was the usual sort of place: big bungalow with a deep porch overlooking mangroves, a dozen researchers from around the world. Everyone had spent the bulk of the day out on the water, deep in mucky tidal marsh or soggy maritime forest, arriving back at the station at sunset to mix enormous quantities of guacamole and margaritas, to fry up fresh corn tortillas and reheat the beans and rice cooked for breakfast. The requisite conga line slithered around the dining room table to Jimmy Buffet's "Volcano." Then we ate and ate and fell onto the front porch in any number of fat little groups.

The lamp light from inside the house cast a weak glow on the porch but had no effect on the jungle pitch. Soon a lovely calm fell upon the merrymakers, and there was only the drone of tropical nightlife: frogs whining and chucking, bats swooping, bugs humming, the constant crunch and patter of all the common nocturnal beasties.

Gwen and two others moved off the porch, down the stairs into the ill-lit margins and tangled velvet pitch. They were playing kick the coconut. They kept hitting each other's shins and tripping over roots. And then it began—Gwen's laugh, swinging and soaring into the lush, balmy night. It was like Tarzan's verdant yodel, only wilder and more heart stirring. Gwen's laughter impaled my imagination, sending me flying along the tropical vines with each of her exquisitely heaved guffaws.

She left the next morning for her usual stint at the Smithsonian Tropical Research Institute in Panama. I watched from the porch as she and a friend walked down the trail to their vehicle. The island green swallowed them up quickly and the rumble of the waves abnegated their voices—or nearly. I did catch the rise and whirl of her laughter flying back to me. Not, of course, just to me, but to all wild and expanding tropical climes.

I didn't speak to Gwen again that season, although I heard gossip, which coalesced around a liaison she had formed with one of the true giants of the maritime research world, a scientist of awesome reputation, with amazing longevity and the most virile of vitae. His name was Angus McCaber, also known as the Orangutan. He had been, in his prime, brute force incarnate, hacking and whacking his way through the tangled confusion of tropical forest and topical significance, his specialty the mixing of contrary deities, river and ocean. He had appeared upon the pages of *National Geographic, Smithsonian,* and *People,* not to mention countless celluloid footage for CBC, ITT, and the BBC. Now in his sixties, McCaber directed his estuary empire from an island in the Charlotte Harbor of southwest Florida. His academic progeny peopled the research stations throughout the tropics, but then so did the romantic conquests of his primal years. News of the coming together of Angus McCaber and Jane Gwen was greeted throughout our world with widened eyes and dropped jaws. So perfect, so delectable, as if Burrough's jungle he had finally met Haggard's jungle she. This was not just a battle of the sexes but of generations. He was the embodiment of one, she the hope of another. Would she be the one to break his radical stallion's will? Or would he be the one to still forever her wild and untethered laugh. All that summer shorelines shimmered and shook in breathless anticipation.

Waiting. No word.

I did cross paths with them briefly in Costa Rica late in the season. I was headed back for the beginning of the fall semester and saw Angus McCaber and Jane Gwen boarding a small plane. I spotted them before they spotted me. I hid among the mangos of a fruit stand at the edge of the tarmac so that I could observe their uninhibited interactions. They were waiting as the pilot ran through the final checklist. Gwen, standing behind Angus at one point, slipped her hands underneath his untucked, baggy tropical shirt, her fingers fluttering briefly in the gray fur that spilled over his shirt lapels. He turned, suddenly, surprising her, and me, and drew us in, tight against his massive body. She seemed to swoon in his arms. Who wouldn't?

When I returned to the tropics the following spring, there was no news of Angus and Gwen. Most dismissed the very idea as idle gossip. I knew differently. I knew the effect of Gwen's laughter on a man's soul, of Angus's animal attraction. I remembered too well their passionate embrace on the tarmac. A part of me had climbed aboard that plane too, headed into the heart of some tangled, tropical pulse.

I ran into Angus in Panama City start of the next field season. He was there for a conference and collecting. I was getting ready to meet up with Gwen in La Selva. Gwen joined me there every year to help with the first census of a group of lichen. We would have plenty of time to explore the truth about her and Angus. Plenty of time between tracing lichen moves and hacking through rainforest trails to hear her tall tales, to elicit her soaring, swinging laughter, to reclaim the bits of my heart her ramblings rescued. Running into Angus along the crowded main drag of Panama City, I wanted not to mention Gwen, but Angus McCaber always could mangle my resolve.

"Miles!" he cried with a naughty grin when I told him where I was headed. "La Selva. Not sure I'll make it out this year. I need to get back to the Pine Islands. But tell the crew hi for me."

I nodded, smiled coyly as I added in spite of my initial resolve not to, "Gwen too? You know she'll be joining me."

"Jane Gwen. Really?" He seemed to ask reluctantly, the full-blown sails of his usual fast-frigate ways slowing, faltering.

Yes, I said to myself, yes, by god, she's blown him clear off course, shown him up for the weather-worn old tub he is. I could hardly contain the pleasure in my voice. "Of course."

"Give her a big wet one for me, will ya, Miles?"

Then he leaned into me as if to give me her due. I teetered, I'm afraid, and he bellowed, his pensive face erupting into a tentative grin.

I thought I saw the truth behind Angus's bravado. I saw the spent sails, the wind-wrecked masts, the warping rudders. She'd tossed him about plenty, my gale force Gwen. Demagnetized his old compass and sent it spinning. I felt some small measure of pity for Angus. Amazing!

Gwen and I met up at La Selva. The census obsessed us for the first two days. The weather was on our side for a change and we were able to reach every site with little event. The last night of our trek, strung up in our separate hammocks, listening to the light rain hitting the tarp we shared, I decided that it was time to pass Angus's message along, albeit in my own inimitable fashion. The light from our kerosene camp stove was low, casting whimsical patterns, turning our faces into shadows, our words into faces. She was telling me some story of her misspent youth, stories of soldiers and teenage angst and revolutionary desires. I turned to watch her face in the camp light. She had taken her thick, wire-rimmed glasses off and her eyes were big and black and defenseless, at once catlike and childlike, dangerous and demur. How best, I prayed, to bring Angus before us? Here, in the dark, when we were so close and comfortable, hidden, together. I reached carefully into her hammock and found her hand pressed up against her thigh, and something else I'd been hoping for too: her water bottle. I raised it quickly, clicking the top open with my thumb and squirting her full in the face.

"Wha-wha-what the hell?"

"From Angus," I said quietly. "He told me to plant a wet one on you."

"Angus!? Angus this."

Then she gave my hammock a spin that sent me face first onto the damp forest floor.

"Now, what about Angus?"

"He doesn't seem the same, Gwen," I began, as I carefully climbed back into my hammock. "Oh, yes his closing remark was typical, full of hot air and machismo but before, when he first asked about you . . . his face seemed pained, reluctant."

"Pained?"

"Broken, bent, missing some vital part."

"Angus? Angus McCaber . . . missing . . . broken?"

"Sad."

She sank and turned away from the light of the camp stove and into the moist, cooling night air. I could sense that her thoughts were agitated, her emotions wavering, like the flickering firelight. I heard her sighed mea culpa, as her hand shot for a moment to her chest, to catch her breath or calm her troubled heart.

"So it's back to the grind tomorrow," I offered as if I hadn't heard her plaintive sigh. "Back to Florida. Pine Island field station out on Demere Key. I've got some patches of lichen I'm mapping along the Matlacha Pass. Might as well use their digitizer to put all my plottings in the computer. Come help if you want. You could check on Angus, out on his island. Anyway, I could pay you for a week of work."

"Sure, Miles. I should. I really should."

I responded with a smile and a renewed sense of hope, thinking, yes indeed, soon we will both return to him. Who knows what we'll find?

*

On the third morning after our return to Demere Key and Pine Island, Gwen left to visit Angus. She was staying with me and I woke to her awkward attempt to muffle the coffee grinder with one of my alpaca sweaters. I heard her sneak out soon after. McCaber was a notorious early riser. Chances were that she would find him at this early hour sunning outside his cabin on North Captiva.

She took the station's skiff over to the island. I followed quietly, some distance back, in my motorized dinghy. I could see the weight and worry of her task in the odd anglings of her shoulders, in her long gazes out over the water. Open runs of water, thick maritime forest trails, currents changing and tricky, any of these would have been less of a threat to Gwen than facing the Angus she feared having left behind.

She reached his pier well ahead of me and started up the path to his compound. I tied up too but took a steeper, quicker path to a clearing behind the house. There I spotted Angus sitting atop a small table, his broad back to the morning sun, stocky legs akimbo, hunched over, reading a journal and occasionally sipping from an enormous, steaming bowl. Quickly I searched out the best climbing palm and made my way up into its protective, leaning canopy. I had a perfect view. The birds were going nuts by now, warning Angus of an unexpected presence on his island. He had just climbed off his table and was standing, naked and furry and bulky, a strangely tantalizing combination of primate and aging Apollo. His eyes scanned the trees. I wanted him to look up and see me. I wanted him to set me free. That's when Gwen climbed onto the clearing and their eyes met.

Angus covered his eyes, squinting, as if to reassure himself that it was truly Gwen approaching through the intense morning light and not some mythical spirit. And then he looked away, back to the house. Ready to run so soon, Angus? I wondered. Ready to run and hide? He looked back to Gwen again and managed a smile. His smile brought tears to my eyes. She must have felt such relief and release at the sight of him.

"How are you Angus? You look fit," I heard her say. And then she offered a small, inhibited laugh – not her rightful laugh at all, weighed down as it was by the harm she feared she'd done him.

Her care brought another brief smile to Angus's clearly troubled face. He looked again to his hut and back to Gwen with an even weaker, pained smile.

Run away, Angus McCaber, I whispered from my lofty viewing place. Try now to run from the truth, from all those you've caught and tossed aside, from the undeniable verdict that stands before you. You are no longer the god you once thought yourself to be. She has had you, McCaber, finished with you, and comes back now only because of me. Me. This, poor McCaber, is little more than a sympathy call. A visitation of pathos and pity. And your fear of her, of her rejection, of her limber embraces, your fear fills your face, beats hard against your boastful barreled chest. Soon it will be all that fills your arms at night, that lies next to you in bed. Oh those arms, that bed! Fear, McCaber, fear and loss and dulling memories are all that will remain for you, while around your crumbling flesh the loves you've tossed aside will rise triumphant into the new night.

By god, I was in a frenzy. Who wouldn't be? For below in capsule all the great stories were playing out before me. Passion facing pain. Force facing form. Old facing new. I was breathless with anticipation, trembling in my own impassioned empathy. And then the palm beneath me, the vegetation all around came alive. Every bird on the island echoed in kind. Below Angus and Gwen looked up into the trees, each taking a step closer to the other, in sympathy, in cautious care for what might be lingering in the jungle shadows. Then a most unexpected call rang out across the morning air.

"Ah-ah-ah-gus. Ah-ah-ah-gus."

Gwen, Angus, and I turned toward the sound. There it was,

sounding from the door of Angus's hut. The voice took form, a form I knew, that everyone clearly knew. It was Brigit Norton, tall, lean, blonde, gorgeous, and naked as a drenched anhinga.

"Ah-ah-ah-gus. Ooh. Aha. Jane Gwen? Gwenie! How are ya, girl?"

Our gaze, that of Angus, Brigit, and me, turned to Gwen, who took a step backward, and then another, gaining perspective, absorbing the view. The emotions that ran across her face, so fast and furious, the full spectrum, lit up her eyes and charged her face with a bright, white aurora of wonderment. And then it began, somewhere down deep in the earth, or perhaps slowly condensing in the heavy morning dew: Gwen's laugh. It began to fill the clearing, wrapping around Angus's embarrassment and breezing through Brigit's bare aplomb. Gwen's laughter spun around the clearing and in one great wave blew up into the surrounding jungle green and out over the bare hillside to the blue of the ocean. And soon everyone was laughing her laugh, Angus, Brigit, me, every bird and beast, the vines, the trees, the earth and air, the sun itself: all shaking with untamed laughter, all going effervescent in an ecstasy of Gwen-filled grace.

Up in my tree I was weak with surprise, lightheaded and suddenly free, and before I knew it I was falling head first from my perch toward the hard ground below. I swear, however, that for a second or two Gwen's laughter bore me up and I floated like a rare butterfly, just shorn of its old, confining cocoon, full flutter amidst the glorious green.

The next thing I remember, Angus was carrying me to his cabin, his embrace every bit as devastating as I'd imagined. I slid my arms around his thick neck and opened my eyes long enough to see Brigit and Gwen laughing up ahead, hand in hand, glancing back at me from time to time, smiling sweetly and laughing all the more.

I suspect I should have been mortified, but I confess I was not. The coast, the islands, the tropics taught me long ago not to exaggerate or avoid my own excesses. And what is one man's exaggeration worth in a place that holds the grand flights and displays of cormorants and ibis, white and brown pelicans, great blues, tricolors and greens, wood storks, marbled godwits, stilts and terns and bitterns, swallow-tail kites, rosy hued spoonbills and rare souls like Angus McCaber and Jane Gwen and Brigit

Norton and—if I may be so bold—the colorful displays of my
own transformative flights? I was not much broken in spite of
my fall, and I and the others spent the day in glorious revelry.

Gwen knew first, of course, as you may already have
guessed, the true source of my tropical spill and the need for this
confessional retelling. It was, after all, her laughter that finally set
me free. I can feel the heat of blush upon my face as I come to
the close, can hear the sanctifying peal of Gwen's laughter as I
read aloud to her my final words:

I—I myself—was in love—with—ANGUS!

Deluxe Scrabble

For Mother's Day, I buy myself the Deluxe Scrabble that comes with a lazy Susan. I delete the Amazon confirmation from my Inbox because Harry will freak if he realizes I spent $119 on a board game no one in our family besides me will play. It comes in a blue box with a cream-colored border, reminding me of the fancy placemats we had when I was a kid, and the fancy cloth napkins, each a different color. My mother would fold them into pretty shapes that looked like half-peeled bananas. My mother used to starch and iron those napkins. In contrast, my napkins are wrinkled around the edges. When Harry folds and puts away laundry, he mixes those napkins up with the tea towels. He and our son, Noah, are seemingly indifferent to the distinctions and will pull out whatever's on top of the stack and use it to wipe their greasy hands during meals.

When I was a kid, I had this friend named Sunshine. Sunshine's house was filthy, and if I walked barefoot on her family's tile floors, the soles of my feet would turn gray-black. Always there was a stray grape or blueberry on the floor in the kitchen or the papery red husk of an onion, sometimes a grocery receipt, a twisty tie, a hairpin. But I spent nearly every day of the summer at Sunshine's house because her mother Desiree was what people in those days called a housewife, and she loved games. The three of us, Sunshine, Desiree, and me, would play games for hours at a time: Yahtzee, dominoes, Sorry, and, my favorite, Scrabble.

I thought Desiree was the most beautiful name I'd ever heard. She insisted I call her Desiree, whereas my mother went by "Mrs. Brock." It's a formality she maintained. She never told Harry to call her Livia, so he avoided calling her anything at all, which made dinners with my mother awkward, Harry waiting until he could look her in the eye to address her. "It's too bizarre to call my mother-in-law of fifteen years 'Mrs. Brock!'" he used to complain.

The few times Sunshine visited my house, I felt self-conscious about how formal everything was. I saw it all through her eyes: it was like sinking into an underwater world. Without really speaking aloud why, the two of us soon settled into a routine of spending all our time together at Sunshine's house.

After we played a game of Scrabble, Desiree and Sunshine and I would look at the completed board and pick out our favorite words, the coolest words, not the ones that scored the most points. I remember feeling proud when Desiree chose my word "banshee." She maintained it was worth getting fewer points, or even wasting an "S," if you could spell something interesting like "fiasco," or line your word right on top of another word, so the two words looked like prone lovers, or neat shelves. "That's so elegant," Desiree would say, and I realized that despite her sticky house she embodied an elegance materially different from my mother's napkin folding.

Desiree taught me that being good at Scrabble was all about memorizing the two-letter words. "Cheating," is what Harry calls those words. Nothing will annoy him more than when I admit I don't know what "Xi" means, but I know it's a word.

Some summer mornings when I entered the kitchen through the screened door in Sunshine's garage, I was greeted by the warm, burnt-sugar scent of homemade blueberry crumb cake. Those were the best days. Desiree had no rules about portion size or the number of servings we were allowed to eat, or how close it was to dinner time. Sometimes we polished off an entire cake, playing round after round after round.

But eventually, after a honeymoon of perfect days, there came days when Desiree was distant or a little short-tempered or just strange. The first time, I remember there weren't more than a few words on the Scrabble board when Desiree pushed herself up from the table and said, "I'm done." She disappeared down the hallway that led to her bedroom, and we didn't see her again that day. I'd been the last one to play before she quit: "ice." I remember the word because, ridiculously, I wondered if I'd disappointed her, if I was the reason she abandoned us.

I had always been a little scared of Sunshine's dad. In fact, I tried to keep an eye on the clock in the afternoons to make sure I left before he returned home from work. He seemed made of stone, or encased in stone, like it might take a pickaxe to chisel him out. He didn't seem like the kind of man who'd have a daughter named Sunshine.

Once in a while, though, he'd come home smiling and

laughing. His cheeks seemed rosy on those days, his hair fluffier. The day that Desiree said she was done was one of those days. I stayed at Sunshine's house late into the afternoon because her mother had already abandoned her, and I didn't want to do the same.

When Sunshine's dad walked into the kitchen, leaving his umbrella in the garage to dry—it had rained all afternoon—he patted her on the head like she was a dog. "How are my girls?" he said, and for a moment, I thought he meant me and Sunshine. Then he said, "Where's Dez?"

I remember wincing, to hear Desiree's beautiful name chopped into something that sounded like a pill you'd pop in a glass of water, which would make the water cloud and fizz. But also, it made me think about how my father always called my mother "Your mother," as in, "Where's your mother"? As if she had no name or independent identity aside from that role, her production of us, her folding of napkins into their lovely, stiff shapes.

"She's in the bedroom," Sunshine said, and her father nodded and said, "Will you hang up my coat, Princess?"

Funny: the things one does and doesn't remember. I remember his coat, the color of toast, lined in red plaid, and I remember noticing, for the first time, the coat-hooks on the wall of the foyer, not hooks at all, but round like doorknobs. But I don't remember the name of Sunshine's father. I don't remember why he frightened me, though I certainly remember watching the kitchen clock to see if it was getting close to 5:00, and I remember how much I wished that clock was in my bedroom. It was one of those cat-shaped clocks with a long tail and eyes that slid from left to right, like the cat was thinking, weighing possibilities. I wondered: if I could see all that cat saw when I wasn't at Sunshine's house, would I understand her parents any better? Would I understand my own?

When Sunshine's father disappeared into her parents' bedroom, Sunshine suggested we go outside and look for frogs. There were almost always frogs in the grass after a good rain. Some of them were as small as Scrabble tiles. Sunshine said they fell from the sky. That didn't make any sense to me, but I couldn't offer up a better explanation of where they'd come from. When we placed them on our palms, the frogs peed, but we didn't mind. They were so delicate. They tickled our skin.

I imagined back then that whatever was going on with Desiree on the days that she retreated from us was of soap opera proportions. She watched *Days of Our Lives*, which was on in the background for an hour each day. Usually, we played something kind of brainless during *Days* so that she wouldn't miss anything important—new developments about the Salem Strangler or various love affairs. When she clicked on the television, Desiree would say, "I know it's dumb." Or, "It's my one vice." I don't think I had any particular plot in mind when Desiree hid out in her bedroom all day, but I imagined her bedroom as dark and kind of sinister. I pictured Desiree in a satin nightgown, something sexy as opposed to the frilly, fuzzy nightgowns my mother wore.

When Sunshine and I went back inside and washed our hands after handling frogs, there was a frozen pizza on the kitchen counter, along with a sticky note that read, "For you and Millie. You can watch a movie." I knew the tiny, neat print was Sunshine's dad's handwriting because I knew Desiree's handwriting from her keeping score. Her handwriting was sloppy, like her kitchen floor. Her handwriting took up space.

"You like pepperoni, right?" Sunshine asked me, but even though I did, I was seized with an urgent desire to leave. It was as if that dark, sinister bedroom had reached out to encase everything else. Even the cat clock on the wall, the clock I'd always loved, seemed menacing instead of vigilant. The ticking noise its tail made was signaling to me go, go, go.

"I promised I'd be home for dinner," I said.

Sunshine looked at me, surprised and then unsurprised. It was as if my defection was something she'd been waiting for: like those characters on *Days* when they receive some awful but long-anticipated news.

＊

That same summer, my mother's little Yorkshire terrier, Boswell, who had a face like a Muppet, died. He was fourteen. She earnestly referred to him as her "firstborn," as though he had come into this world the same route I had. But the way she loved him was starkly different from the way she loved me. She dressed both of us up in ridiculous, uncomfortable outfits, and she tried tirelessly to train us to obey, but she doted on that dog. Practically the only time I saw my mother smile was when Boswell sat on her lap, and she scratched him behind his ears. When I was really little, I was so jealous of Boswell that I schemed about ways to murder him.

But Boswell's death taught me that murdering him when I was younger wouldn't have made my mother dote on me more. I was the one who found him that June morning, his legs stretched out stiffly, so he looked like a footstool tipped over on its side. "Mom!" I'd called, though I usually called her Mother. She cried when she saw him, but when I said, "Poor Boswell" and tried to hug her, she shook her head and crossed her arms protectively. In bed that night I cried, not because I felt sad about Boswell particularly—he'd always ignored me, except when I was near the cabinet where my mother kept a cookie jar of dog biscuits, and then he'd whine and nose the back of my legs. I cried because I kept visualizing my mother's wet, cold eyes. I was convinced she blamed me for finding him.

One evening when I returned home from Sunshine's house, my mother said at dinner, "I don't know that I like you spending every day at that girl's house. I bet her mother would like some peace and quiet." With her long dark hair and erect posture, my mother reminded me of Morticia Addams, but with less charm.

When I told her that Desiree played board games with us, my mother raised her eyebrows, but said nothing more.

This was sometime after Desiree abandoned Sunshine and me in the middle of that Scrabble game in which I played "ice." It was also after the game of Scrabble in which Sunshine tried to play "passion," but she spelled it wrong, and Desiree laughed and said, "Passion with one lonely 's.' That's hilarious." Sunshine had said, "Don't make fun of me." She'd crossed her arms and sulked. Desiree had looked startled. "Oh, hon, I wasn't making fun of you." She'd leaned over and kissed Sunshine on her head. "You are the most important thing in the world to me." Not long after that, though, Desiree said she didn't feel good and was going to take a bath. She slid her remaining tiles back into the black pouch.

I believe I told my mother about Desiree playing games with us to defend myself—to clarify that I wasn't imposing—but once I said it, I thought about those two abandoned games and I wondered if maybe my mother was right.

It certainly didn't occur to me that anything about that exchange could be upsetting to my mother. I'd forgotten all about it when my father knocked on my bedroom door later that night, sat on my bed, and said, "Hey, Chicken: you made your mother feel bad."

That summer, I kept oscillating between having a grandiose sense of power and feeling utterly insignificant. As an example of the first, I felt responsible for Boswell's death, because years ago, I'd fantasized poisoning him. When my mother looked at me with her red, teary eyes, she'd seemed to accuse my jealous, seven-year-old self. On the other hand, I was shocked that anything I could say would wound her. I had no idea what my father was even talking about that night. That was long before I was trained in couples counseling, as well as in required so-called personal development classes at work, to take ownership of my feelings and to separate my feelings from facts. Back then, I had no qualms with the idea that other people, my mother especially, could be responsible for my feelings, but the reverse was unfathomable. And why wouldn't it be? My mother had trained me to raise my hand if I needed to speak to her and to wait to be called on. This wasn't just for occasions on which she had company and so to prevent my interrupting conversation. My mother explained that she startled easily and that children were abrupt.

Even when my father explained himself, I just stared at him.

Then he said, as he had several times over the years, "Your mother had a rough childhood. It follows her, you know?" I didn't know. My father never elaborated on this statement. I pictured a hooded, shadowy figure, like a jailor, standing in the corner, its eyes tracking my mother.

✳

Sunshine's birthday was on the solstice. "The longest, hottest day of the year," Desiree said as she brought out a white-frosted cake covered in rainbow sprinkles.

For the occasion, Sunshine's father had set out a blue tarp and covered it in soapy water so that if we ran and leaped onto it, we slid all the way across. He'd put out buckets of water and blue sponges that Sunshine and her cousins threw at each other.

It was a family birthday party, except for me. That could have been awkward, especially since I didn't know Sunshine's cousins, and Alexandra in particular was intimidating, with her purple eyeliner and feathery bangs. But Desiree put her arm around me, and said, "This is Millie. Millie's honorary family." It's hard to describe how special that made me feel. It made me want to cry.

My memory, as noted, is unreliable: it's like a piece of linen that moths have gotten to, full of lacy holes. But just today, when I was sitting by myself at our dining room table (Noah at soccer practice, Harry who-the-fuck knows where), playing myself at Scrabble (Millie against Amelia, no one has called me "Millie" for at least fifteen years), that whole party unfurled in my mind. I was arranging the letters in Millie's rack—HORROR, HONOR, HOAR—and then I realized I could use them all if I played on the Y. Once that clicked, the memory clicked as well, like a Scrabble tile locking into a slot. I saw the wet blue tarp, I heard the smack and slide of bodies, I felt Desiree's warm arm around my shoulder.

I remembered how Sunshine said my present was the prettiest of the bunch—shiny rose-colored paper wrapped in a fancy white bow that reminded me of a sea anemone. The wrapping was pretty, I suppose, but the word that came to my mind was *gaudy*. My mother wrapped it. She picked out Sunshine's gift, too. I had wanted to buy Sunshine a bracelet kit I'd seen at Target, but from across our dining room table, my mother had frowned. She said, "She's your best friend. Let's get her something special."

My mother perked up then. She said we'd make a day of it. She'd take me to lunch at that restaurant that does the tea service with the platters of little sandwiches with their crusts cut off and mini quiches and pastries, where your tea is served with a bowl full of sparkling sugar cubes. She said, "Doesn't that sound fun?" My father smiled. He gave me a pointed glance. I thought of poor little Boswell when my mother tried to trick him to get inside his dog carrier to go to the vet. She'd place a dog biscuit all the way in the back. Boswell knew it was a trick. He'd look at the treat, then look at my mother and whimper.

That's how I ended up giving Sunshine a Precious Moments figurine of two girls holding hands. The base on which the girls stood read, "Two Friends, One Heart."

When Sunshine lifted the figurine from the box, her cousin Alexandra smirked. One of Sunshine's aunts said, "That's just darling." It was probably a hundred degrees outside, but I was mostly sweating from embarrassment.

Sunshine was sweet about it. She thanked me and gave me a hug. Maybe she really did like the figurine, but that wasn't the point.

The point was I had been too worried about my mother's feelings to insist on picking out my best friend's birthday gift. Standing there in my dripping swimsuit in Sunshine's yard, I hated my mother.

That evening, when my mother asked what Sunshine thought of her gift, I said, "She liked it." I even smiled at my mother. But I wasn't really seeing my mother at all. I was imagining Desiree across the table from me—Desiree, my honorary mother. I was thinking how she loved me like I was her own daughter; how she loved me in a way my own mother was incapable of.

The following March, right before I turned twelve, though, that illusion was shattered when Sunshine and Desiree moved to Montana. As they got into their packed station wagon, my and Sunshine's faces wet with tears, Desiree spoke only of my and Sunshine's friendship: "You'll write each other letters. You'll talk on the phone. Distance will make your friendship all the more special, you'll see."

Distance didn't.

And it comes to me today, this strange, sad, lonely Mother's Day—a holiday that my husband and son didn't even remember this morning, because let's face it, it's stupid, created by Hallmark to sell cards; a holiday my own mother always disdained, though ironically, this is the first anniversary of her death—that here's another meaning for "honorary": a family member that only contingently belongs.

George Singleton

Here's a Little Song

This lawless, irretrievable, scar-inducing event occurred near the end of my father's Barter Years. I didn't know about his unplanned and unfortunate annulment with cash until later, and I'm not sure even my father understood how his wallet molded from disuse. He'd traded an aluminum canoe for a 1970s Fisher model metal detector. He'd gotten the canoe for a tandem bicycle, and this whole bartering system took place, I'm guessing, because my mother took off to live with "my great aunt Virginia, who's in need of some help not falling." Without her, he needed no bicycle built for two. He'd gotten that unsafe and archaic two-wheeler in trade for some masonry work he completed at one of the rich people's houses up above the mill village. I learned later that those people didn't need a tandem bicycle, what with their new ponies. When I learned the entire story years later, I wondered how my father held back—how he didn't blame my mother's absence on the pony-people, somehow, and didn't sneak on their property and, out of vengeance, open their stalls and gates.

During that last Barter Year, we lived about the best we'd ever lived: in a rental house in a mill village, surrounded by neighbors about to die at age fifty from brown lung, or unemployable after the cotton mill's demise seeing as they held ninth grade educations. This was before crack epidemics, before crystal meth and heroin and fentanyl. I couldn't imagine living in this particular mill village now. I'm talking 1990. Before the Barter Year, my father worked steady at a number of things: brick layer, house painter, lawncare specialist, small engine repair mechanic. At one point he delivered newspapers until he figured out that the cost of gasoline was more than he could make monthly, back in 1979 during the Oil Embargo, when I could barely tie my shoes.

Sometimes I ask people about their first memories. Most involve Christmas, or a vacation at Myrtle Beach, or a tracheotomy victim blowing balloons out of his neck-hole. Me, I remember going off on a pre-dawn adventure with my father, following his old seventy-mile morning paper route, though we never delivered the morning news.

I turned fifteen toward the beginning of the Barter Year. There, in the back yard, my father sweeping the metal detector around the yard, he said, "Always respect the Law, Renfro." I stood there with a little shovel in my hand. "The Law, but not the *laws*. There's a difference. If you get pulled over by the Law, say 'sir' or 'ma'am.' Do what they ask of you. But don't respect the laws. Do you hear me?"

I pointed at an old beer tab in the grass, a pull-tab. I said, "Don't step on that," because my father walked around barefoot.

My father handed over his beer and told me I could drink the rest of it. He lit a cigarette, took a few puffs without taking it out of his mouth, then handed it over to me. He said, "Against the law for you to drink and smoke. But do you see the world stopping on its axles? Do you see birds flying north for the winter?" He went on and on. My father had some good ones. I figured that he'd been brooding over things for some time. He said, "Is Hell in the sky and Heaven in the middle of the Earth?"

I said, "What are the chances we'll find something worthwhile in our yard, Dad? Why don't we take this detector out to, I don't know, a place where maybe people dropped money. Like at the fairgrounds, or a parking lot?"

At the time I didn't know that he searched for his wedding band. I didn't know that my mother accused him of cheating on her—that he'd taken off his wedding band at some bar, because he wanted to appear single—at Smiley's, Ronnie's, Godfrey's, the Spinning Room, the Ramada Inn bar two towns away, wherever. I didn't know that my mom left to "take care of Great Aunt Virginia" only because she'd had enough. How could a fifteen-year-old know his mother's hopes and dreams? She wanted to attend the local technical college, study hard, and become a phlebotomist. What good son understands his mother's infatuation with bloodletting at a regular hospital or free clinic?

"I'm getting a good beep right here," my father said, waving the wand over a patch of dead grass. "I don't remember ever standing right here, but maybe it's it."

I dug into the grassless soil and pulled out a roofing nail. I said, "Come on, man, tell me something."

My father swiped sweat off his forehead with a forearm that

446

looked more and more like a butter knife. He'd not been taking care of himself. This is when I learned the truth: "We're looking for my wedding ring. Goddamn. If I can find this thing, your mother will come back."

I tried not to look up at the neighbors on four sides, plinking their cheap Venetian blinds to see what we did. "Where's the septic tank? Maybe your wedding band fell off when you washed your hands," I said. I think I had seen a TV movie where this happened.

My father dropped his metal detector. He took off the head-phones. He grabbed me by both biceps and kissed me on the lips for the first time. I could taste gin, bourbon, beer, and vodka, all at once.

✳

My father became a certified brick mason, then house painter, only because he could buy a jointer trowel, block brush, brick tongs, nylon mason's line, and so on. Roller, drop cloth, six-inch brush, caulk gun. He'd taken courses in the high school's vocational studies program only because he hated math, science, English, and social studies. He took woodworking, masonry, elementary electricity, and whatever those other classes were. I'm going to go ahead—this is embarrassing—and mention how I, for whatever reason, somehow, fucking aced every class and, even though I made no real friends what with my station in life, graduated high school salutatorian. I still don't understand all the Nature v. Nurture stuff, or DNA, or genetics, or "generation skipping" theories, but I hailed from a phlebotomist-wishful mother and a scam-daddy.

My first memory went like this: "Come on, Renfro."

"You are *not* taking Renfro with you," my mother said.

"Goddamn right I am," my father said. "We ain't got no dog no more. You drunk and wanting to drive around? You take a dog. No good cop comes between a man and his riding retriever. You sober and don't want to get caught by the Law? You take a toddler. No deputy stops a man going off to buy Pampers."

"You ain't right," my mother said, but she laughed. She said, "Where y'all going?"

My father said, "To the going-place. You don't worry none."

Oh, if only I knew grammar back then—I could've pointed out a number of double-negatives, of missing verbs, of verb tense shifts.

This may or may not've been a time before child seats, about laws that babies and toddlers needed to be in back somewhere, faced away from the front of the car. I don't know. But I remember having to stand in the front seat of my father's cool F-150 Ford truck, kind of a forest green/pale green motif, and reaching into people's mailboxes, looking for envelopes.

"Good boy, Renfro," my father said when I found one and handed it over. "We get back home, I'mo make a waffle for you for breakfast," he said. "You like ice cream? I'mo put ice cream on your waffle."

This memory came back to me without the aid of a psychologist. My father, from his ex-newspaper-delivering days, remembered that people—especially country people—still put out their monthly newspaper dues in the mailbox, without threat or worry. Back then, the monthly seven-days-a-week paper cost something like nine-fifty a month. I might be wrong by a dollar or two, either way. I just know this: Where we lived, in the middle of nowhere, people didn't put their monthly subscriptions on a credit card, and they didn't mail in checks to either the deliverer or the newspaper itself. They walked out to their mailboxes, slung up the red flag to let the newspaper deliverer know another month's been paid, and forgot about it. Where we lived, most people didn't pay in check. Sometimes I pulled out an envelope so heavy in nickels the gummed innards strained. It didn't matter. My father turned on the truck's inside lights and said, "Count it, boy," and I'd go, "Five, ten, fifteen, twenty…."

Then he'd turn off the inside light and look into the rearview mirror because, I figured out later, he didn't want the real newspaper deliverer, the one who took over after my father quit, throwing papers and checking mailboxes—and thinking I guess these people will all pay tomorrow—catching up behind us.

This entire episode ended up with my father gathering his stolen money, then going down to Snoddy's Lumber and Supply, and paying, in cash, for all the handyman accouterments he'd need to start a business. I stood there at the cash register when Mr. Ellis Snoddy himself said, "You come into some money or something, Chesley? You drive over to one them other states and win the lottery?"

My father stared a hole through the man. Even as a little kid

I felt uncomfortable with the silence. He said, "Yeah. Me and Renfro just come back from Indiana." I can't know for certain now, but I bet that prolonged silence took place because my father tried to think of another state that wasn't South Carolina, and one that Mr. Snoddy'd not visited and wouldn't know if a lottery took place there.

"Indiana," the man said. "I hear it's nice there. Flat."

"It surely was," my father said. "Especially around all them shorelines." It took me a few years to understand that my father had Indiana confused with Michigan.

Anyway, all those masonry and painting tools came to about a dime below what my father and I had stolen from people's mailboxes. I'm not sure how he accumulated money to afford photocopied fliers to put in the very same mailboxes, advertising "Ware House Improvement." Not "Ware's." I would bet that half of his prospective customers threw away their fliers thinking they didn't need to improve a warehouse.

※

My mother, I didn't know at the time, had taken a job at her friend's cousin's motel on the outskirts of I-26, some sixty miles away. She didn't even have a Great Aunt Virginia, prone to imbalance. My mother took a job cleaning rooms, got free rent/shower/electricity/color TV and in-room phone, plus maybe fifteen dollars a day paid under the table. She called home twice a week, always at a time when my father was out. She said things like, "Aunt Virginia's holding on the best she can," and "I have to help her in and out of the tub." She said, "Are y'all eating okay?" and "Are you getting your school work done?" She asked, "Is your father going out every night to one of his bars?"

I gave honest answers, or at least deflected. "I love cube steak," I said once, which was true, though we'd not come close to eating even Hamburger Helper since my mother's absence. I said, "American history is more interesting than I thought it would be," though our idiot teacher found it necessary that we all memorize the forty-six counties of South Carolina, something I'd already done in seventh grade for, of all things, a class called South Carolina History.

One time I said, "Is Great Aunt Virginia going to die?" I wanted to tell her about my passing the written part of the driver's exam.

My mom laughed. "Everyone's going to die, Ren. There's just nobody else on my side of the family to help out."

There'd always be some buzzing in the background, which I learned later to be the window air conditioning unit. I'd say, "What's that noise?" Sometimes cars honked in the near-background and I'd say, "Does she live close to an intersection or something?" I'd hear people yelling in the background, a pounding noise, someone screaming about an ice machine. "Where are you, again? I forget."

"Indiana," my mother said.

※

I'd passed the thirty questions of the driver's test, and practiced, most days after school, with my father in the passenger side of that same green-and-green Ford truck. My mother had taken our other car—a 1980 two-door Buick Skylark that, I bet by now, is one of the hottest low-riders east of the Mississippi, somewhere. All of this is to say, I would have to drive my father's junker truck to pass the test. While my mother was gone our days went like this: My father said he had a job somewhere, doing something, which ended up not being so true. I took a school bus to high school. I came home. We messed with the metal detector for a couple hours. And then my dad would say, "Hey, it might be a good idea for you to practice that parallel parking again."

It just so happened that his favorite liquor store had parallel parking out front. Normally my father came up with this idea twenty minutes before seven, and in South Carolina it's the law—the bad kind of law—for package stores to close at seven o'clock. So we didn't get to spend a lot of time, I don't know, taking left turns, or passing other cars, or taking right turns, or figuring out etiquette at a four-way stop. I didn't practice those arm signals that South Carolina required everyone to exhibit— for left turn, right turn, slowing down—even though no one ever demonstrated such, outside of grown men on bicycles, some years later, wearing Spandex, plus the occasional moped victim. Mostly I knew how to turn on the headlights returning from the liquor store, seeing as it got dark by then. Sometimes I got to click on the high beams.

"When are you going to let me take the test?" I asked my father more than once.

"We need to find that wedding band," he always said.

"I can pass. Everyone I know at school has taken it and passed," I said. "It's kind of embarrassing riding the bus to school."

"You ain't got no car. I need the truck for work. Your momma's got the Buick. Why you need to drive so bad?"

"'Ain't got no car' is a double negative," I'd say, then brace myself for his punch. I learned how to drive a truck while getting punched in the right arm hard. That should've been on the actual test. The driver's exam bureaucrat from the Department of Motor Vehicles should've figured out a way to flat-out punch the driver mid-road test, seeing as, at some point, it would happen to most drivers in South Carolina.

"If I get my real license, I can take you to work, drive myself to school, come pick you up when I get out, take you to a number of bars so you don't get another DUI, get you back home," I said.

"I know your mother's been calling you," he said. "You ain't been telling her nothing, have you?"

I said, "That's another..." and then stopped. I couldn't take another bruise. I said, "Well."

My father pounded the dashboard. "She's been calling you? How's she know when I'm not around?" He'd say, "She ain't called me. Listen, Renfro, I have never cheated on your mother, and I can prove it. Next time you talk to her, tell her she needs to talk to me. I might have to use some notes, but I got it all down, explaining."

I said, "Well."

"Goddamn it to hell," my father said, during that last little father-son practice drive. "Get us back home and I'll prove it."

We were already in the ten-yard driveway, next to the clapboard house. I said, "We're here, Dad."

He got out of the truck. He stomped—holding a brown bag with one of the cheaper bourbons—out back. My father turned to me—I'd turned off the ignition, but forgotten to turn off the headlights—and said, "Meet me on the back porch."

How did my father hide the fact that he owned a pawn shop acoustic guitar, a Martin, no less? What kind of Honor Roll child was I who never snooped around to find such an instrument in our house? When did guitar playing become one of the prerequisites of a vocational school education, along with woodworking and masonry?

I got out of the truck, and locked it for some reason. Of

course I locked the keys in the ignition. I followed my father, who had gone through the back door of the house, and emerged with his six-string and a Blue Horse spiral notebook. He sat down on an old wooden spool that most of our neighbors used for outdoor tables, one of those things that once held cable. I walked up and said, "What are you doing?"

He'd traded his spare tire—I didn't know this at the time—for the guitar. He'd quit looking for handyman jobs, and practiced playing from eight until three. My father said, "I might not be the smartest man, but I learned that I can still do this."

And then he started playing. I'm talking he picked that guitar in a way that would've made an angel weep. He stared down at his shoe the entire time. Me, I reached over, grabbed that brown paper bag, and uncapped a bottle of Kentucky Gentleman, took two swigs, and tapped my foot. My father didn't stop me. I could've pulled out a hypodermic needle and shot up heroin at this point. My father took off on some kind of instrumental collusion that could've stopped the ocean's tides had we lived closer to the beach. Then out of nowhere he eased into "Lost Highway" by Hank Williams. I didn't know the song at the time—me, I'd somehow learned about punk music—but I understood my father's ability and significance. And soul. As much as my missing mother wanted to be a phlebotomist, my father wanted to be a country singer, and by god, he deserved it.

He said, "Listen to this song I wrote by myself, Renfro," and I felt myself cringe.

I said, "If I get my driver's license, then I can take you down to the grocery store and we can get some good cube steak, and more of those boxes of macaroni and cheese. Spam."

I didn't pay attention enough to my father's lyrics, though I swear he sang out in a way that would've made any National Anthem soloist proud. I think it went like this: "You tell me I can't go to the bar no more/You say heaven ain't going to glitter down manna/When's the last time I slept on the floor?/When's the last time I left for Indiana?"

Oh, the song went on, a real narrative, something about a man hoodwinked and accused, about a man misunderstood and pitiful. I stood there watching my father, there in the mill village where his wedding band may or may not have hidden itself in a way to prod my mother elsewhere.

*

As it ended up, we did get out shovels and dig down into the septic tank. It would've been easier to call up a Rotor-rooter-like company, and have them do whatever they do, but my father got down to the coffin lid, pulled it out, then said, "I learned this little thing in high school. It might have to do with either physics or aqueducts."

My father turned the garden hose on full blast and stuck it down into the septic tank. He let it go for two minutes straight. I stood there while he counted out to 120. I'm not sure why that was the magic number. Then he turned off the spigot, un-wrenched the hose, and set it down on the ground, pointed toward our neighbors to the west. I stood there—if I ever write a memoir it's going to be titled *I Stood There*—and watched as our bodily fluids chugged a seeping path to the neighbor's yard, then behind toward their backyard neighbor's yard. I imagined our septic tank's contents eventually making its way to a creek, then that creek carrying it to a major river going to a town with a real water supply instead of a plague of wells. Don't ask me how toilet paper didn't clog up the hose. Don't ask me about the smell.

"If the ring comes out, it'll just set itself right here near the mouth of the hose pipe," my father said. "You can stay out here if you want. I need to go inside and practice."

To make sure he knew what I meant, I said, "This whole malodorous escapade is not going to get us into untroubled cir-cumstances."

He stopped on his way to the house. My father stomped his boots. "That'd almost make a good song-line," he said. "Work on it." Then he looked up at the sky. I could tell he worked his brain, conjuring rhymes for "circumstances."

*

"Evidently it takes only one dog hanging himself by accident to understand, from that point forward, to measure out a chain and make sure the dog can't still jump the fence tied up." My fa-ther used to say that. When I was younger I'd say things like "Did you have a dog that accidentally hanged himself?" or "What was your dog's name?" or "How tall was the fence?" As I got older– maybe ten to twelve—I said, "Dogs shouldn't be on chains in the first place," or "Is that what happened to Roger, and you wouldn't tell me?," Roger being the dog that disappeared overnight. And then—right when my father admitted to, then displayed, his dream of becoming a musician–I realized that he was talking about himself. All along my father said the thing about the hanging dog because *he'd* done something wrong, and my mother made it a point to disallow another misadventure.

He owned variations. On a couple occasions, after performing a less-than-stellar parallel parking maneuver in front of Shupee's Party Shop, I walked in with my dad and, without any kind of prompt or recognizable segue, he'd blurt out, "It ain't so much I'm on a short leash. She let me circle the stob until I got all twisted right facedown to the ground." No one at the liquor story felt confused by the non sequitur. Other times my father might walk up to a complete stranger and say, "Don't ever pee in your empty water bowl, my man, thinking it's better off filled with anything available."

Then—and I learned later in life this isn't a normal financial transaction—my father argued back and forth until he offered a Craftsman circular saw for, I don't know, two half-gallons of lower-shelf bourbon. One time he traded a crescent wrench for a half-pint of Schnapps.

The septic tank drained. I stayed out there for a while. My father locked himself in his bedroom and strummed his guitar. I wish I'd've owned a tape recorder back then so I could prove to anyone—maybe my wife now—this song that started off with his crooning, "I had a horse, I named it Homer/I owned a cow, whose name was Peg/I loved my mule, that went by Gomer/I miss my pig—I ate its leg." It went off for another ten or twelve verses, a regular barnyard elegy. Or eulogy.

Understand that this was a time before Caller ID and cell phones. I still thought my mother lived in Indiana, taking care of Great Aunt Virginia. So I did the only thing I could do at the time, and that was to get down on my knees and pray to God, the other gods, and Electricity Itself that my mother would call at this point. I concentrated. I started off with "Dear Lord" and "I don't know your name, but you're the one with eight arms," and "Dear Thomas Alva Edison, in connection with Southern Bell."

I could barely concentrate over the noise outside, made up of people yelling out, "Goddamn, what's that smell?" and "Somebody's septic's done overflowed," and "What's them people's names rented that house a while ago?" meaning us.

Then the phone rang. I got off the floor in such a way it probably looked like I had starting blocks, from track, to help my initial surge. I picked up the receiver after less than one ring and said, "Hello?" quietly. In the background, my father sang about a goat named Sam that ended up tasting like Underwood Deviled Ham.

My mother said, "Are you alone, Renfro?"

I shook my head No.

She said, "Are you shaking your head either up or down, or sideways? I can't see you, you know. Are you alone?"

I told my mother about Dad in the bedroom. I whispered everything about his looking for his wedding ring in the septic tank, like how it might've fallen off when he washed his hands or wiped himself. I said, "He can play the guitar. Did you know this?" There was a lot of silence on the other end. I said, "I can't see you nodding or shaking your head."

My mother said, "I guess I might've made things worse."

"He's not that bad," I said. I said, "I'll be the first to admit that I'm not a connoisseur of any kind of music, seeing as we don't have much of a record player or album collection, but his voice comes out in pleasant tones."

That's what I said: "pleasant tones," like some kind of pussy. I can hear it in my head now. Not to mention "connoisseur."

My mother said, "Yes." On her end of the line I could hear someone yelling about a pool being more of a *cess*pool. I heard, "We're from Michigan, so it ain't too cold for us, but this pool you got here is disgusting."

I thought of the septic outside. People still yelled out there. My father dropped his original tune and started singing that song about the lonesome whipporwill. I said, "Please come home. I might never get my drivers license if we don't have two cars here."

She said, "*I* have your daddy's wedding band, Renfro. I need-ed some time off, and took it off the bedstand so he wouldn't go pawn it off for more booze. Or trade it for a nail gun. It ain't much of a ring in terms of bartering abilities." I don't know why she thought it the perfect time to admit her ruse, and offer me perfect instructions to find Two Pines Motel, straight up I-26 north of us, then a couple miles to the left after the second North Carolina exit. I could hear her exhale a cigarette. "I got his ring on a chain around my neck, for some reason. I guess so people around this motel think I'm a widow."

I said, "Well." I said, "I'm no professional critic, but he's good. I wish you'd come home and listen to him."

My mother said, "There are dogs that'll scratch a spot raw, even after the fleas been gone, Renfro. They'll scratch and scratch themselves until they bleed." She said, "Your daddy promised me he'd quit his music dream, after it got him in so much trouble. But I guess maybe I should've never," and then we got cut off.

Never what? Gave him a chance? Cared? Should've made some ultimatums long ago, then left years later? Never understood the nuances of songwriting?

My father, in the background, over the neighbors yelling, went into another original, I guessed. He even said to himself, "Here's a little song I wrote," as if talking to an audience, then began a song that involved end-lines that rhymed cube steak/birthday cake/streak-of-lean/Patsy Jean. I could tell my father wished to write a traditional love song.

Patsy Jean was my momma's name.

✳

I woke up the next morning to find my father gone. This was a Saturday. The truck stood in the driveway, but he wasn't around. I looked out the window to see if he worried the garden hose. The inside of the house smelled septic. Finally, around eight o'clock, I went outside to find a note beneath the windshield wiper. My father'd taken off, too. He'd packed a suitcase, grabbed his guitar, and hitchhiked to Nashville. He wrote, "I know it's both inconsiderate and irresponsible to leave you alone. If you call your momma, or she calls you again, tell her I'm gone, and that I'll stay gone until I've made it big enough for us to buy our own house. She'll come home, I know, if I'm not there."

Listen, I didn't care about his being inconsiderate and irresponsible, but there for a good ten minutes I felt sorry for myself. I wondered what I did to drive both parents out of the home.

He continued with, "Stay by the telephone all day, just in case she calls. Or me. Also, because I had this all planned out, there are two cans of Lysol spray beneath the sink. Please go spray the back yard."

I'll probably be judged by this if there's an afterlife. I know that I should've never told my wife this story, all these years later, after both my parents had died. I didn't go sit back down by the phone, waiting for the phone call from an errant parent, a mother and father with broken dreams, et cetera. First, I thought, I will never end up like the Ware side of my family. Then I went into my father's bedroom, found a half bottle of bourbon, took it out to the truck, loaded up the metal detector, figured out how to use a wire hanger to pull up the door lock (which should be part of the driver's test, if you ask me), and drove off, illegally, of course, to all of the poorer churches' parking lots—I'm talking Pentecostal and Baptist—because I had a feeling that those congregants probably had holes in their pockets and lost spare change on regular Sundays. Boy, was I right. Then I went beneath the stands of the high school football field. Bingo. I drove to the town of Inman, where there was a Hardees and McDonalds, parked, meandered over to the drive-through windows and got more than a dollar at both places.

In between, I played this little game with myself to take a swig of whiskey for every dollar I found, which meant four swigs in about two hours. I found enough change—I didn't know this at age fifteen, seeing as we didn't have to take an economics course in high school—to pay for the gas used up by that truck.

This particular incident, as it ends up, caused me to write that one song, recorded by you-know-who, that made me enough money to quit songwriting altogether, back in the day, before I got all caught up starting the non-profit to give free blue tarps to bad-roofed people. Anyway, I returned home, feeling good about myself.

The phone rang. I picked up and probably slurred out, "What you want now?"

It was my father. He said, "I'm so sorry, Renfro."

I looked at the clock on the kitchen wall. I didn't know when he left, but I doubted he made it all the way to Nashville by this point. I said, "I found your wedding ring!" like that.

He said, "The world isn't like it used to be."

I said, "I'm just kidding. But I know where your wedding ring is. You didn't lose it."

My father said, "I'm on a pay phone so I might have to talk fast. Hey, if I call back collect later, be sure to accept the charges."

In the background it sounded a lot like when I talked to my mother—cars and trucks honking, people yelling about stuff. I said, "Where are you?"

He said, "I made it as far as the other side of Asheville."

"Nashville?" I said. "That's pretty good for hitchhiking, right? How many times did you have to put your thumb out?"

He yelled into the receiver, "Asheville!" which wasn't that far away at all. It was only an hour away, at most. I tried to do some math in my head, but that bourbon squelched my abilities, evidently.

I said, "Asheville, North Carolina? That's it?"

"This truck driver picked me up, then had to let me out, and I kind of forgot my guitar. I have my suitcase, but I ain't got my guitar," he said. "It's in that boy's semi. You got to come pick me up."

Well, well, well, I thought. I said, "Can't do it, Dad. I ain't got no driver's license. You understand my predicament, right? I ain't got no. I ain't got no." I said, "Now, I could've come to pick you up had you found time to take me over to the DMV at some point, after I got my learner's permit. But I wouldn't want to test the Law, you know. I don't mind *breaking* **laws, but what if I get pulled over by** *The* Law? That could be an ugly sight and an indelible mark on my record." I might've said some other things. I might've passed out a little in between, then awakened to continue the conversation.

"I'll walk back home—it'll take me three days—and kick your ass, boy, if you don't come pick me up."

I kind of sobered up quickly. Of all the bad things my father had said over the years, he'd never sounded so determined.

Still, I wasn't so sober so as not to say, "Sing it, Dad. Sing me how to come reach you."

❋

My mill village rental house to my father's spot at a Petro truck stop went like this: Take a left out of the driveway, drive a couple miles to the interstate, take a right, drive sixty miles, take a right, find Dad sitting there still next to the pay phone, on his haunches. I don't want to say that I was a natural driver, but nothing happened, outside of a few people hitting their horns when I drifted from the right lane to the left. I still had the metal detector in the back of the truck, and for some reason I thought that if I got pulled over by The Law, I'd say something about how I was a gold miner, and so on.

"This life is turning out worse and worse,"my father said after he got in the cab.

I said, "You want to drive?"

He said, "Why? So I can drive both of us off a cliff? Goddamn I should've gone to college. I should've studied accounting, and gotten a good job with H&R Block."

And then he leaned his head back and fell asleep immediately.

I put the truck in reverse and got out of the parking lot. You probably already see what's going to happen, if you've paid attention to the geography and mathematics: I drove fifty miles south, then turned right at the next-to-last exit before the South Carolina line. I turned right, and drove straight to the Two Pines Motel, this time not drifting so much into the passing lane, but holding on tight to the steering wheel so as not to veer into the emergency lane.

He didn't know—how could he have?—of my wish to reconcile my odd parents.

My father didn't know this wasn't Indiana.

I slowed down and took a left into the gravel parking lot. I hit the horn in an SOS fashion, because I'd learned Morse Code. My father awoke, sat up, and said, "Do we need gas?" and "Do we need to put some water in the radiator?"

My mother came out of room 11, looking withered. I turned toward my father in order to see his face and wondered if he'd go all wide-eyed There's My Wife. I wondered if he'd turn to me and look You Bastard. My mom held some kind of dust rag. She appeared beautiful, beautiful.

She waved that rag at me and smiled. She said, "Hey! Hey! It worked. You learned how to drive!" She said, "Hold on," and went back into one of the rooms.

My father looked around at the surrounding mountains. My mother returned, holding one suitcase, flashing that wedding band on a string around her neck. She pointed to the passenger-side front tire and said, "You got an almost-flat tire."

My father asked how long he'd been asleep, then began humming what appeared to be a dirge. Some years later, in college, I learned that someone said all stories were either about a stranger coming to town, or a character going on a journey. When the professor mentioned this, I rose my hand.

Marjorie Tesser

Miles & Myles

I find out through a music blog that my old pal DV has a show
booked in the city, and I message him right away. He texts
right back, for him, late the next week. *Devin my man it's been a
minute. You're on the list.* The last time DV had been in New York I
hadn't been able to get into the city; we'd just adopted Nico. Now
the baby's almost two and I can get out once in a while as long as
we plan it right.

The day of the show, I have to stay late for a faculty meeting.
My colleagues discuss minutia with excruciating thoroughness
while I shift in my seat. I race home. Kai, the sitter, is feeding
Nico. I give the baby a kiss, wipe his sticky applesauce off my
lips, shrug out of my work clothes. After a full day of teaching,
the sofa is inviting. But I rally; I've been looking forward to the
show, to DV. He'd been looking kind of rough the last time I'd
seen him. I hope he's gotten shit together.

I drive down the West Side, experiencing a nostalgic hum of
expectation at being out at night in the city. On into Brooklyn,
where I circle for parking. When I'd lived here, the streets were
always empty. I wonder whether DV will think fatherhood has
altered me. Forty-one, but I still have my long hair, I eat healthy,
keep fit. I buzz in at the tall concrete building and it's three
long flights up to a metal door. Inside, hiply-dressed people mill
around in front of a cage of a box office.

"Guest list," I say to the young guy in the cage.

"Name?"

"Devin Myles."

"No, *your* name," he says.

"It's Devin Myles," I say.

"Is this a joke?"

"No man, I'm a friend of DV's. We have a similar name.

✳

We met in the principal's office, the first day of school.
There had been a mix-up; he, DeVon Miles, a fourth grader, had
been assigned to a third-grade class. I, Devin Myles, belonged in

third but had been sent to fourth. Sitting on hard wooden chairs in a corner of the office, we whispered while the paperwork was corrected. We liked the idea of another person with the same name, a mirror self. He and I gravitated toward each other on the playground whenever our two grades were out at the same time. We both liked video games and skateboarding; we were each "only" kids with one white parent. He went by DV; he called me "Little Dev" because I was younger, though even then I was taller.

Our parents worked and were out all day. We'd hang out at whichever home had the better snacks, usually his place, since my mom was a nutritionist. In any case, his house was nicer, one of those grand Victorians with curlicues and bright-painted trim and a million rooms. DV's family had moved up from the city that summer. His dad was a doctor; his mom, an artsy type, opened one of those little Main Street boutiques the tourists love. DV was pissed at his parents for making him leave the city and his friends, though he soon had more friends than I'd ever had, and I'd lived here since I was a baby. We spent our afternoons zapping demons on his new PlayStation 2, or out in the street, rolling on boards or bikes. He was the more daring, first to try a new bike route, skateboard trick, and later, smokes, beer, graffiti. I envied his confidence and followed, with a glance over my shoulder.

DV couldn't wait to get out of our town; he called it Whoville, like in the Dr. Seuss book. "I need to be where more is going on."

"You mean, to go back to the city?"

"Nah. Maybe Japan, Europe. I don't know. I go forward, not back."

Actually, I loved our town. I played town rec t-ball and soccer with kids I'd known since preschool; we marched in parades down Main Street for Memorial Day, sweating in stiff polyester band uniforms while our parents clapped from folding chairs at the curb along the route. On Halloween, all the stores decorated and gave out candy. Families and groups of friends devised insane costumes for the Halloween parade. DV and I coordinated—he was Batman, I, Robin; he was a hamburger, I, ketchup. One year we switched identities. To mimic each other's hair would have been impossible, so we shoved his crunchy curls and my straight mop up inside identical baseball caps. Wearing DV's cargo shorts and t-shirt, his leather bracelet and Cons high-tops, I found myself bopping down the street with his signature bounce, while he perfectly mimicked my casual slouch.

The new skate park became our second home. It was set in the lower section of the leafy town park, with a clear view of the river. One day we'd been skating from the moment school ended, a whole golden afternoon of flying together, our wheels singing. The sun had begun to set. Pools of shade spread dark and deep beneath the big trees. A shadow twin lurked under each piece of playground equipment. The kids that had been rolling with us all afternoon peeled off one by one, home for dinner, or to hang on a corner with others who had no particular dinner to go to; one or two of the older ones headed out to part-time jobs. The playground to our left emptied and passed into dark. DV and I skated and skated and then I rolled to a stop. I looked down at the slate-colored river, the ripple and swell of it. Big rocks along the shoreline and a family of ducks bobbing. A cool breeze came up off the river and ruffled the hair at the back of my neck. The sun focused down to a narrow orange eye zapping rays of yellow and gold that bounced off the Hudson in long glints. I glanced up and saw DV, at the far side of the skate park, smoking a ciga-rette and gazing out. "Nice, huh?" I called.

"What?" he said.

"The river, man. We're lucky, right?" At that moment, as we both looked out, I felt as close to him as if we were sitting right next to each other, the long concrete ramps, the distance between us, nothing. DV shook his head. "I was looking at the bridge."

I looked back at the sweep of the span, arcing south before it veered back towards Westchester, all lit up to show the way out. All the red taillights leaving Rockland.

✳

"Sorry, sir. I don't have you on my list," says the box office guy. Is that a smirk?

"Are you sure? Devin Myles?"

He shakes his head, lips pursed.

"Can you call DV? Or his manager, Ellen?" Was she even still his manager?

"Can you please step to the side a moment so I can help these other folks," he says, with excessive politeness. I move aside and a young couple takes my place at the window.

✳

In middle school I developed a secret crush on DV, athough

to tell the truth I didn't know if I wanted him or wanted *be* him. Luckily, I soon discovered my first boyfriend, which saved us from potential awkwardness. When I finally came out to DV it wasn't a big deal. He was straight, as far as I knew, and spent time with the prettiest girls in school but no one owned him. I was quiet in those years, but DV, still a grade ahead of me, had gotten in with a group of tough guys. He could be kind of a jerk when he was hanging out with his older friends, ignoring me in the halls, teasing me about my band uniform, getting into some stupid shit that got him sent to detention, but he also saved me a couple of times. When I was dumped by that first boyfriend, DV comforted me. "No shit man, you are awesome. You'll find someone better." And when some assholes started ragging on me, saying "That's so gay," with knowing looks in my direction, DV shut them down.

In DV's eighth-grade year, his dad died of a sudden heart attack. Dr. Miles had been a respected doctor and a contributor to the community. The local paper ran a two-page obituary detailing his rise from poverty, his emigration to the US, where he'd worked three jobs to put himself through school, his stellar professional career, his charitable work on behalf of his native Haiti. It mentioned that he was survived by his wife Corinne (but said nothing of their recent separation), and one son, DeVon. It hit DV hard. He'd come over and we'd walk, down to the park, or all the way up Broadway to the craggy path that led down along the river. DV's dad had set high standards for him, and he felt he'd never lived up. My own dad had died when I was young. I somehow figured out what to say. "He was tough because he loved you, man. You don't have to see him to feel that."

By high school I cast off my anonymity. A musical polymath, I was a band teacher's dream—though I'd trained on cello and sax, I could fake it on pretty much any instrument. I saved more than one performance by filling in, though officially I was only in Band and Jazz Combo. DV hung out with different sets, art students, theater kids, a bunch of older guys into the Metal scene in town. But we were still tight. We even had a band together for a couple of years, Miles & Myles. He was on synth; I played guitar and acted as lead vocalist. DV didn't sing, but even then, he had that lead-singer charisma, a persona and high style, with his billowy 'fro and tight gymnast's body, a kind of glow he gave out.

The kids loved his inventiveness, our sense of play, my nimble riffs. We'd feel a true high after our shows. Packing up, or hanging at the American Dream Diner for a bite after the show, DV would talk about playing bigger venues, maybe the city. He knew a guy whose friend worked with a promoter, maybe they'd put us on a bill. We'd get a van and tour, "Get the hell out and have a look around," DV said. But we never got it together and then we graduated.

※

The Master of the Box Office admits the couple that had been behind me in line. Telling myself that I shouldn't feel wounded and forgotten, I move up to the window and cough up the twenty-five-buck admission. I'm directed to another steep staircase up which ends in a small vestibule with exposed brick walls. A girl with cherry red hair and an armful of programs tells us to wait, the company is still setting up. "Unless you're on the guest list," she adds. "Those on the guest list can enter right now." Three people brush by me and go in.

※

I was waitlisted at Berklee. U of Rochester's Eastman School of Music had a strong department with the option of a music education track, which I added, upon being strongly urged by my mom. After college I came back downstate and lived in a shared apartment in Williamsburg. I played bars and coffee houses solo, and local dives with two different indie bands, each with its own small cadre of dedicated fans. I busked in the subway one winter. I gave guitar lessons and took other random jobs to supplement, and waited for one of my gigs to click, my career to take off.

DV got a full scholarship to Cal Arts and went off to make weird sounds in a setting which, the one time I visited, had the kinetic creativity of a Burning Man festival. He left school after a couple of years to do his thing. Based near LA, he became a solo artist, playing small venues up and down the West Coast. Then his career seemed to catch on; he started getting gigs in other cities, Chicago, Atlanta, even New York.

When he had a New York show, I'd go, to the loft in an industrial neighborhood of Queens or the seedy club on Attorney Street. I couldn't wait to see which DV he'd be—he developed a different persona for each trip, shifting through hair styles and costume changes. The music changed too; one time he'd have all the newest tech and the next he'd be performing on a vintage Moog, an old boxy Hammond organ. And he did vocals—I regretted that he'd never sung in our high school band because he had a resonant, memorable voice. He was truly experimental; he didn't wait till a piece was perfected but just put it out there. DV loved the improvisational, the serendipitous, the interaction of the emerging piece with the now. Most times he pulled it off. Music bloggers and zines started to cover him. "Do you consider your work to be hip hop, jazz, experimental, avant-garde?" they'd ask. "Naaah, man," he'd drawl, "it's just music."

Soon, his shows merited larger and tonier venues—a barge on the Hudson, a millionaire's penthouse. DV travelled in the circles of the better-known forward-thinking. He collaborated with dancers, singers, playwrights and poets, but never with me, to my tender annoyance, unjustified, because our musical styles had diverged, but still a sore spot—at many a show he'd be working with a guitarist I could've played rings around. After the show I'd go out with DV and his posse and the conversations I got to listen to were amazing, like a second show for me. Sometimes someone would be polite and ask where I'd been gigging. "Lately? Mongrels, The Lizard Room, California Pete's…" "California Pete's?" someone would reply. "I played there back in the day. Fuckin' dump!" I may have been hanging in there as a musician, but DV was living the life.

The day I turned twenty-eight, my mom sent me a notice of a job as a music teacher at Edward Hopper, my old middle school. Both bands I'd been playing with had recently broken up. I was tired of hustling gigs for applause but no coin, tired of living with increasingly immature, inconsiderate, and progressively younger roommates, even bored with the social scene. When I started at Hopper, I was the youngest teacher in the school. Teaching was a challenge, paperwork, rules; I was supposed to manage pre-teens at the most hormonal, volatile time of their lives. On the plus side, I got my own decent-sized place in town, a three-room apartment for less than I'd paid for my minuscule room in the city, and connected with a group of new friends. I even played music weekly, at a local jazz club's open mic.

DV's career kept going. Summers, he toured Europe with an experimental music festival. When he came through New York, I'd take the train in to catch his show. "We have to catch up, man," he'd say. "Can't believe you're back at fucking Hopper. A teacher! Wow!" "Come up any time, open invitation," I told him. But then someone else would command his attention and that was that. I dreamed about his drafting me to play on one of his projects, but it never happened. Out at cafes and clubs after the show, I had even less to say to his friends than I had when I lived in the city.

My town's cool but I doubt I'd have stayed this long if I hadn't met Tyler. He opened his wine bar on River Street a few months after I moved up; I went there one evening and Tyler and I immediately felt a chord. Six months later he asked me to move in. It seemed too soon; also, he was ten years older. But love won. I moved into the tiny house he was renting on the river then, our little nest, and we've been together ever since.

For DV, things seemed to go south. The New York gigs were farther between and booked in smaller, seedier clubs. The last show I got to, DV was playing cover songs of eighties pop hits, in a black cowboy hat, studded belt and bolo tie. He'd gotten very thin. He wore a long-sleeved hoodie in the midst of a summer heat wave, and slurred long, vague stories into the mic. He still gave me the big hello but was cagey about what he'd be doing after the show. Then there was a long gap where he didn't come back East at all. My mother spoke to his mom on the phone; they'd kept in touch, on and off, all those years, even though Corinne had moved away when DV went to college. She mentioned that DV was living in Las Vegas with a wealthy older woman, acting as a sort of companion. She hadn't seen him in ages; she missed him.

That was about the time Ty and I started talking about adopting. I was hesitant. Things between us were great. We'd rescued a floppy-eared mutt and I'd thought that was enough. Tyler thought we should start looking into it; who knew how much time it might take? His wine bar was doing well, my job was tenured and secure, he wasn't getting any younger. We put a down payment on a bigger house in town and started investigating options. By the next time DV was in town, I was a dad.

After almost two years off the grid, DV booked a comeback show out in LA, at a tony old-school cabaret. Performing in the persona of an aging crooner trotting out all the old standards, he played selections of his own older work. Some music blog covered it as this genius of the avant-garde coming out of seclusion. The critic lauded DV's inventiveness and range through the years, and gave an appreciative wink to the sly self-parody of the act. On the strength of that publicity, DV booked a national tour, first stop New York.

✳

More and more people are coming up the steps to crowd into the little vestibule. I shrink against the brick wall and check my phone. It's a text from Ty with a video of Nico in the bath. Our kid is so damn cute. The redhead finally opens the door and we squeeze into the room, a black box theater. All the good seats are taken except one, in the front section roped off with a purple ribbon. I make for it but the usher in the aisle shakes her head. *Guest list only.* Of course. I climb to the back row, duck my head under a protruding pipe and wedge myself into the one available seat. The view turns out to be okay, if I hunch and keep my head turned slightly.

The show is good; actually, great. DV does the cabaret character for the first act, swanning around in a silver lamé jacket and then, after a short intermission, some cool electronic stuff in a changing light-scape of blues and greens and flashes of video, like vague thoughts or half-visions. When he's done the audience springs to its feet, applause echoing off the concrete walls. He bows once and walks off. We all wait. After a several minutes, DV emerges from the wings in sneakers and a grey sweatshirt. He walks to the front of the stage, and stands in a small circle of white light. He starts slowly and builds, a haunting twenty-minute chant, backed only with a beat box, that dissipates to soft mutters and finally, silence. There's a moment in which the audience doesn't move, and then a burst of wild applause. People walk out quiet, with the dazed expressions of those who know they've seen something memorable. DV was amazing. The energy, the concentration you need to perform with that intensity.

It's like teaching, how you have to be on from the moment the kids walk in. My job is actually okay. Of course, there are the annoyances—faculty meetings, early practices, paperwork, official crap. But my schedule meshes well with Ty's later one; we each get time with the baby and only need part-time child care (and for fill-ins, my mom helps out, thrilled to find herself

a grandmother when she'd given up hope). My principal is open
to innovative programming and loves the arts. And the kids are
terrific, so smart, funny, full of potential. It's an awkward age
but they're rocking it. I love that moment when they *click,* go
past playing the notes to making music; that connection when
everyone realizes we're all together in one big vibration, this flow.

I wait around with maybe twenty other people from the
audience after the show to say hello. DV finally comes out from
the back and is immediately surrounded. When most of them are
gone I walk over. He looks over the head of the girl he's talking
with and throws up his hand for me to bump like when we were
kids. "Devin, my man, come here. This is Simone, this young
lady is Astrid. And the dude over there is Heinz, we're all talking
about doing a thing. Guys, meet Devin, my friend from way back.
He knew me before I was me."

"Yeah, if we're such great friends," I give him shit, "you'd
think I'd be on the guest list!"

"Fuck me, did that not work out? I thought I told...so how'd
you get in?"

I rubbed my fingers together.

"You had to pay? Sorry man. I owe you fifteen bucks."

"Twenty-five," I say, keeping it going. Despite our lives on
polar coasts, the years since we've been together, we slide into
our old banter, its affection and edge. "So how you doing, man?"

"Alright. And you, still a teacher? And you're a daddy now,
right?"

I'd messaged DV to invite him up to our place, to meet the
new baby, when he was in New York two years earlier. He was
in for a show and couldn't fit in a trip upstate to visit. But he did
send a gift, a cute rainbow teddy bear, from Europe that summer.
I have my phone ready to show off the video of Nico but he
says, "Hey we're going out. Let me buy you a drink."

"I hate to admit it, I'm dragging; I've been up since six. Plus,
it's a school night and I have a forty-minute ride home, best-case,
no construction on the bridge." He's not persuaded. "These folks
are cool; we met in Iceland; they're fun and smart. Besides, this is
my last New York gig for a while. I'm doing a Europe thing."

"It sounds great," I say, and mean it, but shake my head.
"Next time, for sure." The truth is, I'd rather get home to Tyler
and Nico. He looks in my eyes, and he's quiet for a beat. Close-

up, there are new lines around his eyes, a strong vertical crease
between the brows. He's still thin, but not as skeletal as the last
time I saw him. The ropy muscles have softened, and a little belly
rounds over his thick black studded belt. There's a grayish cast to
his skin, but he doesn't look unhealthy now, only too much time
indoors, too many late nights.

"Devin?" he says. "Rachel's gone. She left, man."

Rachel? I thought he'd been with a Jen last time. But he
looks sad, so I give him a clumsy hug. "I'm sorry, DV." He grabs
and gives me one hard, quick squeeze, then one last try. "A drink
for old times' sake?"

I never did find it easy to say no to DV. Which is why I find
myself crammed in a corner booth with him, the Iceland contin-
gent, some side musicians, a roadie, and a slight grey-haired guy
who turns out to be the new tour manager. They're all scarfing
down tapas, plates full of salty fish in oil, some kind of mush-
room thing, olives as big as golf balls, an eel dish, with hard
crusty bread, washing it all down with huge draughts of wine.
Despite the din reverberating off the tin ceiling, they're in an
animated discussion of the new tour they're planning, which will
fuse American soul and electronics with traditional Icelandic folk
music. As usual, I'm an audience of one, the fly on the wall. I feel
the weight of the day in the back of my neck and my shoulders,
and a pull in my center toward home, Nico, and Ty, our cozy bed.
I'm kind of drifting off when I hear DV's voice cutting through
the clamor. "My man Devvy can do it. How about it, Little Dev?
Up for a road trip?" Turns out they can use an American guitar-
ist, someone versatile enough to handle the soul riffs and insert
some cutting-edge guitar/electronic interface; a sort of condi-
ment to the main course of the music.

The European tour is set to begin in May, a month before
the end of my school term. It will run through the summer,
playing medium size concert halls, festivals, and the like. I answer
automatically. "Can't, DV. I've got a job. I have a kid." But he
coaxes. "Come on man, it's going to be amazing. We'll have a
luxury bus, get a chance to see the sights between gigs. Your job
will let you off, right? And your partner can watch the kid. Heinz
here has a family. He doesn't let it get in the way of his music." I
can picture it, the sleek tour bus wending down picturesque roads
through quaint towns, into hip cities. The food, the sights, the

conversations. And the crowds, all up for the show, moving to the beat, singing along; the energy, the tremendous rush. Like what I'd known, but on a scale I'd never known it. And I'm calculating. Can I add up all my unused vacation days and leave school early? Could my mom be drafted to help with Nico? And Ty, he's used to being on his own. He'd get by. But I know it's a fantasy. What about the Spring Concert I'd planned, the fun rock medley I'd put together for the band to take on? And Nico; what changes would I miss out on? Would he be talking more when I got back; would he have grown a size? And wouldn't he miss me? Not to mention Ty. So I shake my head. "Think about it and get back to me," DV says. "But don't wait too long." They're planning on going out to a club, but I beg off.

"No worries," he shrugs. "Great to see you man. Miles & Myles, forever, right? Great to see your face."

We all walk out together. We hug, a real one. Then, I head down the street to my car and he goes the other way, one arm draped around the tall blonde woman, the other, the brunette.

It must have rained when we were inside; awnings are dripping and the city street gleams as if it's been polished. Every streetlamp is haloed in mist. Of course, there is construction on the bridge. I inch across. The whole way I'm thinking about the show, our conversation. Second-guessing it, thinking about what it would be like to live that life.

On the parkway north, fog is rolling in from the river; I'm caught in a net of cloud. In less than a mile, visibility is nil; my headlights illuminate only white. I'm driving blind, unsure what's the road, what's the shoulder. I creep around a curve and spot, way off, the sparks of a pair of taillights ahead of me, going slow, but going. Showing me the way. I keep pace, trailing his sparks of red for the ten miles to my exit.

I get home after two, let myself in, and peek in at Nico, tiny fingers clutching Gabby Giraffe. Tyler's been home from work for a while. He's in bed with the light on and a book in his hands but his eyes are closed. He hears me moving around and opens them and I lean in.

"You smell of smoke," he says.

"Not smoke, just the city. I'll wash up."

In the bathroom, I catch a glimpse of myself, the tired eyes, the lines starting to etch themselves around my mouth. A middle-aged middle school teacher, not the guitar star I once thought I'd be. I shower and towel off and climb into bed with Tyler. Our bodies reach for each other, breathe each other in.

"How was it?" he asks. "You're home late."

"Good. And actually, this is early; they were going out to a club. But I was beat."

Tomorrow after work maybe I'll get the guitar out, play some with Nico. The last time I did it, Nico started to sing–at two, he can actually carry a tune– and clap his sticky hands; my kid's my best audience. When Nico's older, I'll teach the kid to fly, like we did, at the local park; I've even saved my old skateboard. I'll get back to playing at the local jams again, maybe get together a band. But no rush. With Nico and Ty, I have such joy I sometimes overlook it; that's how much I'm blessed. To want anything other than this would be crazy. Right?

Rebecca Thomas

Root Bound

When Amanda, Richard, and his mother returned from dinner, tagging covered their fence. OCAX3. Silver. Paint dripped under the c, as if the letter wanted to slip away. The graffiti was big this time, taking up a fourth of the red cedar boards that separated their side yard from the dirt lot.

Heart in her ears from the alcohol at dinner, Amanda could practically hear the hiss of the spray can. It was only eight. What does it mean that it was so early? she wondered. She took a step back, wished she had a sweater on. She wanted to wrap something around her. But it was May, and it was hot.

Amanda glanced at her mother-in-law for a reaction, but Katherine only stared. Somehow this had been the first time their house had been tagged with Katherine there. The graffiti had gone quiet every other time she visited, as if the neighborhood understood that an upper-middle-class white lady from a gated community wouldn't understand tagging even though she sure as shit understood property boundaries.

"Are you calling the police?" Katherine's voice spilled down the street.

Amanda glanced around, but no one was out. "Let's go inside. You want some tea?"

Inside, they moved swiftly. Amanda in the kitchen asking Katherine to get the cups while Richard grabbed the paint can in the front closet and went outside.

"Does this happen often?" Katherine asked.

Amanda shrugged. "Rarely. Once or twice. It's nothing really."

Katherine drummed her fingers on the countertops. "Oh, it's something."

※

In the morning, Amanda laced up her running shoes in the living room while Katherine still slept. Richard sat on the couch with his coffee and kept his eyes on the paper. "You up for that?" he asked.

"It's either that or murder your mother." Amanda's voice was too harsh. She could feel it. Dr. Clements's voice came to her. *Give the other the benefit of the doubt.* He said it their first session five months ago. The last time she ran—four days ago, the day after her miscarriage—she passed out for a second while waiting for Richard to get her. Richard's coming from a place of concern, she reminded herself. "I'll take it slow." She made her voice gentle. She put her hand on his arm. "Thank you."

"Take your time. Call me if you need help."

Before she was even two blocks away, she felt tired. Her body ached, cramped. The pregnancy had been a surprise. Amanda had thrown out her birth control when Richard was first diagnosed over a year ago. The chemo was supposed to fry his sperm, and so she thought she was safe when he went into remission. But apparently, like cockroaches, his guys could survive radiation, and one swam and settled and burrowed. Cells multiplied and formed until they let go last weekend in the vegetable department at Von's.

They hadn't told anyone about the baby yet—they were going to tell Katherine this weekend for Richard's birthday. So at least there was that, Amanda thought. At least, they didn't have to suffer through more pity. For three months, it had been their secret. They guarded it, hoarded it. After spending eight months fielding cancer questions, they needed something that was just theirs. And like cancer, once the pregnancy got out, the questions and advice would begin.

The sun hadn't yet hit the neighborhood. Sprinklers shushed as she ran, splashing her legs, water creeping into her socks. A half a block down, when the bars on windows were replaced with stained glass, her body ached. Her breath caught and suddenly her heart covered her, invaded her belly. But she pushed on, passing the university where Richard taught, passing the high school, moving until the Craftsmen and Victorians gave way to tract houses, where there once was nothing but fields and citrus. On the corner between a tan stucco house and a white one, she stumbled, caught her hand on the wrought iron fence, gripped it, and tried to find her breath.

Now still, her thoughts caught up with her, tripping over her heels like a dog. Her body twinged, an arc that ran from her side to her heel, and she sat on the curb, head between her legs, willing herself not to pass out. Not again, she commanded her body, as if her body would listen.

Four days ago, she ran. Still bleeding, she strapped on a pad and let herself go. Pushed herself until she tasted iron. Pushed herself until she forgot that just the day before she had a baby and then she didn't. But then she stumbled. Andthen she threw up. And then stars covered her eyes until she sat down and called Richard to come get her.

She wouldn't do that again today. Turn around, she told herself. Go home, and she did.

When she rounded her corner, she checked the fence to see if they needed another coat to cover the letters.

OCAX3.

Larger this time. Two of them. One on either end.

She swore, low, long, under her breath, her heart already too loud in her chest. Looking up, she saw that the rest of the neighborhood had been hit too: the old farmhouse across from her, the mission-style two-bedroom, the cinderblock wall that separated her neighborhood from the university's parking lot. She just hadn't noticed it earlier. Car doors slammed one block away at the old packinghouse as vendors arrived for the weekly farmers' market. It was still early, Amanda reminded herself. Katherine might not even be up yet. She went inside and got Richard.

Minutes later, Richard stood in front of the fence next to her. "What does it mean?" he asked. "Why again?"

She stared at the two markings. "I don't know. Probably nothing."

"They used to come round a few times a week. Now twice in a day?"

"They got the whole neighborhood. They just must have been out."

They both looked down the street at the damage, the buildings all a patchy tan from years of painting.

"Just remind your mom it's a nice place to live, okay?" Amanda bent down, dipped a brush in paint, and got to work.

"She knows."

Amanda saw Richard's hand clutch the brush a little tighter. She could see his jaw work. Does she? she wanted to ask. She wanted to be catty, but she thought of Dr. Clements and stopped herself. They hadn't even gone to therapy since the pregnancy.

They had started going when the cancer went into remission and they found that they didn't know how to go forward, but once the baby appeared, they didn't want to know what Dr. Clements would have to say. They told each other it was the money. Babies are expensive and so are therapists. They told themselves this, but they knew that really they couldn't afford any more vulnerability. They didn't want to sit next to Dr. Clements' spider plants and begin talking about household chores—Richard always did dishes; Amanda always vacuumed—and end with their fears about the other—Amanda was afraid that Richard didn't respect her intelligence or her job; Richard was afraid that Amanda thought he was uncaring. There were only so many times that they could admit how deeply scared they were during the cancer and how deeply they depended on the other.

It was as if the pregnancy suspended everything. All resources went to the baby. It reminded Amanda of the cancer: everything focused on survival. Except this time, it didn't work. Maybe Richard's stronger, Amanda thought. Maybe if he was pregnant the baby would have stayed. But, she reminded herself, Richard would never have allowed a baby in the first place. She saw his shoulders tense in a line when she told him the news. She saw him pick at a string on his shirt, twirling it and pulling it until it began to unravel.

It was quiet but for the whisper of the traffic a few blocks away, the shushing of the brush on the wood as they painted. "She'll be gone tomorrow, "Richard said. "This will all stop soon."

"And if it doesn't?" Amanda asked.

"We'll figure it out. We always do."

✻

But the writing was back after brunch. Amanda saw it from the backseat of their Prius before she realized she was looking for it. "Richie," she said and then stopped herself.

Katherine pointed. "Someone did it again. Don't they know you can't do this?"

"That's kind of the point, Mom."

"Well, who does that? Is it safe here? Are you two safe?"

"It's just graffiti."

"But this is from a gang isn't it?"

"Yes, but this isn't some television show." Richard's hands

gripped the steering wheel. "They're a gang. It's not warfare."

"Call the police, Richard," Katherine said.

He pulled into the driveway, stopped the car. "We know what we're doing, Mom."

"Call the police, Richard. Or I will." They were sitting in their driveway. Katherine looked behind her to the street. "You should get a gate. If you're not going to use your garage, you should get a gate."

Amanda sighed before she could stop herself. "We don't need a gate, Katherine. Nobody comes in here."

"It'll make you feel better," she said, and Amanda knew she was right.

※

They waited for the gang unit to come and take pictures of the writing before painting over it. When the police arrived, Katherine insisted on greeting them even when Amanda and Richard said that it wasn't necessary, that the police take their pictures for the database and go.

"Son of a bitch," Richard said and Amanda looked up to see another marking.

"That's the fourth time in less than twenty-four hours," she told the police officer.

"Fourth?" Katherine said, but Amanda ignored her.

"What does it mean? Are they trying to send us a message?" Amanda's hands felt shaky.

"It means they have too much time on their hands, ma'am," the man said, but he wouldn't look her in the face. He spoke staring past her right shoulder.

"What are you going to do about it?" Katherine asked.

"Mom."

"Ma'am?"

"What are you going to do about it?" She pointed to the wall. "About this?"

"The pictures go in our database, so we have clear documentation of the gang if we need to prosecute or compile evidence. It helps us sort which is the real gang and which is just kids tagging."

"So you aren't going to stop it?"

"Mom." Richard stood between his mother and the officer. "What can they do? They can't patrol the neighborhood all the time. If someone wants to mark something, they'll find a way. You know this."

"I also know how gangs work, Richard." Katherine's voice cut through the air, and Amanda could imagine the force that she used to be in the classroom, making college freshman everywhere shit themselves and switch into sociology rather than anthropology. "Don't lose control of your space." She turned back to the officer. "So you've seen this a lot, yes?" She pointed to the wall. The man nodded. "Is this the actual gang?"

"It looks like it."

"Are you planning on using this evidence any time soon?"

"What?"

"Do I need to be worried about the safety of my family?" Katherine asked.

"We've got this, ma'am." The officer said, and Amanda's hand went to her stomach for just a moment even though she knew that the baby was no longer there.

When she first found out, when she sat in their bathroom while Richard was at yoga, she cried. Hard. They both taught and had enough of taking care of other people's children. They didn't need to watch over another. Richard went away for months during the summer to research, and while she could come to his digs too, hanging out in the Mojave was not her idea of summer vacation. She felt her patience run thin every day with her fourth graders. How was she going to handle a baby? She wasn't certain that she even wanted the baby until it left. It was only when she felt that sudden pain, the trickle of blood, the certainty that something *was not right*, that the certainty of needing that child, of wanting that child, formed. But by then, of course, it was too late.

Later, the three of them sat out in the yard, their heads under the shade of the umbrella, their legs stretched out in the sun. Their cat lounged in the space that they had cleared for a garden when they first moved in, but they never got the plants in the ground. Now weeds had grown thick from the winter rain and not yet fried by the heat.

Richard had made them a pitcher of margaritas. Amanda had brought out the chips and guacamole. It would have been nice if it had been the two of them. They could have sat in silence and dozed or read, but Katherine kept tapping her toes on the cement.

"You know what it is," Katherine said. "It's just like—"

A rattle on the other side of the fence.

They froze.

A hiss.

Amanda stared at Richard. "What the fuck?" she mouthed.

Richard shook his head.

She checked the time. It was two o'clock. She held up the phone. He shook his head again. Her fingers traced the sweat on the cup. She stared at that time. Two o'clock. "What the fuck," she whispered. "It's two o'clock." Her voice louder.

Katherine shushed her.

"It's two o-fucking-clock," she shouted it this time. She pushed her chair back.

"Where are you going?" Richard got up, reached out to her.

"It's not even night." Amanda marched to the gate.

"Amanda," Richard said. She heard his feet behind her. "Stop."

Her heart was in her chest just as it was at work whenever she'd have to break up student fights. But she could break up fights. She'd done it before. She'd caught kids—sixth graders— once smoking out in the bathroom, and she broke that up too. She rounded the corner. "It's two o'clock," she yelled before she saw him. "What the fuck do you think you're doing?" And then she looked up and saw the boy. Maybe fifteen. She could picture him in her class five years earlier, and the thought made her slow.

The boy stood at the fence, paint can in hand. "Fuck you, lady." He started to run, but she ran after him, caught the tail end of his white t-shirt.

"What the fuck do you think you're doing?" she said.

"Amanda," Richard shouted behind her. "Stop."

The boy pushed Amanda back. Hard. She fell. He started to run, but she grabbed the edge of his khaki shorts and tripped him. "Leave our fence alone."

He kicked at her. His foot caught her teeth. Iron flooded her mouth. Blood. She cupped her mouth, and he pushed away.

She reached out for him, blood on her palms, but she swiped at air. He was already down the street. Dust caught in her eye. Richard ran after the boy.

"Richie, stop," Amanda shouted. "Stop."

He turned around, kneeled in front of her. "What are you doing?"

"Something needed to be done, Richard."

He pulled her up. "How bad is it?"

She took a step away from them, one hand on her stomach, the other on her face. Blood dripped through her fingers. "It was never going to stop. We can't just pretend it away. Pretend it didn't happen."

"I'm not pretending," Richard said. "I'm being realistic."

"Well, fuck you and your realism."

Katherine put her hand on Amanda's shoulder. "Let's get you some ice." She turned to her son. "Richard, get your wife some ice." He started to speak. "Go," Katherine repeated.

For a moment, it was just the two of them. Their silhouettes outlined on the fence, falling on the unfinished graffiti. *I had a miscarriage*, Amanda wanted to say. *We don't talk about it. Your son was relieved.* But it wasn't her secret to tell. It was theirs. Richard would be the one dealing with the aftermath, and his mother already hovered because of the cancer.

"Richard can be too practical at times," Katherine said. She touched Amanda's arm for just a second, a rub on her elbow, before pulling away.

When they got inside, Richard held up a bag of frozen peas and had two Advil on the counter. "Bamboo," he said.

"What?"

"Let's get bamboo for the fence. It'll be a barrier. It'll look nice."

That night, after four trips to the nursery and sixteen bamboo plants stuffed into their Prius, Amanda, Katherine, and Richard dug in the dirt. Amanda's body ached. Blood lingered in the back of her throat. But the dirt under her nails felt good. She was in motion. She kneeled on a blanket and pressed into the dense, clay soil, pulling out rocks, breaking up the earth hard from drought until she had a hole twice as wide as deep. Her knees sank into the ground, and it was only when she bent over that she realized she was still searching in her mind for the effects of the miscarriage.

It was hard not to take the miscarriage personally. Fertility, like cancer, might be explained in biological terms, but Amanda still found herself searching for reasons why, searching for any evidence of something that she did to make it slip away. Because, like cancer, it was easier to understand if it was something that she did. If it was because of exercising too hard, stress, eating fish. When Richard first got sick, they were flooded with advice: a friend beat cancer with organic food, with a positive mindset, with yoga, with a juice cleanse. As if Richard only needed to think and eat the cancer away. As if it wasn't a disease filled with mutating cells that crept into his body like mold. "He needs to take control of that cancer," her hairdresser told her, and Amanda had to sit tight lipped for the next thirty minutes as the woman finished. She knew that cancer was biology, that he couldn't have changed it. She knew the same about the miscarriage, and yet, there she was, wondering. When she drove to work, when she was making dinner, when she was in the shower, she listed the things she could have done differently. She searched for ways that she could have been proactive.

The sun hadn't yet disappeared behind the cinderblock wall. It hit Amanda in the shoulders, warming her, making her sweat. She ducked her head and found the shadow. Bending, Amanda dug, pushing the shovel into clay, letting the handle press into her palm until she knew that tomorrow she'd still have a mark. It felt good, this work, this ache in her body that she created.

"This won't stop them," Katherine said. "Not right away at least. The plants will need to grow in first. And even then... They can still get to your fence."

"It's something," Richard said. "At least it'll mask it. It's the best we can do."

Amanda paused and measured the hole with the plant. "Give yourself space," the man at the nursery had said. "You need more room than you think." And so she dug until she was sure. She broke the plastic away from the plant, cradling the bamboo shoots in her fingers as she put the container aside. Her hands broke into the snarl of roots, dirt embedding under her fingernails. The roots curled into each other, a swirl of white. Amanda twisted the root ball, snapped a few apart. "Treat the plant rough," the man had said. "You don't want it root bound." She shook the bamboo, the roots now dangling, soil trailing to the ground. Grabbing a handful of compost, Amanda filled the hole, put the plant inside, and pressed until the ground became firm. She patted her hands together. Earth caked the lines of her palms. She got up and moved to the next.

Erica Williams

Finding Funerals

My obsession with watching funerals online started by accident. I'd worked from home for months because of the pandemic. I opened my computer, searched for a new hire's previous employer, and stumbled upon a funeral home website broadcasting a service. It was a lovely ceremony, rife with emotion and vast floral sprays of roses and daisies. The family's grief was affecting. Their sadness beamed through me like X-Ray waves. As an experienced HR specialist, even on my busiest days, I finished by midafternoon. I spent the rest of my time finding funerals.

I often wondered about my mama's funeral. My grandmother Ruby Belle—folks called her Belle—didn't let me attend. I was eight years old, and Grandma Belle said that I had endured enough trauma surrounding the death of my mama. She didn't want my final remembrance of Mama to be lying in a casket. I would've preferred that to be my last memory instead of her collapsed in a pool of blood. But had I said that twenty years ago, Grandma Belle would've chastised me for talking back.

Today I watched a mother lay her daughter to rest. A parent should never have to bury their child, Grandma Belle always said, breathing out a sigh saddled in grief. The mother slumped over the casket, letting out a wail so loud I turned down the volume.

The day Mama died, I was preparing to spend the weekend with my father, Oakdale, whom everybody called Oak. When he arrived, I was in my room and knew not to come out until told to do so. Mama had business to tend to with Oak. At first, her voice was at a respectable level but rose with thunderous intensity as she accused him of half-ass paying child support. My stomach twisted in knots. Even though they weren't together anymore, I knew Mama still loved Oak and never got over the humiliation of him tramping around Baton Rouge while they were married. I heard her threaten to take him back to court and then slapping sounds, followed by a muffled scream and a popping noise that sounded like a firecracker even though it wasn't the Fourth of

July.

At the next funeral, I watched a little girl sitting on the front pew, ankles crossed. She looked about seven or eight years old and wore a black dress with frilly white lace draped around the collar. Her braided hair sported white beads dangling at the ends. She listened with her head down as neighbors, co-workers, and friends memorialized the woman I understood to be her mother.

I had peeked out the bedroom and saw Oak holding what the detectives later referred to as a thirty-eight revolver. Mama lay sprawled on the floor as liquid, the color of red paint, oozed from her neck. I screamed and burst into tears. Oaks' eyes were wide and wet, still in shock when he called 911. He told me it was an accident. They were arguing, and she grabbed the gun from his pocket. When he tried to take it from her, it discharged. If anyone asked me what happened, tell them I saw the entire thing.

The girl rocked her feet back and forth, in a daze, as she stared at the cherrywood casket trimmed in gold. I wished I could use telepathy to tell her she was lucky she didn't have to grow up wondering if the funeral home workers fixed her mother's hair properly. Mama loved her curly afro and referred to it as her lion's mane. People often told me I was my mama's twin, with the same voluminous hair, double dimples, and skin the color of brown sugar.

I contemplated the stories told at Mama's funeral. Did they mention she woke me up every morning saying, 'Hello Sunshine,' as I caught a whiff of buttered grits and eggs, and heard pan sausage frying, crackling through the house like electricity? Or how she loved to buy us matching dresses? My favorite, the yellow one with the ruffled sleeves. Did they play upbeat gospel music like the kind we danced to on Saturday mornings while cleaning the house, or Aretha Franklin's gospel that she listened to alone with tears in her eyes while sipping a beer?

The pastor, a husky man with a baritone voice, wore a tight, ill-fitting black suit. He ended his eulogy, reminding the family that weeping may endure, but joy chased its tail. Along with others on the front row, the girl walked to the coffin to pay final respects. Her jaw dropped. She looked bewildered, like when I saw Grandma Belle get filled with the holy ghost at church for the first time. As they wandered away one by one, she and a man remained. Finally, the preacher urged the family along, saying they needed to get to the gravesite. The man scooped the girl in his arms. She erupted into tears and cried Mama as the pallbearers carried the casket out.

I closed the laptop. I thought of Oak, who'd moved to Atlanta years ago after being cleared of any wrongdoing. And Grandma Belle, who told me she'd buried Mama in the yellow dress.

I walked to the kitchen and drank ice water from a mason jar, not stopping until it was almost empty. I sat back down and opened my computer, searching until I found another funeral. Good. This one just started. I had all day.

Anna Young

Stalls

The school got sick to death of us bullying each other, so they took the doors off the girls' bathroom stalls.

They must have thought, if we could watch each other shit, we might not write mean graffiti on the pink shellac. Or something. They threatened to put cameras in there, but my mom told me they can't really do that.

It was funny. I never once drew anything until the week before they took the doors. All's I drew was a little frog wearing a top hat, right at eye level. Third stall in the row of four.

I dunno what I drew it for. I didn't even use a Sharpie like most girls—all I had was the stub of a golf pencil I shoved in the pocket of my hoodie real fast before I asked Ms. Chandler if I could use it. She almost didn't let me, but I'm a good kid and quiet and don't seem like the graffiti type.

Anyway, it's funny to think my Abe Lincoln frog might have been the last straw. I can just see Principal Donahue foaming at the mouth and shredding report cards with his teeth like a rabid dog, thinking of all the graffiti in the girls' bathroom.

✳

It's Friday, and me and Simone Beck are heading to the peek-a-boo bathroom because it's the only one us sixth graders can use. There's a perfectly normal one in the seventh and eighth grade wing, but the hall monitors will give us little tykes detention if they catch us down there. Apparently it's for our own good. They've had problems with the big kids kicking the puke out of fish fry like us.

Simone is on her period, and she wants me to keep a lookout while she changes her tampon. Most girls don't dare use the stall-less bathroom, but I guess she doesn't have a choice.

Simone and I are both in cross-country. We've got a nice symbiotic relationship that only makes me a little jealous all the time. She likes me because I repel boys—I like her because she attracts them, with her perfectly loose long blond braid and her blue eyes. Eyelashes like butterfly legs. She's also tall and obviously she's got her period. My older sister tells me I don't want it, but I feel even more like a scrawny little baby around girls like Simone.

I think she can tell, too. She's the fastest girl on the team, and one of those nice Mormons. I can never tell with them if it's all an act or what.

But we've got a thing going, so I stand like a bouncer with my legs spread and my bony arms crossed over my stupid flat chest. I've got a tiny pocket knife I always keep tucked away, and I use it to clean under my fingernails while I wait. Simone thanks me for standing watch over and over again like I'm doing a real service. As if any of my classmates couldn't easily shove me over and bang up my head on the dirty white tile. I'm barely over five feet. The girls keep tabs on stuff like that.

But Simone goes on and on anyway. "You're a lifesaver, Nikki." *Rrrrip*, goes the paper packaging on her tampon. "This is so embarrassing." A stifled silence where…well, where something happens. Everyone's been pretty mum on tampon details with me.

"It's fine," I say, kinda bored. My voice echoes in the hollows of each stall.

Simone sniffles. I wrinkle my nose since she can't see. Is she crying or something? "I really appreciate it."

"You'd do the same for me," I say. "Well, you know—"

"You're *so* lucky you don't have it yet. Seriously."

A flush, and she taps my shoulder to let me know I can stand down. She goes past me to wash her hands.

I look at her face in the grimy reflection. Even her fakey Mormon blush looks like it's on purpose, like rosy watercolor swished over her nose.

"Yeah," I say. "I read that girls who have their periods put off, like, pheromones and stuff that attracts boys. That's probably why they're always chasing you down."

"Ugh. Boys." She says it like I would know anything about the troubles of being super pretty and talented. I don't get a chance to respond 'cause she sticks her hands under the air dryer and it roars and screams like a waterfall full of drowning victims.

❋

The school puts the doors back after a few weeks per parental complaints. I dunno if anybody could have actually sued, but it sure shut the school board up. But there's a new development—they had Remy the janitor paint all the stalls black. Now we have a goth bathroom.

I dunno why they thought that would stop anyone. All the girls just went out and bought silver Sharpies or found them in the swampy grass around the middle school. I even picked one up off the blacktop when I saw it.

After cross-country practice the next week, I have to pee so bad I know I won't make it home—the bus bounces like it's got damned Moon Boots strapped to the wheels. Simone says she would wait up if she didn't have Family Home Evening tonight, but don't care.

As I clear out my bladder, I stare at the words in front of me. Neat, looping handwriting, in silver Sharpie: "Simone Beck is a stuck-up bitch."

I consider it for a while, elbows balanced on my naked knees. Once I haul up my sweaty shorts and flush the toilet, I think about writing "Anyone who thinks" before it, and "is a fat dumbass" after. That way I could get vengeance and not wreck the nice handwriting.

But after a minute, I just slip my pocket knife from the band of my training bra—both leave an indent on my ribs—and scrape it off.

The pink shellac glares through from underneath.

Lucy Zhang

Bonchon Chats

The grim reaper once told her that she'd fall in love in her fifteenth life. But here she was, seated on a squeaky office chair in front of a desk too low for her elbows, back hunched and eyes squinting at the monitor whose blue glow lit up her face like a halo but in reality, it was just luminescent contrast thanks to one of the room light bulbs dying last year. The room was always too dim after the sun went down, and the sun had gone down hours ago. Most of her coworkers had left and she remained, sorting through rows and columns on spreadsheets, cross-checking Twitter for the latest scandal one of the employees had blown a whistle on, managing compensation bumps so they'd stop shouting their complaints into the internet ether, not that she approved of bribing employees to stay silent or preaching to the faceless Twitter trolls. Young people were like that, trying to fight for fair compensation and correcting injustices and toxic office behavior, but as long as she had good medical insurance, she didn't care much, not in this life. She just needed to pay for rent and groceries and, in theory, the rest of the company could deal with the press. Except, somehow, she was the one left to handle the escalating situation by some osmosis of responsibility. Upper management and the employees thought she was reliable. Fifteen lives later, and she still failed to learn how to slack off. She click click clicked and slammed the save key-chord three times. The paranoia carried through every life.

The grim reaper was a smart but socially out of tune fellow with a preference for Bonchon and deep loathing of KFC. "It has garlic, soy, umami," he sang every time he invited her to a meal. "Double fried in spicy-sweet gochujang-saturated sauce."

"Please listen," she said, folding and unfolding a brown compostable napkin capable of scratching your mouth off if you applied enough pressure. "I've got work to do without you getting grease on my desk. When's this love supposed to enter the stage?"

The grim reaper leaned back on the small couch. It went

mostly unused unless others needed to complain to her about their manager or coworker or spouse. Something about her made her a complaint sponge. Maybe it was the old people vibe that persisted from several lives ago after she'd survived through the Taiping Rebellion without her children starving to death. Or the fact that she'd gone through three divorces: twice she was divorced because they found her too "out of touch," and the third time she initiated the divorce because she had been curious how it'd feel to be on the other end. She felt bad about it, but there were no hard feelings since the divorcee had been cheating on her with a pole dancer who cooked a superior curry—the secret was Fuji apples, she learned three lives later after enrolling in culinary school, so it was a win-win.

"It'll happen, you gotta live in the moment," the grim reaper said, licking one of his fingers coated in sauce. "Chill out, don't work so much. Not good for the blood pressure, you might die again."

She had died from overwork once. It was uneventful and pathetic. She had been a history teacher at a blue ribbon, Ivy League feeding high school and spent all of her free time enhancing and rewriting the provided textbook with her memories. At some point, she'd neglected to take her insulin because she'd forgotten diabetes plagued her then-current body and ended up in a coma. According to the grim reaper, the custodian had recycled her drafts of the new textbook. She cried after learning the fate of her thousands of hand-written words and vowed to never try writing a book again. That was the wasted eleventh life.

"You sure I haven't already found love?" She asked. After all, there was Benjamin, the optics engineer who took her to Venice, and bought them ten pizzas because the bread part was "too thin" and they'd never be full. She was young at the time and prone to being hangry, so she appreciated his attentiveness. There was Liutong, the college dropout who went back to China and got featured on a reality TV show because of his nice, feminine face, and she had been one of the hosts of the show at the time and showed him around, recommended the best biang biang noodle restaurants, explained how to select a good diamond that ended up snug on her ring finger. There was Shakespeare-expert Sara who was too shy to go anywhere and clung to her shoulder when they entered public areas, and it was honestly endearing—

how Sara behaved like a duckling. There had been plenty of love. Perhaps it wasn't meant to be something mind-blowingly unique. Plus, the heartbreak had begun to numb after her sixth life, and she felt a tiny bit guilty moving on so quickly.

"Nah, you definitely haven't. If you had, we wouldn't still be doing this."

"What is 'this'?" She asked, gesturing to herself and the office and the paper box of crumbs and sauce and a single piece of leftover chicken.

The problem was, the grim reaper was a romantic. He didn't consider much outside of his fried chicken and Korean dramas and smut novels. When she'd asked him why he put her through not one but three wars—Taiping Rebellion, World War I, and the Napoleonic Wars—he claimed wars made the most passionate couples. "You don't know if you'll ever see each other again, there's no time to waste on bickering about who's taking care of the kids. It's tragedy and love in its purest form!" He'd said. But she was convinced what he loved most was the tragedy part, how someone ended up dead and someone stayed alive and they wallowed into despair because humans were, according to him, creatures who could not live without love. That was the market-ed story. She had gotten by fine when her loved ones died. Not immediately, and not without pain, but slowly she'd recovered and resumed road tripping or experimenting in the kitchen with torches and cumin or designing tennis skirts for women in the 17th century.

"This! Everything! A wealth of opportunity and chances is what," he proclaimed. "The world is your oyster, an infinite supply of oysters, uh, if the ocean holds up. I think you've got something of a climate issue going on."

"I need an opportunity to stay dead," she said.

"Maybe that too is a form of love," the reaper replied. Because really, she had outlived most of her children, seen more Olympics than she'd ever cared for, visited Antarctica which took until her tenth life to finally accomplish because her daughter was a polar guide and nautical captain leading a tourist expedition through Drake passage and there was an extra spot in the cabin so she tagged along. It was not, she insisted, because she was tired of living. She liked many aspects: waking up to the first coffee or tea or milk or orange juice-with-cereal (depending on that life's taste buds), opening a fresh jar of sesame paste—the pressure in the cap popping, the fragrant scent, watching her twins laugh together with a rose-scented candle in the dark living room as they waited for power to return and the hurricane to pass, crushing lobster shells with her knife as she prepared to stir-fry the crustacean with ginger and scallion and how strong she felt to be able to cut through the fiery armor, reach the interior of sweet flesh, suck it out with her tongue and teeth.

"You got any of those potstickers left?" The grim reaper liked potstickers, although not as much as the fried chicken. The potstickers were filler foods. Tasty, but still filler.

"No, I don't make potstickers anymore, remember?"

"Ah right, that was during your housewife days. Good times, eh?" He took a sip from his styrofoam cup of Calpico he had nabbed from her mini-fridge.

It was her previous life. The fourteenth. She'd been a house-wife married to an upper-middle-class real estate agent who had no idea how to handle his own money, so she ended up the one negotiating their first house purchase, installing AT&T Fiber, switching out the light switches with smart ones so they could control all the rooms with an app, fixing the microwave when it went crazy (they never did figure out why it'd beep randomly; she ended up silencing it completely). Her husband had been the one to make dinner reservations for them at posh omakase restaurants, compile a list of gynecologists for her to vet, buy the kids a dog and teach them to ride bikes without training wheels, have them learn the guqin because the violin and piano were too boring. He had been the one to invent protein-coupled receptor modulator compounds as a hobby and tried to explain to their son how pineapple juice contained bromelain which digested other proteins, and how marinating the beef required less effort, although their son preferred the mallet tenderizer and would slam it into cuts of meat like a whac-a-mole, enjoying the vibrations sent through the counter. She, who had seen enough bayoneted bodies for multiple lifetimes, said violence wasn't necessary. Her husband said boys will be boys and it wasn't like anyone was trying to beat up a human—just meat fibers. Their relationship worked because of the incongruity. He made the best Elvis PB&J; she made the dumplings. She'd made potstick-ers before, but this life had been the first time she made them in such a luxurious kitchen on an island made from white marble and surrounded by counters that seemed to stretch into infinity. There was a levity to her crimps, a kind of freedom from repetition, and it must've made a decent end product because the grim reaper had eaten a whole plate when he visited. And then she died because she was already scheduled for death because cancer rolled around like a whirlwind, unstoppable, full of conviction, the final hurrah of cells gone haywire.

"Not really," she muttered. Nothing was really a "good" time anymore, and it certainly didn't help that her coworkers thought it was ok to bribe their direct reports to prevent them from posting scandalous screenshots on Twitter or Facebook or Reddit or whatever it was they used these days. "And I won't die from overwork." She also decided she'd keep herself too busy for love, which was why she joined this company and plunged headfirst into its political dumpster fire in the first place, but she didn't tell the grim reaper that.

CONTRIBUTORS

HUSSAIN AHMED is a Nigerian poet and environmentalist. His works are featured or forthcoming in *POETRY, Kenyon Review, Transition Magazine, AGNI* and elsewhere. He is currently an MFA candidate in poetry at the University of Mississippi. He is the author of *Harp in a Fireplace* (New Found, 2021) and *Soliloquy with the Ghosts in Nile* (Black Ocean, 2022). He lives in Oxford.

NOAH ALVAREZ is a Cuban-American author from Lexington, Kentucky, now living in North Carolina.. He writes fiction and nonfiction. This is his first published story. You can reach him at noahalvarezsports@yahoo.com.

ZEINA AZZAM is a Palestinian American poet, writer, editor, and community activist. Her poems appear in literary journals including *Pleiades, Gyroscope, Passager, Mizna, Sukoon Magazine, Beltway Poetry Quarterly, Split This Rock, Barzakh: A Literary Magazine,* and *Voice Male* and in the edited volumes *Tales from Six Feet Apart, Bettering American Poetry, Making Mirrors: Writing/Righting by and for Refugees,* and *Gaza Unsilenced.* Zeina's chapbook, *Bayna Bayna, In-Between,* was published by The Poetry Box in May 2021. She earned an M.A. in Arabic literature at Georgetown University.

DANIEL R. BALL holds an MFA from Stonecoast in Maine, where he studied under Rick Bass. His writing has appeared in *The Fourth River, FLDQ, The Whitefish Review,* and elsewhere. He lives with his wife and daughter in Massachusetts.

BRETT BIEBEL teaches writing and literature at Augustana College in Rock Island, Illinois. His (mostly very) short fiction has appeared in *Hobart, SmokeLong Quarterly, The Masters Review, Wigleaf,* and elsewhere. It's also been chosen for Best Small Fictions and as part of *Wigleaf's* annual *Top 50 Very Short Stories. 48 Blitz,* his debut story collection, is available from Split/Lip Press.

LORI BRACK is the author of *A Case for the Dead Letter Detective* (Kelsay, 2021), *Museum Made of Breath* (Spartan Kansas City, 2018), and *A Fine Place to See the Sky* (The Field School, 2010). Her essays and poems have appeared in *Another Chicago Magazine, North American Review, Atlas and Alice, Entropy Magazine, Mid-American Review* and other journals and anthologies. She lives on the prairie two blocks from the Garden of Eden and 14 miles from the geodetic center of North America.

OFELIA BROOKS (she/her) is a Black, Latiné, first-generation writer and lawyer. Her work appears in *Drunk Monkeys, Amplify, Spillover, Honeyfire,* and *Diem.* She can be found on Twitter and Instagram @ofeliabrooksesq and at ofeliabrooksesq.com.

VICTORIA BUITRON is a writer and translator with an MFA in Creative Nonfiction from Fairfield University. Her work has been featured or is upcoming in *Barren Magazine, Bending Genres, Lost Balloon,* and other literary magazines. Her debut memoir-in-essays, *A Body Across Two Hemispheres* (Woodall Press, 2022), is the 2021 Fairfield Book Prize winner.

CHRISTINE BUTTERWORTH-MCDERMOTT'S latest poetry collection is *Evelyn As* (Fomite, 2019). She is the founder and co-editor of *Gingerbread House Literary Magazine.* Her poetry has been published in such journals as *Alaska Quarterly Review, The Normal School, The Massachusetts Review,* and *River Styx,* among others.

SARA SIDDIQUI CHANSARKAR is an Indian-American writer. Her work has appeared in *SmokeLong Quarterly, Reflex Press, Flash Fiction Online,* and elsewhere. She is currently an editor at Janus Literary and a Submissions Editor at *SmokeLong Quarterly.* Her debut flash fiction collection, *Morsels of Purple,* was published in 2021.

APRIL DARCY'S fiction can be found in *Shenandoah,* where she was the recipient of the Shenandoah River Fiction Prize, and her nonfiction can be found in *North American Review,* where she was a finalist for the Torch Nonfiction Prize. She is the recipient of fellowships from Writing by Writers, the Napa Valley Writers Conference, and the BookEnds program at Southampton Arts of Stony Brook University. She received a 2020 Elizabeth George Foundation grant, and a 2022 Fellowship from the New Jersey State Council on the Arts, both in support of her forthcoming novel. She holds an MFA in writing and literature from the Bennington Writing Seminars, and lives and teaches creative writing in New Jersey.

LAUREN DAVIS is the author of *Home Beneath the Church* (Fernwood Press), *When I Drowned* (Aldrich Press, forthcoming), and the chapbooks *Each Wild Thing's Consent* (Poetry Wolf Press) and *The Missing Ones* (Winter Texts). She holds an MFA from the Bennington College Writing Seminars. Winner of the *Landing Zone Magazine's* Flash Fiction Contest, Davis lives on the Olympic Peninsula in a Victorian seaport community.

LESLIE DOYLE'S essays and fiction have appeared in *Front Porch, MARY, The Fourth River, The Forge, Gigantic Sequins, Signal Mountain Review, Electric Literature, Rougerou, Tupelo Quarterly Review, The New York Times,* and elsewhere. She lives in New Jersey and teaches at Montclair State University.

Born and raised in Georgia, **MONIC DUCTAN** now lives in Tennessee, where she teaches creative writing and literature at Tennessee Tech University. Ductan's work has appeared in numerous literary journals, including *Southeast Review, Shenandoah, Oxford American, Still: the Journal, South Carolina Review, Water~-Stone Review, The Fourth River,* and *Arkansas Review.* She received the 2019 Denny C. Plattner Award in nonfiction from *Appalachian Review* for her essay "Fantasy Worlds," which was also listed as notable in *Best American Essays 2019.* She's at work on a story collection and a novel.

HANNA FERGUSON is a nonfiction writer and poet whose work can be found in *The Oneota Review* and elsewhere. She's a recent graduate of Luther College and lives in Chicago with her husband and sweet kitty Minka.

PATRICIA FOSTER is the author of *All the Lost Girls: Confessions of a Southern Daughter, Just Beneath My Skin,* and *Girl from Soldier Creek.* She has won a Pushcart Prize, a Dean's Scholar Award, the Hoepfner Award, the Clarence Cason Award for Nonfiction, and other prizes. Seventeen of her essays have been listed as notable in the *Best American Essays* series. She was a professor for 25 years in the MFA Program in Nonfiction at the University of Iowa and has taught in Australia, Italy, Spain, and the Czech Republic.

ROBERT FANNING is the author of four full-length collections of poetry: *Severance, Our Sudden Museum, American Prophet,* and *The Seed Thieves,* as well as two chapbooks: *Sheet Music* and *Old Bright Wheel.* His poems have appeared in *Poetry, Ploughshares, Shenandoah, Gulf Coast, The Atlanta Review, Waxwing, THRUSH, The Cortland Review, The Common,* and many other journals. He is a Professor of English at Central Michigan University, as well as the Founder/Facilitator of the *Wellspring Literary Series* in Mt. Pleasant, MI, and the Founder/Director of PEN/INSULA POETRY, a resource for Michigan poets.

KATE HANSON FOSTER'S collection of poems, *Crow Funeral,* was published in March 2022 by EastOver Press. She is also the author of *Mid Drift,* a finalist for the Massachusetts Center for the Book Award. Her writing has appeared in *Birmingham Poetry Review, Comstock Review, Harpur Palate, Poet Lore, Salamander, Tupelo Quarterly,* and elsewhere. A recipient of the NEA Parent Fellowship through the Vermont Studio Center, she lives and writes in Groton, Massachusetts.

EMILY FRANKLIN has been published in *The New York Times, The London Sunday Times, Guernica, The Cincinnati Review, New Ohio Review, Hobart, Blackbird, The Rumpus, Epoch, River Styx,* and *The Journal* as well as featured on National Public Radio, and named notable by the Association of Jewish Libraries. Her debut poetry collection *Tell Me How You Got Here* was published by Terrapin Books in February 2021.

JUNE GERVAIS grew up on the south shore of Long Island and holds an MFA from the Bennington Writing Seminars. Her work has appeared or is forthcoming in *LitHub, Writer's Digest, Big Fiction, Sojourners, The Common, Cordella, The Southampton Review,* and elsewhere, and she was a Sustainable Arts Fellow at Rivendell Writers Colony. *Jobs for Girls with Artistic Flair* is her debut novel.

ELISE GREGORY received her MFA from Eastern Washington University. She's the author of two poetry chapbooks, as well as the co-editor with Emily Gwinn of the anthology *All We Can Hold: Poems of Motherhood. The Clayfields,* a novel in stories, was released in Fall 2022 as part of the Legacy Series. She lives with her family and animals on a hillside in western Wisconsin.

MOLLY GAUDRY is the author of the verse novels *Desire: A Haunting* and *We Take Me Apart,* which was a finalist for the Asian American Literary Award and shortlisted for the PEN/Osterweil. She is the founder of *Lit Pub* and teaches at Stony Brook University.

PAULETTA HANSEL'S eighth poetry collection is *Friend: Epistolary Poems Written in the Early Days of the Pandemic.* Her writing has been featured in *Oxford American, Rattle, Appalachian Journal, Still: The Journal,* and *One,* among others. Pauletta was

Cincinnati's first Poet Laureate (2016-2018), and is past managing editor of *Pine Mountain Sand & Gravel*, the journal of the Southern Appalachian Writers Cooperative.

KHANH HA is the author of *Flesh, The Demon Who Peddled Longing,* and *Mrs. Rossi's Dream.* He is the recipient of the Sand Hills Prize for Best Fiction, the Robert Watson Literary Prize in Fiction, The *Orison Anthology* Award for Fiction, The James Knudsen Prize for Fiction, The C&R Press Fiction Prize, and The EastOver Press Fiction Prize. *Mrs. Rossi's Dream* was named Best New Book by *Booklist* and a 2019 Foreword Reviews INDIES Silver Winner and Bronze Winner. His short story collection, *All the Rivers Flow into the Sea,* was published by EastOver Press in 2022.

JEFF HARDIN is the author of six collections of poetry, most recently *No Other Kind of World* and *A Clearing Space in the Middle of Being.* His work has been honored with the Nicholas Roerich Prize, the Donald Justice Prize, and the X. J. Kennedy Prize. His poems appear in *The Gettysburg Review, The Southern Review, Hudson Review, North American Review, Poetry Northwest,* and many others. His seventh book, *Watermark,* was published in spring 2022. He lives and teaches in Tennessee.

MARC HARSHMAN'S *Woman in Red Anorak,* Blue Lynx Prize winner, was published in 2018 by Lynx House Press. His previous collection, *Believe What You Can,* (Vandalia/West Virginia University Press) won the Weatherford Award. His fourteenth children's book, *Fallingwater,* with co-author Anna Smucker, was published by Roaring Brook/Macmillan. He is co-winner of the 2019 Allen Ginsberg Poetry Award and his Thanksgiving poem, "Dispatch from the Mountain State," was recently printed in *The New York Times.* Poems have been anthologized by Kent State University, the University of Iowa, University of Georgia, and the University of Arizona. His newest title, *The Shadow Testimonies,* is forthcoming from Salmon Press, Ireland. Appointed in 2012, he is the seventh poet laureate of West Virginia.

DUSTIN M. HOFFMAN is the author of the story collection *One-Hundred-Knuckled Fist,* winner of the 2015 Prairie Schooner Book Prize. His second collection *No Good for Digging* and his chapbook *Secrets of the Wild* were both published by Word West Press. He painted houses for ten years in Michigan and now teaches creative writing at Winthrop University in South Carolina. His stories have recently appeared in *Faultline, Wigleaf, DIAGRAM, Redivider, Fiddlehead,* and *Alaska Quarterly Review.*

STEPHEN HUNDLEY is the author of *The Aliens Will Come to Georgia First* (University of North Georgia Press, 2021). His work has appeared in *Prairie Schooner, Cutbank, Carve,* and other journals. He serves as a fiction editor for Driftwood Press and is a Richard Ford Fellow at the University of Mississippi.

BEN KAUFMAN is a Chicago-based writer and multimedia storyteller. He is most interested in stories that upset the mundane and force characters to confront their own shortcomings. Kaufman draws upon his own background as a dual-citizen of Israel and the U.S. to tell intimate stories that connect family history to personal experiences.

JOHN LANE is Emeritus Professor of Environmental Studies at Wofford College and was founding director of the college's Goodall Environmental Studies Center. He is the author of over a dozen books of poetry and prose. In 2014 he was inducted into the SC Academy of Authors. He, with his wife Betsy Teter, is one of the co-founders of Spartanburg's Hub City Writers Project.

CHARLOTTE LEBARRON hails from the rural "Hilltown" region of Western Massachusetts, but currently resides in Brooklyn, New York. She obtained dual degrees in Accounting and Communication from Boston College, and earned licensure as a Certified Public Accountant. Having recently fled her job as an auditor, Charlotte researches corporate governance at New York University's School of Law, daydreams about becoming an academic, and fiddles with words. This is her first published story.

CHRISTOPHER LINFORTH is the Editor-in-Chief of *Atticus Review*. He is author of three story collections, *The Distortions* (Orison Books, 2022), winner of the 2020 Orison Books Fiction Prize; *Directory* (Otis Books/Seismicity Editions, 2020); and *When You Find Us We Will Be Gone* (Lamar University Press, 2014).

NATHAN ALLING LONG's work has won international competitions and appears on NPR and in various journals, including *Tin House, Story Quarterly, Witness,* and *The Sun. The Origin of Doubt,* a collection of fifty stories, was a 2019 Lambda finalist; Nathan's second manuscript was an Iowa Fiction Award semi-finalist and Hudson Fiction Manuscript Prize finalist. They live in Philadelphia.

GEORGE ELLA LYON's recent poetry collections include *She Let Herself Go, Many-Storied House,* and *Voices from the March on Washington,* co-written with J. Patrick Lewis. A freelance writer and teacher, Lyon is particularly interested in the poetry of witness. She served as Kentucky Poet Laureate (2015-2016). She is the co-founder, with Julie Landsman, of the I Am From Project, a national project to gather new poetry in response to the troubled state of the nation. See more at https://iamfromproject.com/about/.

YASMINA DIN MADDEN is a Vietnamese American writer who lives in Iowa. Her fiction and nonfiction have been published in *The Idaho Review, PANK, Necessary Fiction, The Forge, The Fairy Tale Review,* and other journals. Her short stories have been finalists for *The Iowa Review* Award in Fiction and *The Masters Review Anthology.* Her flash fiction stories have been finalists for the Fractured Micro-Fiction Contest and *Wigleaf Top 50 Very Short Fictions.*

KIM MAGOWAN lives in San Francisco and teaches in the Department of Literatures and Languages at Mills College. Her short story collection *Undoing* (2018) won the 2017 Moon City Press Fiction Award. Her novel *The Light Source* (2019) was published by 7.13 Books. Her second story collection, *How Far I've Come,* was recently published by Gold Wake Press. Her fiction has been published in *Atticus Review, Cleaver, The Gettysburg Review, Hobart, Smokelong Quarterly, Wigleaf,* and many other journals. Her stories have been selected for *Best Small Fictions* and *Wigleaf's Top 50.* She is the Editor-in-Chief and Fiction Editor of Pithead Chapel.

LOUISE MARBURG is the author of two collections of stories, *The Truth About Me* and *No Diving Allowed.* Her third collection of stories, *You Have Reached Your*

Destination, was published by EastOver Press in November 2022. Her work has appeared in such journals as *Narrative, Ploughshares, STORY, The Hudson Review,* and many others. She has been supported by the Sewanee Writers' Conference, the Kenyon Writing Workshops, and the Virginia Center for the Creative Arts. She lives in New York City with her husband, the artist Charles Marburg.

E.M. MARIANI holds an MFA from the Bennington Writing Seminars. This is her first published essay.

TIFFANY MELANSON is a poet and arts educator with an MFA from the Bennington Writing Seminars. She is the author of the audio chapbook *What Happens* (EAT Poems), and her work has recently appeared in *POETRY Magazine, Bridge Eight,* and *Compose Journal,* among others. She teaches poetry and oral interpretation at Douglas Anderson School of the Arts in Jacksonville, Florida, where she is faculty sponsor of *Élan,* a student literary magazine, and co-director of the Douglas Anderson Writers' Festival.

JIM MINICK is the author of five books, the most recent, *Fire Is Your Water,* a novel. *The Blueberry Years,* his memoir, won the Best Nonfiction Book of the Year from Southern Independent Booksellers Association. His honors include the Jean Ritchie Fellowship and the Fred Chappell Fellowship. His poem "I Dream a Bean" was picked by Claudia Emerson for permanent display at the Tysons Corner Metrorail Station. His work has appeared in many publications including *The New York Times, Poets & Writers, Tampa Review, Shenandoah, Orion, Oxford American,* and *The Sun.*

CAROLYNN MIREAULT is a Leslie Epstein Fellow and the Senior Teaching Fellow in the MFA program at Boston University. Her work has recently appeared or is forthcoming in *Louisiana Literature, FEED, The Westchester Review, South Shore Review, Abandon Journal, Misery Tourism, Across the Margin* and *BULL.* Access her most recent publications at carolynnmireault.com.

EMILY MOHN-SLATE is the author of *The Falls,* winner of the 2019 New American Poetry Prize (New American Press, 2020) and *Feed,* winner of the 2018 Keystone Chapbook Prize (Seven Kitchens Press). Her poems and essays have appeared or are forthcoming in *Romper, AGNI, New Ohio Review, Racked, Crab Orchard Review, Muzzle Magazine, Tupelo Quarterly, The Adroit Journal,* and elsewhere. Her poems and essays have been anthologized in *The Long Devotion: Poets Writing Motherhood,* nominated for the Pushcart Prize, the *Best of the Net Anthology,* and highly commended in the Gregory O'Donoghue International Poetry Prize competition.

THERESA MONTEIRO lives in New Hampshire with her husband and six children. She is a former teacher and holds an MFA from the University of New Hampshire. She has had poems published in *The American Journal of Poetry, On the Seawall, River Heron Review, Pittsburgh Poetry Journal, Tipton Poetry Journal, Black Fork Review, Presence, The Meadow, Banyan Review, Cutbank Literary Journal,* and *Dunes Review.* She received the Dick Shea Memorial Prize for poetry in 2019.

ROBERT MORGAN has published several books of poetry, including *Dark Energy* (Penguin, 2015). A native of western North Carolina, he teaches at Cornell University.

ANNA NGUYEN is a PhD student and instructor in the Faculty of Arts and Social Sciences at Leibniz Universität Hannover in Germany [an1]. Her research centers on literary studies of science, science and technology studies, literature on food, and social theory. She is especially interested in theoretical creative non-fiction, where social theory, thinking about food, and first-person narrative blend without enforcing academic conventions. She hosts a podcast, *Critical Literary Consumption*.

LIAM OCTOBER O'BRIEN grew up on a small island. Some of his recent work can be found in *Joyland, Bennington Review,* and Nightboat Books' *We Want It All: An Anthology of Radical Trans Poetics*. He received his MFA at the Iowa Writers' Workshop, where he was an Iowa Arts Fellow.

DAVID ISHAYA OSU is a poet, memoirist, and street photographer. His work has appeared in magazines and anthologies across Nigeria, Uganda, the UK, the US, Australia, Canada, Austria, Bangladesh, India, France, South Africa, and elsewhere. He is the poetry editor of *Panorama: The Journal of Intelligent Travel*. David currently runs a virtual coffee shop where he showcases poems, pictures, plays, prompts, perspectives, psyches. David currently lives in Australia.

LISA PARKER is a native Virginian, a poet, musician, and photographer. Her book, *This Gone Place,* won the 2010 Appalachian Studies Association Weatherford Award and her work is widely published in literary journals and anthologies. Her photography has been on exhibit in NYC and published in several arts journals and anthologies.

Poet, playwright, essayist, and editor, LINDA PARSONS is the poetry editor for Madville Publishing and copy editor for *Chapter 16*, the literary website of Humanities Tennessee. She is a poetry mentor in the MTSU Write certificate program and has published in such journals as *The Georgia Review, Iowa Review, Prairie Schooner, Southern Poetry Review, The Chattahoochee Review, Baltimore Review,* and *Shenandoah*. Five of her plays have been produced, and her fifth poetry collection is *Candescent* (Iris Press, 2019).

CASEY PYCIOR is the author of the short story collection, *The Spoils* (Switchgrass Books/NIU Press, 2017), and he was awarded the 2015 Charles Johnson Fiction Award at *Crab Orchard Review*. His work has recently appeared or is forthcoming in *South Dakota Review, The Laurel Review, Beloit Fiction Journal, Midwestern Gothic, Harpur Palate, BULL, Wigleaf,* and *Crab Orchard Review* among many other places. He is an Assistant Professor of English at the University of Southern Indiana and serves as Fiction Editor of *Southern Indiana Review*.

C.R. RESETARITS has had work recently in *December, Southern Humanities Review, Modern Language Studies, North Dakota Quarterly, Confrontation,* and *Native Voices: Indigenous American Poetry, Craft and Conversations* (Tupelo Press.) She lives in Oxford, Mississippi.

SHAWNA KAY RODENBERG is the author of *Kin* (Bloomsbury.) She holds an MFA from the Bennington Writing Seminars and her reviews and essays have appeared in *Consequence, Salon, the Village Voice,* and *Elle*. In 2016, Shawna was awarded the Jean Ritchie Fellowship, and in 2017 she was the recipient of a Rona Jaffe Foundation Writer's Award. A registered nurse, community college English instructor, mother of five, and grandmother of two, she lives on a hobby goat farm in southern Indiana.

RON RASH is the author of the PEN/Faulkner finalist and *New York Times* best-selling novel *Serena*, in addition to the critically acclaimed novels *The Risen, Above the Waterfall, The Cove, One Foot in Eden, Saints at the River,* and *The World Made Straight;* four collections of poems; and six collections of stories, among them *Burning Bright,* which won the 2010 Frank O'Connor International Short Story Award, *Nothing Gold Can Stay,* a *New York Times* bestseller, and *Chemistry and Other Stories,* which was a finalist for the 2007 PEN/Faulkner Award. Twice the recipient of the O. Henry Prize and winner of the 2019 Sidney Lanier Prize for Southern Literature, he is the Parris Distinguished Professor in Appalachian Cultural Studies at Western Carolina University.

ROLLI is a Canadian author, cartoonist, and songwriter. He's the author of many acclaimed books for adults and children, including *Kabungo and The Sea-Wave.* Rolli's fiction, poetry, essays, cartoons and drawings are staples of *The New York Times, The Saturday Evening Post, Playboy, The Wall Street Journal, Reader's Digest, The Walrus,* and other top outlets. Visit Rolli's website (rollistuff.com) and follow him on Twitter at @rolliwrites.

DANIEL ROMO is the author of *Moonlighting as an Avalanche* (Tebot Bach 2021), *Apologies in Reverse* (FutureCycle Press 2019), *When Kerosene's Involved* (Mojave River Press 2014), and *Romancing Gravity* (Silver Birch Press 2013). He received an MFA from Queens University of Charlotte, and he lives, teaches, and bench presses in Long Beach, CA.

MICHELLE ROSS is the author of three story collections: *There's So Much They Haven't Told You,* winner of the 2016 Moon City Short Fiction Award, *Shapeshifting,* winner of the 2020 Stillhouse Press Short Fiction Award (2021), and *They Kept Running,* winner of the 2021 Katherine Anne Porter Prize in Short Fiction (2022). Her fiction has appeared in *Alaska Quarterly Review, Colorado Review, Electric Literature, Witness,* and other venues. Her work is included in *Best Small Fictions, Best Microfiction, the Wigleaf Top 50,* and other anthologies. She is fiction editor of *Atticus Review* and was a consulting editor for *Best Small Fictions 2018.* www.michellenross.com

MORIEL ROTHMAN-ZECHER is a Jerusalem-born novelist and poet. His first novel, *Sadness Is a White Bird,* was a finalist for the Dayton Literary Peace Prize, was longlisted for the Center for Fiction's First Novel Prize, and was the winner of the Ohioana Book Award, among other honors. His second novel *Before All the World* was published by Farrar, Straus and Giroux in October 2022. His poetry has been published or is forthcoming in *ZYZZYVA, The Common, Barrelhouse, Paper Brigade,* and elsewhere, and he is the recipient of a 2018 National Book Foundation '5 Under 35' Honor and a 2020 MacDowell Fellowship. Moriel lives with his family in Yellow Springs, Ohio.

JOHN SAUL is the author of the collections of short fiction, *Call It Tender, The Most Serene Republic,* and *As Rivers Flow,* as well as the novels *Heron and Quin* and *Seventeen.* With stories appearing in publications throughout the UK and internationally, he has had work in *Dalkey Archive's Best European Fiction 2018* anthology and *Best British Short Stories 2016.* He lives in west London.

E.C. SALIBIAN is a nonfiction writer who lives in Rochester, New York, with two cats, Gadu Meg and Gadu Yergoo. Her work has appeared in *The Sun, Fourth Genre, Los Angeles Review of Books,* and other publications. Salibian is senior editor of Rochester Beacon, a digital publication and community forum that looks in depth at the Rochester, New York, region's complex challenges. Born in Casablanca, Morocco, she also is working on a memoir about her continent-spanning Armenian family.

TATIANA SCHLOTE-BONNE received an MFA at the University of Iowa in The Nonfiction Writing Program. Recent essays have appeared in *F(r)iction, The Iowa Review, The Los Angeles Review,* and *Narrative Magazine.* She lifts weights and plays "Magic: The Gathering" in Iowa City.

LEONA SEVICK is the 2017 Press 53 Poetry Award Winner for her first full-length book of poems, *Lion Brothers.* Her recent work appears in *Orion, Birmingham Poetry Review,* and *Blackbird.* Her work also appears in *The Golden Shovel Anthology: New Poems Honoring Gwendolyn Brooks.* Sevick was named a 2019 Walter E. Dakin Fellow and a 2018 Tennessee Williams Scholar for the Sewanee Writers' Conference. She serves as poetry reader for *Los Angeles Review* and advisory board member of the Furious Flower Black Poetry Center. She is professor of English at Bridgewater College in Virginia, where she teaches Asian American literature.

GEORGE SINGLETON has published four collections of stories, two novels, and a book of nonfiction. His stories have appeared in *Georgia Review, Atlantic Monthly, Harper's, Zoetrope,* and elsewhere. He teaches fiction writing at the South Carolina Governor's School for the Arts in Greenville.

DARIUS STEWART's poetry and creative nonfiction appear or are forthcoming in *The Brooklyn Review, Callaloo, Cimarron Review, Fourth Genre, Gargoyle, Meridian, The Potomac Review, Salamander, storySouth, Verse Daily,* and others. Stewart received an MFA in poetry from the Michener Center for Writers at the University of Texas at Austin (2007) and an MFA from the Nonfiction Writing Program at the University of Iowa (2020). In 2021, the East Tennessee Writers Hall of Fame honored him with the inaugural Emerging Writer Award. He is currently a Lulu "Merle" Johnson Doctoral Fellow in English Literary Studies at the University of Iowa, where he lives in Iowa City with his dog, Fry. His poems "On the Bus" and "Poem to a Son" were previously published in his chapbook *The Terribly Beautiful.* Stewart's first full-length collection of poems, *Intimacies in Borrowed Light,* was published in 2022 by EastOver Press.

MARJORIE TESSER's short fiction has been published in *Sunspot Lit, Breadcrumbs, Exoplanet, Fifty More or Less,* and others. A recent MFA Fiction graduate of Sarah Lawrence College, she received an Academy of American Poets prize. She is the author of two poetry chapbooks and editor of *Mom Egg Review.*

REBECCA THOMAS' work has appeared in *Prairie Schooner, ZYZZYVA, The Massachusetts Review,* and other places. She is the senior editor for *Ms. Aligned 3* and received an MFA from West Virginia University. Originally from Orange County, California, Rebecca now lives and teaches writing in Charlottesville, VA.

BEN WEAKLEY spent fourteen years in the U.S. Army, beginning with deployments to Iraq and Afghanistan and finishing at a desk inside the Pentagon. His work appears in the anthology *Our Best War Stories* by Middle West Press. Other poems appear or are forthcoming in *The Line, Wrath-Bearing Tree, Black Moon Magazine, The Ekphrastic Review,* and *Vita Brevis,* among other publications. His poetry won first prize in the 2021 Col. Darron L. Wright Memorial Writing Awards and first place in the 2019 Heroes' Voices National Poetry Contest. Ben lives in Northeast Tennessee with his wife, their children, and a red-tick hound named Camo.

BETH WEINSTOCK is a poet and physician living in Columbus Ohio. In 2019, she completed an MFA in Poetry at Bennington Writing Seminars, and now teaches poetry workshops to medical students, veterans, and incarcerated individuals. Her poems have been published recently in *Greensboro Review, The MacGuffin, Global Poemic, Harpur Palate, Headline Poetry and Press, South Florida Poetry Journal,* and *High Shelf Press.*

DANA WILDSMITH's newest collection of poems is *One Light* from Texas Review Press. She is also the author of a novel, *Jumping,* an environmental memoir, *Back to Abnormal: Surviving with an Old Farm in the New South,* and five additional collections of poetry. Wildsmith has served as Artist-in-Residence for Grand Canyon National Park and Everglades National Park, as Writer-in-Residence for the Island Institute in Sitka, Alaska, and she is a Fellow of the Hambidge Center for Creative Arts and Sciences.

ERICA L. WILLIAMS received an MFA in Creative Writing Fiction from Vermont College of Fine Arts. Her writing has appeared in *The Rumpus, Blood Orange Review, Entropy Literary Magazine, Necessary Fiction, Vol. 1, Brooklyn, Kansas City Voices,* and elsewhere. She currently resides in Baton Rouge, LA.

WILLIAM WOOLFITT's poems, short stories, and essays have appeared in *AGNI, Blackbird, Tin House, The Threepenny Review, The Cincinnati Review,* and elsewhere. He is the author of three poetry collections, most recently *Spring Up Everlasting,* (Mercer University Press, 2020).

ANNA YOUNG is a summa cum laude graduate of the creative writing program at Washington State University and an MFA candidate at Western Washington University. She published in Crack the Spine's *The Year* anthology in 2022.

CYNTHIA ROBINSON YOUNG is a native of Newark, New Jersey, but now lives and writes in Chattanooga, Tennessee. Her work has appeared in journals and magazines including *The Writer's Chronicle, Grist Journal, The Amistad, Sixfold, The Ekphrastic Review,* and *Catalpa: a Magazine of Southern Perspectives.* For her chapbook, *Migration* (Finishing Line Press) she was named Finalist in the 2019 Georgia Author of the Year Award in her category.

ABDULBASEET YUSUFF is a Nigerian writer. His works appear or are forthcoming in *Brittle Paper, Rattle, Glass: A Journal of Poetry, Up The Staircase Quarterly, Pidgeonholes, The Indianapolis Review,* and elsewhere.

LUCY ZHANG writes, codes, and watches anime. Her work has appeared in *DIAGRAM, Three-Lobed Burning Eye, Four Way Review, The Cincinnati Review, The Portland Review, West Branch,* and elsewhere. Her work is included in *Best Microfiction 2021* and *Best Small Fictions 2021.*

MARY ZHENG is a first-generation Chinese American writer. A former Ameri-Corps and Peace Corps volunteer, she lives in Philadelphia where she works as an emergency department social worker. She is currently working on a book about her year solo hitchhiking and busking around the Mediterranean without a single plan other than learning to trust in this world--a time when she broke bread with refugees and anarchists alike in an attempt to understand what it means to be human.

CYNDIE ZIKMUND's essays have appeared in *Under the Gum Tree, Pink Panther Magazine, Magnolia Review,* and *The Literary Traveler.* Her book reviews have been published by *River Teeth* and *Southern Review of Books.* She is an editor for *Magnolia Review,* and served as Creative Nonfiction Editor for *Qu Literary Magazine.* She has an MFA from Queens University of Charlotte. See some of her work at www.cyndiezikmund.com.

EDITORS

KEITH LESMEISTER is the author of the story collection *We Could've Been Happy Here* (MG Press, 2017). His fiction has appeared in *American Short Fiction*, *Gettysburg Review*, *North American Review*, *Redivider*, *Slice Magazine*, and many others. His nonfiction has appeared in *River Teeth*, *Sycamore Review*, *The Good Men Project*, *Tin House Open Bar*, *Water~Stone Review*, and elsewhere. He lives and works in rural northeast Iowa. Visit Keith's website at keithlesmeister.com.

DENTON LOVING lives on a farm near the historic Cumberland Gap, where Tennessee, Kentucky, and Virginia come together. He is the author of the poetry collection, *Crimes Against Birds* (Main Street Rag). He is also the editor of *Seeking Its Own Level: an anthology of writings about water* (MotesBooks). His fiction, poetry, essays, reviews and interviews have appeared in over 120 publications including *River Styx*, *CutBank*, *Iron Horse Literary Review*, and *The Chattahoochee Review*. You can follow Denton on Twitter @DentonLoving and visit his website at dentonlovingblog.wordpress.com.

KELLY MARCH is a writer in North Carolina. A former newspaper reporter and editor, she is currently working on her first collection of essays.

WALTER M. ROBINSON is a writer and physician in Massachusetts. His collection of essays, *What Cannot Be Undone*, won the 2022 River Teeth Prize for Nonfiction and was published by University of New Mexico Press in 2022. His recent essays appear in *wildness*, *Ruminate*, *Months To Years*, *The Sun*, *The Literary Review*, and *Harvard Review*. You can follow Walter on Twitter @WRobinsonWriter or visit his website at wmrobinson.com.

CPSIA information can be obtained
at www.ICGtesting.com
Printed in the USA
JSHW061526271222
35407JS00004B/15